# COMMUNITY COLLEGES

**Recent title in**
**Educational Policy in the 21st Century**

Educational Leadership: Policy Dimensions in the 21st Century
*Bruce Anthony Jones*

# COMMUNITY COLLEGES

## Policy in the Future Context

*Edited by Barbara K. Townsend
and Susan B. Twombly*

Educational Policy in the 21st Century, Volume 2
*Bruce Anthony Jones, Series Editor*

ABLEX PUBLISHING
Westport, Connecticut • London

**Library of Congress Cataloging-in-Publication Data**

Community colleges : policy in the future context / edited by Barbara K. Townsend,
Susan B. Twombly.
    p.   cm.—(Educational policy in the 21st century ; v. 2)
   Includes bibliographical references and index.
   ISBN 1–56750–522–8 (cloth)—ISBN 1–56750–523–6 (paper)
    1. Community colleges—United States.   2. Higher education and state—United States.   3.
Education, Higher—Aims and objectives—United States.   I. Townsend, Barbara K.   II.
Twombly, Susan B.   III. Series.
   LB2328.15.U6C655   2001
   378.1'543'0973—dc21          00–025326

British Library Cataloguing in Publication Data is available.

Library of Congress Catalog Card Number: 00–025326
ISBN: 1–56750–522–8
        1–56750–523–6 (pbk.)

First published in 2001

Ablex Publishing, 88 Post Road West, Westport, CT 06881
An imprint of Greenwood Publishing Group, Inc.
www.ablexbooks.com

Printed in the United States of America

∞™

The paper used in this book complies with the
Permanent Paper Standard issued by the National
Information Standards Organization (Z39.48–1984).

P

To S. V. Martorana (1919–2000)
Friend, scholar, and teacher who planted the seeds and nourished the field of
community college policy studies

# Contents

# Introduction

*Barbara K. Townsend and*
*Susan B. Twombly*

As the 20th century comes to a close and the 21st century begins, community colleges are poised to assume a new, and increasingly important, role in higher education. For most of the 20th century, community colleges operated on the margins of the educational system to provide transfer, occupational, and remedial/developmental education, as well as short-term training. From a four-year-college perspective, the community college has sometimes been viewed as a poor cousin of elite liberal arts colleges and research universities. This place on the margins was cemented in early decades of the 20th century when four-year universities continued to offer the first two years of a college education in spite of the development of the two-year college (Cohen & Brawer, 1996). Despite the boost community colleges received from national initiatives such as the 1947 Truman Commission Report on Higher Education, they have remained secondary to four-year colleges and universities. However, for individuals and communities served by community colleges, these schools are, and have been, anything but marginal institutions. Community colleges provide status and income to the towns and counties that support them, as well as low-cost access to higher education and job training for literally millions of individuals. Yet, as recently as 1996, the Education Commission of the States argued that policy makers failed to recognize the importance of community colleges when planning for postsecondary education.

Now, however, a number of forces are aligning to catapult community colleges to the center of the federal and states educational policy agendas. Among these forces is the rapidly globalizing economy, with its insatiable demand for information and technical education, the largest factor for expansion of the higher education system since the 1970s (Adelman, 1999). Other forces include shrinking public resources to support higher education and public demands for accountability and quality. President Bill Clinton gave great impetus toward shifting community college policy to the center when he stated that at least 80 percent of adults should attain at least an associate degree (Adelman, 1999). As some college education becomes as nearly as universal as high school graduation, policy makers are beginning to think differently about the educational system. A mere 15 years ago, higher education was considered distinctly separate from K-12 education, with community colleges occupying a gray area between the two sectors. Now, however, policy makers talk about a seamless K-14 or K-16 educational system. Their language and resulting actions reflect a significant change in how community colleges and their role in the system are viewed.

This book is the result of the belief that community college policy is now taking a central place on policy makers' educational agendas. At the state and national levels, policy related to community colleges has been dominated by an overarching concern for workforce development (Grubb & Associates, 1999) and the related issues of equity and access. By addressing policies affecting how community colleges operate at the close of the 20th century, the book illustrates how this policy perspective has shifted in emphasis over the years. Parameters of the book include a focus on policies affecting public two-year schools and, more specifically, community colleges, defined as institutions offering the associate degree through a curriculum that includes transfer/general education, occupational education, and remedial/developmental education.

Each of the authors has addressed a significant policy issue affecting community colleges at the federal, state, or institutional level. Some chapters provide a perspective or conceptual framework in which to view policies (e.g., Richard C. Richardson Jr. and Gerardo de los Santos's chapter describing a typology for viewing the governance of two-year colleges and Margaret Orr and Debra Bragg's chapter on K-14 initiatives). Other chapters take a specific topic or issue and examine current (1990s) state policies on this topic (e.g., Rosa Cintrón, Connie Dillon, and Tammy Boyd's chapter on instructional technology). In some cases the effect of specific policies is described, as in Kathleen Shaw's chapter on remediation and George Higginbottom and Richard Romano's chapter on general education.

The book is divided into three parts. Part I provides a context for understanding specific policies influencing community colleges through its examination of major forces driving these policies. An obvious major force is governmental policy making. Arthur Cohen, in Chapter 1, provides a historical overview of the development of state and federal policies affecting community colleges, including their organization and governance, financing, staffing, enrollments, and curriculum. In Chapter 2 Cheryl Lovell further demonstrates the impact of federal policies on individual community colleges and makes a case for the tendency of institutional leaders to shape this influence to meet their own, local needs. As Cohen illustrates in Chapter 1, local community colleges are addi-

tionally influenced by policies developed at the state level. To further understanding of how states develop policies pertaining to community colleges, in
Chapter 3 Richard Richardson Jr. and Gerardo E. de los Santos present their
State Community College Governance Structures Typology. Based on a study
of seven states' governance structures, the typology provides a new classification
system for understanding how states currently govern their community colleges.
Part of state governance involves the issue of institutional accountability for the
use of state dollars. As community college funding has shifted so that most
states are the dominant source, state policies concerning institutional accountability have escalated. In Chapter 4, Frankie Santos Laanan documents the accountability movement, including emerging issues and trends affecting community colleges.

Although state governance systems and federal and state policies are major
forces moving or shaping institutional decisions and behaviors, they are not the
only ones. In spite of their local orientation, community colleges are not immune
from the influence of globalization, as John Levin clearly illustrates in Chapter
5. He documents this emerging influence in his portrayal of community colleges
as institutions both "buffered" and "buffeted" by globalization.

Moving from the level of international and national forces influencing community college policy, Part II provides examples of how state-level policy issues
influence community college operations. Driven by concerns for educational
efficiency as well as effectiveness, state leaders have moved from accepting the
fact that students drop out from one educational sector to the next to desiring a
seamless transition between and within sectors. The first step in developing a
seamless system is to create initiatives linking K-12 with the first two years of
college. Many of these initiatives are described in Chapters 6 through 8. In
Chapter 6, Margaret Orr and Debra Bragg present a broad picture of current
policy initiatives linking community colleges with secondary schools through
collaborative efforts designed to prepare high school students for college or the
workforce after attendance at the community college. State policies shaping the
role of community colleges in workforce development are more specifically
described by Kevin Dougherty in Chapter 7. In Chapter 8, Anthony Girardi and
Robert Stein detail the growth of dual credit or dual enrollment programs, which
are designed to encourage high school students to attend college, whether at a
community college or a four-year school.

Once within higher education, students face the possibility of moving between
the two-year and four-year college sectors. Jan Ignash and Barbara Townsend,
in Chapter 9, focus on linkages between these sectors through state policies on
transfer and articulation. Their chapter illustrates how state policies can facilitate
or hinder this transfer. Also at issue between the sectors is where remediation
should occur. In Chapter 10 Kathleen Shaw discusses current approaches to
remediation, including the growing support for relegating it to the two-year
sector. Her study of how remedial education has developed within Massachusetts
and Maryland illustrates how different state policies about remedial education

affect a state's entire educational system as well as the treatment of remedial education at the institutional level.

Part II concludes with a look at state-system policies regarding educational technologies. In Chapter 11, Rosa Cintrón, Connie Dillon, and Tammy Boyd examine seven states' policies and draw conclusions about states' responses to the impact of technology on teaching and learning in higher education, including community colleges.

Although state policies affecting community colleges are developed and designed from a systemic perspective, they are ultimately experienced or played out at the institutional level. Some demonstration of this effect is provided in Part III, which moves the focus of community college policy to the institutional level. In Chapter 12, George Higginbottom and Richard Romano illustrate how one governing body's systemwide policy on general education affects a particular community college (Binghampton Community College, part of the State University of New York system). The authors provide a faculty perspective on trustees' efforts to change the curriculum, traditionally considered a faculty prerogative. The curriculum also affects student persistence or retention, a growing concern given research demonstrating the link between degree completion and individual economic benefits (Grubb & Associates, 1999). Thus, it is vital for community colleges to increase student retention to the point of degree or transfer. Romero Jalomo Jr., in Chapter 13, provides an overview of institutional programs affecting the retention of first-year community college students and provides campus policy makers with several policy recommendations regarding these programs.

In the concluding chapter, we review the policy issues covered in the book and provide a conceptual framework—Scheurich's (1997) policy archaeology—suggesting that these policy issues may have been derived from a traditional policy perspective in which policies serve as solutions to perceived problems. An alternative perspective is that the problems are socially constructed and the solutions derive directly from the particular definitions of the problems. Thus, policy solutions addressing these problems may instead only exacerbate them. Viewing problems and solutions as social constructions is critical for understanding them both, and readers are urged to read each chapter with this framework in mind.

Intended audiences for this book include faculty and students in graduate programs focusing on higher education and, especially, the community college. With its single focus on community college policy issues at three levels (national, state, and institutional), this book is unique among current literature on the community college. Other audiences include both state and institutional community college leaders who are desirous of placing institutional and state educational policies within a broader framework. For example, community college presidents will better understand the influence of federal policies on their institution after reading Cohen's and Lovell's chapters dealing with federal policies. Similarly, Richardson and de los Santos's chapter on statewide governance structures will assist institutional leaders and state policy makers in understanding how their state's governance structure facilitates or hinders institutional and sector collaborative efforts. Levin's chapter reminds policy makers and community college leaders that the institution is not immune to global forces shaping the economy. Finally, individuals interested in a specific higher education policy issue such as remediation or the use of instructional technology to facilitate educational access will have the opportunity to learn how the issue specifically affects the community college.

While not every possible policy issue affecting community colleges could be included, this book provides an introduction to some key policy issues that currently dominate the functioning of community colleges. Thus, the book may serve as a catalyst for determining what other policy issues need to be considered in any comprehensive look at community college policy in the 21st century.

## REFERENCES

Adelman, C. (1999, January/February). Crosscurrents and riptides: Asking about the capacity of the higher education system. *Change*, pp. 21–26.

Cohen, A., & Brawer, F. (1996). *The American community college* (3rd ed.). San Francisco: Jossey-Bass.

Grubb, N., & Associates (1999). *Honored but invisible: An inside look at teaching in community colleges*. New York: Routledge.

Scheurich, J. J. (1997). *Research method in the postmodern*. London: Falmer Press.

## PART I

## NATIONAL LEVEL

*Chapter 1* _____

# Governmental Policies Affecting Community Colleges: A Historical Perspective

*Arthur M. Cohen*

Government affects every enterprise. In the private sector it provides subsidies; levies taxes; mandates rules governing employment, wages, hours, and workplace safety; and, through numerous other measures, advances or retards the course of all types of industry. Government influence is even more pronounced in the public sector, where various organizations are developed and supported under governmental aegis. Federal, state, and local governments create, build, merge, and collapse agencies and institutions dedicated to myriad endeavors.

This chapter traces the influence of governmental forces on several aspects of the nation's public community colleges. It considers college organization and governance, finance, staffing, enrollments, and curriculum, pointing up how different levels of government, especially the states, have affected the colleges at different stages of their development.

## COLLEGE ORGANIZATION AND GOVERNANCE

The American community colleges started as neighborhood schools. Subsequently, state plans guided their development. The federal government had little to do with them. In fact, excepting special circumstances such as a college for the deaf, a college for blacks, and the military academies, the federal government was not involved in the establishment of colleges at any level. Its only direct connection with junior colleges was during the Great Depression of the 1930s when it organized a few colleges as part of its workforce development effort. But in the main, the building of institutions was left to local, and then state, governments.

A community college is defined as any institution accredited to award the associate degree as its highest degree. Although private junior colleges and two-year proprietary schools are included in that definition, the 1,050 or so publicly supported comprehensive institutions are the dominant form; hence, this discussion concentrates on them. Located in every state, these colleges provide occupational programs, the first two years of baccalaureate studies, basic skills development, and a variety of special interest courses to nearly half the students beginning postsecondary education.

The community colleges' main contribution has been to expand access to postsecondary studies for the millions of students who would otherwise not have an opportunity to participate. The first question then becomes, why did the states not expand their universities sufficiently to accommodate the rising tide of demand that has been apparent since early in the twentieth century? Why form an entirely new type of institution? Many interpretations have been brought forward attributing the organization and growth of the community colleges to broad social forces. One contention is that the colleges were sponsored by upper classes wishing to maintain their social position by restricting access to the universities that their offspring attended. Accordingly, they supported institutions that would deflect the aspirations of lower-class youths. This argument is bolstered by quotations from university presidents who sought to convert their institutions into research and graduate schools exclusively. And its proponents use as evidence the differential progress into society made by young people from families of high- and low-socioeconomic status. The thesis is especially appealing to people seeking reasons to account for a class-based society and for the inequitable distribution of social goods.

A reciprocal thesis resting on social forces contends that the community colleges arose out of an alliance between working-class groups and middle-class reformers seeking to counter the upper-class effort to stratify and limit educational opportunity. This position holds that the working class has always supported publicly funded education that allows its youth to progress to higher levels of schooling through access to education that has a common or general curriculum, not just a vocational orientation. Thus, community colleges, emphasizing both occupational studies and collegiate curriculum, provided an avenue of opportunity that young people from the lower classes could travel. Accordingly, working-class groups welcomed them and lobbied for their establishment.

A tangential argument holds that the colleges were built because of the desires of professional educators. Here the proponents point to the support for community colleges exhibited by university presidents in the early years. Since the universities wished to distance themselves from the students they did not care to serve, they sponsored community colleges in their own interest. Complementarily, public school officials advocated community colleges for the prestige and higher-status professional positions they yielded, as teachers became professors and superintendents became presidents. This position that the education community itself created the colleges has been supported especially by those who contend that the colleges were transformed from prebaccalaureate to vocational institutions in the 1970s because their leaders were seeking a secure niche in the structure of higher education.

At one level it is engaging to consider broad social forces, especially when a writer can postulate a conspiracy of the elite, a populist alliance, or a clique of professional educators. But great and complex developments typically have great and complex causes, and no one set of arguments seems more plausible than any other. It is perhaps more informative to cast the discussion in the context of specific legislative acts and institutional development that can be supported by the evidence of history.

## THE COLLEGES EMERGE

Educational institutions in the United States grew from the bottom and the top, with a gap in the middle that was not filled until more than a century had passed after the formation of the nation. In the colonial era and until well in the nineteenth century, public schooling for the vast majority of youth stopped at the sixth or eighth grade. For a few it picked up again at the college level. In the late nineteenth and early twentieth centuries, however, the center was filled in as public high schools were built in every state and education was made mandatory through age 16 in most states. Meanwhile the universities were expanding upward. Enamoured of the German research and freedom-of-inquiry model, the universities added master's and doctoral programs featuring selective admissions and an independently functioning faculty. This was as true of the vocationally oriented universities that had been formed under the Morrill Act of 1862 as of the older institutions. Rather than reach out to the rapidly growing numbers of high school graduates, many universities attempted to excise the freshman and sophomore classes. Where they opened to most high school graduates, as in the Midwest, universities endeavored to maintain collegiate standards by dismissing a sizable proportion of the matriculants before the end of their freshman year.

These moves toward upper division and graduate study left the lower-school districts to engage in their own form of upward mobility by adding grades 13 and 14 to the high schools. Rationalized as completing the students' general education, that is, helping them become good citizens, homemakers, or workers, the schools were actually filling in the gap. As state after state passed child labor legislation, the number of students staying in school and graduating high school grew rapidly. Since a primary benefit of a year of schooling is to provide a ticket enabling a person to attend the next year of schooling, the pressure for postsecondary education became evident. Accordingly, in many states the community colleges were organized and funded by local school districts following the model already in place for their elementary and secondary schools. Community colleges rose into a vacuum, as it were, well ahead of state authorization or planning.

Although, over the past 40 years, responsibility for funding and governance has moved in the main to the state level, community colleges still reflect their lower-school roots. The policy of admitting all students who apply, the patterns of funding on the basis of student attendance, the qualifications and working life of the faculty, and the generality of the curriculum all betray their origins. Even where the colleges were organized originally under state legislation, the authorizing acts usually directed the local district to petition for the establishment of a college, and state support typically was provided on an average-daily-attendance or full-time-student-equivalent basis.

The other major form of development, although a distant second in terms of number of institutions, was the two-year college built by the universities. Some were formed as branch campuses and others as colleges within colleges, responsible to the parent university but with their own staff and admissions policies (with the latter always proving more liberal).

## EARLY STATE LEGISLATION

Prior to mid-century, statewide plans for organizing community colleges were hardly seen and national influence was even less apparent. Even though President Harry Truman's Commission on Higher Education (President's Commission on Higher Education, (1947) concluded that half of the nation's young could benefit from extending their formal education through grade 14, tangible federal support was slow to develop. Most of the states, however, were considering ways of coordinating college organization. And although the head of the American Association of Junior Colleges (formed in 1920) could still say that the colleges "had been growing without plan, general support, or supervision" (Bogue, 1950, p. 137), change was imminent.

By the 1960s state plans were mushrooming across the nation, leading to a period of tremendous expansion with some 50 new colleges opening each year. Half the states in the nation were commissioning studies, writing master plans, passing legislation, and building toward statewide systems of community colleges. The early leaders in statewide planning and development included California, Florida, Illinois, Michigan, and North Carolina. Indeed, these became the states with the most comprehensive sets of colleges. A review of developments in 15 states reveals the patterns.

Maryland had had public junior colleges since 1927 but in the 1960s it moved toward a state system by authorizing local boards of education to establish colleges that would be partially funded by the state and by authorizing the issuance of bonds. Furthermore, state funds for campus construction would be provided to the local districts on a matching basis.

Oregon's first community college opened in 1949 under a law stating that a public school district could be reimbursed for providing grade 13 and 14 classes. With a new law passed in 1961, the state provided funds for full time equivalent (FTE) operations plus 75 percent of building costs. Supervision was manifested in a community colleges section of the state department of education.

North Carolina's Community College Act was passed in 1957, providing construction funds (on a matching basis) and other small grants to the four municipally supported community colleges then functioning. The public community colleges emphasized prebaccalaureate programs, while a separate system of industrial education centers offered vocational training. In 1963 a law stated that a department of community colleges, operating within the state board of education, would combine the two systems. The state would match local funds for capital construction and would pay up to 65 percent of the operating costs.

New Jersey had been the recipient of six colleges funded by the federal government under the Emergency Relief Administration, beginning in 1933. However, federal support was withdrawn toward the end of the 1930s and four of the six colleges closed. Not until 1962 did New Jersey pass legislation establishing county colleges. The costs for capital would be shared equally by state and county and the state would provide a maximum of $200 per FTE student toward operation. The colleges were directed to provide both prebaccalaureate and technical studies. By the end of the 1960s, 12 colleges had been established.

In Washington some of the high schools had tried extending secondary programs as early as 1915, but these proved unsuccessful. Beginning in 1925 independent junior colleges were established, but not funded, by the state. In 1945 the legislature enabled the junior colleges to again become part of school districts, and in 1961 a law was passed designating community colleges, with strict control from the legislature. The state was to provide around 80 percent of the operating budgets, with the remainder coming from tuition. The colleges were formed from the local school districts but, because prior to 1961 the districts were not allowed to organize colleges in counties that had state colleges or universities already there, the institutions were slow in developing. By 1967 the legislature divided the state into community college districts, each with a board of trustees. A separate coordinating council for occupational education was also established.

Michigan's first junior college opened in 1914 with a traditional liberal arts curriculum. The colleges that opened over the years were locally controlled and funded. By 1961 an amendment to the state constitution was passed providing for the establishment and financial support of community colleges that would be supervised by locally elected boards. The amendment further stated that a state board for community colleges should advise the state board of education on the general planning for such colleges and their requests for annual appropriations. Thus Michigan became unusual among American states by naming the community colleges in its constitution. In subsequent years the state provided somewhat less than half the cost of capital outlay and operating expenses, but in 1964 a legislative act was passed authorizing the local boards to offer both collegiate and noncollegiate programs, award associate degrees, and, in general, maintain flexibility in the types of students that they might matriculate and for whom state support would be provided. The law also allowed the local boards to levy property taxes and issue bonds for the support of the colleges. In the latter 1960s most of the community colleges broke away from the lower-school districts and established their own districts.

In Texas several junior colleges were originally founded as two-year church colleges dating from 1898. Others grew out of the public secondary schools. Well into the 1960s, the colleges were making moves toward becoming baccalaureate-granting institutions. Prior to the 1940s, the 22 public junior colleges in operation were still financed entirely from local funds. Subsequently, the legislature agreed to pay a portion of the operating costs on a per-student basis. Still, the majority of the funds for capital construction were local and most of the operating costs were carried by the sponsoring districts and the students. Not until the mid-1960s did state appropriations nearly approximate the operating costs for the colleges, and by the end of the 1960s the state was, for the first time, paying the full instructional costs in the colleges.

Pennsylvania's Community College Act was passed in 1963. Prior to that time, the state's higher education included an abundance of 164 institutions, public and private, many with branches or extension centers. When the community colleges were formed under the new act, local boards of trustees were elected and operating expenses were shared on a one-third basis by the local districts, the state, and the students. This expectation put Pennsylvania among the states with the highest tuition right from the start. The Community College Act also divided governance powers among the state board of education and other state agencies and the local school districts. A subsequent amendment directed that capital expenses were to be shared equally by the state and local districts. The law noted that the community college instructional program should include "preprofessional liberal arts and sciences, semiprofessional business studies and technology, trade and industrial education, developmental training and adult education" (Yarrington, 1969, p. 154).

California's two-year colleges date from 1907, when a legislative act authorized high schools to offer postgraduate courses, and they were given impetus in 1921, when an act authorized establishment of separate junior college districts. Subsequent acts dealt with state support and included the junior colleges within the state's constitutional definition of free public education. In 1961 state funds were authorized to be used for capital construction. However, the California Master Plan, enacted into law early in the 1960s, added a provision to the education code stating that "the public junior colleges are secondary schools and shall continue to be a part of the public school system of this State." Another part of the same act said that public higher education included each campus of the University of California, all state colleges, and "all public junior colleges heretofore and hereafter established pursuant to law" (cited in Yarrington, 1969, p. 159). The state provided around one-third of the funding for operations through the middle 1970s, with the balance made up by the local districts. At the end of the 1970s a proposition effectually eliminated the colleges from the likelihood of finding funds from their local tax base and funding subsequently reverted almost entirely to the state.

The succession of legislative acts authorizing junior colleges in California led to some institutions being formed by high school districts, some by unified districts, and some by separate junior college districts, the latter split between those having an administration shared with the public school districts, and those having a separate board of trustees. In the 1960s this duality was overturned when the local districts were directed to separate from the unified schools and to form independent community college districts. The State Board of Education set rules for forming a district that mandated a certain minimum student potential and a certain local assessed valuation. In the late 1960s a state-level board of governors was created with members appointed by the governor to assume all of the responsibilities previously vested in the state board of education and most of its staff and most of its rules were transferred over directly from the state department of education. The dual status of community colleges as part of both the lower schools and higher education has continued as subsequent acts guaranteed funding for the community colleges just as for the lower schools, while others gave much more latitude to the colleges in terms of staffing. The state continued to mandate admissions expectations and to set student fees, which have remained the lowest in the nation.

Illinois claims the first public community college in the nation (Joliet Junior College), dating from 1902. Over the next 30 years the state's community colleges grew, despite the absence of specific legal sanction. State aid for operating costs was provided in 1955 and, ten years later, for capital construction. In 1965 the Illinois Junior College Board was formed and took over the functions formerly carried out by the state superintendent of public instruction. It designated the junior colleges as part of the higher-education system, in contrast to their former status as an element in the lower school system.

Minnesota's local school districts had started junior colleges as early as 1915, with financial support entirely the responsibility of the local school district. In 1957 the legislature authorized state aid for operating costs, and in 1963 the legislature created a State Junior College Board to manage the system: to determine the location of new colleges, prescribe tuition rates, provide for uniform faculty salaries, and find funds for construction. Thus, Minnesota established the most restrictive state system, which endured into the 1990s when the community colleges were merged with the technical institutes and the state colleges into an even more comprehensive statewide system.

The Kansas legislature passed the first enabling act for junior college in 1917; it was a permissive law authorizing boards of education in local school districts to add grades 13 and 14 to their schools. In 1965 the state passed a Community Junior College Act providing for the superintendent of public instruction to be the state authority, naming various state agencies as oversight groups, enabling the junior colleges to have their own separate boards with taxing powers, and authorizing state aid, including tuition, to be paid by counties lacking community colleges, whose residents had to attend classes outside the district. By 1968 the state was providing operating funds on a per-credit-hour basis, but 40 percent of the operating costs were being borne by the local districts and 10 percent by the students.

In Virginia the community colleges were funded entirely by the state, including operating costs and capital outlay. No local funds were needed, although student tuition carried some of the burden. The colleges themselves were either two-year branches of state universities or vocational schools operated as extensions of the public schools. In 1966 a State Board for Community Colleges was established and the Virginia Community College System began operations. The board, appointed by the governor, was responsible for creating local community college boards for each institution. The state provided operating funds and capital construction, but the local units were responsible for site development. According to the state rules, the community colleges were to include occupational education, prebaccalaureate education, general education, adult education, remedial programs, special training for new industries, and noncredit community service—in short the entire range of community college activities.

When the public colleges of Georgia were organized into a system under the control of the board of regents in the 1930s, eight junior colleges were in existence. Four of those were converted to senior colleges during the ensuing 25 years, and no new junior colleges were established. Subsequent to 1958, seven new junior colleges were opened and two community-operated colleges were taken into the system. By 1968, four more junior colleges were converted to senior colleges. The Junior College Act of 1958 authorized local communities to develop and operate colleges with the assistance of state funds for operating expenses. No provision was made for site development or construction.

The public junior colleges of Mississippi were established with local districts and the state sharing responsibility. Most of them were an outgrowth of county agricultural high schools, dating from 1908. Legislation enacted in 1922 provided that any such high school located not less than 20 miles from a state college could add freshman and sophomore courses. The law also set standards for instructors and library holdings, but made no state appropriation to support college work. A 1928 law established a Junior College Commission as a regulatory agency for the colleges and provided some state funds for support. The local counties were placed into junior college districts in 1964 and allowed to levy local taxes. The state provided funds on a matching basis for constructing vocational-technical facilities.

## STATE PLANS

In the late 1960s additional legislation was passed in several states, much under the impetus of the federal Higher Education Act of 1965, which directed the states to create higher-education coordinating commissions if they wished to qualify for various federal aid programs. State master plans for community college development continued evolving. By the end of the 1960s, comprehensive plans specifically detailing college development and support were in place or imminent in 19 states, while legislation providing generalized guidelines had been passed in several others (Hurlbert, 1969). The state plans typically described organized systems, including the ways in which the colleges would be funded, and pointed out what separate communities had to do in order to develop their own institutions. One of the main arguments in favor of state planning was the recognition of the states' responsibility for equalizing the financing of community colleges so that students from low-income districts would be less disadvantaged. Another was the realization that for the community college to be a player within a higher-education system, some guidelines for curriculum, student access, and professional standards had to be established. The imminence of federal funding and regulation was also recognized, and contentions were raised that only through statewide coordination could the requirements and opportunities set down by the federal government be realized.

The plans were always rationalized with the idea of providing equal opportunity for all of the state's residents and a sense of the importance of preparing them to take their place within the state's workforce. Access for the widest number of the state's population was usually mentioned, along with the characteristics of the community colleges that would serve both prebaccalaureate and occupational aspirants. Typically, although the plans might have referred to remedial and general education, those terms were not well defined. In some instances the state plans stated specifically that the community colleges were to serve commuters, with the institutions cautioned not to build residence halls. However, this expectation was not universal, and residence halls were developed in many states where students were attracted from distant locations.

Equity throughout a state was also furthered by plans showing districts or regions where community colleges would be developed. Especially noted were areas where opportunities for postsecondary education were limited. Here the plans pointed toward the special necessity of developing colleges so that all of the state's residents would have an opportunity to attend. The goal in all cases was that 95 percent of the population would be within reasonable commuting distance of a junior college.

By way of ensuring that communities build colleges only where there were sufficient numbers of potential students, many state plans specified minimum enrollment expectations: 300 in Massachusetts; 400 in Virginia; 500 in New Hampshire and Texas; 600 in Colorado; 1,000 in Illinois, Michigan, and Ohio. Maximum enrollments were rarely specified. Admission was often noted as being open for everyone, including high school dropouts. Some of the plans noted faculty qualifications: for example, Kansas and Oregon endorsed the master's degree or equivalent for instructors in prebaccalaureate areas. Other plans noted minimum years of experience in the vocational areas in which instructors were teaching. Some plans recommended funding for prospective faculty members who could obtain additional graduate school credits.

Many of the plans indicated the percentage of operating costs that the state would pay; this was usually around half the total cost, ranging from 30 percent in California to 65 percent in North Carolina. Several states adopted minimum foundation plans in which each district would contribute in accordance with its ability to pay.

State contributions to capital outlay were quite varied. Michigan called for funding for up to 100 percent of the initial building program; Illinois, 75 percent; and New Hampshire and Colorado, 100 percent of building construction, provided that the local community purchase and prepare the site. Virginia and Oregon also did not permit the use of state funds for site acquisition. In Kansas, state funds could not be used for constructing residence halls. The plans typically also commented on tuition. At one extreme was California, with tuition-free higher education, while at the other was New Hampshire, which took a stand against low tuition as being a subsidy to students that disregarded family income. Most states allowed tuition to vary from around 10 to 50 percent of operating costs.

As for organization, state departments and state boards were often recommended, with local boards filling in with additional responsibilities. It is possible to see the trend developing toward separate boards for community colleges even as the statewide authority was vested in a state board of education or a state board of higher education. In some cases the state boards for junior colleges had representatives on a coordinating council for all of higher education: California, Illinois, and Pennsylvania exemplify that type of coordination. Overall, the state plans had to create systems of community colleges out of uncoordinated groups of institutions.

Inserted in most of the plans was the expectation that the state supervisory agency would conduct a continuing study of student access and college operations. This put a research responsibility into the state departments, but one that depended on local cooperation, that is, the individual colleges were going to have to supply the data that the state agency needed to summarize trends and events in the colleges. This expectation proved difficult to bring about because it demanded a uniform set of reporting, which was, in effect, a violation of the idea that each college would be able to determine its own categories and criteria. At the same time, few state agencies developed a capacity for collecting data according to consistent criteria. Every time a state agency tried to define a category, a number of local college leaders typically responded that the criteria did not recognize the unique circumstances within their own institutions.

Research at the local level was rarely mentioned. The understanding was that the junior college staff should not have research as part of its responsibilities but would only provide data to the state agencies. Over the years this proved to be a weakness, as the collection of data required local staff to understand its importance and the ways of collecting it. Other weaknesses in the plans were that they rarely specified how staff were to be recruited, leaving that to the local institutions. Nor did the plans suggest specifics regarding transfer procedures and requirements, leaving that to be worked out between the local institutions and the universities to which their students aspired.

The state plans purported to reduce the further development of underfunded, marginally viable colleges, but they confronted some widely held views that the growth of junior colleges depended less on state-level decrees than on the healthy formation of institutions in response to local needs and conditions. The concept of locally controlled community colleges was still firmly in place, and many commentators viewed with suspicion the development of institutions controlled from distant state capitals. As Hurlbert noted, "Without the aspirations, pride, and initiative of local communities, many community colleges would never have come into existence" (1969, p. 5). He recognized the delicacy of balancing state and local control and proposed master plans that would coordinate systems even while allowing for a significant portion of grass-roots management and goal setting. Lombardi (1968) also commented on the care taken in the legislation establishing California's board of governors to mention that local boards of trustees would maintain a sizable proportion of responsibility. Even as control and funding moved steadily toward state capitals over the next 30 years, the belief in the value and importance of local control would not die. It became rather like the nostalgia for the ivy-covered, autonomous four-year college, free of external interference, a nostalgia that persisted long into an era when every aspect of institutional management and support was influenced by court rulings and civil legislation.

## LATER STATE LEGISLATION

Reviews of state legislation passed in the 1970s and 1980s demonstrate the evolution of state policy. In 1976, the first of Martorana and colleagues' (Martorana & McGuire, 1976) many reports on legislation affecting community colleges classified the legislative actions under the headings of finance, state-level concerns, institutional concerns, personnel, students, and academic concerns. Predictably, most of the legislation dealt with finance: appropriations for operations, capital funds, and financial procedures. State-level administration and statewide coordination also came in for a share of concern, along with institutional administration and tuition. A total of 334 legislative enactments among the thirty states was reviewed.

Increases in appropriations were seen in most of the states at a time of enrollment growth. The states authorized bond issues to fund capital improvement in many cases. Legislation affecting financial procedures tended toward yielding greater financial flexibility, on the one hand, and legislative control of expenditures, on the other. Some states were going one way and some the other. Several bills related to coordination, with two states (California and Florida) proposing the establishment of regional coordinating councils. A few states passed laws establishing a legal basis for community colleges so that the local districts would have taxing and bonding authority: Texas, Connecticut, and Arkansas were among them.

Under institutional concerns the legislation dealt with issues of liability, and either permissive or mandatory actions related to what local boards and administrators might do. Among the latter, five states dealt with provisions for electing trustees. Laws were also passed in Oklahoma and Mississippi authorizing or providing for the establishment of new colleges. Name changes during this era were also authorized, generally moving the institutions from the category of "junior" to "community."

Several states authorized collective bargaining for faculty during the mid-1970s, including Connecticut, Michigan, Washington, and Florida. Other states expanded protection for faculty members, extending due process procedures for those terminated. Nevada, in effect, granted tenure to the faculty.

Among laws affecting students included those providing for tuition waivers for veterans, disadvantaged students, and senior citizens. The continuing tendency toward access is revealed in these types of bills. Scholarship funds were increased in Michigan, Hawaii, and Arizona, while Iowa and Illinois opened up their student aid programs to part-time students.

Several enactments related to curriculum tended to be proscriptive. Tennessee required all students to complete a minimum number of credits in U.S. or state history; Hawaii resolved that environmental education should be required; Texas required nursing programs to grant credit for experience. Other laws dealt with establishing economic education or law enforcement centers.

The states reacted to the federal Higher Education Acts of 1965 and 1972, which directed them to establish procedures for coordinating public higher education within their boundaries. Community colleges were typically represented on the so-called 1202 commissions (state planning commissions) established during this era, but there was much foot-dragging as questions of state and local responsibility and of public versus independent higher education were considered. Still, several states created governing or coordinating boards covering all of public higher education. The states also reacted to federal influence on student financial aid, as when they provided for veterans' benefits and for administering federal aid to students.

The legislative activity of the late 1970s continued to focus especially on finance and administration, with more than half the legislation falling into those two areas. General appropriations for community colleges were increasing, with operational costs and capital funding bills being enacted across the board. Much of the legislation related to procedural matters and taxing structures, but the trend toward state control of finances was definitely in place.

The legislation affecting governing local and state governing bodies "focused on board composition and procedural execution of policy rather than substantive issues of authority" (Martorana & Broomall, 1981, p. 27). Massachusetts established a state board, and New Jersey and Arizona passed legislation affecting the composition of local boards. The legislatures were also enacting bills providing for various types of studies and surveys, including general studies of the role of the community college and specific surveys of subcategories of students, such as those with learning disabilities (Virginia) and foreign and out-of-state students (Tennessee). However, in general there was "a continued trend among state legislators to view the community college more as an element within postsecondary education or state government and less as a unique educational entity" (p. 60).

Other trends were that legislative attention to academic affairs focused increasingly on occupational education that and legislation directed toward students came in the form of bills providing for tuition waivers for special groups, such as senior citizens, the academically gifted, people unemployed due to the closure of major industries, and those for whom English was a second language. Notable for its absence was legislation directed toward enhancing community or adult education or toward strengthening the articulation between community colleges and secondary schools.

The level of legislative activity increased through the 1980s, with an average of 18 pieces of legislation affecting community colleges passed in each state. Finance and administration accounted for five out of every eight laws; the others dealt with personnel, students, and academic programs, while physical facilities and institutional growth seemed lowest in levels of activity. A growing concern for quality was apparent as legislators passed more bills concerned with academic programs.

Although several studies examining community college mission were conducted, few changes were occurring. These commissions recommended increases in vocational education and economic development, but the provision of funds or directives to establish particular types of programs was slow in coming. Most of the commissions stated the major functions of the community colleges but left to the institutions the magnitude of emphasis that they would place on one function or another. Nonetheless, some states recommended strongly that the community colleges be involved with economic development. As an example, in its 1982 Master Plan for Higher Education in Ohio, the state board of regents suggested that two-year colleges become partners in local efforts at economic revitalization, establish adult learning programs related to employment, and contract for training employees of local businesses. The question of when the states became concerned particularly with the access and progress of ethnic minorities can be raised in association with these reports of legislation. Apparently, the federal government was much more concerned about such matters at this time. Another question is when the states became interested in distance education; nothing in the reports from the mid-1980s and earlier suggests that they were.

By 1990 the tempo had picked up, with almost twice as many pieces of legislation being passed as in prior years (an average of 32 per state). The topical areas were similar across state lines, as though imitation was guiding the policy makers. Governance issues remained prominent, with seven states enacting legislation to change or substantially modify governance structures. Academic issues were gaining in attention, now running a close third to administration and finance, and laws concerned with students were now fourth.

The trends toward access remained intact. Several states considered legislation that would establish funds for prepaid tuition or tax credits. Michigan was the first state to create a guaranteed tuition savings plan, followed by similar legislation in Alabama, Louisiana, and Massachusetts. Texas created a college savings bond program.

The requests for data continued taking specific turns. Pennsylvania was first to require that colleges report the level of crime on their campus. Coordinating bodies also continued to evolve, for example, the boards for state technical colleges and community colleges in Connecticut were merged into a single board. However, some states acted to ease bureaucratic controls on specific institutional functions: Arkansas, New Jersey, and New York were in this group.

In academic affairs, top concern was given to occupational training, but there also seemed to be a growing interest in program articulation with high schools and with universities. Much attention was being given to the ability of community college students to transfer to senior public universities, while other policies were enacted to allow high school students to matriculate in community colleges. At the same time that articulation between community colleges and universities was being laboriously streamlined in some states, the two-year upper-division universities that had been built in Texas, Florida, and Illinois were being expanded so that they could include freshman and sophomore students. Nonetheless, institutional competition in general was not a public policy issue. Interest in tracking students on a statewide basis was growing, along with issues related to the use of part-time faculty.

The number of states seeking institutional accountability grew gradually during the 1990s. In 1997 the Kentucky Postsecondary Improvement Act included provisos for educational quality as revealed by data on student outcomes, including pass rates on licensure examinations; student progress, with data on time to degree; the effectiveness of remedial programs; and persistence and graduation rates (Kentucky Council on Postsecondary Education, 1997). South Carolina attempted to base its appropriations to higher education on performance indicators that included 37 criteria for judging institutional performance (Schmidt, 1997).

Moves toward uniformity in curriculum and graduation requirements were revealed in a 1992 law passed in Indiana that required colleges and universities to jointly identify at least 30 credit hours of comparable general education courses fulfilling graduation requirements (Indiana State Commission for Higher Education, 1996). Florida also attempted to standardize requirements for baccalaureate programs and general education by mandating that common degree program prerequisites be established and that general education requirements be stabilized at 36 hours at all colleges and universities (LeMon & Pitter, 1996).

Issues of personnel qualifications, employment, and dismissal continued to be codified. A bill enacted into law in California in 1990 removed the requirement that instructors possess a state teaching credential and allowed local districts to set standards for instructors and policies for employing and evaluating them. It put forth the concept of shared governance, stating that groups representative of faculty, administrators, students, and classified staff (business officers, custodians) be consulted on all policy decisions. Faculty were to be involved in evaluating administrators.

The California pattern, of responsibility shared by a state board and local trustees, points up how the evolution of community colleges from local institutions to state control has proceeded fitfully. A merit system administered by a state personnel commission has authority over the local trustees in matters involving the classified staff. The state board of governors, working within the framework of the state education code, defines rules relating to administrators with responsibility for academic affairs and student services. The local boards employ the administrators, who can be dismissed at any time (as long as due process is followed) unless they have been granted an expressed contract, which is limited by the code to four years. The state does not provide for administrative employment rights except to say that administrators must be notified if they are to be terminated (Lau, 1997).

To summarize, the flurry of state legislation that began in the early 1960s had several effects. It typically spelled out the responsibilities, funding, and management issues shared by state and local authorities, while separating the colleges from the public school districts, which had constructed many of them. Despite assurances that local boards would maintain certain prerogatives, it is obvious that control was gravitating toward the state capitals. Under federal prodding, nearly all the states created coordinating bodies for all public higher education, including community colleges. The states sponsored studies of need and feasibility that projected population growth, employment opportunities, and college demand. They also set tuition policies, reimbursement schedules, and guidelines for capital expenditures, often leaving a portion of the latter to the local districts. A few built state systems encompassing all governance and funding, but most sustained hybrids.

Other areas, such as course requirements and staff responsibilities, were less strictly controlled. But by the 1990s, more micromanagement was apparent, as the state agencies sought evidence of college effects, especially in remedial and occupational education. Various groups lobbying on behalf of their members were active in gaining state approval for all sorts of special action, from faculty salaries to intercollegiate athletics. Oregon's State Board of Education set instructor standards. The Texas Higher Education Coordinating Board mandated an academic skills test and began linking approval of new associate degrees to the college's job-training record. Florida's state board of regents set uniform general-education requirements across all colleges and universities and limited the number of credit hours toward degrees for which it would provide reimbursement. Having established rules for college formation and support, the states moved steadily toward more detailed regulations. Little fell outside their purview.

## FEDERAL POLICIES

Federal policies affecting community colleges may be clustered under headings of access, funding, and curriculum. Under access the primary policy was the Servicemen's Readjustment Act of 1944, commonly known as the GI Bill. By placing funds for college-going in the hands of the veterans of World War II, the bill marked a major shift in the direction of federal influence. For the first time federal monies were given to individuals rather than to the institutions. Each veteran was authorized to attend any college or university that would admit him, and the government agreed to pay the tuition, pay for books and supplies, and pay a monthly stipend for living expenses. Since many veterans did not qualify for university admission or chose to attend the community colleges in their hometown, veteran enrollment swelled the two-year college campuses.

A second set of acts affecting access came in subsequent years as numerous forms of antidiscrimination legislation were passed. The civil rights acts of the 1960s and 1970s forbade discrimination in college admissions on the basis of race. Title IX of the Education Amendments of 1972 prohibited gender bias in college admissions. The Rehabilitation Act of 1973 and the Americans with Disabilities Act of 1990 mandated access and special facilities for individuals with disabilities who otherwise met academic and technical standards. The Age Discrimination Act of 1975 prohibited discrimination on the basis of age in programs or activities receiving federal financial assistance.

Numerous court rulings pointed to the specifics in these acts enhancing access. In the 1970s a federal district court ruled in favor of two 16-year old plaintiffs who had sought entrance to Sonoma County Junior College in California. The court reasoned that the institution's requirement that students be 18 years old was not rational in relationship to the state's interest in educating qualified students. Also in the 1970s the U.S. Supreme Court ruled that Southeastern Community College (North Carolina) was within its rights in denying the admission of a severely deaf student to its nursing program because the student's disability would preclude her taking part in the clinical aspects of the nursing program and would create serious difficulties in practicing the profession. However, in other cases the courts have ruled that students must be admitted if reasonable accommodations can be made that would enable them to participate in educational programs. Accordingly, the colleges were directed to build access ramps for physically disabled students and to make accommodations in science laboratories so that visually handicapped students might participate.

Federal funding for students was continued through the Pell Grant program, along with supplemental educational opportunity grants, guaranteed student loans, and college work-study aid. Since the Pell Grant program began in the early 1970s, students in community colleges have received between 18 and 26 percent of the awards each year. It is more difficult to estimate an exact federal contribution to students in the form of guaranteed loans because students who receive the loans are expected to repay them. The contribution of the federal government appears in the form of interest that is paid while the student is enrolled and when the government pays the banks if the student defaults. Because, compared to students in the universities, the students in community colleges tend to be from lower socioeconomic classes and the dropout rates are higher, default rates in the community colleges have been higher than those for university students. This, then, represents a type of student subsidy.

Amendments to the Higher Education Act of 1965 have been made several times, most recently in 1998. A review of these amendments shows some effects on community colleges, of which a few are direct but most are tangential. Among the direct effect, the 1992 amendments established a Community College Liaison Office in the U.S. Department of Education and provided Presidential Access Scholarships for students in two-year programs. Among the less direct effects, the amendments extended Pell Grant eligibility for students attending part time, authorized grants to colleges enrolling high proportions of Hispanic students, and allowed colleges to petition for funds to support child care services for disadvantaged students.

The 1998 amendments sharply increased the maximum Pell Grant award while denying Pell Grants to students in colleges with 25 percent or greater default rates over a three-year period. Some community college students were affected because their colleges were struggling to keep from crossing the 25 percent default line. The amendments also demanded more disclosure of campus crime rates and mandated that colleges distribute a voter registration form to each enrolled student.

Federal government influence on community college curriculum has been felt primarily in the occupational areas. Beginning with the Vocational Act of 1963, which authorized federal funding of occupational programs in postsecondary institutions, the community colleges have been handsomely supported by this form of federal financing. Actually, the Vocational Education Act was not the first piece of legislation to authorize federal funds for community colleges. In the 1930s several colleges were receiving federal money for occupational education that had been appropriated under the 1917 Smith-Hughes Act and the 1937 George-Deen Act. The colleges slipped in under those acts because, as Eells (1941) pointed out, they did not "mean that the *institution* must be of less than college grade—only that the particular *work offered*, for which federal aid is received, must be of less than college grade" (1941, p. 29). However, the 1963 act and the amendments of 1968 and 1972 vastly augmented federal funds for vocational education. The Carl D. Perkins Vocational Education Act of 1984 further modified the guidelines for distributing federal funding, and by 1985 the community colleges were receiving around 22 percent of the Perkins money. Other federal programs providing funds for community college vocational education include Job Training Partnerships, Job Opportunities and Basic Skills, Omnibus Trade and Competitiveness, Worksite Literacy, and Cooperative Education.

Compared with the federal funds running to occupational education, federal support for other studies has been minuscule. The National Endowment for the Humanities (NEH) has sponsored a few programs addressed to community college education, but funding does not reach more than a couple of percentage points of that which the federal government makes available for occupational studies. Some colleges have taken advantage of programs sponsored by the Fund for the Improvement of Postsecondary Education and the National Science Foundation. Most federal legislation does not specify institutional type; however, Title III (Developing Institutions) has benefited the colleges. Also, the Tribally Controlled Community Colleges Act singles out a particular group for direct support. Other funds appropriated by the federal government often loop through the states for administration. Many are block grants that can be used by the states to assist the colleges in developing curriculum, providing funds to various categories of students, training teachers, and so on. The federal interest in these areas goes all the way back to the various types of vocational education support appropriated early in the century.

## CONCLUSION

The history of state and national policy affecting community colleges points up how the institutions have developed within a federated system, ranging from the U.S. government to the local school districts. But without a doubt, the state governments have been most influential, especially since the 1960s, when nearly all of them stepped up efforts to coordinate public higher education within their borders. State policies allocate decision-making authority to state agencies and college officials. State regulations promote or inhibit institutional growth. State databases reveal college operation and compliance with regulations. State funds provide for operating expenses and capital outlay. Some states have imposed standards for associate degrees and certificates and for the types of courses qualifying for reimbursement; others have established staff qualifications. Although the colleges are still localized institutions, drawing their students and character from their neighborhood, they operate within a myriad state regulations. The influence of the federal government pales in light of state rules and support.

A stable set of institutions has been the main effect of state control. From the start, the states have demanded minimum numbers of students and reliable funding sources. The college leaders know what to expect; their communities are not faced with unforeseen closures, mergers, or reconstitutions as different types of schools. There is little tolerance for weak, drifting colleges that are hardly worthy of the name. The community colleges are reliable players in each state's education system.

Some of the other consequences of state influence have been institutional expansion and a lateral curriculum. Most states fund on the basis of student enrollment. Since enrolling more students results in the receipt of more money, the college leaders have developed a mindset favoring growth, which stems from the knowledge that without augmented enrollment, leaders cannot fund salary increases, new programs, and all the changes that make their colleges appear innovative. The institutions are reimbursed for students taking classes, whether these are, from one term to another, the same or different students. There have been few incentives for increased rates of program completion; thus, the leaders react with alarm when states impose enrollment caps or request data on graduation or job-attainment rates. The federal government has colluded in this "growth is good" presumption through its ever-expanding student grant and loan programs.

Curricular breadth is a corollary of the growth dogma; more courses designed to serve more students with different aspirations enhance enrollments. Here again the federal government is a contributor. If it had not funded occupational education heavily, the colleges could not have developed the numerous vocational programs that have expanded their curriculums. Taken together, the enrollment growth and the curricular breadth have yielded the community colleges' greatest contribution to American postsecondary education, access, and their second greatest contribution, workforce development.

In the coming years, governmental influence will continue along the channels developed over the past several decades: federal support for students and state support for the colleges on a broader basis. The trend toward state-level coordination, in place for over one-third of a century, will continue. The requests for data on program outcomes will increase, and pressures for funding on the basis of outcomes will become ever more insistent. Perhaps the latter evidences public distrust of the colleges; perhaps it suggests that they are so important a part of the social system that it is unconscionable for their staff to imply, "Send us the funds and don't ask questions." In any event, a set of institutions attuned historically to process is being turned laboriously, gradually, toward a concern for product. Are community colleges players in the global economy? Purveyors of education to people around the world? They began as schools serving their local communities, and there they will remain, as public perceptions hold them in the place from which they arose.

## REFERENCES

Bogue, J. P. (1950). *The community college*. New York: McGraw Hill.

Eells, W. C. (1941). *Present status of junior college terminal education*. Washington, DC: American Association of Junior Colleges.

Hurlbert, A. S. (1969). State master plans for community colleges. *ERIC Clearinghouse for Junior Colleges Monograph Series* (Number 8), Los Angeles.

Indiana State Commission for Higher Education. (1996). *Transferring Ivy Tech credit to public institutions: 1996 progress report*. Indianapolis.

Jones, D., Ewell, P., & McGuinness, A. (1998). *The challenges and opportunities facing higher education.* San Jose, CA: National Center for Public Policy and Higher Education.

Kentucky Council on Postsecondary Education. (1997). *The status of Kentucky postsecondary education: In transition, 1997.* Frankfort.

Lau, R. (1997, April 2). *Employment rights of administrators in the California community colleges.* Compton, CA: Compton Community College District.

LeMon, R. E., & Pitter, G. W. (1996). *Standardizing across institutions: Now that we all look alike, what do we look like?* Tallahassee, FL.

Lombardi, J. (1968, October). Unique problems of the inner city colleges. Speech presented to California Junior College Association, Anaheim, CA. ERIC ED 026057.

Martorana, S. V., & Broomall, J. K. (1981, June). *State legislation affecting community and junior colleges, 1980* (Report Number 37). Pennsylvania State University Center for the Study of Higher Education.

Martorana, S. V., & Garland, P. H. (1986). *State legislation and state-level public policy affecting community, junior, and two-year technical college education, 1985.* Pennsylvania State University.

Martorana, S. V., & McGuire, W. G. (1976). *State legislation relating to community and junior colleges, 1973–75.* State College: Pennsylvania State University Press.

Martorana, S. V., et al. (1991). *State legislation and state-level public policy affecting community, junior, and two-year technical college education, 1989.* Pennsylvania State University.

President's Commission on Higher Education. (1947). *Higher education for American democracy.* Washington, DC: U.S. Government Printing Office.

Schmidt, P. (1997, April 4). Rancor and confusion greet a change in South Carolina's budgeting system. *Chronicle of Higher Education,* pp. A26–A27.

Yarrington, R. (1969). *Junior colleges: 50 states, 50 years.* Washington, DC: American Association of Junior Colleges.

## Chapter 2

# Federal Policies and Community Colleges: A Mix of Federal and Local Influences

*Cheryl D. Lovell*

It is common to consider community colleges as "local" institutions. This local label is indeed true when most community colleges talk about their service region or community district. A local label is also accurate when referring to the typical community college student who attends the community college in his or her local geographic region or neighborhood. Nonetheless, though local in many aspects, the community college of today and tomorrow has more connections to the federal government in Washington, DC, than one might realize. The level of federal influence is great for many community colleges, and this involvement and influence show no signs of reversing anytime soon. Thus, community college leaders must understand the far-reaching arm of the federal government and the opportunities for "localizing" that influence.

Although the history of the community college movement has been well documented (Brint & Karabel, 1989; Cohen & Brawer, 1989; Cohen, Brawer, et al., 1994; Goodchild & Wechsler, 1997; Ratcliff, Schwarz, & Ebbers, 1994) little, if anything, is known about the extent of federal influence on local community colleges. The focus of this chapter is on federal involvement with community colleges and the means by which this relationship can influence and, in some cases, drive the activities and focus of the local community college. An examination of the federal influences will be presented in six sections. First, a context for understanding the federal role in postsecondary education will be presented. Typically, federal involvement with postsecondary education is apparent in four broad areas, and each of the areas will be explored in the subsequent five sections. The second section will discuss the important area of federal research support of community colleges. The third section will detail how federal tax policies influence community colleges. Fourth, how the federal government provides support for student financial aid will be examined. Fifth, mandates, both funded and unfunded, will be discussed in terms of their interest to community colleges. Finally, the chapter will conclude with a discussion of the significant issues in the federal-community college relationship that will shape the community college campuses for the next century.

## CONTEXT SETTING: THE FEDERAL ROLE IN POSTSECONDARY EDUCATION

Even though education is constitutionally a state responsibility, the federal government has a long history of involvement in education. Dating back to the 1700s, there are examples of the federal government enacting laws and statutes that aided the establishment and support of postsecondary education. The Northwest Ordinance of 1785 is a prime example of such support (Pulliam, 1991). Other examples include the Morrill Act of 1862, The Smith-Hughes Act, the GI Bill, the National Defense Act (Brubacher & Rudy, 1976), and countless other legislative acts displaying the interests of Congress to ensure a quality higher educational system in this country.

Evidence of federal support is noted as "federal outlays for student aid and research and development (R&D) far exceed those of the states, industry, and other donors," according to Gladieux and King (1998, p. 217). They go on to say: "[T]he federal impact on campuses and on students is substantial, diverse, and constantly changing. It is the product of deeply rooted traditions but also short-term decisions" (p. 217). Further, Lovell (1999) notes continuing influence from the federal government across many areas of higher education. Thus it is clear the federal role has the potential to significantly affect community colleges. Specifically, the expenditures of federal monies and interests tend to be clustered around four major dimensions of involvement: research funding, tax policies, student financial aid, and mandates. What follows is an examination of each of the four dimensions in terms of its immediate interests to the community college campus.

### Federal Research Funding

There is a long history of federal support for research in America's colleges and universities. Federal support to agriculturally based, land grant universities proved beneficial for applying and sharing knowledge. More recent support of new knowledge for science occurred during World War II (Gladieux & King, 1998). Wartime activities created new demands on technology, and developing new scientific knowledge to aid this country's war efforts became a critical area for the federal government. Universities were the major benefactors of the influx of federal research dollars. Federal dollars have continued to flow to colleges and universities for research and development (R&D) (National Science Board,

1998). The most recent data show around \$14.1 million in federal dollars for support of academic R&D (National Science Board, 1998, p. 284). Much of this money flows to research universities (National Science Foundation, 1998), with relatively few institutions receiving the bulk.

Historically, community colleges have not received research support from the federal government. However, this trend is changing with passage of the 1994 Advanced Technological Education (ATE) Program (AACC, 1999e). The ATE is a National Science Foundation program that is intended to provide financial support to community colleges for improvements in the curriculum of technological education. According to the AACC, about 160 grants focused on the quality of advanced technological education in the science and engineering fields, basic math, and core science programs (AACC, 1999e) have been awarded since 1994. Community colleges have also been able to use the funding to establish Centers of Excellence to identify "systemic approaches to technician education within specific disciplines" (AACC, 1999e, p. 1).

To continue the support of community colleges for research advancements in the fiscal year (FY) 2000 budget, the administration has designated additional funding to support three National Science Foundation programs within its Division of Undergraduate Education (DUE) (AACC, 1999e). Institutions can submit proposals dealing with curriculum and laboratory improvements. In addition, the U.S. Department of Agriculture accepts proposals from community colleges through its demonstration site programs. Some smaller programs are also available to community colleges through the U.S. Department of Commerce. Community colleges have been able to leverage federal support to enhance local programs and collaborate with industry (AACC, 1997). The participation in federal research programs can play a significant role in shaping the local community college curriculum and its programs. This support also shows a clear sign that the federal government plans to continue to support community colleges in the research dimension.

### Federal Tax Policies

Tax policies provide a form of assistance to community colleges in a variety of ways. Some are applied directly to the institution, whereas others are utilized directly by the students or parents of students who attend the college. Nonprofit postsecondary institutions benefit with a designation as a 501(c)3 by the Internal Revenue Service (IRS). This tax classification allows the institution to receive tax-deductible charitable donations and gifts. Consequently, both the donor and the receiving institution benefit. The donor can take an income tax deduction, and the institution receives important contributions that it might not otherwise gain.

Another important institutional tax benefit includes tax incentives for corporations that invest in university-based research and donate research-related equipment. This deduction has had a roller coaster past since the early 1980s.

According to Gladieux and King (1998), in 1981 corporations were given tax credits for investing in university-based research; this deduction was eliminated in 1986; and finally, in 1993, this tax break was restored for corporations to increase their collaborations with institutions.

Moreover, another tax policy that relates to postsecondary colleges involves the Unrelated Business Income Tax (UBIT) laws. These tax laws require the institution to pay federal taxes on income earned if the income was earned through means not related to the institution's primary educational mission (Lovell & Pankowski, 1989). Significant attention to taxable revenue is warranted when considering the range of potentially taxable sums of revenue in bookstores, housing, and dining facilities, for example. Thus, colleges have to be careful to avoid engaging in activities that are not education related for fear of violating UBIT laws.

A growing area for community colleges includes the establishment of non-profit foundations to support and enhance institutional activities. Tax policies in this arena are important for community colleges. Campus leaders must consider IRS tax policies carefully as they continue to establish these foundations.

Regarding individuals, federal tax policies provide several tax incentives for participation in higher education. One of the most noted tax policies is the personal exemption deduction that parents can take for dependents between the ages of 19 and 24 who are enrolled in college. In addition, individuals receive a tax break on profits from U.S. Savings Bonds if they are used for participation in postsecondary education.

Community colleges might benefit from Section 127 of the IRS tax code as it allows individuals to receive a tax exemption for educational benefits provided by their employers. Community colleges may primarily benefit, as these campuses tend to have the curricular offerings to provide quick, tailored, job-skill improvement programs, in contrast to the typical research universities, for example. This tax policy benefit has also had a difficult past because it was not allowed as an itemized deduction in 1993, but it was restored in 1995. It was disallowed again in 1996 but recently was extended for three additional years (AACC, 1998a).

Recently, individuals have been granted new tax deductions for participation in postsecondary education. For example, President Clinton signed the Taxpayer Relief Act of 1998 into law, providing for two significant educational tax credits, the HOPE Scholarship and the Lifetime Learning Tax Credit (U.S. Department of Education, 1998). The HOPE Scholarship is not what the name might imply; rather, it is a tax credit for up to $1,500 for the first two years of college for students who attend at least half time (AACC, 1998a). An individual is eligible for this tax break regardless of the type of institution attended as long as he or she is enrolled in a degree, certificate, or other program leading to a recognized education credential (AACC, 1998a). However, some consider the real benefactor to be the community colleges (Brindley, 1997), since their average tuition costs are so low. Community college students can deduct most, if not all, of the tuition charges for the first two years which may booster community college enrollments. Not only does this definitely reflect a support for community colleges but these tax deductions also help support the national policy of providing access to higher education.

The Lifetime Learning Tax Credit provides a similar tax deduction for individuals, but this time it applies to students who attend less than half time. A 20 percent tax credit is allowed for the first $5,000 in tuition and fees for junior, senior, graduate students, or adults who take a course to advance their career (U.S. Department of Education 1998). This program is intended to apply after the HOPE Scholarship tax credit covering the first two years has already been utilized.

Students may also deduct the interest or qualified student loans under certain circumstances. The Education Individual Retirement Account (IRA) also can be used on a tax-free basis for qualified higher-education expenses (IRS, 1997). Again, these are individual tax benefits, but they do provide further support for postsecondary education through federal tax policies.

Community colleges may be more influenced by these tax credits than private, independent institutions because tax credits to individuals through these new programs will probably cover most of the tuition for an associate degree. It is important to community college leaders to keep their students informed of this new tax option.

## Federal Student Financial Aid

Federal support for higher education through student financial aid has been demonstrated in earnest over the last 50 years. A plethora of federal policies has been enacted, starting with the Servicemen's Readjustment Act of 1944, which provided federal financial aid to support access to higher education (Brubacher & Rudy, 1976). Other mass efforts from the federal government included the 1965 Higher Education Act, which made "an explicit commitment to equalizing college opportunities for needy students" (Gladieux & King, 1998, p. 229). Since a primary public policy focus for the federal government has been to provide access to students through financial aid, this has created an environment offering students a greater array of postsecondary options. Federal support for financial aid has been achieved through several grant and loan initiatives. Up until about 1980, grants comprised the majority of the appropriations for federal financial aid (College Board, 1998). In total, AACC reports that federal financial aid provides the bulk of all aid awarded to college students (AACC, 1996). Therefore, it makes sense for community college leaders to understand the breath and depth of the federal financial aid programs. An overview of the federal financial aid programs administered through the U.S. Department of Education may assist community college leaders.

*Grants.* The federal appropriations for Pell Grants exceed $6 billion for 1997–1998 (College Board, 1998). Pell grants are distributed based on financial need (as determined according to a federal need analysis) and are not required to be repaid. In terms of magnitude of impact of the federal Pell Grant program, community college students receive about 30 percent of all Pell awards (AACC, 1996). Baime notes, "The Pell Grant program remains the critical bedrock of federal financial aid for community college students" (AACC, 1996, p. 2). The Pell program is designed to increase access for students with the most financial need, Baime indicates that more than two-thirds of all Pell recipients had an annual income of less than $20,000 (AACC, 1996).

A second federal grant is the Supplemental Education Opportunity Grant (SEOG), which is awarded to postsecondary students based on "exceptional financial need," as determined by the federal need analysis formula. There is less money in the SEOG program than in the Pell program. For example, during 1997–1998, just less than $600,000 was allocated for the neediest students (College Board, 1998).

*Loans.* The biggest shift in the federal financial aid arena has been in the area of increased reliance on loans over grants. Much of the growth in the loan area has occurred since the federal caps were increased on the total amount a student could borrow, as was the case during the 1992 reauthorization of the Higher Education Act (Gladieux & King, 1998). Loans are a big part of the financial aid environment, and it is important to note the different types of loan programs that may be utilized by community college students.

Federal loans now predominate the financial aid mix with just over 59 percent of all financial aid coming in the form of loans and a total of $30 billion being distributed in 1996–1997 (Lee, 1999). The Federal Family of Educational Loan Program (FFEL) provides two major types of loans: subsidized and unsubsidized. The Stafford Loan–Subsidized represents 60 percent of all loans (Lee, 1999). Subsidized loans are available to students based on financial need. The loan does not accrue interest as long as the borrower maintains enrollment. The federal government covers the interest or "subsidizes" it during this enrollment. Nationally, approximately $12 billion was awarded to students in the form of subsidized loans (College Board, 1998). Unsubsidized loans, on the other hand, begin to accrue interest from the time the loan is made. Also, financial need is not an issue in determining how much a student is eligible to borrow. More and more federal dollars are being allocated to the unsubsidized loan program, with close to $8 billion allocated in 1997–1998 (College Board, 1998).

The Perkins Loan Program provides both undergraduate and graduate students with low-interest loans directly lent by a banking institution. Under this loan program, the institution is responsible for determining how much a student should receive based on the federal needs analysis. Distribution of loan payments and collection of repayments are the responsibility of the institution. The Perkins program received an appropriation of just over $1 billion in 1997–1998 (College Board, 1998).

The PLUS loan is available for parents of college students. It is a federal loan program available to students who are enrolled at least half time. The key to this federal loan program is that the money is lent to the parents and not directly to the student. A typical credit check is required before the loan can be issued to the parents. Just over $1 billion was allocated for this loan program during the 1997–1998 year (College Board, 1998).

The Consolidation Loans Program allows borrowers to combine several loan programs into one. This program provides more flexible repayment options and is intended to assist students and parent borrowers with easier repayment schedules. It may be appealing to borrowers as the interest rate could be lower through the consolidation program than the interest on the separate loans. For many students and their parents, consolidation loans may be a valuable tool to support continued enrollment in higher education.

*Work-Study.* The total outlay of financial aid received by undergraduates in the form of federal work-study monies was less than 2 percent of all financial aid monies in 1996–1997 (College Board, 1998); this federal program received just over $1 billion in appropriations. Work-study eligibility is need based, and hourly rates vary depending on the type of work. Students are encouraged to work in areas of the campus to support their academic interests if possible, with options to work off-campus under certain circumstances.

Federal financial aid programs are critical. Community college administrators need to know which programs exist and how students can utilize them. It is important to note that community colleges do not receive a majority of their revenues from federal financial aid (AACC, 1996); however, these programs can be an important means for some students to participate in postsecondary education.

## FEDERAL MANDATES: FUNDED AND UNFUNDED

The federal government can control and direct the activities of community colleges, as with all institutions, through mandates and regulations. Gladieux and King's (1998) framework for understanding the federal government's role in American higher education does include the area of regulations or mandates. However, there is no distinction between those requirements that are funded and those that are not funded. Since governmental regulation is increasing and many of the regulations or mandates are not supported with funding, it is imperative that the framework be expanded and that community college leaders understand this growing policy area. These regulations are typically called "unfunded mandates," meaning that the government sets forth a regulation that must be implemented and followed, without any monetary support. Burdensome regulations often require community colleges to allocate institutional monies to comply with a new federal law. It is impossible to discuss every example of these unfunded mandates and regulations, but some of the more current, and often burdensome regulations include several aspects important to the federal government, such as Integrated Postsecondary Education Data Systems (IPEDS), Student Right to know (SRK) legislation, the Americans with Disabilities Act (ADA), the Occupational Safety and Health Act (OSHA), vote (voter registration, Family Education Rights and Privacy Act (FERPA), and immunization law.

### Unfunded Mandates

The Integrated Postsecondary Education Data Systems (IPEDS) require each institution receiving any federal funding (direct or indirect) to report data to the federal Department of Education, through its National Center for Education Statistics (NCES), on a variety of data areas. Institutions respond to a series of surveys requiring data on students, faculty, staff, facilities, revenues, and expenditures. The intentions of the IPEDS program are meritorious in that data for all institutions can be aggregated to describe the condition of postsecondary education. Also, there are many analytical advantages to having one repository of postsecondary institutional data. However, the time and effort required by some institutions to complete the IPEDS surveys can be extensive. This is especially true for community colleges with limited data collection and analytical staff. Some community college systems have attempted to make some IPEDS reporting easier for campuses by coordinating data collection and reporting from the system office. But these data reporting requirements can still be a strain on campuses with limited budget and staff.

Equally important, the Student Right to Know (SRK) and campus crime legislation of 1990 requires institutions to make available to students, prospective students, and employees data regarding several important elements, such as graduation rates and crime activities on campuses. NCES also serves as the repository for these databases. Community colleges may be limited in institutional research staff and thus have difficulty in reporting these data to the campus community and to the federal government.

One significant law that applies to all public and private institutions is the American with Disabilities Act (ADA), which requires that all institutions provide access and accommodation to students needing special assistance. The intent of the law was to make facilities more accessible to people with disabilities, and it can be extremely expensive to gain full compliance. ADA requires a twofold approach for postsecondary institutions: both physical and academic/programmatic accommodations must be made. Thus institutions need to provide physical accessibility to all students by altering older buildings (i.e., adding elevators) and have some type of accommodation for the curricular offerings to be accessible (i.e., having books in Braille or providing notetakers for classes). The resources necessary to make all accommodations can be particularly burdensome for community colleges with limited budgets. The construction costs are extensive when a campus retrofits older buildings, and the curricular accommodations to make needed programs accessible to students with disabilities can easily double academic budgets. Since community colleges tend to be open enrollment institutions, they may be more inclined to have more students who need either physical or academic enhancements.

The Occupational Safety and Health Act (OSHA) also applies to community colleges. OSHA regulations are intended to protect workers in hazardous work environments by assuring safe and healthful working conditions (OSHA, 1990). The law is important to community colleges because many of these institutions have programs in the technical science areas, automotive sciences, environmental technologies, and trades/vocational related programs that could cause instructional staff and students to be exposed to hazardous materials if precautions are not followed. The OSHA regulations are potentially of more concern to community colleges than to other institutions that do not specialize in these kinds of programs. It is often costly for institutions to comply with environmental regulations and meet the guidelines set by the OSHA laws.

There are several federal social policies that often require higher education institutions to enforce laws that might not otherwise have anything to do with their function as an educational institution. For example, voter registration and immunization laws are important social agenda items that postsecondary institutions are required to provide information about or monitor to comply with federal mandates. Yet these laws are not related to postsecondary education. Congress requires that community colleges provide information about voter registration to all students and require that students have certain vaccinations prior to enrolling in college programs.

## Funded Mandates

Congress also can provide funding to carry out certain federal programs and initiatives. The programs are often targeted to certain social agendas but also may come with appropriate monies to begin and, sometimes, carry out the program. Some of the more recent noted funded legislative enactments that are important to community colleges include the Workforce Investment Act and the Perkins Vocational Act of 1998. Technically, these specific legislative enactments are not required for community colleges, but for many institutions, they are the only way to acquire additional, new monies to support the curricular offerings of the campus. Many community colleges leaders often feel compelled to participate. Thus, these legislative regulations have the effect of a mandate, but in this case, participation comes with much-needed funding.

The intent of the major federal work-related legislation is to keep a competitive workforce and to keep citizens employable. Historically, some of the older programs include the Manpower Development and Training Act of 1962 (AACC, 1998g) the Comprehensive Employment Training Act (CETA), and the

Job Training Partnership Act (JTPA) (Katsinas & Swender, 1992). Congress made an attempt in the early to mid-1990s to combine several vocation-related programs and to streamline the federal efforts to improve America's workforce. These initiatives are considered some of the most important reforms in the job training area during 1985–2000 (AACC, 1999a).

The Workforce Investment Act (WIA) is intended to reform federal job-training programs and to establish a "one-stop" system of services to assist American workers. Many believe community colleges are principal players in such efforts as they have had very close ties to local community and business leaders (Shults, 1997). When this legislation was signed into law, the community colleges were guaranteed a key role in each local one-stop office, which is to have at least one community college represented (AACC, 1998d). Each state is to establish a workforce investment board to assist in the development of a statewide plan for providing job-training services to the state. Each local community can also establish its own local workforce board to implement a local version of the statewide plan. The community college leaders are prime participants in this effort, as they have been "doing this for years," according to former U.S. Secretary of Labor Robert Reich (Reinhard, 1994, p. 26). Partners in the one-stop centers provide assistance for job training, adult education, and vocational rehabilitation, and community colleges will have a key role in delivering these training and education (AACC, 1998d). Within the WIA, Congress also included a bill entitled the Adult Education and Family Literacy Act (1998b), which also gives community colleges an opportunity to receive funding for workplace literacy services.

Another program, the Carl D. Perkins Vocational and Technical Education Act of 1998, has recommitted the federal government to vocational education (AACC, 1999g). This act provides greater flexibility for states to utilize federal funds. The states receive a lump sum fund that is to be distributed for statewide and local programs to improve areas of the state that are in need of vocational and technical education. A requirement to have 85 percent of the funding distributed to local programs is a key feature for community colleges (AACC, 1999f).

With both the WIA and the Perkins act, accountability measures are increased. This increase is another reason why funded mandates become burdensome to community colleges. The reporting requirements for the institutions that receive these federal funds are very extensive. Each funded program is to provide data that show performance indicators regarding student attainment of academic, vocational, and technical skill proficiencies and completion, placement, and program retention rates (AACC, 1999f).

## CONCERNS FOR THE FUTURE FEDERAL–COMMUNITY COLLEGE RELATIONSHIP

The involvement of federal influence with the local community college is not abating. Rather, it has become an entrenched way of viewing the postsecondary education system in the United States. Where this relation will go is not yet known. One certainty is that this way of doing business—of carrying out public policy through funded and unfunded regulations—will continue and most likely grow. The effective community college leader must understand how to use this external influence to harness resources for the local campus. It is important to know when to apply for certain federally funded programs and to be aware of ways to collaborate with local industry and other local institutions to maximize the monies received and take advantage of the changing environment. It is also important for community college leaders to know of the continuing problems with these federal efforts and to know how the federal programs may provide unique issues for their institutions. Lobbying federal agencies and legislators to better understand issues of the community college is of paramount importance to community college (AACC-ACCT, 1999).

It is also important for community college leaders to stay informed on key legislative activities (AACC, 1998f; AACC, 1998c). There are many efforts in Washington, DC, that will continue to focus on community colleges, for example, the recent efforts to help shape federal rules based on the Reauthorization of the Higher Education Act of 1998 (H.R. 6, 1998; AACC, 1999d). Community colleges are key players in linkages with K-12 and postsecondary education (Hodgkinson, 1999), and community colleges support access to a growing population of students who want education and training on demand. To be successful in this demanding environment, community college leaders must know the laws and regulations and understand how they may affect their campuses. Federal support for research, tax policies, financial aid, and mandates has been explored in this chapter. Of these dimensions of federal involvement with colleges, financial aid policies are particularly critical and affect the campus in many ways. It is important to note specifically how crucial this domain of federal involvement interests community colleges.

Regarding federal student financial aid, community colleges are confronted with a whole host of issues that do not apply to certain other institutions, such as research universities. The key areas of concern for community colleges regarding federal financial aid relate to issues of satisfactory academic progress, remedial education, and ability to benefit. Federal student financial aid regulations require students who receive financial aid to make sufficient progress toward completing their program of study. This means that a certain number of credit hours should be attained by within a given time frame. Community colleges also need to be sure students are enrolled in credits that count toward a recognized program of study.

Remedial education is a significant concern for many institutions, but it is a primary concern for community colleges, as it may make a participating student ineligible for federal financial aid under certain circumstances. Some states, such as Colorado, for example, only provide funding for community colleges to provide remedial education. Baccalaureate institutions in the state may offer some remedial coursework, but they must pay for it from their own budgets. This puts the community colleges in the primary role of providing the needed remediation and with limitations on how federal financial aid can be used to cover remedial course work, community college administrators must monitor course-taking patterns of its students in a manner that baccalaureate institutions do not.

Ability to Benefit (ATB) requirements pertain to institutions with open enrollments. The intent of the regulations is to ensure that students who receive federal financial aid have a chance of being successful in completing their program, that is, that they have some ability to benefit and gain from the educational experience. This safeguard is in place to make sure students do not receive financial assistance if they have no chance of completing the program. Prior to the student becoming eligible for federal financial aid, community colleges must assess his or her ability to determine whether the student has the potential to complete a program.

These are just a few of the many areas of federal financial aid that greatly influence the community colleges in ways different from other postsecondary institutions. It is paramount for community colleges to be aware of the federal requirements and to monitor institutional actions to maintain eligibility for federal student aid programs.

All federal regulations, whether funded or unfunded, generally require extensive accountability. Community college leaders also need to be aware of the data-reporting requirements and the outcome accountability associated with each federal mandate. The Perkins and Workforce Investment Acts are just two of several funded federal programs that place a burden on the receiving institution. Accountability measures and performance indicators are required in exchange for the funding. Community college leaders need to demonstrate success in a plethora of ways and become as knowledgeable as possible about these and other federal requirements.

Leadership for tomorrow's community college requires a keen awareness of federal activities and efforts. A good community college administrator is one who can combine and localize federal money in a way that supports the particular institutional mission (AACC, 1999b, 1999c). This kind of leadership will be essential for all community colleges. The key will be for campus leaders to know how to get the needed federal support without sacrificing local direction and control.

## REFERENCES

AACC (American Association of Community Colleges) (1996). Community college students and federal student financial aid. Available: http://www.aacc.nche.edu/leg/ White%20Papers/FIN_AID/FIN_AID.htm

AACC. (1997). Testimony of Alfredo de los Santos at hearing on FY 1998. Available: http://www.aacc.nche.edu/leg/testimony/Alfredo.htm

AACC. (1998a, August 3). About the Hope Scholarship and other tax benefits. Available: http://www.aacc.nche.edu/leg/HOPE/hopenews.htm

AACC. (1998b, October 1). Adult education and family literacy act. Available: http:// www.aacc.nche.edu/leg/legisu/workforce/aepofWIA98.html

AACC. (1998c, October 30). Higher education act reauthorization. Available: http://www.aacc.nche.edu/leg/legisu/heareau/heareauth.htm

AACC. (1998d, August 19). Highlights of the Workforce Investment Act. Available: http://www.aacc.nche.edu/leg/legisu/workforce/wjobsum.htm

AACC. (1998e, October 13). Hope Scholarship tax credit information. Available: http://www.aacc.nche.edu/leg/HOPE/hope.htm

AACC. (1998f, October 12). Summary of the higher education amendments of 1998. Available: http://www.aacc.nche.edu/leg/docs/acheasum.htm

AACC. (1998g, October 13). The workforce investment act: Implications for community colleges. Available: http://www.aacc.nche.edu/leg/doc/WIA.htm

AACC. (1999a). The DOL issues an interim final rule. Available: http://www.aacc.nche.edu/headline/041599head 1.htm

AACC. (1999b, March 24). Fiscal year (FY) 2000 funding. Available: http://www.aacc.nche.edu/leg/legisu/apps/apps.htm

AACC. (1999c, April 15). Government relations. Available: http://www.aacc.nche.edu/leg/legislative.htm

AACC. (1999d, March 24). Higher education act reauthorization: Implementation of higher education and negotiated rulemaking. Available: http://www.aacc.nche.edu/leg/legisu/heareau/heareauth.htm

AACC. (1999e, March 24). The National Science Foundation authorization/appropriations issues. Available: http://www.aacc.nche.edu/leg/legisu/NSF/nsf.htm

AACC. (1999f, March 24). Vocational education: The Carl D. Perkins Vocational-Technical Education Amendments. Available: http://www.aacc.nche.edu/leg/legisu/voced/voced.htm

AACC. (1999g). Workforce education and training. Available: http://www.aacc.nche.edu/leg/legisu/workforce/workforce.htm

AACC-ACCT. (1999). AACC-ACCT Community college agenda for the 106th Congress. Available: http://www.aacc.nche.edu/leg/legagenda/105th/106th.htm

Baime, D. (1996). *Community college students and federal student financial aid: A policy framework for the next administration*. Washington, DC: AACC.

Baker, G., & Reed, L. (1994, April/May). Creating a world-class workforce. *Community College Journal*, 64 (5): 31–35.

Bergman, T. (1994, October/November). New resource for training: The national workforce assistance collaborative. *Community College Journal*, 65 (2): 43–47.

Berson, J. (1994, June/July). A marriage made in heaven: Community college and service learning. *Community College Journal*, pp. 14–19.

Boone, E. (1997). National perspective of community colleges. *Community College Journal of Research and Practice, 21,* 1–12.

Brindley, D. (1997). The complex impact of the new tax law. *US News & World Report, 123* (9), 78–80.

Brint, S., & Karabel, J. (1998). *The diverted dream: Community colleges and the promise of educational opportunity in America, 1900–1985*. New York: Oxford University Press.

Brown, L., & Dalziel, C. (1993, October/November). Federal support for information super highways: A review of pending legislation. *AACC Journal*, pp. 26–29.

Brubacher, J., & Rudy, W. (1976). *Higher education in transition* (3rd ed.). New York: Harper & Row.

Bryant, D., & Kirk, M. (1997). Legal and technological issues of the School-to-Work

Opportunities Act of 1994 (In E. I. Farmer & C. B. Key (Eds.) School-to-work systems no. 97, (pp. 89–96). San Francisco: Jossey-Bass. *(New Directions for Community Colleges)*.

Burd, S. (1997, April 4). Community college and 4-year institutions split over proposals on Pell Grants. *Chronicle of Higher Education*, p. A28.

Cohen, A., & Brawer, F. (1989). *The American community college*, (2nd ed). San Francisco: Jossey-Bass.

Cohen, A, Brawer, F., et al. (1994). *Managing community colleges*. San Francisco: Jossey-Bass.

College Board. (1998). Trends in student aid. Washington, DC: Author.

Culp, M., & Helfgot, S. (Eds.). *Life at the edge of the wave: Lessons from the community college*. Washington, DC: National Association of Student Personnel Administrators (NASPA).

Gladieux, L., & King, J. (1998). The federal government and higher education. In P. Altbach, R. Berdahl, & P. Gumport (Eds). *American higher education in the 21st century: Social, political, and economic challenges* (pp. 217–250). Boston: Boston College Center for International Higher Education.

Gladieux, L., & Swail, W. (1999). The virtual university and educational opportunity: Issues of equity and access for the next generation. *Policy Perspectives*. Washington, DC: The College Board.

Goldstein, M. (1993, October/November). Technology and the law: What every community college leader needs to know. *AACC Journal*, pp. 31–33.

Goldstein, M. (1997). Financial aid and the developmental student. In J. Ignash (Ed.), *Implementing effective policies for remedial and developmental education* (New Directions for Community Colleges, No. 100, pp. 81–86). San Francisco: Jossey-Bass.

Goodchild, L., & Wechsler, H. (1997). *The history of higher education* (2nd ed.). Needham Heights, MA: Simon & Schuster.

Gray, T. (1993, October/November). New regulatory opportunities in telecommunications technology. *AACC Journal*, pp. 33–35.

H.CON.RES. 68. (1999). Concurrent resolution on the budget for fiscal year 2000. Available: http://www.aacc.nche.edu/leg/legisu/apps/HconRes68.htm

Hendley, V. (1994, June/July). Community college leaders meet federal education leaders in Washington. *Community College Journal*, pp. 35–38.

Hodgkinson, H. (1999). *All one system: A second look*. Washington, DC: The National Center for Public Policy and Higher Education.

H. R. 6 (Public Law 105–244). (1998). Higher education amendments of 1998. Available: http://thomas.loc.gov/cgi-bin/bdquery/z?d105:HR00006:@@@D

Internal Revenue Service. (1997). Available: http://www.irs.ustreas.gov/prod/hot/not97–603.html

Katsinas, S. (1994, April/May). Is the open door closing? *AACC Journal*, pp. 22–28.

Katsinas, S., & Swender, H. (1992, June/July). Community colleges and JTPA: Involvement opportunity. *AACJC Journal*, pp. 18–23.

Kelly, K. (1997). *School-to-careers: Background paper and technical support*. ERIC Document No. 414441.

Lee, J. (1999). How do students and families pay for college? In J. King (Ed.). *Financing a college education: How it works, how it's changing*. Phoenix, AZ: ACE/Oryx Press.

Lederman, D. (1998, August 14). Congress approves plan to consolidate job training and adult-education programs. *Chronicle of Higher Education*, p. A29.

Lovell, C. D., & Pankowski, M. (1989). Living with the unrelated business income tax: A new challenge for continuing higher education. *Lifelong Learning, 12*(5), 20–22, 28.

Lovell, C. D. (1999). Past and future pressures and issues of postsecondary education: State perspectives. In B. Fife & J. Losco (Eds.), *Higher education in transition: The challenges of the new millenium* (pp. 109–139). Westport, CT: Greenwood Press.

Malik, J., & Petersen, J. (1993, August/September). Higher education act reauthorization. *AACC Journal*, pp. 15–16.

National Science Board. (1998). *Science and Engineering Indicators—1998*. Arlington, VA: National Science Foundation.

National Science Foundation. (1998). *Data brief* (NSF 98–303). Arlington, VA: National Science Foundation.

Occupational Safety and Health Act (OSHA). (1990). Public Law 91–596. Available: http://www.osha-slc.gov/OshAct_data/OSH_ACT1.html

Orr, M. (1998). Integrating secondary schools and community colleges through school-to-work transition and education reform. *Journal of Vocational Education Research, 23*, 1–17.

Phelps, D. (1994, August/September). What lies ahead for community colleges as we hurdle toward the 21st century. *Community College Journal*, pp. 22–25.

Pulliam, J. (1991). *History of education in America* (5th ed.) New York: Macmillan.

Ratcliff, J., Schwarz, S., & Ebbers, L. (1994). *Community colleges*. Needham Heights, MA: Simon & Schuster.

Reinhard, B. (1994). The federal challenge to our community colleges. *Journal of Career Planning and Employment, 54* (4), 26–30.

Ross, D. (1994, April/May). The reemployment act of 1994: New opportunities for America's community colleges. *AACC Journal*, pp. 16–20.

Salomon, K. (1993, October/November). Federal support for educational telecommunications. *AACC Journal*, pp. 35–36.

Shults, D. (1997). *The School-to-Work Opportunity Act and community college preparedness*. ERIC Document No. 40939.

State Higher Education Executive Officers (SHEEO). (1998). Focus on information from Washington. *Network News, 17*(4), 1–2.

Suksi, J. (1994). Educational reform: A new dimension for tech prep at the community college. *Community College Journal of Research and Practice, 18*, 57–70.

Tarricone, C. (1997). House panel approves "tech-prep" measure. *Chronicle of Higher Education*, p. A33.

U.S. Department of Education. (1998). *Investing in quality, affordable education for all Americans: A new look at community colleges*. Washington, DC: Office of Vocational and Adult Education.

U.S. Department of Education. (1999, February 8). Federal student financial assistance programs—distance education demonstration program. *Federal Register, 64*(25), 64 Fed. Reg. 16880.

*Chapter 3* _____

# Statewide Governance Structures and Two-Year Colleges

*Richard C. Richardson Jr. and*
*Gerardo E. de los Santos*

Most of the literature on the statewide governance and coordination of higher education has historically focused on four-year colleges and universities.[1] Since the 1970s, state governance and coordination of community colleges has been the focus of only a small number of community college specialists.[2] Yet during the past decade, as the 20th century drew to a close, writers looked increasingly at community college issues as part of the larger question of achieving integrated designs that respond in cost-effective ways to the entire range of a state's needs and priorities for higher education. This new focus is overdue. Campus-based and state-level community college practitioners have received little guidance in their efforts to achieve an appropriate balance between growing state account-ability concerns and their continuing commitments to the communities they serve. The tension has been aggravated by the failures of both state and local governments to provide adequate funding for enrollment increases, threatening the community college access mission by making users responsible for an ever-increasing share of operating costs.[3]

Adequate state financing is far from the only policy issue confronting com-munity college leaders, and it may not even be the most important. For example, referendums in California and Washington have eliminated affirmative action practices that operate on the basis of race or ethnicity, and courts have chal-lenged such practices in Texas and Michigan. Two of the three largest higher-education systems in the country have eliminated remedial education in four-year institutions. One of the early proposals advanced for the City Univer-sity of New York (CUNY) would have eliminated remedial education in the university's community colleges as well. Some 14 states have initiated or taken under consideration plans similar to the Georgia Hope Scholarships, which award public financial assistance on the basis of merit rather than need. Distance education, credit by examination, greater emphasis on competency-based and proficiency-based learning, and limits on the number of state-subsidized credits that are applicable to degrees not only threaten traditional learning practices, but also call into question the formulas that have been used to allocate resources to community colleges. In every state, legislators call for better K-12 linkages to higher education, improved articulation between two- and four-year institutions, and stronger school-to-work connections. Additionally, the mushrooming costs and capabilities of technology raise questions about service boundaries and interinstitutional collaboration.

While these few examples only begin to identify the complex issues that surround the statewide governance and coordination of higher education, they serve to remind us that state community college governance is laden with ever-changing dynamics and competing interests. Since the inception of public, two-year colleges nearly 100 years ago, administrators have been challenged to walk the "tightrope" of coordination with four-year colleges and universities. Elected state leaders have expected that all publicly funded institutions will work co-operatively instead of competing to admit freshman and sophomore students. More often than not, however, the reality has been competition and protectionism, as manifested in student transfer difficulties and increased costs. Now, under the influence of constrained resources and with the aid of new information technologies, states are moving to address long-standing issues of coordination and collaboration through renewed attention to the linkages between state government and all forms of higher education.

We begin this chapter by tracing the evolution of statewide governance and coordination for community colleges. Next, we propose a way of thinking about statewide structures that takes into account the various approaches states have adopted for coordinating and governing the public two- and four-year institutions they support. We developed the State Community College Governance Structures Typology to compare the strengths and weaknesses of arrangements currently in use across the nation's 50 states in the context of recent developments. In addition, we suggest that some arrangements are better designed than others to respond to the demands of the 21st century. In this regard, we differ from some of our predecessors who have suggested that success or failure in state-level coordination depends more on the philosophy and approach of the state director and staff than on the structure or range of powers of the organization.[4] Finally, we summarize current arrangements and suggest a number of issues that must be considered in the 21st century as states give renewed attention to the chronic problem of how to create integrated and collaborative systems out of the disjointed institutional arrangements that they inherited from the growth era of the 1950s and 1960s.

## HISTORICAL PERSPECTIVE

The explosive growth of community colleges during the 1960s, combined with the movement to separate these institutions from the public school districts, under whose auspices many had been founded, led to the establishment, not only of local community college governing boards, but also of new, state-level boards charged with the responsibility for coordinating new systems of community colleges. Examples include Arizona, Illinois, Colorado, Washington, Maryland, North Carolina, and Florida. Other states chose not to establish a specific coordinating board focused exclusively on community colleges, but instead strengthened coordinating arrangements for new or developing community college systems, either through a division within a coordinating board responsible for all educational services (Pennsylvania) or, more commonly, through a board with coordinating responsibilities for all postsecondary education institutions (Missouri, New Jersey, and Texas). Some states (generally the less populated) addressed coordination issues by placing all public institutions under a single governing board (Hawaii, North Dakota, South Dakota, Rhode Island, and Utah).

Prior to the mid-1970s, the activities of state coordinating boards focused primarily on the management of growth. During this era the literature suggests little, if any, criticism of their operations. Beginning in the mid- to late 1970s, however, coordinating boards were called on increasingly to administer legislative interventions and budget cuts, resulting in a marked deterioration of relationships with institutional boards and administrators (Glenny, 1979).

The list of external influences impinging on both local and state boards is a lengthy one. Both local and state boards were increasingly caught in a multifaceted decision-making process, in which ultimate accountability was distorted by the many agencies and interests that intervened. Executive orders, lapsing and allocation procedures, accounting requirements, informational demands, contract controls, legal opinions, audits, and program and budget controls were only some of the influences identified as emanating from a variety of state agencies (Mundt, 1978). During the 1970s and early 1980s, some events that added to these influences include equal access/equal opportunity legislation and regulations, collective bargaining, and proviso language restricting the use of appropriated funds (Owen, 1978). Thus, it is apparent that state coordinating boards were only one part of the web of increasing state regulation about which institutions complained. Furthermore, actions taken by a wide range of state and federal agencies were commonly channeled through state coordinating or governing boards, making them, from an institutional perspective, the most visible constraint on autonomy.

The reasons for the increase in state interest in regulation and accountability during the 1980s and early 1990s were not difficult to discover. Chief among them was the growing importance of community colleges as major users of state revenues. When community colleges derived most of their resources from a local property tax, it was a simple matter for the legislature to control state expenditures by using formula-driven appropriations that changed more slowly than the rate of inflation. In that era, community college leaders complained about being ignored in the legislative process. By the 1980s, with state appropriations running from 75 to 90 percent of the total expenditures for community colleges in many states, these institutions had become major competitors for tax dollars. The stage was set for the accountability movement that came to fruition in many states during the current decade and threatens to become the norm in the 21st century (see Chapter 4).

Given the nature of community colleges as resource-dependent organizations, the ideal of local autonomy will always be something to be pursued rather than an attainable end. Hence, community college presidents will never have all the autonomy they would like. Many of the regulations adopted by state coordinating boards have their genesis in the requirements of other state and federal agencies. Beyond agency intervention, the magnitude of state tax dollars required to maintain the enterprise guarantees continuing close scrutiny from legislators and governors. Most community college leaders accept the reality of state-level coordination and governance, particularly as it applies to budgeting and allocating resources fairly; being accountable for state appropriated funds; planning for statewide access to an appropriate range of programs, including the use of technology to deliver distance education; assuring barrier-free articulation and transfer; and providing credible information to elected state leaders and the general public about services and performance. Less accepted realities are actions that cap enrollments, require high-stakes tests of student competencies, specify admission eligibility, mandate responsibility for remedial education, limit program or course availability, mandate faculty governance arrangements, or base allocations on state-specified performance criteria.

Given the movement toward increased state coordination during the past two decades, it is not surprising that a considerable amount has been written on how to minimize conflict between state and local boards. The delineation of functions, the approach chosen by California when the board of governors was created in 1969, is particularly appealing because it holds out the promise of preserving the highest degree of local control and autonomy by defining responsibilities so that they appear mutually exclusive and by assigning them to either one board or the other (Clark, 1980). Of course, in real life there is a high degree of interdependence, both between functions and between boards. As a result, the delineation of functions approach worked in California only as long as the board of governors chose not to exercise its prerogatives and the funding arrangements for community colleges placed the major burden on the local property tax. By 1980, however, it was apparent that board functions, as they pertained to issues of mutual responsibility, were paramount. Therefore, the more important question to ask was no longer, "Who did what?" but, rather,

"What can we do together that otherwise cannot be done?" (Callan, 1981; Clark, 1980).

Despite calls for state and local boards to work closely together, most writers who have examined the interface between local and state-level boards have not been sanguine about their findings. Tillery and Wattenbarger (1985) described local state relationships as characterized by an inadequate delineation of authority and by the appearance that the state always wins the arguments. A decade later, Tschechtelin (1994) asserted that dualistic advocacy remained a major challenge. State governments expected community colleges to appreciate state priorities and to be accountable, while community college leaders resisted intrusion and valued autonomy while expecting strong financial support.

The functions of governing institutions cannot be defined so as to make them exclusively a local or a state responsibility. Autonomy, rather than an unqualified virtue, is desirable to the extent that those to whom it is granted can demonstrate superior performance. Local boards function to ensure responsiveness to local needs, while state boards ensure accountability for state funds. Communication between state and local boards, as well as among other community college participants, is indispensable to achieving effective results under conditions of interdependency.

## TOWARD A NEW TYPOLOGY OF STATE COMMUNITY COLLEGE GOVERNANCE STRUCTURES

A recent study of higher-education coordinating and governance arrangements in seven large states developed a new approach to classifying systems based on the answers to two key questions:

• Does the state system have a coordinating board/agency with at least some statutory authority for serving as the interface between higher-education institutions and state government for the four central work processes: budgeting, program planning and approval, information management and dissemination, and articulation and collaboration? (Coordinating boards do not have authority over such decisions as the appointment and removal of presidents or day-to-day management and operation of the institution.)

• Does the state system have more than a single governing board for all of its degree-granting, postsecondary institutions, including community colleges and technical institutes? (Governing boards have legal authority to operate the institution, including appointment and removal of presidents and all other decisions not specifically reserved by the state for purposes of coordination and accountability) (Richardson, Bracco, Callan, & Finney, 1998).

If the answer to the first question is "yes," then the state higher-education system is classified as "federal" because policy makers have chosen to separate the powers of institutional governance and advocacy from responsibility for representing the public interest in a way that reflects the influences of federalism in the U.S. Constitution.[5]

If the answer to the first question is "no," then we move to the second question. If the answer to the second question is "no," then the system is unified. If the answer to the second question is "yes," then the system is classified as segmented. Institutions in segmented systems are divided into two or more sectors, each with its own governing arrangements. There is considerable variation among states in the degree of segmentation, ranging from Michigan, where almost every institution has its own governing board, to states such as Florida and Arizona, where there may be only a single governing board for all public four-year institutions.

We can summarize the three basic designs that the answers to these questions yield:

- Segmented systems have two or more governing boards that supervise single institutions or groupings of institutions. No single statewide agency has statutory authority over all four of the key coordinating work processes: budgeting; program planning and approval; articulation; and providing information to elected policy officials and the general public.

- Unified systems place all degree-granting, public higher-education institutions under a single governing board, which works directly with the governor and the legislature on budgeting; program planning and approval; articulation; and determining the available information about capacity and performance.

- Federal systems organize degree-granting, public institutions under some range of governing boards that are required to work directly with a statewide coordinating board with legislatively delegated authority for representing the public interest in such key areas as budgeting, program planning and approval, articulation and collaboration, and information collection and reporting.

So far, our classification system has considerable overlap with the most widely used taxonomy, which was published by the Education Commission of the States (1997). While the most recent version of this sourcebook gives expanded treatment, over earlier versions, to associate degree institutions, the publication still provides less clarity about state governance of community colleges than is desirable for our purposes. The typology developed in this chapter draws sharper distinctions among state governing and coordinating arrangements for community colleges by asking the same two questions for community colleges that we earlier asked about the entire state system:

- Do community colleges and technical institutes have a coordinating board/agency with some statutory authority for serving as the interface between these institutions and state government in such key areas as budgeting, program planning and approval, articulation and collaboration, and information collection and reporting? If the answer is "yes," then the community college system is classified as federal. If the answer is "no," then we move to the next question.

**Table 3.1**
**Conceptual Model of State Structures for Community Colleges**

| | State Governance and Coordinating Arrangements for All Higher Education | | |
|---|---|---|---|
| | FEDERAL | UNIFIED | SEGMENTED |
| State Governance and Coordinating Arrangements for Community Colleges — FEDERAL | FEDERAL 1 [2] | FEDERAL N/A | FEDERAL 5 [10] |
| UNIFIED | UNIFIED 2 [7] | UNIFIED 4 [9] | UNIFIED 6 [7] |
| SEGMENTED | SEGMENTED 3 [11] | SEGMENTED N/A | SEGMENTED 7 [5] |

- Does the state system of community colleges and technical institutes have more than one governing board? If the answer is "no," then the system is unified. If the answer is "yes," then the system is segmented.

The answers to these two sets of questions create a 3 × 3 table that permits grouping all 50 state systems into seven categories. Since state systems are not as neat as our taxonomy, we have had to make a number of "judgment calls" about where to place specific states that exhibit characteristics of more than one category. Our reasons for these judgments are explained more fully in the comments on strengths and weaknesses.

Table 3.1 shows the seven possible conceptual categories. Unified state systems, by definition, cannot have federal or segmented arrangements for community colleges. The boldface numbers in brackets in each cell indicate the number of states using that arrangement. The bracketed numbers total to 51 because New York appears in both the segmented federal and the segmented unified cells.

## Applying the Typology

In this section of the chapter, we discuss groupings in the order in which they appear in Table 3.1.

*Federal/Federal States.* Only two states, Illinois and Washington, have a coordinating board for all higher education, a separate statewide coordinating structure for community colleges, and local governing boards. In Washington, the governor appoints local boards, the community college coordinating board, and the coordinating board for all higher education. This arrangement seems to produce fewer jurisdictional problems than in Illinois, where local board members are elected. Significantly, however, the governor's 2020 Commission recently recommended narrowing the authority and responsibilities of the Washington Higher Education Coordinating Board (governor's 2020 Commission, 1998). In 1995, the coordinating board for all higher education in Illinois (IBHE) rearranged the priorities for capital projects submitted to it by the state community college board. This action precipitated an effort by some community college leaders and legislators to remove the community college board from the jurisdiction of the IBHE. The legislation passed both chambers by wide margins but was vetoed by the governor. Nonetheless, it was widely interpreted as a wake-up call for the IBHE to exercise greater sensitivity to the concerns and priorities of community colleges.

Two state-level coordinating boards, one reporting to the other, represent a considerable amount of state oversight for institutions that have, in addition, their own local governing boards. Illinois adopted this arrangement in 1965, and Washington, in 1967. Maryland had a comparable arrangement between 1988 and 1992, when it abolished a state board for community colleges that had been established in 1969. While state higher-education systems seem likely to receive more, rather than less, planning and collaboration in the 21st century, there are clearly limits on the amount of state bureaucracy that can be expected to add enough value to offset its costs and complexity. While current arrangements seem to work reasonably well in both Illinois and Washington, these states are probably at the outer limits of cost-effective state governance and coordination.

*Federal/Unified States.* Seven states, Alabama, Colorado, Connecticut, Kentucky, Massachusetts, Tennessee, and Virginia, have statewide coordinating boards for all higher education and a single statewide governing board for community colleges and technical institutes. In Massachusetts and Tennessee, the statewide governing board for community colleges also oversees a system of four-year colleges and universities, excluding the state's flagship university. The Massachusetts Board of Higher Education, which governs community and state colleges, also serves as a coordinating board for the University of Massachusetts system. In Colorado, three small community colleges still retain their locally elected governing boards, but most of the state's community colleges are governed by the statewide board, which is appointed by the governor. The trend in Colorado seems to be in the direction of having all community colleges governed by a single board.

Kentucky established its statewide governing board for community colleges only within the past year. Previously, community colleges were part of the University of Kentucky system. None of these states (with the exception of Colorado) has any tradition of local governing boards. In states where community colleges have been governed by the same board that governs some four-year institutions (Kentucky, Massachusetts, and Tennessee), there is evidence that community colleges have been held back in their development or less well utilized than in states where they have their own governing arrangements. Certainly this was a factor in the changes that were made in Kentucky, and it was a part of the recent discussions by a special higher-education study committee in Tennessee ("Sunquist Targets Higher Education Reform," 1998). The advantages of statewide governance in an age of technology can be clearly seen in the Colorado Electronic Community College, an imaginative organization that would not have been feasible in the absence of structural arrangements that permitted the pooling of resources across a state system of collaborating institutions.

*Federal/Segmented States.* Eleven states, Arkansas, Indiana, Louisiana, Maryland, Missouri, Nebraska, New Jersey, Ohio, Oklahoma, South Carolina, and Texas, have both a statewide board that coordinates all higher education and more than one community college or technical institute with its own governance arrangements; this is, by a slim margin, the arrangement most frequently observed. States using this approach are highly diverse, ranging from such relatively well-developed and orderly systems as those in Maryland, Missouri, New Jersey, and Texas to the mixed models in Arkansas, Louisiana, Ohio, and South Carolina, where evolutionary combinations of two-year branch campuses, community colleges, technical institutes, and their diverse state and local governing arrangements often defy description.

Indiana really deserves its own category. In the 1960s, an influential president of the University of Indiana succeeded in blocking the development of Indiana community colleges. One corollary has been the state's consistently poor college-going rates, a performance that numerous grants awarded by the Lilly Endowment have done little to change. Very recently, the governor proposed that the state's sole community college (Vincennes University Junior College) should collaborate with the state's system of technical colleges (Ivy Tech) to offer comprehensive community college services across the state.

The consequences of high levels of segmentation in the absence of a coherent state plan for comprehensive, two-year, postsecondary services can be observed even in some of the more orderly systems. Oklahoma, Texas, and Louisiana have a history of legislatively converting two-year colleges into four-year institutions. Oklahoma provides the most recent example in the conversion of Rogers University to four-year status. Louisiana may finally overcome some of the legacy of its dual system as it moves to implement the statewide community college system adopted in 1998. If federal/federal models provide too much of a good thing, then the more chaotic federal/segmented systems may well provide too little.

*Unified States.* Nine states, Alaska, Hawaii, Idaho, Montana, Nevada, North Dakota, Rhode Island, South Dakota, and Utah have a single board that governs all degree-granting institutions of higher education. These states tend to be less populated and to have fewer institutions and less complex systems.

There is considerable diversity in unified systems, and even some anomalies. For example, the community college in Valdez retained independent status when other Alaskan community colleges were swept into the University of Alaska system in the mid-1980s. In Idaho, a single board governs both K-12 and higher education. Some elected leaders in Idaho argue that this arrangement has contributed to the state's failure to develop a coherent system of community colleges. In Montana, a 1994 reorganization merged former vocational technical centers into two of the state's universities and strengthened the powers of the board of regents, which functions as the governing board for all four-year public institutions. However, the board exercises primarily coordinating authority over the state's community colleges, which continue to be governed by locally elected boards. Although South Dakota does have several technical institutes that operate under local boards, there are no public community colleges in the state. In Rhode Island, a single community college operates a number of campuses statewide. Many of the Western states in this category have tribally controlled community colleges that are primarily funded by the federal government. Typically, such institutions are not involved in state coordination activities.

Unified systems seem to serve the needs of their respective states effectively. No state using this arrangement has chosen to modify it other than by providing greater authority to the central governing authority. Some states encourage greater responsiveness to local needs by providing for appointed boards at each institution to which the unified board delegates specified authority. As was the case in the federal/unified structure, boards with the responsibility for governing both two- and four-year institutions may be tempted to neglect the needs and development of the former in order to have more resources available for baccalaureate and graduate programs.

*Segmented/Federal States.* Ten states, Arizona, California, Florida, Georgia, Kansas, Mississippi, New York (State University of New York), North Carolina, Wisconsin, and Wyoming have two or more governing boards for higher-education institutions, along with a coordinating or governing board for community or technical colleges. Nine of the states in this category and all of those in the two that follow have no single statewide agency, either governing or coordinating, with delegated authority for all higher-education institutions in the key decision areas of budgeting, program planning and approval, articulation and collaboration, and information collection and dissemination. Only Kansas, with its 1999 legislatively mandated system redesign, has designated the board that governs four-year institutions as a coordinating board for community colleges and technical institutes, which also retain their own local governing boards. This arrangement is similar to one used by New York, which we have listed both here and in the segmented/unified category because all public institutions in that state are divided into two heterogeneous systems, each with its own governing board. Both two-and-four-year institutions outside the city of New York make up the State University of New York (SUNY). In SUNY, each community college is governed by an appointed local board, and the board of trustees of SUNY serves as a coordinating board for all SUNY community colleges. The City University of New York (CUNY) is a unified system in which ` community colleges, baccalaureate and master's degree–granting institutions, and a graduate center are all governed by the same appointed board.

The degree of segmentation in these nine states varies considerably. Arizona, Florida, Georgia, Mississippi, North Carolina, Wisconsin, and Wyoming have only two statewide boards, with one governing all public four-year institutions and the other coordinating or governing a system of community or technical colleges. Kansas has a single statewide board that governs both systems. Georgia operates a postsecondary vocational education system under the auspices of the state board of technical and adult education, as well as 15 public two-year degree-granting colleges that are governed by the Board of Regents of the University System of Georgia. A similar arrangement in Wisconsin assigns responsibility for governing all four-year institutions and most campuses offering the first two years of a baccalaureate program to the Board of Regents of the University of Wisconsin system. Technical colleges, including the three that offer college transfer programs, have their own governing boards and receive statewide coordination in selected areas from the Wisconsin Board of Vocational, Technical and Adult Education.

California divides its four-year institutions into two segments, each with its own governing board. Community colleges have elected governing boards, and the community college segment is coordinated by a board of governors. Both California and Florida have weak statewide coordinating agencies, which have some advisory responsibilities for all higher education, including community colleges. States with this governing arrangement have experienced a variety of problems that seem related both to the nature of their local governance arrangements and to the absence of a statewide structure with enough authority to accomplish meaningful coordination for all higher education. Articulation between two- and four-year institutions remains an issue for most of these states, although less so in states like Georgia, New York, and Washington, where a single board has at least some responsibility for both two- and four-year institutions. The hope for improved articulation was certainly a factor in the approach to system redesign chosen by Kansas.

Community college governance is perhaps most controversial in California, where a board with essentially coordinating powers (Board of Governors of the California Community Colleges) thinks, and sometimes acts, like a governing board and locally elected boards of trustees have the responsibility for negotiating collective bargaining agreements with employee unions, which are largely responsible for their election. Since the passage of Proposition 13, however, these same boards no longer have responsibility for raising local tax rates to pay for the generous agreements they negotiate. A legislative attempt to fix the problems in 1988 by mandating "shared governance" simply made matters worse in the opinion of most community college leaders. By the late 1990s, knowledgeable observers were questioning whether some California community college districts had become ungovernable. A recent citizen's commission has recommended extensive changes, including the elimination of locally elected boards and the negotiation of collective bargaining agreements on a statewide basis (California Citizens Commission on Higher Education in the Twenty-First Century, 1998).

Florida is often cited as one of the states most subject to legislative micro-management. Long noted for its CLAST (rising junior) exam, the state recently implemented one of the first performance funding plans for community colleges. Florida also has more legislation applying to student transfer between community colleges and universities than any other state, although California runs a close second. Higher-education leaders in New York have questioned the wisdom of having the same board that governs one of the nation's largest higher-education systems also serve as a coordinating board for a very large system of locally governed community colleges.

The combination of locally elected boards and a statewide community college coordinating board is clearly one of the most volatile arrangements for community college governance. States with appointed local boards (Florida, New York, Mississippi, Georgia, and North Carolina) seem to report fewer jurisdictional problems and appear to provide more examples of interinstitutional collaboration than combination states like Arizona, California, and Wyoming.

*Segmented/Unified States.* Seven states, Delaware, Maine, Minnesota, New Hampshire, New York (CUNY), Vermont, and West Virginia have two or more statewide governing boards for higher education, one of which has responsibility for community colleges or technical institutions. Only Delaware, Maine, and New Hampshire have separate governing boards for community colleges or technical institutes. In the remaining four states, community colleges are governed by a board that also has responsibility for baccalaureate and graduate degree–granting institutions. This arrangement is very recent in Minnesota, which merged separate state college and community college systems in 1995, and relatively new in West Virginia, which adopted similar arrangements in 1989.

In none of these states is there any tradition of local governance for community colleges. Delaware, like Rhode Island, is served by a single community college that operates multiple campuses. The Community College of Vermont operates statewide, but in a noncampus format. Vermont also has a two-year residential technical college. The extremes in population, demographics, rural/urban character, and geographic size characterizing these states suggest that they have adopted relatively centralized forms of state governance to address unique population needs under conditions of resource constraint. Recent adoptions of this structural arrangement suggest the continuing search in many states for designs that promise the most services for the least cost.

*Segmented/Segmented States.* Five states, Iowa, Michigan, New Mexico, Oregon, and Pennsylvania, have two or more governing boards for higher education, local governing boards for community colleges, and no statewide agency with effective coordinating or governing responsibilities for community colleges and technical institutes. All of these states except New Mexico assign some coordinating or regulatory responsibilities for community colleges to state boards that also have responsibility for coordinating and regulating K-12 education. Judging from recent efforts in Kansas and Iowa to create specific boards charged with the sole responsibility for overseeing community colleges and technical institutes, state governance arrangements that call for the same board to oversee both K-12 and postsecondary institutions work no better now than they did in the 1950s and 1960s, when many junior colleges were governed by the same boards that were responsible for public schools.

Of all the states, New Mexico has one of the least systematic approaches to providing postsecondary services. Three of the state's universities operate their own systems of state-funded two-year branch campuses. There is a unique residential two-year college with its own board, appointed by the governor. The cities of Hobbs and Farmington operate comprehensive community colleges with locally elected boards that levy property taxes to pay for the same types of services the state funds in other communities. The same pattern is followed by the former vocational technical institutes in Albuquerque and Luna, which now have the status of locally controlled community colleges. Santa Fe, thanks to a special legislative dispensation, seems to have the best of both possible worlds, with state funding and a locally elected board. This description scarcely does justice to the full range of institutional arrangements to which the state's weak coordinating agency, the commission on higher education, is charged with bringing coherence. Not the least of the problems caused by this approach involves the criteria for deciding where services are to be provided. Institutions compete to provide services where revenues exceed costs and seek to avoid areas where costs exceed revenues. Many people in New Mexico believe this arrangement gives excessive weight to market forces.

States in the segmented/segmented category give the appearance of a work in progress. Community colleges in Pennsylvania receive little leadership, guidance, or advocacy from the state board. Those colleges that have the misfortune of operating under school district sponsorship must devote large amounts of time and energy to securing approval from their members for budgets that include no more than 15 to 20 percent of local tax dollars. In Michigan, all two-year, and most four-year, institutions have their own governing boards. All four-year institutions have constitutional status; only voluntary arrangements exist for coordination and collaboration. Statewide articulation policies are spelled out in a voluntary 1978 agreement developed by the Michigan Association of Collegiate Registrars and Admission Officers, which has never been signed by the University of Michigan. In the absence of any effective mechanism for encouraging institutional responsiveness to state priorities, legislators and citizens must be satisfied with whatever programs and services institutions decide to deliver.

Segmented/segmented systems are at the opposite extreme from their federal/federal counterparts. Boards of Education preoccupied with K-12 problems seem able to devote only regulatory attention to the postsecondary institutions that they have been assigned, almost by default. Only the governor and the legisla-

ture have ongoing, statewide responsibilities for making certain that state resources in aggregate are wisely used and for ensuring that the sum of what
institutions deliver is equal to what citizens need. If federal/federal designs provide more coordination than absolutely essential, it seems likely that segmented/
segmented systems provide considerably less.

## SUMMING UP

As this chapter shows, state-level higher education coordination and governance arrangements can vary significantly from state to state, and the issues that
surround such coordination are often complex and dynamic. Here we summarize
arrangements and suggest a number of important issues that states must address
in the 21st century.

Almost half the nation's states (23) have chosen to have community colleges
and technical institutes governed by a single statewide board to which all higher-
education institutions report. In 15 of these states, two-year institutions are part
of consolidated systems that also include at least some of the state's four-year
institutions. While these states seem well positioned to respond to the requirements for articulation and collaboration that will confront all systems in the 21st
century, boards with combined responsibilities for two- and four-year institutions
often fail to make optimum use of the two-year sector, thus leading to problems
in both coherence and efficiency. Community colleges and technical institutes
provide access and school-to-work solutions that their more traditional four-year
counterparts rarely develop. Community colleges and technical institutes also
provide these functions at lower cost than four-year institutions, and with greater
flexibility and shorter lead times. Boards that supervise both two- and four-year
institutions sometimes spend more time refereeing disputes over students, programs, and fiscal resources than worrying about how to best serve the public
interest.

Eleven states have created coordinating boards that focus exclusively on community colleges. An additional 19 states assign responsibility for coordinating
community colleges to a statewide board that also has responsibility for all
public higher education. These 30 states include most of the largest and most
complex higher education systems in the country.

As they confront the challenges of the 21st century, states that have used
federal principles in the design of their governance systems for community colleges will enjoy three inherent advantages. First, federal systems are dynamic.
Through frequent, smaller adjustments, they avoid the major restructuring that
segmented and unified systems must occasionally undergo as the price for their
capacity to resist change. Second, federal systems divide responsibility for representing the public interest from institutional advocacy, leaving the latter to
governing boards and assigning the former to the coordinating board. This arrangement is more realistic than expecting the same board to do both. Finally,

federal systems have empowered a statewide agency with the capacity to provide leadership on such key 21st-century issues as collaboration in the use of technology and in achieving barrier-free access and mobility for increasingly diverse student populations.

However, states with federal systems do not face the millennium free from the need to address some very pressing problems. A number of states with federal systems, either for community colleges or for all institutions, confront problems of coherence and system development. Some have strange combinations of technical institutes, community colleges, and branch campuses that suggest more attention was paid to political compromise than to planning or the public interest. Some states, like Indiana, are simply cases of arrested development. Others have elected local governing boards that worry more about defending their turf from state incursions than about finding ways to collaborate with other colleges to effectively and efficiently serve the needs of their constituencies. Also, states where collective bargaining legislation or taxpayer initiatives have drastically altered the environment for higher education often lack ways of making complementary changes in the way colleges are governed.

Now that Kansas has moved into the segmented/federal category, only five states have segmented community college systems operating in segmented structures involving all of higher education. On the basis of their own assessments, as well as ours, this group of states seems the least well positioned to respond to the challenges of a new century. Their arrangements incorporate many of the problems and few of the advantages we reported for other designs. With the exception of Michigan, where legislators talk about higher education as the fourth branch of state government and seem resigned to accepting whatever the institutions choose to deliver, these states seem likely candidates for change.

All states will face complex issues in the 21st century, but some will have to do so with the disjointed, underdeveloped, and inefficient community college systems inherited from the 20th century. Predictably, such states will have more difficulty in producing relevant and efficient responses than states that bring with them from the past quarter-century more coherent and responsive systems. In the 21st century, all states will need better integrated, more synergistic, and less bureaucratic state governance arrangements to meet the issues already visible on the horizon. Those that have not yet developed coherent and efficient systems will need to do so quickly or fall even further behind in the global competition that they are already experiencing. The recent attention devoted to restructuring in such states as Indiana, Iowa, Kansas, Kentucky, and Louisiana offers evidence that at least some policy makers in these and other states share this assessment. We hope the conceptual perspectives offered in this chapter will be helpful to elected and appointed higher education leaders in all states as they confront the increasingly important tasks of assessing and modifying their systems of higher education to keep them both competitive and responsive to the public interest.

**NOTES**

1. See, as examples, the following: L. Glenny (1971), *Coordinating higher education for the '70's* (Berkeley: University of California at Berkeley, Berkeley Center for Research and Development in Higher Education); R. O. Berdahl (1971), *Statewide coordination of higher education* (Washington, DC: American Council on Education); J. D. Millett (1984), *Conflict in higher education: State government coordination and versus institutional independence* (San Francisco, CA: Jossey-Bass); E. B. Shick, R. I. Novak, J. A. Norton, and H. G. Elam (1992), *Shared visions of public higher education: Structures and leadership styles that work* (Washington, DC: American Association of State Colleges and Universities); T. J. MacTaggert et al. (1998), *Seeking excellence through independence: Liberating colleges and universities from excessive regulation* (San Francisco, CA: Jossey-Bass).

2. The best known include L. W. Bender, S. V. Martorana, and J. L. Wattenbarger.

3. D. Campbell, L. Leverty, and K. Sayles (1996), "Funding for community colleges: Changing patterns of support," Chapter 8 in *A Struggle to Survive: Funding Higher Education in the Next Century*, edited by D. S. Honeyman, J. L. Wattenbarger, and K. C. Westbrook (Thousand Oaks, CA: Corwin Press) document these trends and point out the degree to which available data is skewed by the California experience.

4. See, for example, L. W. Bender's (1975) *The states, communities, and control of the community college* (Washington, DC: American Association of Community Colleges). The more contemporary study by Schick et al. (1992), *Shared visions of public education*, reached a similar conclusion.

5. See C. Handy's (1992, November/December) 1992 "Balancing corporate power: A new Federalist Paper," *Harvard Business Review*, 70(6), pp. 59–72, for an extended discussion of concepts underlying the idea of the federal model.

**REFERENCES**

California Citizens Commission on Higher Education in the Twenty-first Century. (1998). *A state of learning.* Los Angeles. Center for Governmental Studies.

Callan, P. M. (1981). Declaring interdependence. *AGB Reports, 23*(1), 30–31.

Clark, G. W. (1980). *The essentials of local autonomy: A contemporary focus on control and responsibility.* Sacramento: California Community and Junior College Association.

Education Commission of the States. (1997). *State postsecondary education structures sourcebook: State coordinating and governing boards.* Denver, CO: Education Commission of the States.

Glenny, L. (1979). The state budget process: Roles and responsibilities. In F. F. Hlarcleroad (Ed.), *Financing postsecondary education in the 1980s* (pp. 35–45). Tucson, AZ: Center for the Study of Higher Education.

Governor's 2020 Commission on the Future of Post-Secondary Education. (October 1998). *Learning for life.* Olympia, WA: Governor's Executive Policy Office.

Mundt, J. C. (1978). State vs. local control: Reality and myth over concern for local autonomy. In C. F. Searle (Ed.), *Balancing state and local control* (New Directions for Community Colleges, No. 23, pp. 49–61). San Francisco: Jossey-Bass.

Owen, H. J. (1978). Balancing state and local control in Florida's community colleges.

In C. F. Searle (Ed.), *Balancing state and local control* (New Directions for Community Colleges, No. 23, pp. 25–31). San Francisco: Jossey-Bass.

Richardson, R. C., Bracco, K. R., Callan, P. M., & Finney, J. E. (1998). *Designing state higher education systems for a new century.* Phoenix, AZ: Oryx Press.

Sundquist targets higher education reform as showpiece for second term. (1998). *The Tennessee Journal, 24* (23), 1–2.

Tillery, D., & Wattenbarger, J. L. (1985). State power in a new era: Threats to local authority. In W. L. Deegan & J. F. Gollattscheck, (Eds.), *Ensuring effective governance* (New Directions for Community Colleges, 49, 13, pp. 5–23). San Francisco: Jossey-Bass.

Tschechtelin, J. D. (1994). The community college and the state. In A. M. Cohen & F. B. Brawer (Eds.), *Managing community colleges* (pp. 101–122). San Francisco, CA: Jossey-Bass.

# Chapter 4

## Accountability in Community Colleges: Looking toward the 21st Century

### Frankie Santos Laanan

> No institution in American education plays a more difficult role than the community college.
>
> —Cohen & Brawer (1996), p. 440

A little shy of celebrating its centennial anniversary, the American community college moves toward the twenty-first century with numerous challenges ahead. Known for its open access and high-quality education, this segment of higher education provides educational opportunities for a diverse constituency (Cohen & Brawer, 1996; Koltai, 1993). According to the American Association of Community Colleges (1998), approximately 10.4 million-credit and noncredit students were enrolled in the 1,100 public and private two-year colleges during the 1997–1998 academic year. About half the nation's undergraduates and half of all first-time freshmen are educated by community colleges, which clearly play a critical role in the postsecondary segment. However, in the last decade, external constituencies have raised questions regarding the effectiveness of these institutions. As the nation's community colleges make the transition to the 21st century, many issues about their missions, functions, and level of effectiveness remain at the forefront.

Like the rest of higher education, the most immediate challenges facing community colleges are diminishing fiscal resources, increasing student diversity, and the growing demands for responding to accountability mandates, both at the federal and statewide levels. Community colleges are facing greater expectations to demonstrate their effectiveness as educational institutions. Some of the buzzwords that have emerged in various federal and state policy with respect to accountability include "student outcomes," "performance measures," "performance indicators," "performance-based accountability," and "performance-based funding," to name a few.

Community colleges distinguish themselves from four-year institutions by their multiple functions and missions, which have been inherent from their early beginnings. Historically, these functions have been part of the foundation of what can be considered American education's most democratic institution. With this comes the challenge and complexity of responding to, and demonstrating the successes and failures of, institutional effectiveness. Some writers maintain that community colleges have lived in the shadow of the research university (Dyer, 1991; Hudgins & Mahaffey, 1998) and, as a result, have historically been measured by university standards. The typical results are unfavorable to the community college, not because the standards were too high but because they were the wrong standards for this institution (Clark, 1960; Pincus, 1994; Zwerling, 1976).

The purpose of this chapter is fourfold: (1) to define accountability in the context of higher education, and more specifically, community colleges; (2) to outline different models of accountability systems; (3) to discuss issues and concerns regarding accountability in the 21st century; and (4) to raise policy recommendations for the future.

## ACCOUNTABILITY DEFINED

Accountability, while not a new concept in education (Southern Regional Education Board, 1998), has had changing definitions. *Merriam-Webster's Collegiate Dictionary* defines accountability as "an obligation or willingness to accept responsibility or to account for one's actions" (1998, p. 12). The term *accountability* has a very specific meaning and is often used synonymously with the concepts of evaluation, assessment, measurement, accreditation, and monitoring. Accountability refers to the systematic collection, analysis, and use of information to hold educational institutions (e.g., schools, colleges, universities, and educators) responsible for students' performance (Education Commission of the States, 1998). Two important aspects of accountability in public higher education are specifying one's obligation and remaining answerable for meeting it (Gaither, 1995; Neal, 1995). Accountability can be said to have two major emphases (California Community Colleges, 1989): institutional or program compliance with financial and operational standards, policies, and legal requirements and institutional or program effectiveness in achieving expected performance outcomes.

In their book, *Encyclopedia of Educational Evaluation*, Anderson, Ball, Murphy, et al. (1975) defined accountability as "responsibility, explicability, and answerability. . . . [A]ccountability has traditionally been used with reference to service in the public interest, where the stewardship of public funds requires obligatory accounting" (p. 1). The authors further provide a working definition of accountability:

- Accountability represents acceptance of responsibility for consequences by those to whom citizens have entrusted the public service of education.
- Accountability acknowledges the public's right to know what actions have been taken in the schools it supports and how effective these actions have been.
- This definition of accountability suggests that the "redress" implicit in the concept is more than the citizen's right to demand the imposition of penalties for failure in accomplishment.
- Rather, it suggests that educators should be required to redesign educational activity to achieve educational effectiveness and efficiency (p. 2).

Accountability is also generally defined as *what* performance to measure and *how* to measure it. The most basic definition of accountability terms it a response to legislative mandates calling on educational institutions to become more accountable for monies spent (Cox et al., 1992). Another definition of accountability relates to external relationships and the extent to which college leaders demonstrate the cost-effective implementation of the college's mission to its various publics (Hudgins & Mahaffey, 1998).

Most state policy makers are concerned about the quality and cost-effectiveness of higher education, and elected officials are interested in obtaining results that speak to the returns on investment of dollars spent on educational programs (Ewell, 1997; Hudgins & Mahaffey, 1998). Two issues are prevalent with respect to the quality and cost-effectiveness of higher education. The first is the increasing cost of public higher education along side limited state resources. The second is the concern and interest among policy makers about the extent to which students are academically prepared and whether graduates possess the technical skills, knowledge and abilities to enter and compete in a global economic workplace.

The major driving forces behind assessment have been and still are the external needs for evidence of effectiveness (Erwin, 1993). In the last few years, external demands for accountability have heightened. Calls for accountability in higher education have led to state mandates and accreditation standards (U.S. Department of Education, 1998a) requiring that the value of programs and services be demonstrated.

## Background of Increased Accountability

According to Ewell (1994), two major factors that caused accountability to emerge can be explained in terms of fiscal and political forces. The popularity and growth of accountability initiatives have been associated with limited resources. Another factor is rooted in the public's sense of the purposes of higher education. That is, as early as the 1980s there has been strong and visible interest in requesting public officials to report the extent to which attending colleges and universities would yield public benefits in terms of quality of life and workplace revitalization.

Referred to as the "new accountability" (Ewell, 1994), this paradigm shift caused state initiatives to emerge that centered on it. The very heart of this paradigm is the notion of higher education's role in society. The former concepts of accountability viewed public higher education as a "public utility" in that the benefits to citizens were in the form of increased social mobility and improved quality of life. The focus of this type of accountability was access and efficiency. However, with the new paradigm shift in accountability, higher education was now perceived as a strategic investment in which policy makers and other external agencies were most interested in assessing or evaluating the return on investment. Although old measures of efficiency and access remained relevant, new accountability mandates emerged that required the assessment of educational results and these began to receive immediate attention.

Scholars assert that accountability is being addressed because of declining public resources and the sense that colleges and universities are ill prepared to meet needs of the 21st century (Ewell, Wellman, & Paulson, 1997). In the last decade, policy leaders at the state and federal levels have struggled to improve higher education's responsiveness. Evident is the challenge and frustration among policy makers to impact the way in which colleges and universities behave. Deregulation and downsizing are two political factors that have been attributed to the dialogue about accountability in recent years. This new accountability movement saw the outgrowth of specific definitions of results in the form of performance indicators. These definitions emphasized efficiency over quality and, increasingly, "consumer information" and "marketplace mechanisms" as substitutes for direct regulation (Ewell, 1994).

## Federal versus State Accountability

For community colleges, responding to accountability mandates has taken center stage (Sanchez & Laanan, 1998). In the early 1980s, the concern for measuring educational effectiveness surfaced as a major new focus for all of higher education, including community colleges. The two-year colleges were not exempted from this new movement of accountability. In fact, there was growing interest among local constituencies and state officials in requiring community colleges to demonstrate that their programs and services worked. Moreover, legislatures and the public demanded that colleges begin documenting evidence as a condition of continued support. In the last decade, community colleges have witnessed an emergence of new federal and state accountability mandates. In considering different types of accountability, it is important to distinguish between federally and state-mandated accountability measures.

*Federal-level Accountability.* At the federal level, the goal of developing accountability initiatives is to implement them at the macro level, that is, for the whole system nationwide. Typically, once federal legislation has been signed and becomes law, guidelines are written and reported in the *Federal Register* that describe how states are to develop, implement, and report on various accountability systems. An example of federal accountability is the Carl D. Perkins Vocational and Technical Education Act of 1998 (VTEA). Referred to as Perkins III, VTEA was signed into law on October 31, 1998, as the reauthorization of the 1990 Perkins act (also known as Vocational and Applied Technology Education Act, or VATEA). The central goals of Perkins III are (1) to further develop the academic, vocational, and technical skills of vocational students through setting high standards (2) to link secondary and postsecondary vocational programs, (3) to increase flexibility in the administration and use of federal funds, (4) to disseminate national research about vocational and technical education, and (5) to provide professional development and technical assistance to vocational educators (American Vocational Association, 1998). In addition, Perkins III helps to ensure that students acquire the skills and knowledge needed to meet state academic standards and industry-recognized skills standards and prepares students for a wide range of opportunities in high-skill, high-wage careers.

An important component of VTEA is the focus on quality. Perkins III focuses the federal investment in vocational and technical education on high-quality programs. These programs must be able to integrate academic and vocational education; promote student attainment of challenging academic, vocational, and technical standards; provide students with strong experience in, and understanding of, all aspects of an industry; address the needs of individuals from special populations; and develop, improve, and expand the use of technology.

With respect to accountability, the law specifies the need to promote continuous program improvement by creating a state performance accountability system. Also evident in the new law is the move toward increased accountability, which is viewed as the cornerstone of the new act. Unlike its predecessor (VATEA of 1990), in which states were required to develop core standards and measures of performance to evaluate the quality of their vocational education programs, Perkins III requires that states develop levels of performance for a number of "core indicators" specified in the law. A challenge faced by many states is the wide interpretations of the law's accountability requirements, as they are complex and not easy to measure or assess. Each state, in cooperation with the U.S. Department of Education, must set expected performance levels in four categories: (1) student attainment of vocational, technical, and academic skill proficiencies, (2) acquisition of secondary or postsecondary degrees or credentials, (3) placement and retention in postsecondary education or employment, and (4) completion of vocational and technical programs that lead to nontraditional training and employment (meaning fields in which one gender accounts for less than a quarter of the participants).

The Workforce Investment Act (WIA) is another example of federal accountability. Signed into law on August 7, 1998, WIA reforms federal employment, adult education, and vocational rehabilitation programs to create an integrated "one-stop" system of workforce investment and education activities for adults and youth. Entities that carry out postsecondary vocational and technical education activities that are assisted under the Perkins VTEA Act are mandatory partners in this one-stop delivery system. The most important aspect of WIA is "its focus on meeting the needs of businesses for skilled workers and the training, education, and employment needs of individuals" (U.S. Department of Education, 1998b, p. 4).

In terms of accountability, states, local areas, and providers of those services will become more accountable for meeting the specified needs. The measures apply to both statewide and local performance. Some of the proposed measures include rates of basic skills and work readiness or occupational skills attainment, attainment of a high school diploma (or its equivalent), and placement and retention in postsecondary education, advanced occupational training, apprenticeships, the military, or employment. Additional measures will also be established relating to the customer satisfaction of both participants and employers.

*State-level Accountability.* In the last decade, numerous state community college systems have developed accountability systems. The common theme among state systems is the need to report specific performance measures in an effort to demonstrate institutional effectiveness across different indicators, as reflected in their stated missions. This section briefly synthesizes the different accountability initiatives that have been previously, and recently, implemented across state community college systems.

In 1988 the California legislature passed Assembly Bill 1725, a landmark piece of reform legislation for California's 106 community colleges (California Community Colleges, 1989, 1990). The law required that the California Community Colleges Board of Governors develop a comprehensive community college educational and fiscal accountability system. Referred to as the Model Accountability System, the immediate intent of this model was to report information that assesses community college educational and fiscal effectiveness. Its ultimate purpose was to maintain and improve the quality of the institution and enhance the community colleges. Five major outcomes were outlined: student access, student success, student satisfaction, staff composition, and fiscal condition. The model accountability system was to serve as a source of information for the system and local districts to use to assess their effectiveness, plan their budgets, and develop programs and services. Today, these same outcome measures are still used and reported on statewide as well as on the local level.

In Illinois the 49 community colleges provide annual reports to the Illinois Community College Board (ICCB) about their improvements in productivity. The annual *Priorities, Quality and Productivity* reports, began in 1991, are submitted by the colleges and provide evidence of the ongoing review processes. These reports are in place to ensure that high levels of quality and productivity are achieved for programs and services considered to be of the highest priority to each college's mission (ICCB, 1997). In response to the Priorities, Quality and Productivity (PQP) policy initiative, the fundamental goal is for colleges to assess their broader functions as they relate to meeting their mission and priorities. Employing a program review process, colleges examine targeted programs and services to assess their ability to meet their intended purpose in a cost-effective, high-quality manner. The five PQP focus areas in which colleges provide information are the following: (1) college priorities, (2) the strengthening of linkages and integrating planning, budgeting, program approval, and program review around collegewide priorities, (3) faculty roles and responsibilities, (4) enhancements in the use of educational technology, and (5) assessment of effectiveness of instructional technology. Another initiative in Illinois that demonstrates the system's commitment to strategic planning for the next century is referred to as Vision 2000 (ICCB, 1993). Based on input from across the state in which information was gathered from regional town meetings, five educational goals were advanced: teaching and learning, student access and opportunity, accountability, community, and resources.

In 1989 the North Carolina General Assembly adopted a provision that mandated the state board of community colleges to develop a "Critical Success Factors" list to define statewide measures of accountability for all community colleges (North Carolina Community College System, 1993). Congruent with the specific mission of the college, the community colleges were responsible for developing an institutional effectiveness plan. Also stipulated was that the plan be consistent with the Southern Association of Colleges and Schools criteria. The intent of the critical success report was to present data that would measure the performance of the system. A few years later, the general assembly passed a special provision on accountability that mandated the state board of community colleges to review the critical success factors and measures and establish performance standards that would indicate colleges' progress in addressing system goals. An accountability task force was established during summer 1993 and began the process of reviewing the critical success factors and measures and establishing performance standards. Critical success factors have been defined as "the key things that must go right for an enterprise to flourish and achieve its goals" (North Carolina Community College System, 1999, p. 2). These factors are viewed as both planning and as evaluation and accountability tools. In addition to the state's Critical Success Factors, other accountability tools exist, including curriculum standards, review of institutional plans and programs, program and financial audits, program monitoring, and accreditation. The seven identified success factors are student success, resources, access, education continuum, workforce development, community services, and program management and accountability.

## MODELS OF ACCOUNTABILITY

In a report published by the Education Commission of the States (ECS), *Charting Higher Education Accountability: A Sourcebook on State-Level Per-*

*formance Indicators*, Ruppert (1994) posits that since 1990, state policy makers have been particularly interested in the educational quality, productivity, and effectiveness of public colleges and universities. Factors such as decreased state funding for higher education, increased costs, and growing demands for access have been attributed to the movement toward greater accountability (Ewell, 1997; Ewell & Jones, 1994; Gaither, 1995). Unlike federal accountability mandates, elected officials have looked to state-level accountability measures to guide state planning and budgetary decisions and to monitor the "public investment" in higher education (Ruppert, 1994). This section presents a background analysis of performance indicators. Systems of indicators, performance-funding mechanisms, and an effectiveness model in community colleges are also discussed.

## Performance Indicators

The adoption of performance indicators (PIs) has been a growing trend among states in response to accountability (Banta & Borden, 1994; Borden & Bottrill, 1994; Neal, 1995). PIs are common measures employed by colleges and universities to assess and report their performance. They can be viewed as barometers, or "dials," to regulate the supply of resources (Klein & Carter, 1988); as signals (Kells, 1993); or as "tin openers" (Klein & Carter, 1988) to unlock areas for further exploration. Another definition is that PIs are used to measure trends in performance, as opposed to current value or level of activity (Cave, Hanney, & Kogan, 1991). Finally, PIs have also been used as guidelines for making strategic decisions that affect the future direction of an institution (Taylor, Meyerson, Morrell, & Park, 1991). According to Ewell and Jones (1994), indicators can best be described

as policy-relevant statistics produced regularly to support overall policy planning and monitoring at the national, state, or system level. . . . In the context of higher education, indicators are used to provide an indirect overview, often through the use of proxy measures designed to reflect trends and conditions accurately and effectively. They include statistics both about current practices (e.g., the proportion of freshman classes taught by full-time faculty) and about key features of the higher education enterprise (e.g., the proportion of undergraduate curricula that requires a thesis or "capstone experience" to obtain a degree). (pp. 6–7)

Examples of indicators include results that are quantifiable statistics, such as faculty-student ratios, and more qualitative measures, such as plans to increase minority student enrollment. Typically, these indicators are published in annual reports, or "report cards," for the purposes of providing information for institutional-level comparisons. More important, such written reports are used to provide easily understandable information to a wide constituency. States identified as being leaders in the accountability movement and that are using performance indicators include Colorado, Florida, Illinois, Kentucky, New York, South Carolina, Tennessee, Texas, Virginia, and Wisconsin (Ruppert, 1994).

There is no generalizable finding about different states' responsibility for identifying or establishing indicators of performance. Arguably, there is variation among the states, given their unique political structures, political actors, and fiscal climates. In some instances, coordinating or governing boards, state legislatures and special committees or commissions have played integral roles in the development of indicators. In general, states tend to share a common set of indicators, such as degrees awarded, graduation rates, and transfer rates, and yet the number of indicators can still range from 15 to 25 elements (Ruppert, 1994).

Four major forces were identified by Ewell and Jones (1994, pp. 7–8) as giving rise to state-level interest in, and justification of, the use of indicators in higher education: first, increasing the complexity and size of the higher-education enterprise as a whole; second, rising costs in delivering higher education and an eroding state resource base; third, growing concerns about improving the linkages between public colleges and universities and the wider society; and, finally, particular concerns about revitalizing undergraduate education in state higher-education systems.

As with any accountability system, there are no perfect measures and data systems that will answer all the questions posed by policy makers and various external constituencies. Ewell and Jones (1994, pp. 8–9) reported the strengths and weaknesses of using indicators as policy tools. Three primary strengths of using indicators are as follows: they can enhance the process of state- and institution-level goal development; they can help mobilize concerted action within the higher-education community, as well as support for higher education among the public at large; and they can support and reinforce the development of a rational set of state policies and institutional actions directed toward ongoing improvement. Conversely, the three weaknesses of using indicators are: they seldom tell policy makers and the public directly what they want to know; they tend to create false short-term incentives for action; and they can focus attention on information gathering itself, rather than on real action to change conditions.

## Indicator Systems

There are four commonly used statewide indicator systems in higher education (Ewell & Jones, 1994, pp. 10–11). The first approach is the inputs-processes-outcomes system, which tends to be the most familiar system used in accountability reporting for K-12 education. The production process is the underlying model, and the primary output is to measure *value added*. Typical indicators include number of entering students, their characteristics and ability levels, instructional expenditure per student, and types of instruction provided (e.g., curriculum design). A second approach is referred to as resource efficiency and effectiveness. In this model the most common indicator is to monitor efficiency; that is, to what extent physical resources, such as faculty, space, and equipment, are utilized and organized. A third approach is referred to as state need and return on investment. In understanding this model, policy makers are interested in assessing the current and future needs of the state in terms of preparing a skilled workforce for positions that require a set of skills and the extent to which graduates produced by public higher-education institutions are going to meet the needs. The final approach is referred to as customer need and return on investment. In this model, the customer is the focus and the primary purpose is to inform consumers of historical performance measures. With recent account- ability mandates, citizens, employers, and the public at large have the right to know about past performance (e.g., rates of persistence, degree completion, and employment) of public higher-education institutions.

Ewell and Jones (1994) posit that "effective indicator systems are best de- veloped for a statewide system or higher education as a whole" (p. 13). They maintain that the focus should be on identifying the strengths and weaknesses of the system and determining how performance can be improved. Components of an effective indicator system should have multiple perspectives representing internal and external parties, in which a balance is established about the way in which goals are measured and reported. For effective indicator systems to work, Ewell and Jones (1994, pp. 14–16) raise questions that policy makers need to ask:

- Does the indicator provide policy leverage for action to correct deficiencies?
- To what extent is the indicator susceptible to manipulation without real changes in the things that it is trying to measure or reflect?
- Is the indicator easily understandable to, and credible for, lay audiences?
- Does the indicator reflect the perspectives and concerns of multiple constituents?
- Against what benchmark will the indicator be compared in order to chart success or progress?
- To what extent is the indicator reliable and valid as a piece of data in itself, and how robust is it under typical conditions of missing or biased data?
- To what extent is the indicator practically obtainable at a reasonable cost?

### Performance Funding

Higher education has witnessed the transition of moving from assessing and reporting results in the 1980s to funding performance in the 1990s (Burke & Serban, 1998). Due to competition for scarce government resources and dissat- isfaction about the level of productivity and performance of public higher ed- ucation in the 1990s, legislators and governors reexamined their funding formulas (Burke, 1998). This trend gave rise to the concept of performance funding. In the literature, two types of performance-funding mechanisms are discussed: performance funding and performance budgeting. Both mechanisms are tied to results. For performance funding, earmarked funds are tied directly to the achievement of public colleges and universities on individual indicators. On the other hand, in performance budgeting, legislators and governors take into account the level of achievement based on established indicators and determine the total budget for higher education (Burke & Serban, 1997).

In April 1997, the Rockefeller Institute conducted a study to collect information about performance funding and performance budgeting (Burke, 1998). Specifically, state higher-education financial officers (SHEFOs) from the 50 states, Puerto Rico, and the District of Columbia were contacted via telephone. The primary objective of the study was to determine states' current and/or previous status with regard to performance funding or performance budgeting for public higher education. According to the study, of the 10 states (Colorado, Connecticut, Florida, Kentucky, Minnesota, Missouri, Ohio, South Carolina, Tennessee, and Washington) that reported using performance funding, all except Connecticut and Kentucky were likely to continue using it. Officers from 18 states indicated that there was a good likelihood that their state would adopt performance funding in the next five years.

In terms of performance budgeting, the study found that eight states had adopted performance budgeting (Alabama, Florida, Hawaii, Idaho, Kansas, Nebraska, Rhode Island, and Texas) and six of the eight were likely to continue this (i.e., Alabama, Florida, Hawaii, Idaho, Rhode Island, and Texas). In states where performance budgeting is not currently implemented, eight states, including the District of Colombia, indicated that in the next five years it might be implemented. Although it is still too early to ascertain the ultimate impact of performance-based funding, the true test to "determine the effectiveness of performance measures will be whether a positive change occurs in teaching and learning" (State Higher Education Executive Officers [SHEEO], 1998, p. 3).

## An Effectiveness Model in Community Colleges

Today, community colleges are faced with many organizational changes and are operating in an increasingly turbulent market. Some of the changes taking place in community colleges include reliance on information and support from external stakeholders in the areas of program development and delivery of services to customers (Alfred, 1998). Beyond traditional academic indicators that have been reported as a result of institutional self-studies or accreditation reporting, this segment has witnessed a growing interest among external constituencies to provide other types of indicators not already reported. According to Alfred (1998), this shift is referred to as moving from a closed system approach to a more open-systems approach for assessing effectiveness. As a result, new indicators that are difficult to measure are beginning to influence the assessment of effectiveness among many community colleges. In the past, traditionally based effectiveness models that measured student performance were valued as useful and informative; however, from an open-systems approach, new models for measuring effectiveness will need to be developed.

**Figure 4.1**
**Effectiveness Stakeholders in Community Colleges**

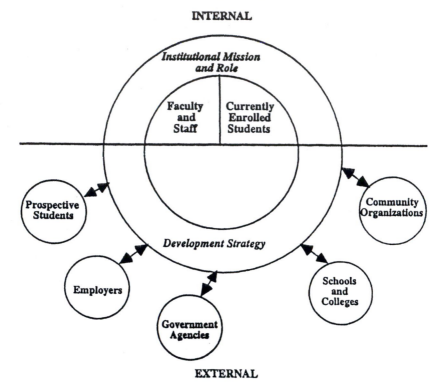

*Source*: Richard Alfred (Fall 1997), "From Closed to Open Systems: New Designs for Effectiveness in Community Colleges," *Journal of Applied Research in the Community College*, 5(1), 15. Used by permission of New Forums Press.

In his discussion of institutional effectiveness stakeholders in community colleges, Alfred (1998) presents his conceptualization of two categories of stakeholders (see Figure 4.1). The first category is the environment or external stakeholder; it includes prospective students, employers, government agencies, schools and colleges, and community organizations. These five groups define a college's external environment and influence the definition of important elements of its development strategy. The second category is referred to as internal stakeholders and is comprised of faculty and staff and the students that are currently enrolled. Within the community college's environment, the types of programs and services delivered to customers are influenced and defined by the external stakeholders. Further, the college's institutional mission and role heavily influence the internal stakeholders.

Based on his model, Alfred (1998) maintains that the "critical purpose underlying effectiveness assessment is to develop and maintain a meaningful re-lationship with each stakeholder" (p. 14), a process that involves identifying the stakeholders' requirements. The challenge is for community colleges to consider the demands of the external stakeholders and, at the same time, the interests of internal stakeholders in the development of indicators to include in an effect-iveness plan. By approaching the process in a strategic manner, the expectations of the diverse stakeholders are addressed in the plan and the college is positioned to respond to the needs of a variety of constituencies.

## LOOKING TOWARD THE TWENTY-FIRST CENTURY

Accountability in higher education and, more specifically, in community col-leges is definitely here to stay. Institutions can expect to see a growing trend of accountability initiatives both at the federal and at the statewide levels. Cur-rently, states are in the process of developing, designing, and operationalizing their responses to the various federal initiatives. At the statewide level, com-munity college systems are working vigorously to respond to initiatives such as Perkins III and the Workforce Investment Act.

Because of the prevalence and variation in sophistication of the data systems in place, some states are experiencing more challenges than others. Some of the more successful states have brought in consultants from the private sector and the universities to assist in the development of comprehensive accountability systems. It is evident that the pressures of external forces demand that com-munity colleges exhibit their effectiveness in numerous outcomes, as defined by specific indicators. The following are some issues and concerns pertaining to accountability that the nation's community colleges face in the next century.

*Changing Demographics*: Emerging trends and issues of change, diversity, quality, growth, and leadership have shaped the 1990s. As we approach the 21st century, the challenge facing the nation's community colleges is to provide quality educational opportunities to the citizens of a nation that is experiencing dramatic change, demographically, economically, and culturally. The students in community colleges will continue to pose unique challenges for the future. Their differing learning styles, levels of academic preparedness, multiple edu-cational objectives are only some of the factors that will require community colleges to respond to a variety of needs and interests.

*Performance-Based Funding*: Community colleges, like the rest of higher ed-ucation, face a common, but unwelcome, dilemma—to prove their worth to an increasingly skeptical and critical public. Legislators, policy makers, governors, parents, students, and other constituencies are all now aware of the numerous accountability mandates. As we move toward the 21st century, states that have adopted performance-based funding systems will have had a few years to reflect on the impact on this type of accountability system. More research and docu-mentation of these types of accountability mechanisms will have to be investigated. Furthermore, the impact of such systems at the institutional level also needs to be examined.

*Political Structure*: Given the political structure of the legislative branch of government with respect to elected representatives, a fundamental challenge that community colleges face at the national and statewide levels is term limits for elected officials. Prior to this movement, elected officials had the opportunity to hold offices for long periods of time, some lasting decades. As a result, the public saw the perpetuation of national and state policy. Term limits, in particular, negatively impact states in their attempts to develop and implement a coherent approach to higher-education policy. It is to the interest of community colleges to continue lobbying Washington as well as state capitols in order to ensure that their interests are advocated and supported. As funding for higher education decreases, the challenge will be for higher-education leaders to successfully play the political game in search of securing continuous support.

*Role of Institutional Research*: Institutional research and planning offices at the local, statewide, and national levels are positioned to play an influential role. In the last decade, many community colleges have responded to the growing mandated accountability movement by establishing or strengthening the institutional research function on their campuses. Although accountability requirements may differ from state to state, they all share the same goal—improving educational and institutional effectiveness. It is imperative that institutional research become an essential function of the community college. College leaders will need to determine the most effective organizational model for integrating research into their operations. In the years to come, factors such as the college's size, organizational complexity, available resources, research expertise, and commitment to institutional research will need to be addressed.

*Sophisticated Research Strategies*: Conducting research for the sake of advancing knowledge is not the mission of community college research offices. However, with the growing demands of external agencies that colleges demonstrate numerous outcomes or outputs, research that is cross-sectional in nature will be limited in scope. The many outcome measures (or indicators) advanced by legislators and state governing boards are complicated and thus require the use of multiple data sources in response. More sophisticated analytic methods, such as employing a longitudinal approach to measure institutional or program effects on student outcomes, will need to be the norm for community college institutional research professionals.

*Interagency Collaboration*: Another issue community college researchers face is the challenge of collecting data and collaborating with federal, state, and private agencies. The use of administrative data bases has proven to be a valuable procedure, as evidenced in states like California, Colorado, Florida, Illinois, Texas and Washington, to name a few. In the 1990s, the issue of privacy of student data posed numerous challenges, and in the years to come it will continue to prove an obstacle for policy makers and researchers.

*Improving Public Trust*: For community colleges, the concept of improving public trust must be taken seriously. At the statewide level, community college governing boards will need to develop strategic-planning procedures to educate and disseminate information about the system's effectiveness. Close linkages between college boards and government offices (i.e., executive and legislative branches) will influence the perceptions of lawmakers. At the institutional level, colleges will need to develop ways to involve their local constituencies. Ultimately, only when taxpayers are informed about a community college's functions and understand the different levels of success will they give these institutions credibility and support. For the next decade, community colleges should be in the business of demonstrating their successes to a variety of external stakeholders.

*Multiple Measures of Success*: In the last few years, state community college systems have developed comprehensive accountability systems to measure institutional effectiveness. Outcome variables associated with these models typically include student achievement, retention and persistence, employment success, student/client satisfaction, community responsiveness, and collaboration with business and industry. For state legislators, demonstrating a system's effectiveness will continue to be a challenging task. Also, colleges will continue to be bombarded with accountability measures from the federal level, which may be similar to, or different from, state-mandated accountability measures. For the next decade, the nation's community colleges will have to continue responding to the multiple measures imposed by various constituencies.

*Improving the System's Image*: Finally, an important issue for community colleges is to improve their image. Even today, the challenge has been to convey the role and importance of community colleges as full and equal partners with universities and state institutions. As the community college system looks to the next decade, it will be even more critical that the image and the perceptions held by legislators, business, parents, students and the general public be positively influenced. Every citizen should be knowledgeable about community colleges and know something about their purpose and role in American higher education.

## POLICY RECOMMENDATIONS

Developing accountability systems is a daunting task. Although many state accountability systems already exist, the future of community college accountability will continue to evolve. The following are policy issues and recommendations for the future.

*Purposes and Goals*: Accountability systems can serve a variety of purposes. An accountability system that attempts to respond to too many purposes or functions will likely fail and do none of them well. In designing and developing an effective accountability system, it is important to identify specific purposes and goals. Employing a coordinated accountability system in which different purposes are identified and met at different levels of the education system is a useful strategy.

*Design and Implementation Process*: Developing the technical aspect of an accountability system is a critical procedure. For example, some of the issues involve defining the unit of accountability (e.g., student, college, district); determining how performance and progress are to be measured, compared, and reported; deciding how accountability data will be used to foster change and improvement; and understanding the role that the community college coordinating board plays in the accountability process. Another issue pertains to resources both internal and external to the institution. Also, providing a steady flow of information to the media, legislative and executive branches, colleges, districts, and the general public will help to minimize misinformation. Implementing these measures will increase the credibility of colleges' effectiveness and foster greater understanding and appreciation of the successes of these institutions.

*Rewards, Sanctions, and Other Incentives*: As a policy issue rewards, sanctions, and other incentive are the most controversial factors in higher education. As states begin to move toward the performance-based funding model, community colleges in particular are faced with having to demonstrate successful outcomes and outputs. In states with a large community college system there will inherently be unique institutional differences. Location, student demographics, and economic region are some of the factors that could influence the extent to which various outcomes meet the proposed standards. In most cases there will always be high-performing and low-performing colleges or districts. Important questions that policy makers need to address include how low-performing institutions should be sanctioned, what assistance the state will provide to help low-performing institutions improve, what the rewards will be for high-performing colleges or districts, and what other incentives will be available for institutions as either rewards or sanctions.

*The Public and Results*: The success of any accountability system is determined by the extent to which the public, policy makers, and other external constituencies view and understand the effectiveness of the college, district, or state community college system. A continual challenge for community colleges is to report results to policy makers and the public in a manner that is easily understandable and clear. Lawmakers in particular do not have the patience to sift through voluminous reports. Disseminating information about an institution or system by using report cards or system evaluations is an example of a useful understandable approach. Another critical role for colleges is to educate the public about the accountability system and what it means.

*Evolving Accountability System*: In order for an accountability system to be successful, an ongoing commitment must be present among policy makers in the system's design, implementation, and continuous refinement. Lack of commitment by the important players to an accountability system will ultimately determine its effectiveness and usefulness. Further, as new legislation pertaining to accountability systems emerges, community colleges will be required to monitor new and existing language to ensure consistency with the accountability design. With an evolving accountability system, community college coordinating boards, as well as legislative agencies, will be required to work harmoniously to calibrate and adjust existing systems.

## CONCLUSION

Community colleges are very robust institutions. In the 20th century, this segment of American higher education witnessed dramatic changes, in terms of both student enrollment and the ever-changing demands of the local community. With accountability systems in place, the nation's colleges will be faced with the need to respond to various performance indicators. Although such systems exist, many will have to be realigned and modified to accommodate the changing political tides. The last five years of the 20th century should serve as a good predictor of what community colleges can expect to see in the near future.

There is no doubt that in the 21st century, community colleges will have to address important issues and concerns with regard to accountability. Accountability is here to stay and will need to be a major policy initiative for colleges. Participation from internal and external stakeholders will play a critical role in designing, developing, and implementing a successful accountability system. As Alfred (1998) maintains, the development and maintenance of meaningful relationships with stakeholders will determine the extent to which colleges will be in the position to respond to the needs of their varied constituencies.

It is evident that there is still work to be done in the area of accountability. Community colleges need to be in the position to be proactive in influencing accountability discussions at the national and statewide levels. College leaders are in the critical position to affect the policy discussions in state capitols and in Washington. Ultimately, increasing public trust and legitimacy will determine organizational change.

## REFERENCES

Alfred, R. (1998). From closed to open systems: New designs for effectiveness in community colleges. *Journal of Applied Research in the Community College, 5*(1), 9–19.

American Association of Community Colleges. (1998). *Pocket profile of community colleges: Trends and statistics 1997–1998*. Washington, DC: Community College Press.

American Vocational Association. (1998). *The official guide to the Perkins Act of 1998. The authoritative guide to federal legislation for vocational-technical education*. Alexandria, VA: American Vocational Association.

Anderson, S. B., Ball, S., Murphy, R. T., et al. (1975). *Encyclopedia of educational*

evaluation: Concepts and techniques for evaluating education and training programs. San Francisco: Jossey-Bass.

Banta, T. W., & Borden, V. M. H. (1994). Performance indicators for accountability and
improvement. In V. M. H. Borden & T. W. Banta (Eds.), Using performance indicators to guide strategic decision making (New Directions for Institutional Research, No. 82 pp. 95–106). San Francisco: Jossey-Bass.

Borden, V. M. H., & Bottrill, K. V. (1994). Performance indicators: History, definitions,
and methods. In V. M. H. Borden & T. W. Banta (Eds.), Using performance indicators to guide strategic decision making (New Directions for Institutional Research, No. 82, pp. 5–21). San Francisco: Jossey-Bass.

Burke, J. C., & Serban, A. M. (Eds). (1998). Performance funding for public higher
education: Fad or trend? (New Directions for Institutional Research, No. 97).
San Francisco: Jossey-Bass.

Burke, J. C., & Serban, A. M. (1997). Performance funding and budgeting for public
higher education: Current status and future prospects. Albany, NY: Rockefeller
Institute.

Burke, J. C. (1998). Performance funding: Present status and future prospects. In J. Burke
& A. Serban (Eds.). Performance funding for public higher education: Fad or
trend? (New Directions for Institutional Research, No. 97, pp. 5–13). San Francisco: Jossey-Bass.

California Community Colleges. (1989, October 26). Assessing educational and fiscal
effectiveness in the California community colleges: A framework for AB 725 accountability requirements. Sacramento: California Community Colleges Chancellor's Office. Draft discussion paper.

California Community Colleges. (1990, April). AB 1725 model accountability system.
Sacramento: California Community Colleges Chancellor's Office.

Cave, M., Hanney, S., & Kogan, M. (1991). The use of performance indicators in higher
education: A critical analysis of developing practice (2nd ed.). London: Kingsley.

Clark, B. (1960). The "cooling-out function" in higher education. American Journal of
Sociology, 65(6), 569–576.

Cohen, A. M., & Brawer, F. B. (1996). The American community college (3rd ed.) San
Francisco: Jossey-Bass.

Cox, J. J., et al. (1992). Beyond accountability: Building a model for institutional effectiveness. Paper presented at the Annual Conference of the Community College
League of California, Ontario, California,

Dyer, P. A. (1991, September). Learning and student success: The mission of higher
education. Southern Association of Community, Junior and Technical Colleges
Occasional Paper, 9(2).

Education Commission of the States. (1998). Designing and implementing standards-
based accountability systems. Denver, CO: Author

Erwin, T. D. (1993). Outcomes assessment. In M. Barr et al. (Eds.), The handbook of
student affairs administration (pp. 230–241). San Francisco: Jossey-Bass.

Ewell, P. T. (1994, November/December). A matter of integrity accountability and the
future of self-regulation. Change, pp. 25–29.

Ewell, P. T. (1997). Accountability and assessment in a second decade. New looks or
same old story? In Assessing Impact: Evidence and Action (pp. 7–22). Washington, DC: American Association for Higher Education.

Ewell, P. T., & Jones, E. P. (1994). Pointing the way: Indicators as policy tolls in higher education. In S. Ruppert (Ed.), *Charting higher education accountability. A sourcebook on state-level performance indicators* (pp. 6–16). Denver, CO: Education Commission of the States.

Ewell, P. T., Wellman, J. V., & Paulson, K. (1997). *Refashioning accountability: Toward a coordinated system of quality assurance for higher education.* Denver, CO: Education Commission of the States.

Gaither, G. H. (Ed.). (1995). *Assessing performance in an age of accountability: Case studies* (New Directions for Higher Education, No. 91). San Francisco: Jossey-Bass.

Hudgins, J. L., & Mahaffey, J. (1998). When institutional effectiveness and performance funding co-exist. *Journal of Applied Research in the Community College, 5*(1), 21–28.

Illinois Community College Board. (1993). *Vision 2000: Charting a course for the future: Strategic plan for the Illinois Community College System.* Springfield: Author.

Illinois Community College Board. (1997). *Accountability and productivity report for the Illinois Community College System fiscal year 1997.* Springfield: Author.

Kells, H. R. (Ed.). (1993). *The development of performance indicators for higher education* (2nd ed.). Paris: Organization for Economic Cooperation and Development.

Klein, R., & Carter, N. (1988). Performance measurement: A review of concepts and issues. In D. Beeton (Ed.), *Performance measurement: Getting the concepts right* (pp. 5–20). Discussion Paper 18. London: Public Finance Foundation.

Koltai, L. (1993). Community colleges: Making winners out of ordinary people. In A. Levine (Ed.), *Higher learning in America 1980–2000* (pp. 100–113). Baltimore, MD: Johns Hopkins.

*Merriam-Webster's Collegiate Dictionary.* (1998). Springfield, MA: Merriam-Webster.

Neal, J. E. (1995). Overview of policy and practice: Differences and similarities in developing higher education Accountability. In G. Gaither (Ed.), *Assessing performance in an age of accountability: Case studies* (New Directions for Higher Education, No. 91, pp. 5–10). San Francisco: Jossey-Bass.

North Carolina Community College System. (1993). *Critical success factors for the North Carolina Community College System, 1993: Fourth Annual Report.* Raleigh: Author. (ERIC Document Reproduction Service No. Ed 361 031.)

North Carolina Community College System. (1999). *1999 critical success factors: Tenth annual report.* Raleigh: Author.

Pincus, F. L. (1994). How critics view the community college's role in the twenty-first century. In G. Baker (Ed.), *A handbook in the community college in America* (pp. 624–636). Westport, CT: Greenwood Press.

Ruppert, S. S. (Ed.). (1994). *Charting higher education accountability: A sourcebook on state-level performance indicators.* Denver, CO: Education Commission of the States.

Sanchez, J. R., & Laanan, F. S. (1998). The economic benefits of a community college education: Issues of accountability and performance measures. In J. R. Sanchez & F. S. Laanan (Eds.), *Determining the economic benefit of attending community college* (New Directions for Community Colleges, No. 104, pp. 5–15). San Francisco: Jossey-Bass.

Southern Regional Education Board. (1998). *Getting results: A fresh look at school accountability*. Atlanta, GA: Author.

State Higher Education Executive Officers. (1998). SHEEO/NCES communication, *Network News*, 17 (1). Available: http://www.SHEEO.org/network/nn-feb98.htm

Taylor, B. E., Meyerson, J. W., Morrell, L. R., & Park Jr., D. G. (1991). *Strategic analysis: Using comparative data to understand your institution*. Washington, DC: Association of University Governing Boards and Colleges.

U.S. Department of Education. (1998a, July). The Office of Vocational and Adult Education. Available: http://www.ed.gov/offices/OVAE/vocsite.html

U.S. Department of Education. (1998b, September). *Workforce Investment Act of 1998*. Washington, DC: U.S. Department of Education, Employment and Training Administration.

Zwerling, L. S. (1976). *Second best: The crisis of the community college*. New York: McGraw-Hill.

## Chapter 5

# The Buffered and the Buffeted Institution: Globalization and the Community College

*John S. Levin*

Long viewed and conceived of as a social and educational institution that responds to its local community, offering open access to postsecondary education and providing comprehensive education and training programs to meet the needs of individual students (Cohen & Brawer, 1996; Dennison & Gallagher, 1986; Dennison & Levin, 1989; Roueche, Taber, & Roueche, 1995), the community college has neither the history nor the image of an institution in a global context. Yet, in the last decade, with the rise in public and government emphasis and attention on a global economy, the community college has become, not only a more prominent regional and national institution, but also an institution that is affected by macro-level changes in the external environment. These changes include evolving government policies that reflect both societal and economic concerns, private sector demands for an increase in work-based training, business and industry specifications for skill acquisition, and the drive for efficiency and greater productivity in the public sector. Thus colleges respond by situating themselves closer to the marketplace to meet the needs of resource providers. This can be seen in their embrace of electronic technologies for rapid information processing and training, both to compete with other institutions and to meet the needs of external constituents as well as students, who depend on the college for their future employment. Like other higher-education institutions, community colleges are affected by global forces and respond both to these forces and to the responses of others, including governments.

Yet community colleges are buffered from direct interaction with their external environments to the extent that government policies and funding behaviors, collective agreements between management and labor, institutional structures such as governance committees, federal regulations, and the like separate societal and global actions such as a recession in Asia or a downturn in the North American forestry industry from the colleges. These external actions are mediated by others, and the colleges become subordinate to external players, reactors to others' actions. In reacting, colleges focus on internal mechanisms, internal politics, internal personalities, and members' personal preferences, unaware at times of the global forces acting upon their institutions or, indeed, experiencing government behaviors that themselves are responses to globalization. Not all colleges, however, are distanced or protected from their external environments; furthermore, colleges protected from some conditions, such as state economic recessions, are not protected from others, such as local demographic changes as a result of refugees and immigrants.

Colleges are buffeted by external forces, including global forces such as changing global economies; the rise and expansion of new technologies; the demands of government for greater productivity and efficiency; the changing workplace, with its emphasis on global competitiveness; and the movement of recent immigrants and refugees from Asia, the former Soviet Union countries, and wartorn Balkan countries to communities surrounding these colleges. In almost contradictory fashion, community colleges are both buffered and buffeted institutions, being simultaneously buffered from a global environment and buffeted by global forces.

## GLOBALIZATION

Globalization is a process and a condition; it is a concept and a force; and it is a proxy, or symbol, for large-scale rapid change, as well as modernization (Giddens, 1990; Robertson, 1992). Globalization has been associated with long-term historical change, corresponding with global exploration commencing in the 15th century (Robertson, 1992). Giddens (1990) and Edwards and Usher (1998), among others, emphasize the process whereby the compression of time and space intensify social, cultural, and economic relations and there is increasing interdependence among societies and nation-states (Robertson, 1992). Most prominent is the association of globalization with economic interdependence. Furthermore, globalization, especially economic globalization, has its champions and its opponents: those who praise and embrace free-market behaviors and unlimited economic growth and those who vilify exploitation and economic servitude.

Globalization is not merely an economic condition or process. Global forces and global behaviors are also social and cultural (Appadurai, 1990; Waters, 1996). In addition to its economic role, globalization connects cultures and groups, integrating people and their differences, sometimes resulting in harmony, sometimes in a "complex, overlapping, disjunctive order" (Appadurai, 1990, p. 296). The integration argument suggests that cultural differences are subsumed in a homogenous, overarching structure (Waters, 1996), where Western, particularly American, values are the dominant ones.

It may be that consciousness of a global society, culture, and economy and global interdependence are the cornerstones of globalization (Robertson, 1992), and these—consciousness and interdependency—have saliency in knowledge-based enterprises. Institutional theory suggests that there are organizational fields, such as higher-education institutions or hospitals, for example, where patterns of institutional behaviors become similar across institutions (DiMaggio & Powell, 1983). Thus, there is a certain inevitability that higher-education institutions, because of their cultural, social, and economic roles, are caught up in, and affected by, globalization.

The process of globalization has been connected to numerous alterations in higher education. For example, with emphasis on international competitiveness, economic globalization is viewed as moving postsecondary institutions into a business-like orientation, with its attendant behaviors of efficiency and productivity. The placement of higher-education institutions in closer proximity to the marketplace, through such arrangements as corporate partnerships and associations, is an obvious manifestation of economic globalization.

## INFLUENCES OF GLOBALIZATION

Globalizing forces and the globalization process have impacted community colleges. One prevalent domain is the economic domain, where a global economy affects state revenues, which in turn affect colleges through government-funding alterations and policy initiatives. A second domain is cultural, where local populations reflect international cultures and are a consequence of international events, such as wars and political realignments. Electronic technology signals a third domain—information, including acquisition, dissemination, and the structuring and management of both acquisition and dissemination.

Aside from these three domains is the role of state government—politics—in the organizational behaviors of colleges. The presence and predominant role of government in the behaviors and actions of colleges, however, is related to both the nature and severity of influence of global forces on colleges. On the one hand, government policy and actions detach colleges from the direct impact of globalization; on the other hand, government behaviors place colleges in the vortex of global forces. These domains are referred to as domains of globalization (see Figure 5.1). This chapter is based on a multicase study of colleges in the West. The study determined the effects of globalization on community colleges; specifically, how much and ways in which globalization affected organizational behaviors, processes, and structures (Levin, 1999). The colleges were given fictitious names to maintain institutional anonymity. In this discussion, three colleges in the states of California, Washington, and Hawaii are

**Figure 5.1**
**Domains of Globalization**

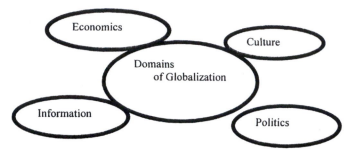

examined, which are named, respectively, Suburban Valley Community College; City South Community College; and Pacific Suburban Community College.


### The Economic Domain

Colleges are connected to global economies largely through state governments, through industry, through local employment conditions and patterns, and through workplace needs. Funding for these colleges relies on two principal sources—government and local students. Colleges are altering this dependency to some extent, first by generating revenues from private sector training and service and second by recruiting international students and securing work contracts with business, industry, and government in other countries. To date, college efforts in generating revenues locally are more successful with government or government agency contracts than with the private sector. International revenue generation is growing, but there are hurdles and hazards, such as problems with costs relative to revenues and, especially, with fluctuations in international economies.

Employment conditions and workplace needs are complex in their effects on colleges. The truism for higher education, that in times of unemployment, enrollments rise, and in times of high employment, enrollments decline, is not borne out by empirical research. In some employment areas where there is heavy demand for workers, such as the computer fields, the health sciences, and business, enrollments rise, and college actions are directed toward providing resources for these program areas. Workplace needs that require basic skills, including English language proficiency, place pressure on colleges to provide instruction in these areas. Student demand appears to dictate this pressure. Workplace needs that require specialized skills, such as computer or managerial skills, have altered college curricula through the influence of program advisory groups, company or corporate officials, and faculty and administrators who interact with employers and observe the workplace.

*Suburban Valley Community College.* Greater productivity and efficiency, the consequence of lessening state support for education, were prominent influences on organizational behaviors at Suburban Valley Community College (SVCC). Actions of restructuring and increasing workloads for college employees were connected to the drive for increased productivity. Furthermore, even though there were limitations to state-supported education, the state was viewed as increasing its influence in college operations. In the latter part of the 1990s, the state instituted performance indicators for monitoring and evaluating college outcomes, although these were largely in the form of quantitative measures such as increasing student numbers. These indicators were intended to be tied to funding, so that increased funding would depend on increases in measures of productivity. Thus, the state directed the college because the college was dependent on the state for revenues.

Economic benefits accrued to the college through offering education as a service. The college developed and offered specific training for local business and industry; and it relied on distance education delivery, both to serve local needs and to position itself as a provider of education via distance education for a national and international market. Thus, education became a commodity.

*City South Community College.* Emphasis on productivity and efficiency, especially in the face of declining revenues, increasing accountability from government, decreasing program demand, and changing workplace requirements, had several effects of substance on City South Community College (CSCC). A restructuring effort of 1995 was a response to what the president viewed as "global forces of change" impacting the college. This effort led to outcomes not unlike those experienced within the larger corporate area of U.S. business and industry—downsizing and layoffs, greater loss of revenues, mission alteration, and greater dependency on resource providers, as well as an increased focus on the private sector marketplace. The 1995 restructuring action was intended to help the college respond better to changing workplace needs. In 1997 college personnel were baffled by the rationale for the restructuring, with many viewing the outcomes as negative, including altered work relations among workers and between workers and administrators and the deprofessionalization of faculty by organizing them into "teams."

While the college president may have acted to save the college from collapse, he did not adapt the institution to a new global economy. There was essentially no plan, no replacing of content to what was altered and jettisoned, and no new programs to take the place of the deteriorating vocational programs.

Although highly influenced by global forces, the college was closely connected to intermediary organizations and systems, which impeded, even determined, college responsiveness. The college was reliant on the performance of the local aircraft industry internationally. Too much economic activity from this sector, however, meant that there was employment and no need for preemployment training; too little economic activity, and the need for trained personnel diminished. The industry demanded specific training outcomes; the college fit the curricula to the industry, but program graduates were not hired in large numbers in the field. For example, from 1990 to 1994, fewer than 25 percent of the 181 graduates in the aircraft maintenance program were hired in their field, according to college records.

College district officials acted to increase efficiencies on campus and to develop a more salable image to the community for the three district colleges as a whole. Thus, district officials acted according to global patterns—they centralized control, information, and decision mechanisms and decentralized production. The district claimed to "subsidize" CSCC, but it also may have been responsible for influencing its management, by selecting and controlling its chief executive officers and by moving the college away from its local community to serve district interests and needs. Again, this behavior of district personnel may indeed have saved CSCC from collapse and from further erosion in state funding.

***Pacific Suburban Community College.*** Pacific Surburban Community College (PSCC) was increasingly an object, a victim even, of economic globalization as external economies (e.g., California in the early 1990s and Japan in the late 1990s) had a significant bearing on the college's actions. The state economy, as several organizational members observed, had a pervasive influence on college behaviors and actions: "Everything pales in comparison to the economy." This economy was dependent on tourism and its related spin-offs, such as retail merchandising. State tourism was declining, as were the revenues associated with this industry. The state was vulnerable to international economic shocks, and the college was, in turn, vulnerable to the state and its economic performance. The island economy, like many of its natural attributes, was fragile (Daws, 1974). The past pattern of expansion ended, and public institutions, such as PSCC, were at a crossroads, either, for the foreseeable future, at the mercy of a declining state economy or preparing to alter sources of funding. The state was not prepared to raise taxes to support the public sector. Observers, such as institutional leaders, saw that the effects of the state's high salaries attributed to the large percentage of unionized workers—approximately 22 percent statewide, as compared to the 12 percent national average—had to be modified by making reductions in the workforce and by curtailing public sector expenditures. But the state's high costs of living, a result, in part, of Asian capital, in the absence of expanded revenues for the state and resultant increases in state expenditures, furthered the existing situation in California of "haves and have nots."

For PSCC, declining state revenues and a declining economy affected organizational behaviors, and managers placed greater emphasis on cost cutting and revenue generation. Productivity and efficiency were emphasized in the middle and latter part of the 1990s, including increased worker productivity and greater institutional attention to student outcomes. The college, along with other community colleges in the state, was permitted not only to keep tuition revenues but also to raise tuition. There were increases in tuition fees of 75 percent from the 1995–1997 period. Remedial education programs shifted from credit to non-credit, enabling the college to use noncredit instructors and increase fees. Distance education delivery was used for efficiency, administrative operations were streamlined, and positions were reduced. In order to generate revenues, the college moved closer to the marketplace, to the private sector, to generate revenues. This action included greater attention to training and to providing services for local business.

### The Cultural Domain

Immigration and local population demographics affect college services and programming as well as college mission orientation. The local population that confronts each college is the primary service area of the institution, although two of these colleges have aspirations to serve a much larger area. The wave of immigration to the West of the United States in the past decade—from Southeast Asia and from the former Soviet Union, in particular—has altered the communities that the colleges occupy. Not only are there cultural changes in these communities, there are also growing populations of nonnative English speakers or second-generation immigrants whose native language is English but for whom English is not a language of competency. Colleges have altered their emphases on culture, becoming more attentive to cultural differences, more pluralistic in their approach to both formal and informal governance, and more responsive, in curriculum and instruction, to multicultural needs. Additionally, cultural awareness and sensitivity have become important qualities in international initiatives for colleges to secure work contracts and recruit students.

*Suburban Valley Community College.* "Multiculturalism" was a persistent term used at SVCC, and it was used in a variety of ways to reflect, not only student demographics, but also institutional behaviors, including instruction and extracurricular activities. At SVCC, there were large numbers of immigrants, especially from non-Western countries. Asian immigration was a consequence of numerous factors, including political conflicts, rapid industrialization, and the promise of economic prosperity in California (Schrag, 1998). The importance of Asia globally was both as a market for products and as a source of labor. This suggested the need to cultivate closer ties to Asian cultures and the need to integrate Asians into other societies. Because of the large Asian population, as well as the other large non-Anglo populations, at SVCC, diversity and multiculturalism were practical concepts. The college responded to its student population by altering programming, curricula, and college social life to fit student ethnic and cultural backgrounds. For example, non-Western writers became more prevalent on course syllabi and extra-curricular activities included international festivals and speakers. Furthermore, new organizational structures were established, such as a college reorganization of units in the mid-1990s to reflect multiculturalism and teamwork, and inter and multi-disciplinarity in curricula gained prominence as the college adapted to college members' understanding of "new learning needs of student," especially part-time learners and nonnative speakers, and concepts of "learning in a global context," as noted by organizational members.

*City South Community College.* The college was situated within a community that had not only a large immigrant population, but also a changing immigrant population as the refugees—the "boat people" of the 1970s—gave way in the 1980s to the Chinese from Hong Kong, and these groups were added to by Eastern Europeans (e.g., Russians). Additionally, as the urban center population moved outward, the local community of CSCC was replaced by a slightly more affluent population as local blue-collar families moved further away from CSCC due to rising housing prices in the metropolitan area.

In the 1990s the college placed increasing emphasis upon multiculturalism and diversity, serving a relatively large immigrant and refugee community population, including many nonnative speakers. The college added (in conjunction with the two other district colleges) a multicultural course requirement for the associate degree (1994) and added a cultural course for the degree (1996). Moreover, a task force on diversity was established and a diversity plan was developed (1996 and 1997) that affected student services and employee hiring.

*Pacific Suburban Community College.* PSCC expanded an already substantial international focus, yet the college simultaneously served the needs of its local students by its emphasis on multiculturalism. While the emphasis on international education had instrumental value—it was intended to attract students and increase enrollments—it had cultural value for organizational members, who were fervent proponents of maintaining a cultural mosaic, both in college student demographics and in curriculum. Thus, cultural events on campus (such as International Week), and courses and programs that had cultural components and multicultural orientations (e.g., culinary arts, humanities, languages, business) were viewed as integral to college behaviors and actions. At PSCC the global was local because of student demographics; the college was a minority-majority college (i.e., visible minorities were the largest class of students on campus), the local community was multiethnic, and the state was populated by large numbers of people with Asian origins or ancestry.

### The Information Domain

Information technologies (e.g., Internet, voice mail, fax, E-mail) affect both instruction and institutional work, including administrative work. The emphasis by managers on productivity and efficiency, as well as the perceived requirement for organizational members to remain current or, indeed, "keep up," steers institutional behaviors toward the increased use of informational technologies. Thus, work has altered at these colleges as a consequence of the use of informational technologies. The industrial model of work and, indeed, of teaching is undergoing change and stress, although the institutions still cling to that model. In order to compete for students, compete globally for international contracts, and satisfy external demands—those of business, industry, and other higher-education institutions—college members support the increasing use of these technologies, as well as the application of informational technologies in instruction.

The World Wide Web, E-mail, and intranet communications have become common structures for instruction.

*Suburban Valley Community College.* The increasing use, and pervasive influence, of electronic technology was a major force acting on the college. Historically, according to numerous administrators and a diverse group of faculty, the college established a reputation as an innovator and educational leader. Thus, such a role, if it is to be maintained, must match external expectations. SVCC adopted electronic technologies such as information technologies (e.g., E-mail, voice mail, on-line registration) and educational technologies (e.g., Web-based instruction) to achieve recognition nationally. Additionally, in order to attract students to increase enrollments and to gain needed revenue, the college offered what the public, business, and industry expected: this included current electronic equipment, user-friendly instructional approaches, and a computer literate student. Finally, the use of electronic technology increasingly supported distance education, a delivery system intended, not only to satisfy the needs of the public (especially the adult, working public), but also to increase productivity, or at least add to enrollment figures. The potential of distance education for revenue generation depended on electronic technology for delivery—including on-line instruction and satellite-broadcast video.

*City South Community College.* In the later part of the 1990s, there was increased use, and greater integration, of electronic technology into CSCC's bureaucracy, such as the use of voice mail to improve customer service and efficiency. Distance delivery of education was in the formative stage, mainly through telecourses, and Internet delivery was slowly integrated into instruction, with plans to expand fivefold between 1998 and 1999. Faculty, in the main, viewed distance education as a threat, especially a threat from the district office, which played a key role in distance delivery. For example, district policy on the use of electronic technology noted that the employer may monitor use. At CSCC in 1997, there were 20 classes of distance education, with 50 full-time equivalency (FTE) students. Yet there was little development in distance education due to limited resources. Other limitations, according to organizational members, included the role of the district office, where district staff made decisions about distance education that affect curriculum on campus, and externally, where institutions such as the Western Governor's University were perceived to be a threat.

*Pacific Suburban Community College.* During the 1990s, there was a rising focus at PSCC on instructional technology, particularly distance education, with one eye on serving the local community and the state's islands and the other eye on the greater South Pacific and Asia as sources for customers of courses and programs. By the latter part of the 1990s, information technology was expanded, driven in part by administrative efforts to improve information systems to support the administrative goal of efficiency and effectiveness.

Technology was also used to alter curriculum and instruction, including program development that both uses instructional technology and trains for the use of information technology (e.g., revised curricula for business computer information systems in 1995–1996). Advances were made in on-line instruction and Web-based instruction, such as expository writing and the biological sciences, and the college was designated as an Auto-CAD (computer assisted drafting) training center.

## The Presence of Government

The behaviors and influences of state governments are dualistic in regard to the colleges. Governments persuade and coerce colleges to increase their productivity, to respond to workplace and business needs, and at least to affect an accountability posture to the public. Colleges respond to workplace demands but also neglect aspects of their mission, and thus their communities, because their focus and their resources are directed to government priorities. Colleges endeavor to increase productivity, but in so doing they precipitate tensions in labor relations, where management asks for, and expects, for example, faculty to teach greater numbers of students and to use technology to support their added responsibilities. In this sense, governments direct colleges to become more efficient and more oriented toward global competition. Governments also shield or detach colleges from global forces, not only by translating these forces for colleges but also by mediating between global and local conditions. Governments use colleges as instruments of policy, and they also protect colleges from market forces by subsidizing their operations. These actions are significant contributors to the condition of colleges, as buffered from, or buffeted by, global forces.

*Suburban Valley Community College.* The role of the state was evident in at least two areas: college finances and accountability. The California system of education funding was based on limits to property tax assessments. This model led to a shortage of funds to support the demands of higher education. Furthermore, the state targeted funding to support specific areas of its interests, but these did not include faculty salaries. While college enrollments either rose or remained stable, and as costs rose, government funding did not keep pace.

The state intervened in college management and operations through its demands for greater productivity and its requirements for increasing accountability. Mandates in the 1990s included a "pay for performance" administrative plan, enrollment fees, performance indicators, and various laws that constrained both the offering of distance education and student registration.

SVCC endeavored to increase enrollments because state funding was enrollment driven. The college also relied on other, non government, funding sources and worked to increase productivity and efficiency, including selecting and expanding program offerings in high-demand areas. As a consequence of less-than-adequate funding from the state, there were union-management tensions over salaries and over the demand for greater productivity. In the 1990s, there was a layoff of staff and elimination of positions; equipment in established instructional areas (e.g., science) was perceived as obsolete; and there were incentives for early staff retirement to decrease salary commitments.

*City South Community College.* According to organizational members, the state, especially through its funding behaviors, treated CSCC as a branch plant operation, much as large corporations behave toward foreign production sites. The state established funding policies and used targeted funding for an agenda not favorable to colleges or students. The state also set tuition fees, used its agency to demand specific forms of accountability, and controlled collective bargaining, in part, by its state salary allocations. Educational policies that might benefit students, such as university transfer articulation policies that facilitate student mobility or support for excellence in student performance, were either nonexistent or below the level of institutional consciousness, as neither organizational members nor institutional documents referred to state policy that had educational salience. Finally, on the far negative side of state influence was the state's Welfare-to-Work program, which, from the perspective of the college, was a regressive action that moved students out of the classroom and onto the streets to look for work, even work offering wages below the poverty level. This policy was viewed as a contributor to the loss of those programs that could help students attain careers and occupations rather than temporary or unstable jobs in a global economy. The program encouraged short-term training and thus detracted from the more educational and long-term employment orientation of two-year associate degree programs. At CSCC in 1998, between 500 and 600 FTE students were categorized as Welfare-to-Work, amounting to close to 20% of the college's total student body.

State influence was largely fiscal, directing programs through enrollment-based funding and operations through the use of performance indicators. Increased government oversight and accompanying decreases in state appropriations placed other stresses on the institution as its enrollments in traditional vocational programs declined and enrollments in academic and other occupational programs did not rise enough to offset declines. Thus, emphasis on increasing productivity, on competition with other institutions, and on bureaucratic procedures to conform to state demands (e.g., performance indicators), along with decreasing revenues, pushed the college to the category of marginality in the "winners and losers" dichotomy of the global economy.

*Pacific Suburban Community College.* The intrusiveness of government, a condition present since the inception of the college and reported as increasingly growing, was expected to diminish, both as a result of declining state fiscal support for the college and due to rising dependence on other resource providers. The state had not moved toward greater accountability measures, likely because of its ability to control and influence higher-education institutions through its policies and, especially, through its bureaucratic and funding relationships (e.g., state-wide contract negotiations for faculty, with government as a third party; state appointment of governing board members). The assumption that a lessening of government fiscal support for the college would lead to greater independence from government is not borne out either by research (e.g., Slaughter & Leslie, 1997) or by the reported experiences of other colleges in this study. Indeed, PSCC may need the state more than it expects, especially if its entrepreneurial actions fail to yield their intended effects. As a board member noted, higher-education institutions in the state have not been economic players or global competitors, and thus they might have to reconsider their future role, including educating and serving the state's population in a changed economy where subsistence may be a realistic condition.

Nonetheless, the state was accused of "micro-managing the . . . college system," and college observers noted that the college was viewed as another department of state government. In short, the state government was not viewed in a favorable light by higher-education system officials. The intrusive role and influence of government in higher education began with the governor's office: the governor not only appointed board members but also became involved in labor relations through collective bargaining. The state legislature influenced the college through policy, through funding and through championing specific programs. "Downsizing is politically popular," noted one college official, showing the impact of political behaviors on college-funding reductions from the state. Indeed, the government in the 1990s was particularly involved in college operations and actions; this included the governor's office, which intervened in, and diverted, a 1997 faculty strike. There was also a state-mandated tuition policy in 1995, whereby in nearly equal amounts, the college retained revenues but government operating monies decreased.

## THE BUFFERED AND BUFFETED INSTITUTION

Colleges are both buffered from their global environments and buffeted by global forces. Several structures aid in buffering colleges from the global environment. That is, colleges are protected and, indeed, detached from their external environments, particularly from macro-forces such as declining international economies, and they are also direct participants in a global environment and impacted significantly by macro-forces. Some college structures, such as governance and labor relations, are responsible for the buffering effects, and external structures, particularly state governments and district offices, are contributors to both buffering and buffeting effects.

## The Buffered College

The buffered college is detached from participation in a global environment because intermediaries translate, interpret, and react to that global environment either before the college encounters external forces or in place of the college. To some extent the buffered college is protected from extreme shocks, such as major funding reductions based on government revenue losses. But the buffered college is also limited in its autonomy to act in response to external forces, as well as impaired in its vision of those forces. The buffered college has limited control over its own actions. More specifically, internal influencers, such as managers, union officials, or governing board members, have little power to direct the institution in responding or adapting to its environment (Mintzberg, 1983).

## The Buffeted College

The buffeted college is exposed to global forces, largely without mediation from external structures. Even the state government does not shield the college from global economic forces. The college is not protected from a downturn in the economy, and revenue losses for the state government are passed on to the college by reductions in allocations. Because the college and the state are seemingly interconnected, both through financial structures and through governance and labor relations structures, the forces that affect the state also affect the college. The buffeted college is exposed to global forces, but the college is not necessarily an autonomous entity able to construct its own responses. Its influence is limited because it is part of a larger system of higher-education institutions and must respond in accord with system demands, controls, and policy.

## Both Buffered and Buffeted

Colleges can be both buffered from, and buffeted by, global forces. As part of a system, colleges are removed from full participation in the external environment and from the full shock of declining revenues. Yet, with their historical connection to workforce training and their service to a large immigrant population, colleges are in the pathway of global forces. A boon-or-bust industrial environment, largely an outcome of global forces and events, affects college programming, enrollments, and revenues. A wave of immigrants from Asian and Eastern European countries affects college programming—increasing the demand for courses in English as a second language—and services.

Colleges can be buffered from global forces through both state government policy and the actions of a college's district office in absorbing some of the shocks from the environment. Colleges can also be buffeted by global forces because of their proximity to, and relationship with, local industries. These ties connect the institution to a global marketplace. Furthermore, a large immigrant population and increasing diversity of students and community members help to situate colleges in a global environment.

### The Impact of Globalization on Three Colleges

Suburban Valley Community College was located in a region that is nationally and internationally renowned and highly competitive internationally in high-technology industries, especially computers and computer software. The area attracted workers internationally, and industry required a trained workforce to maintain its competitive advantage over other countries' lower-paid workers. This external pressure corresponded with the college's increasing use of electronic technology and its programmatic emphasis on computer-based instruction.

Actions of restructuring and increasing workloads for college employees were connected to the drive for increased productivity. Greater productivity and efficiency were behaviors influenced, not only by local industry and its emphasis on electronic technology, but also by the state. Although the state decreased its funding support for education, it was viewed as increasing its influence in college operations. State policy initiatives, such as increased emphasis on the training of students and a greater infusion of technological equipment into the workplace, affected both instruction and administrative and clerical work. The state directed the college because the college was largely dependent on the state for revenues.

The state was not as directive in the area of multiculturalism. Here, the college responded directly to its changing local demographics. These changing demographics were the result of an influx of large numbers of immigrants, especially from non-Western countries.

Some college members and other observers (Schrag, 1998) believed that the 1978 Proposition 13 (initiative to impose property tax limits) initiated the decline of public education in the state. Others were less historically minded but acknowledged a severe decline and considerable college actions to "keep up," to maintain quality, and to attract both students and revenues from the state. College members faced a nearly insurmountable condition: increases in workload; increases in student and public expectations; changing student demographics, with larger numbers of underprepared students; greater accountability initiatives; aging employees, facilities, and equipment; greater workplace expectations for graduates; and, finally, decreasing fiscal resources. While the college was insulated from dramatic global economic shifts, largely because its funding was a state responsibility and not dependent on college entrepreneurship, SVCC was subject to a substantial environmental influence, including influence of a global or international nature, such as immigration and global industrial competitiveness. SVCC was thus both a buffered and a buffeted institution.

City South Community College was buffeted by numerous external environmental forces, encumbered by its organizational history, its leaders were continually proposing, and working on, strategies to respond to externally influenced change. Its geographical location, the demographic characteristics of its local population, and the combination of unskilled employment opportunities and the college's historical emphasis on vocational programming shaped college actions and outcomes over the 1990s. To some extent, the college was a prisoner of its basic environment, its large immigrant and working-class population, and its industrial base, as well as its history and continuing behaviors as a vocationally oriented institution.

Globalization for CSCC was a complex phenomenon, colored by the global connectivity of two state and local industries—aircraft and computer software. The college's history as a vocational institution, ("Paycheck College"), (where students enroll in programs, finish, and obtain jobs with satisfying remuneration, is like a microcosm of the global economy's effects on America in the 1980s. Blue-collar, trades jobs declined, both through automation and through out sourcing to other countries. The call for American competitiveness was, not to address the decline in industrial manufacturing, but to stimulate training in the high-technology fields, in the professions, and in business. CSCC was caught in a "time warp," where old, successful programs lost enrollments because of structural changes in the political economy, yet the college's image and its community demographics limited its movement toward evolving as an advanced educational institution.

The role of the district office cannot be underestimated. While CSCC was an independently accredited institution, it was, de facto, one of three institutions under the oversight of a single college district board and was centrally managed, especially fiscally, by a district office and district executive officers. Collective bargaining, for example, was a district-wide action, and numerous policies emanated from the governing board and the district office. On a day-to-day basis, the district office was viewed by numerous college employees as the major external force acting on CSCC. In this vein, it can be concluded that the district office served as a buffer between global and other large macro-forces and the college. CSCC was both buffered from and buffeted by global forces.

Pacific Suburban Community College continued its historical pattern of contracting geographical distance between South Pacific and Asian countries, as well as within the state, by increasing its development and use of electronic technologies (i.e., distance education) and unifying cultural differences among its various ethnic populations by increasing its emphasis on multiculturalism.

In the mid- and late 1990s, the state witnessed a sharp alteration in its economy, which was largely determined by the decline of tourism. The California recession of the early 1990s and the Japanese economic slide of the mid- and late 1990s translated into fewer Californian and Japanese tourists for the state. The historical dependency of the state on trade and travel and on its strategic location, whether historically for trade or military conquest and defense, altered, not in nature, but in kind: the economy was singly focused on tourists. Other natural resources diminished in their economic worth; the military importance of the state, and thus the resources committed to the preservation of the military, declined substantially. By the mid-1990s, the state economy, which was generally characterized by ups and downs, moved into a period of decline, which since then has not altered in direction. Furthermore, because the state supported the public higher-education sector with the majority of its revenues, supplemented in the mid-1990s by tuition fees, the weakening economy resulted in diminishing state revenues, and thus reduced fiscal resources for institutions. PSCC was captive to a condition of fiscal decline.

PSCC as an institution began to move closer to the marketplace and further from reliance on government in the belief that the private sector would respond and provide needed revenues for the college. Thus, state economic woes meant that some societally beneficial actions by the college—such as the provision of relatively inexpensive training and education—were coming to an end. Once tuition rose (in the mid- to late 1990s), enrollments declined. The pattern suggested that PSCC would generate fewer tuition revenues and suffer a further decline in government funding. The college set itself on a course to raise productivity, and some increases were intended to come from international sources that could access college programs. Once a buffered institution, in the 1990s PSCC gradually became buffeted by global forces of change.

## WORK AND EDUCATION

Whether colleges are buffered, buffeted, or both, in all colleges both work and education are affected by globalization. It is just that in the buffered college and in those colleges where there are buffered areas, alterations to work and education are not as heightened or extreme. Work has changed, and continues to change, becoming aligned with the ideology of global competitiveness and corporatism (Ralston Saul, 1995). Work norms emphasize productivity and efficiency, as evidenced by the increase of speed in tasks and by enlarged workloads. These increases are made possible by the deployment of electronic technologies and computer-based production processes. Furthermore, work is constantly restructured through job reduction and job creation in targeted areas so as to increase productivity. For faculty, productivity is achieved by serving more students and by decreasing costs, specifically labor costs. Both are accomplished by the use of part-time faculty because of their low costs and by incentives for full-time faculty to serve more students.

Education has altered both in programming—that is, curriculum offerings— and in curriculum itself. Programs are added to serve the needs of the job market, not only to match government policy but also to gain government approval. With this approval, resources follow. Students are increasingly viewed and treated as customers or consumers, who are engaging in training and education as private citizens with vocational needs. Curriculum moves toward skill training, which is justified by the need for students to acquire competencies that are valued in the marketplace and workplace. Thus, in the extreme, curriculum is economically determined: colleges gain financially by providing favored programs; students gain economic advantage by their acquisition of specific competencies; and business and industry profit with a trained or preselected workforce.

In this light, community colleges reinforce globalization, likely reproducing its attentiveness to economic, material emphases and its neglect of both social relations (Teeple, 1995) and the public good (Ralston Saul, 1995). But this may not be done completely—or every time, Globalization also brings cultural integration (Waters, 1996) and promotes a conception of the world as a single place (Robertson, 1992) where diverse individuals and groups connect. Through its emphasis on multiculturalism (Gaff, 1992) in both institutional activities and in curriculum, Suburban Valley Community College, City South Community College, and Pacific Suburban Community College place cultural understanding at the forefront of their practices. Although one motive in colleges' emphasis on multiculturalism is economic—to attract more students—another motive is pedagogical, if not moral—to fulfill the needs of learners.

In higher education, globalization theory pertains most emphatically to work—to the changing nature and pace of labor as a result of technological change and the demand from employers and government for increased productivity and efficiency, largely in the name of global competitiveness. While education—curriculum, programming, and instruction—is altering as well, the impact of globalization on this area is not as pronounced. Yet curriculum is becoming more oriented to skill acquisition, programming more connected to the needs of business and industry, and instruction more reliant on electronic technologies. Government policies and funding incentives are decidedly directed at accelerating the pace of change in education, responding to global pressures for increasing productivity, and developing a globally competitive labor force while reducing labor costs.

## GLOBALIZING HIGHER EDUCATION

The implications of globalization for higher education are varied, yet significant. Two prominent implications involve areas of work and education. For institutions of higher education, globalization processes both accompany technological changes, assisting in the transformation of academic work (Aronowitz & Di Fazio, 1994), and situate institutions closer to the marketplace, especially in fields connected to technology and science (Slaughter & Leslie, 1997). Furthermore, education is vocationalized and training is driven by the demands of business and industry. With business and industry increasingly international in focus, having become dependent on global capital, global markets, and a globally defined labor force (Teeple, 1995), higher-education institutions, in following government and public policy toward competition and consumerism, adopt private sector practices and begin to function as corporations (Ralston Saul, 1995; Ritzer, 1998; Teeple, 1995). In order to be competitive, these institutions emphasize efficiency and productivity in work and market responsiveness and relevancy in education.

In the 1990s and at the dawn of the year 2000, community colleges became more market oriented in their goals and more business-like in their behaviors. They expanded their traditional mission by enlarging workforce training and emphasizing skills development. Doing so has resulted in a more overt concentration on private sector interests, which is reflected in changing priorities for student learning.

The shift of community colleges to an entrepreneurial focus and a more overt economic role is linked to both government funding and government policy. Thus, colleges are more decidedly instruments of government, particularly economic interests, than in the past, and yet they are less dependent on government for their total revenues. At the extreme, colleges have become several institutions structured within one institution. They are multi-institutions, combing an entrepreneurial college with a workforce training center, and yet they have preserved much of the traditional institution, which is comprised of a comprehensive curriculum and open admissions practices. They have maintained democratic principles, most notably open access to educational opportunities (a characteristic of "democracy's college") and respond more emphatically to corporate and economic interests of the community. They have shifted from community service to private sector interests, while preserving and expanding education and training opportunities for community members.

Student learning priorities have shifted from an acclaimed focus on individual development and career and educational preparation to skills development and workforce training. Marketplace interests and employment training and retraining have motivated institutional programming patterns. While some traditional vocational programs deteriorated, both in enrollments and in resources, vocationalism insinuated itself in higher-level programming, such as business- and computer-oriented programs. Decidedly less priority was given to remediation and to developmental education.

The changing institutional priorities to student learning include instructional delivery as well as curriculum. Moving in a direction similar to the ubiquitous claim of a paradigm shift in postsecondary education from teaching to learning (Barr & Tagg, 1995; Dolence & Norris, 1995), institutions justified institutional practices from distance education to computer-based instruction as "learner-centered." Institutional rationales parallel the view of education and training as a commodity, students as customers, and business and industry as clients—all reinforcing market ideology.

Institutional change in this direction follows student, employer, and government preferences. Institutional revenues increased significantly in the 1990s, even with claims of government funding constraints. Tuition fees, contract service revenues, and temporary funding not in the base budget, and often competitive government grants comprised a greater share of institutional revenues, suggesting that resource providers, including the private sector, were favorably impressed with institutional responsiveness to economic interests. To what extent this shift to more job market responsiveness at higher costs to students affected both students and community members who were not students is uncertain.

College actions and outcomes demonstrate the expansion of mission, the growth in services, the elaboration of structures, the accommodation of more students, and increasing attention to new methods of instructional delivery and instructional strategies, all during the 1990s. The pattern of the 1990s indicates rising expenditures to support these behaviors. In order to meet the associated expenses and to acquire fiscal resources, community colleges will turn increasingly to the private sector—unless governments significantly increase their allocations. It does not appear that colleges will contract their missions unless that occurs in the vocational, developmental, and remedial areas, where private businesses could replace colleges' responsibilities.

With increasing reliance on fee payers and business and industry, college programs and services will inevitably reflect the needs and requirements of resource providers. This suggests a decrease in the social, community role of community colleges and an increase in their economic role. It also suggests that instruction will develop in line with the needs of educational users, needs that are likely to include more work-based training, more nonclassroom instruction (relying on computer-related technologies), and greater emphasis on employability skills.

For the early decades of the 21st century, the pressures to provide education and training to a diverse student population in order to serve community economic interests and to support institutional operations with more fiscal resources will no doubt increase. As a result, institutions will be caught between the need to turn more to the private sector for funds, especially fee payers, and meeting community demands for traditional education, such as literacy and cognitive development. Simultaneously, institutions will face identity pressures, whether that be to preserve traditional community college missions and values or to expand into a higher-status postsecondary institution. The pattern established in the 1990s toward a more corporate and business-like approach to education and the more traditional education and socializing function of college is likely to be of central concern to governments, inasmuch as they respond to public opinion as well as to private sector interests.

Student learning needs and outcomes and instructional practices constitute only half of the dilemma that faces stakeholders. The second half involves the nature of institutional work. Changes both to work activities and to the workload of organizational members are evident at community colleges. Administrative work has altered, with greater pressure for efficient production and increases in the duration and pace of work. Faculty work has altered in various ways, including responding more directly to management and institutional priorities as well as to public and private sector requirements for employable workers. Faculty workloads have tended to increase with respect to time devoted to communication and to meetings. Also, with a shift to more part-time faculty, greater responsibilities devolve to full-time faculty in their institutional service and administrative tasks. The use of electronic technology increases faculty work, particularly in instructional preparation. Also, student numbers in many instructional areas have grown, with faculty responsible for increasing numbers of students. Finally, support staff, which are fewer in number than in the 1980s relative to institutional size, face increased workloads and greater demands from both administrators and faculty alike. The proliferation of electronic technology increases their workloads as institutional expectations rise with new technological capabilities and the rising speed of information processing and communication.

Stakeholders, especially governing board members and union and management leaders, as well as responsible government officials, while likely cognizant of the working conditions of institutional employees, have made few major overt efforts to mitigate these conditions. With aging employees and increasing work demands, both personal welfare and work outputs may suffer without intervention. In one jurisdiction, a government official wrote to college presidents following the recent deaths of two higher-education leaders and suggested that health check-ups were in order—hardly an antidote to escalating demands from external constituents such as governments and the ever-expanding workload expected of college managers. The pressures from government, business, and industry, as well as from formal institutional leaders, for greater productivity and greater efficiencies, and thus reduced per-unit costs, will result in negative outcomes for both education and work.

## NOTE

This research was sponsored by the Social Sciences and Humanities Research Council (Canada).

## REFERENCES

Appadurai, A. (1990). Disjunctures and difference in the global cultural economy. In M. Featherstone (Ed.), *Global culture: Nationalism, globalization and modernity* (pp. 295–310). Newbury Park, CA: Sage.
Aronowitz, S, & Di Fazio, W. (1994). *The jobless future: Sci-tech and the dogma of work*. Minneapolis: University of Minnesota Press.

Barr, R., & Tagg, J. (1995, November/December). From teaching to learning—A new paradigm for undergraduate education. *Change*, 27 (6), pp. 13–25.

Cohen, A., & Brawer, F. (1996). *The American community college*. San Francisco: Jossey-Bass.

Currie, J. (1998). Introduction. In J. Currie & J. Newson (Eds.), *Universities and globalization* (pp. 1–13). Thousand Oaks, CA: Sage.

Daws, G. (1974). *Shoal of time: A history of the Hawaiian islands*. Honolulu: University of Hawaii Press.

Dennison, J., & Gallagher, P. (1986). *Canada's community colleges*. Vancouver: University of British Columbia Press.

Dennison, J., & Levin, J. (1989). *Canada's community college in the nineteen eighties*. Willowdale, Ontario: Association of Canadian Community Colleges.

DiMaggio, P., & Powell, W. (1983). The iron cage revisited: Institutional isomorphism and collective rationality in organizational fields. *American Sociological Review, 48*, 147–160.

Dolence, M., & Norris, D. (1995). *Transforming higher education: A vision for learning in the 21st century*. Ann Arbor, MI: Society for College and University Planning.

Edwards, R., & Usher, R. (1998, April). *Globalisation, diaspora space and pedagogy*. Paper presented at the annual meeting of the American Educational Research Association, San Diego.

Gaff, J. (1992). Beyond politics: The educational issues inherent in multicultural education. *Change, 24* (1), 31–35.

Giddens, A. (1990). *The consequences of modernity*. Stanford, CA: Stanford University Press.

Levin, J. (1999). *Mission and structure: The community college in a global context: A report*. Tucson: University of Arizona Center for the Study of Higher Education.

Mintzberg, H. (1983). *Power in and around organizations*. Englewood Cliffs, NJ: Prentice-Hall.

Ralston Saul, J. (1995). *The unconscious civilization*. Concord, Ontario: House of Anansi Press.

Ritzer, G. (1998). *The McDonaldization thesis. Explorations and extensions*. Thousand Oaks, CA: Sage.

Robertson, R. (1992). *Globalization: Social theory and global culture*. London: Sage.

Roueche, J., Taber, L., & Roueche, S. (1995). *The company we keep: Collaboration in the community college*. Washington, DC: American Association of Community Colleges.

Schrag, P. (1998). *Paradise lost: California's experience, America's future*. New York: New Press.

Schwantes, C. (1996). Wage earners and wealth makers. In C. Milner, C. O'Connor, & M. Sandweiss (Eds.), *The Oxford history of the American west* (pp. 431–467). New York: Oxford University Press.

Slaughter, S., & Leslie, L. (1997). *Academic capitalism: Politics, policies, and the entrepreneurial university*. Baltimore: Johns Hopkins University Press.

Teeple, G. (1995). *Globalization and the decline of social reform*. Atlantic Highlands, NJ: Humanities Press.

Waters, M. (1996). *Globalization*. New York: Routledge.

**PART II** —————————————————————

## STATE LEVEL

*Chapter 6* _____

# Policy Directions for K-14 Education—Looking to the Future

*Margaret Terry Orr and Debra D. Bragg*

Many educational and policy proposals encourage a seamless K-14 educational system to substantively link secondary schools and higher-education institutions, particularly through community colleges. Increased cooperation between secondary schools and community colleges and other higher-education institutions is thought to improve how well all students are prepared, academically and vocationally, for the future, particularly to meet the demands of growth industries and changing labor markets for the global economy. The current extent and limits of collaboration between secondary schools and community colleges in particular is not well understood, and little is known about the existing educational policies' impact on coordination and collaboration across the disparate levels of these two educational systems. The purpose of this chapter is to provide a conceptual framework for discussing K-14 system formation and its current forms and to reflect on the role of public policy in promoting greater coordination and system building.

## CONTEXT FOR K-14 SYSTEM BUILDING

For purposes of our discussion and analysis, we recognize that K-14 system formation can encompass a wide variety of collaborative activities, ranging from information sharing to joint action (see Langman & McLaughlin, 1993, for an analysis of collaboration forms among public service organizations). We also acknowledge the importance of system building, which will eventually link all of education, from kindergarten through four-year college (K-16). Not discounting the K-16 continuum, we instead emphasize a K-14 system to underscore the importance of community colleges within the educational pathway. In discussions of K-16 system building, it appears to have been easy to overlook community colleges or wrongly assume their contribution is limited. But we argue that this would be a mistake. Indeed, community colleges are an increasingly vital part of the K-16 continuum and, we argue, their importance will continue to grow in the 21st century. Further, we view K-14 system building as being far more than information sharing because it requires the creation of an infrastructure for shared enterprises, with a common mission and objectives that can influence and benefit both school district and community college partners simultaneously.

Interinstitutional relationships such as coordination, integration, collaboration, and partnership are central to the goal of system building and to our discussion here. In our view, coordination represents the purposeful alignment of personnel, infrastructure, resources, and constituents to meet complementary or shared goals. We define integration here as being more extensive than coordination by intertwining K-12 and community college systems in new ways to provide a more cohesive K-14 educational system. For our purposes, we define partnerships as the interpersonal relationships between people in the two systems who work toward a common vision and goals. In contrast, we define collaboration as the interinstitutional relationships formed to support shared purposes and outcomes, including decision making and accountability processes and procedures.

Community colleges and public school systems are well positioned for system integration. They are the two largest, and most broadly serving, public educational systems in the United States. This fact alone helps to explain why K-14 system building captures the attention of policy makers, but there are additional reasons. Both systems are primarily publicly funded, often serving geographically defined communities and similar constituent groups. Both systems primarily respond to local and state priorities, due to the way in which they are funded and governed. Community colleges are well suited to work closely with school districts because of their similar public education mission, specialization in transfer and technical education, low cost, and accessibility. Finally, both systems are pressured by similar public expectations about the role and function of public education for social equity and workforce development.

Community colleges already coordinate de facto with secondary schools, since the colleges enroll a large percentage of high school graduates and design programs to extend beyond secondary education and fill in the gap between high school preparation and college-level studies. Increasingly, community colleges provide remediation instruction to assist students to fulfill the basic academic requirements needed to progress in either academic or technical studies at the postsecondary level (Lewis, Farris, & Greene, 1996). Based on the present college-going patterns of high school students, Baker and Smith (1997) concluded that a K-14 system already exists and that a continuation of this trend of increasing rates of college-going among high school graduates will transform higher education, particularly community colleges.

Public schools and community college institutions are increasingly characterized as interdependent in both purpose and responsibility for educational outcomes, providing yet another reason for their convergence. In evaluating the relationship between the City University of New York (CUNY), a public two- and four-year college system, and the New York City Public Schools, the Mayor's Advisory Task Force on the City University of New York (better known as the Schmidt Commission) concluded: "These two enterprises together constitute public education in NYC. They virtually shape one another for better or worse" (Mayor's Advisory Task Force on the City of New York, 1999, p. 18). The commission observed that "although the public schools and CUNY share a largely overlapping student population and face many of the same educational challenges, they have few common education strategies. Their goals, curriculum and evaluation protocols are incongruent" (p. 97). This lack of common educational strategies and general incongruence on educational matters is not unique to New York City; it represents challenges for the relationship between public schools and community colleges nationwide.

There is historic precedence for a K-14 educational system. Several community colleges began as extensions of local high schools, created as early as the 1920s for continued training and career preparation beyond high school (Callan, 1998; Cohen & Brawer, 1996; Dougherty, 1994). Some still exist as part of public school districts. Callan (1998) concluded that K-16 system collaborations have become more prevalent over the last decade, during which "various types of collaborative arrangements between schools and colleges have proliferated" (p. 43). Importantly, his analysis focused primarily on transition-related collaborations intended to improve minority and low-income students' access to higher education, and not other types, such as school-to-work transition programs, that have also become prevalent recently.

The goal of improving school-to-work transition undergirded the School-to-Work Opportunities Act of 1994, the federal Tech Prep Education legislation, and the federal Carl D. Perkins vocational legislation. Pauley, Kopp, and Haimson (1995) captured this notion, stating: "It is now undeniably clear that many students in the United States need help making the transition from high school to postsecondary learning opportunities and to meaningful, productive, skilled work. State and federal policy makers recognize this, educators recognize it, and so does the general public" (p. 1). It is in this arena—school-to-work transition for youth—that we have seen the greatest push for a realignment of secondary and postsecondary educational systems to better prepare students, academically and technically, for further education and gainful employment.

Other reasons for greater K-14 collaboration are also compelling, particularly as it serves to encourage community colleges to take a leadership role in educational reform and the workforce development of youth. Haycock (1998) stresses that systemic reform needs the active cooperation of higher education and that both K-12 and higher-education leaders must be proactive in forging collaborative efforts. Farmer and Key (1997) underscored the same view, applying it more narrowly to community colleges and explaining that "[a]s an extension of their traditions, community colleges have the power and ethical responsibility to negotiate systemic education reform" (p. 97). They concluded, "Assuming this role, however, will require effort and proactive commitment to collaboration and partnerships with educators, labor and employers" (p. 97). This emphasis on collaboration usually encompasses raising academic standards and improving the academic skill proficiency of youth, both for college preparedness and for the workforce.

Parallel encouragement for collaboration has focused specifically on workforce preparation for youth. Proposals and policies aimed at improving the workforce readiness and advanced technical skills of entry-level workers often encourage K-14 coordination between secondary schools and community colleges. Marshall and Tucker (1992) advocated a system of standards to qualify students for a college preparatory program or entry into a program of technical and professional studies, for nonbaccalaureate occupational programs, and for entering and leaving college. They recommended using a series of standards and certificates of achievement to help students progress through high school and into various baccalaureate and nonbaccalaureate options, particularly for technical and professional careers. While they did not limit their proposals to community colleges, Marshall and Tucker did advocate for an improved system of education: "What [the United States] so sorely lacks and so desperately needs is a system that embraces the great majority of our students and prepares them to become productive members of what could be . . . the most capable front-line work force in the world" (p. 208).

To address workforce needs for skilled employees, Grubb (1996) envisioned a coherent educational system that would link all academic and vocational-technical programs as a "vertical ladder" (p. 123) that "individuals can use to progress from relatively low levels of skill . . . to higher levels of skill and . . . more demanding, better-paid, and more stable occupations" (p. 124). According to his design, such a vertical system would connect public schools, community colleges, four-year colleges, and other educational and training programs through articulation and student-tracking mechanisms in order to ensure that students continue to make progress. He recommended that community colleges become the "linchpin connecting job training programs to the educational system" (p. 135) in order to help a wide variety of people become well prepared for the changing economy and workforce needs, particularly for jobs in the subbaccalaureate labor market.

## THEORETICAL ARGUMENTS FOR K-14 SYSTEM BUILDING

Taken together, the arguments for a K-14 educational system are rooted in three theoretical goals—structural efficiency, social equity, and human capital development. Each argument provides its own unique, but sometimes overlapping, definitions, all of which are related to potential changes designed to link K-14 education in more meaningful and systemic ways. The goals of each theoretical argument are presented in this section, with brief examples of how their objectives could be implemented.

### Structural Efficiency Goals

The structural efficiency goal includes three primary objectives—for improved operational efficiency, cost-effectiveness, and improved quality control of inputs. These three objectives are rooted in what Labaree (1997) describes as an organizational argument about the problems of education. Operational efficiency objectives address the administration of services and resources and capitalizes on the relative expertise that comes from linking school districts and community colleges. This objective is reflected in interinstitutional practices such as dual enrollment, whereby high school students take advanced academic and technical courses at community colleges, thus making use of the available faculty expertise and instructional resources. Another interinstitutional efficiency example occurs when school districts combine resources to purchase services from a community college, such as an on-campus dropout prevention program or driver education classes, as the Community College of Alleghany County (PA) does for some of its local school districts.

Cost-effectiveness goals are reflected in the coordination of the educational functions of K-12 and higher-education systems to reduce service duplication, particularly the need for college-level remediation, and to improve how well high school students are prepared for college-level work and focused on career plans. Parnell (1994) spoke to this goal directly when suggesting that, as a result of Tech Prep, community colleges would enroll more college-ready students, thus reducing the cost of remedial education. Envisioning education as a game to be won or lost, Parnell summarized the cost effectiveness goal of Tech Prep as a primary vehicle for supporting a seamless K-14 education system. He argued that "communities and states will win because cooperation at different levels of education will eliminate unnecessary program duplication, provide for greater efficiency, and more fully develop the human resources of each region" (p. 50).

A third structural objective centers on influencing institutional "inputs" and "outcomes," focusing on improving students' readiness for college and their capacity to complete a degree program. Tompkins (1999) uses this objective to argue for school-college partnerships because of colleges' dependence on high schools' capacity to prepare students well for college-level work: "As universities become more concerned about the sort of 'product' they are receiving from high schools and more concerned about new competition for enrollment, logic would dictate their increased collaboration with K-12 educators to improve this product" (p. 12). The Schmidt Commission (Mayor's Advisory Task Force on the City University of New York, 1999) stressed this objective further in the way in which it evaluated CUNY's relationship with public schools. The commission argued that "it is critical that CUNY's relationship with the public schools be mutually reinforcing rather than mutually destructive" (p. 18). The crux of the commission's recommendations centered on the inadequate academic skill proficiencies of high school graduates: "For too long . . . CUNY has been a passive receptacle for the cumulative failures of the public schools—or, even worse, a contributor to those failures" (p. 43). The commission proposed structural solutions for CUNY and its relationship with the public schools in which "CUNY must develop a comprehensive institutional strategy of raising standards and improving student achievement in NYCPS [New York City Public Schools]" (p. 52), particularly in setting admission standards, providing remediation, and communicating college preparation requirements to the schools. In its final analysis, the commission recommended "a long term vision that encompasses a K-16 continuum and beyond" (pp. 97–98).

Stewart and Johanek (1998) concluded that most policy on school-college connections has focused on administrative issues—particularly the logistics of transitions and connecting the K-16 curriculum—encompassing admissions procedures, assessment instruments, and curricular credit. They described these as primarily alignment and accountability issues, which spell out "in scope and sequence the skills and knowledge to be learned at various points in a learner's academic career in given subject areas" (p. 43). An accountability dimension addresses the quality and effectiveness of teaching. Stewart and Johanek (1998) typify such policy trends as fostering an educational pipeline for a continuum of skill and competency development, which is driven by the standards reform movement. One goal of this pipeline, as they explained, is to reduce waste in educational resources, which is represented in postsecondary education remediation and course duplication; this is similar to the goal for Tech Prep expressed by Parnell (1994).

Several state policy proposals are rooted in structural efficiency objectives, such as promoting greater K-14 system collaboration to reduce the state support of education by eliminating the apparent duplication of high school academic work through college-level remediation. Oregon, for example, has been developing proficiency-based admissions standards as a strategy to improve student preparation for college (Conley, 1996). Several states use their school-to-work initiatives in the high schools to improve student preparation and promote educational strategies such as curriculum integration and performance-based learning (Rubin, 1996). Other state policies aim to reduce education costs through vocational and technical course articulation between secondary schools and community colleges and to eliminate duplication and shorten students' college-degree time and tuition expenses (Sebring, 1996). Policy alignments with Tech Prep and related school-to-work transition efforts also reflect a way to integrate public schools and community colleges around courses of study. An important result of these policy efforts would be a more coherent infrastructure for K-14 education. There may be a downside, however. According to Callan (1998), constrained state fiscal resources, coupled with an increased demand for publicly funded higher education, will lead to decreased access to programs and services, as well as to strategies to reduce the need for remediation.

### Social Equity Goals

The second theoretical goal concerns opportunities for social equity through access and mobility, by maximizing access to college for all students as a way of fostering social mobility to benefit both the individual and local communities economically. Labaree (1997) described the educational goals of democratic equality and social mobility as conflicting because they represent competing visions of education and the structure of education. He defined democratic equality as an ideological tradition "that sees schools as an expression of democratic political ideals and as a mechanism for preparing children to play constructive roles in democratic society" (p. 43). As he explained further, the pursuit of equal access, whereby everyone "should have an equal opportunity to acquire an education at any educational level" (p. 46), is one form of this goal. This goal has made attending a postsecondary education institution a norm, rather than an exception, for high school graduates. The result, Labaree argued, has been tremendous public funding support designed to open up all levels of education to everyone. Institutional ramifications include "the proliferation of programs and courses, the search for ways to improve pedagogical efficiency, the concern about enhancing administrative control, and the stress on fiscal parsimony" (p. 46).

In contrast, Labaree (1997) defined the social mobility goal as providing "students with the educational credentials they need in order to get ahead in [the existing socioeconomic] structure" (p. 50). He saw this as an individual goal, rather than a collective goal, like democratic equality, because social mobility emphasizes "*individual status attainment* rather than the production of human capital" (p. 51, emphasis in the original). He saw the tension between equal access and social mobility as "providing an unlimited possibility for education attainment" (p. 69) so long as there is a "pyramid-shaped occupational structure" (p. 69).

In our view, social equity arguments for postsecondary education attainment combine the goals of access and of mobility, despite their apparent conflict. Labaree (1997) acknowledged that these two goals are expressed in "the market for educational credentials" (p. 71). We find that the combination of these goals is reflected in the common claim that a college diploma is key to future eco-

nomic prosperity (Gray & Herr, 1995), thereby making democratic equity dependent on social mobility. The coupling of these two goals is reflected in public
policy, particularly the federal Goals 2000 Educate America Act (Goals 2000),
which stresses raising academic standards for all students and facilitating their
transition to higher education, thus likewise promoting social mobility opportunities as a part of democratic equity.

Community colleges, with their open-access policies, have become a primary
educational vehicle for fulfilling these two educational goals of access and mobility. They are most equipped to offer high-risk youth avenues for earning a
two-year college degree or transferring to a four-year degree program. Many
poor, minority, immigrant, and disabled students have difficulty in making the
transition from high school graduation to gainful employment (Hamilton, 1990).
As a result, their transition from secondary to postsecondary education and their
academic preparedness for college-level work become critical in fulfilling the
combined goals of equity and mobility.

## Human Capital Development Goals

The third theoretical goal centers on human capital theory, in which improvements in how well young people are educated and trained in advanced technical
skills will have economic returns for the individuals as well as society as a
whole. Labaree (1997) captures this argument in his discussion of the educational goal of social efficiency, whereby schooling is structured to meet the
"demands of the occupational marketplace" (p. 46). The underlying logic of his
arguments are rooted in this perspective: "Schooling supplies future workers
with skills that will enhance their productivity and therefore promote economic
growth" (p. 48). While Labaree focuses on how this goal has influenced the
structure of schooling generally, this argument has been used historically to
expand vocational and technical education in the United States, particularly
postsecondary technical training and two-year degrees. As an illustration of this
argument, Gray and Herr (1995) concluded that the "2-year technical education
has the best potential for a positive return and is critical for the future economic
competitiveness of the United States" (p. 6). Policy proposals based on this
perspective include workforce development efforts that promote early career and
education planning and coordinated sequences of technical skills preparation.
Various federal education policies, particularly Tech Prep and the School to
Work Opportunities Act (STWOA), promote greater secondary and postsecondary education coordination based on this argument. Even the federal Goals
2000 uses an argument based in human capital theory in supporting higher
academic and occupational skill standards to better prepare all students to succeed in the workforce and compete in the global economy.

## THE STUDENT EXPERIENCE

Regardless of the nature of formal relationships between high school and
college, more young people are combining the two educational experiences by

going to college after high school graduation. The U.S. Department of Education (1998) showed that enrollments in postsecondary education increased by 16 percent between 1985 and 1995. By 1996, almost two-thirds of all high school graduates had enrolled in either a two-year or four-year college within a year of finishing high school. Gray and Herr (1995), in their analysis of National Center for Educational Statistics (NCES) data, found that 95 percent of the 1992 high school seniors reported that they planned to go to college (showing that even more would like to go than actually enroll). This level of growth in postsecondary enrollment is encouraging, but there are concerns.

Students who go to college are not always successful, and the problem may be worsening. Halperin (1998), in analyzing NCES postsecondary education data, found that as college enrollment rates rose over the past decade, graduation rates fell. As a result, over 50 percent of college freshmen today do not graduate with a bachelor's degree after five years of college enrollment, in contrast to 40 percent ten years ago. Drawing on his extensive research on college persistence, Tinto (1996) concluded that students drop out for many reasons, but primarily because of lack of preparation for college-level studies, lack of direction, insufficient integration into college-level academic and social life, and other academic and personal difficulties.

Despite the increasing difficulty students have in completing college, enrollments are likely to increase. The U.S. Department of Education (1999) predicts that there will be a steady increase in all higher-education enrollments, including at two-year colleges, over the next decade. According to Gray and Herr (1995), the pressures on all youth to go to college are "intense and relentless" (p. 23) and come from parents, schools, peers, and the media. Social forces add to this pressure, encouraging youth to go on to college regardless of whether they are ready. Gray and Herr argue that there are widespread misconceptions about whether only a four-year college degree provides the best economic return to students. They do not deny these benefits but believe that they may be overstated while other options are discounted. Stressing that a four-year college degree does not necessarily lead to a high-paying career, they urge students to consider two-year technical degree programs that can prepare them for high-skill/high-wage occupations. They argue that the wages are tied to skills, not degrees, and that "the skills required in many high skill/high wage occupations can be learned in associate degree programs in the technologies" (p. 96).

Many high school graduates have reached the same conclusion—that a community college would be a better first college experience than a four-year institution. The American Association of Community Colleges (AACC) (1999) confirms that a growing proportion of high school graduates are choosing to enroll in community colleges. In fact, AACC currently, reports that 47 percent of high school graduates enroll in a community college following graduation. In recent years, first- and second-year undergraduate students were more likely to be enrolled in a two-year than a four-year institution. During the 1995–1996 academic year, 56 percent of second-year students were enrolled in a two-year institution and only 38 percent were enrolled in a four-year college (Horn, Berktold & Malizio, 1998). Together, transfer and vocational-technical enrollments account for the most significant portion of the two-year college curriculum (Boesel & McFarland, 1994; Cohen & Brawer, 1996).

Meanwhile, at a time when more students are going to college, the changing labor market is adversely affecting young people who choose not to enter postsecondary education or who drop out without college credentials. Bernhardt, Morris, Handcock & Scott (1998) studied the first 16 years of work experience for two cohorts of young white men from the National Longitudinal Surveys sponsored by the National Center for Education Statistics and concluded that:

A new generation is entering a transformed labor market, and especially for those without a college degree, the prospects for a living wage, stable employment, and upward mobility are not at all guaranteed. . . . To the extent that wage growth represents upward mobility, it is clear that the prospects for such mobility have deteriorated in recent years. Those without a college degree have clearly gotten hit the hardest, and this represents the majority of workers. (p. 8)

Recent research confirms the relationship of advanced education to higher wages and earning potential but similarly argues the relative economic advantages of a two-year over a high school degree. In his recent review of outcomes associated with subbaccalaureate (two-year) college participation, Grubb (1998) supports the importance of college credentials on economic well-being. He dispels misconceptions that two-year college credentials are not worthwhile, noting serious methodological problems with the prior studies that are cited repeatedly by various community college critics. His review points to concerns with poor-quality data, samples having unknown generalizability, and a lack of conceptual clarity in the selection of comparison groups. Given these limitations, Grubb cites recent studies that he and others have conducted, which show "clear and substantial returns to Associate degrees, though they are, unsurprisingly, lower than the returns to baccalaureate degrees" (p. 12). He correctly points out unrealistic expectations of scholars who lament that two-year college degrees yield fewer economic benefits than four-year credentials. Grubb argues that four-year colleges, by definition, require twice as long a period of learning and are often selective. Given these differences, carefully designed studies consistently show positive economic benefits for two-year college completers over high school graduates and persons with some college, particularly for students in occupational programs, and among these graduates, especially for women.

Yet earning even a two-year degree can be challenging for some students, in part because of the nature of their high school preparation. As more high school students choose to go to college, the college student ranks are increasingly including those who are poorly prepared to pursue college-level work. These students, in turn, sometimes require extensive college-level remediation and support to prepare them for college studies. According to Nunley and Gemberling (1999), "Kindergarten through college has become the typical educational experience for students of widely varying abilities and educational backgrounds, not only elite 'college prep' students" (p. 35). They concluded that greater student success is dependent on the relationship between high schools and colleges. It is likely that high school graduates most needing college-level remediation will seek community college programs, because of their open-access admissions policies as well as their low cost and availability. Thus, of all the higher-education institutions, community colleges are most likely to be responsible for shouldering the work of improving high school graduates' readiness for college-level work. Remediation rates are already soaring at community colleges (McCabe & Day, 1998), and they will no doubt increase further as less prepared students enroll in greater numbers.

The college success of such high-risk students is hindered by the lack of advanced academic skill development in their high school preparation and course taking and the lack of communication about academic skill standards for college preparedness. Bragg (1998) documented this phenomenon in a series of interviews with first-year community college students. She revealed that, when entering community colleges, students struggled to adjust because the learning environment of college was much less structured than in high school. Students talked about the difficulties they had in managing their own learning and were cognizant of the lower expectations of high school teachers compared to their college instructors. They viewed college as far more demanding than high school, saying that college instructors were much less explicit about what and how students should learn. Some students were distressed, and even bitter, about their lack of preparedness for college and the difficulties they were experiencing because of this.

Other problems center on inadequate college guidance in high school particularly for less well prepared students. According to Boesel and Fredland (1999), even students who are poorly prepared for college are being encouraged to go, without being given opportunities to explore other training and preparatory options or learn about what will be required of them academically and their likely completion rates.

Indeed, the gap between secondary and postsecondary education exists for many complex reasons, which are often linked to inadequate high school academic preparation. According to Bragg (1999), "an over-reliance on basic courses limits college readiness" (p. 1). Second, as Bragg explained further, while most high school students go to college, few complete a college-preparatory curriculum at the secondary level. Many high school students take a hodgepodge of courses that are not coherent and are "neither useful for college or work after high school" (p. 1). Larson, Garies, and Campbell (1996, as cited in Nunley & Gemberling, 1999) in their analysis of high school transcripts of community college students, identified course-taking patterns that were associated with different college outcomes. For example, students who did not take challenging academic courses in high schools had a better than 90 percent chance of testing into remediation courses on their college placement tests.

In summary, more students are being encouraged to go to, and more are attending, college than ever before, even though many lack adequate preparation. The academic challenges experienced by many students can be traced to a few fundamental problems in the relationship between the two educational levels. First, there is a lack of agreement about academic and technical standards and insufficient communication about these standards between high schools and community colleges. Second, high schools and community colleges provide limited guidance services to assist students in making decisions about their futures after high school. Third, there is a the lack of early feedback about college-readiness while students are still in high school. Finally, there is a lack of oversight over progress as students make the transition from one educational system to the next.

## INTERINSTITUTIONAL RELATIONS

Community colleges can play a vital role in contributing to a more meaningful K-16 educational system, although their potential to do so is sometimes overlooked. For example, in Timpane and White's (1998) edited volume on higher education and school reform, the discussions of K-16 collaboration center on colleges and universities, with little mention of the unique role of community colleges. Fortunately, this trend may be changing. Community colleges already serve as a first-college experience for many young people because of their accessibility, low cost, breadth of technical and academic programs, and variety of certificate and degree options. In contrast to other types of higher-education institutions, community colleges are well situated across the country, often being located in neighborhoods where they can serve youth who are otherwise under prepared for the changing labor market demands (McCabe & Day, 1999). Community colleges also have developed structures for better analyzing students' academic skills, providing targeted academic support (through remediation and other developmental program experiences), and providing flexibility in their programs and course taking (through regular, evening, and distance-learning classes). Thus, they can complement high school preparation well, accommodating a wide range of student abilities and prior competencies. Finally, they are well equipped to build on high school–level academic and technical curricula to provide for a wide range of workforce opportunities and continued education.

Given that community colleges are increasingly likely to serve larger numbers of the young people who are the least well prepared academically, there is a danger that their role in an educational continuum could narrow, rather than broaden. Therefore, working with local high schools to improve the preparation of their students is crucial. It is imperative that community colleges maintain a broad educational mission and not divert limited resources away from supporting their pivotal role in K-14 or K-16 educational systems. Otherwise, increasing proportions of community college resources will be directed to remediation or later adult retraining, rather than the more advanced academic and technical preparation needed to support student progress through the entire educational pathway.

Presently, various local, state, and federal reform initiatives are, directly or indirectly, pushing these two educational systems to be more closely coordinated, if not integrated, by stressing similar priorities to optimize their resources, encourage more postsecondary education participation for all high school graduates, and enlarge the workforce preparation roles of community colleges and secondary schools. Most central among these are three federal policies—the Tech Prep Education Act of the federal vocational legislation, the School to Work Opportunities Act (STWOA), and the Goals 2000: Educate America Act. All three stress an improved transition to postsecondary education and higher academic and technical skill levels for all high school students, among other priorities (Orr, 1998). At the heart of these policy reforms is improving academic preparation and postsecondary educational access and providing a seamless, progressive educational experience, which would make a community college education (and, eventually, more advanced higher education) more universal.

Improved collaboration with secondary schools would allow community colleges to better address student transition and prior academic and workforce preparation. Such improved preparation and transition could (1) increase the number of students entering community colleges for the first time (Just & Adams, 1997); (2) ensure that more entering students would be better prepared academically, thus requiring less remediation (Just & Adams, 1997; Silverberg, 1993, 1996); (3) increase the percentage of high school graduates who are successful in their postsecondary education programs (Silverberg, 1993); and (4) renew attention to occupational skill development (Orr, 1998).

Orr (1999) recently conducted research on K-14 collaborations addressing the workforce development of youth and identified three common interorganizational barriers to strengthening the K-14 system. The first is logistical—community colleges and local school districts do not have the same scope within their designated geographic service areas. Community colleges usually serve a geographic area that includes one or more school districts. The number of districts was found to have bearing on community colleges' collaborative capacity. Orr found that community colleges with only one or two school districts in their service area were able to forge a common commitment to workforce development and school-to-work transition priorities and to otherwise align their efforts. In contrast, community colleges with many school districts in their service area (as many as 40 for one metropolitan area community college studied) focused more on continuous relationship formation, and limited their partnership activities to only a few of the local districts.

The second barrier was the lack of local leadership priority within the community colleges. Community college officials who made workforce development a priority for their institutions' mission were more likely to be proactive in engaging school district and business and industry participation, reforming their own institutions' curricula, seeking resources, and developing integrated programs with local school districts. Community college officials who did not have a broader workforce development mission were less likely to direct their institutional resources to these activities. Orr found that community college officials who made workforce preparation of youth a priority for their institutions also recognized the importance of a K-14 system and were committed to strengthening K-12 education as well as their own postsecondary education programs. They interpreted the workforce development of youth as beginning early in public schooling and carrying forward through the community college programs, and they understood the importance of fuller integration of the community colleges and secondary schools in forging a seamless transition system (Orr, 1999).

The final barrier was the lack of a common planning and governance structure for the partnership itself. Community colleges and local school districts that could integrate their workforce development planning for Tech Prep and STWOA under one governance structure seemed to be better able than others to undertake more extensive integration for other related efforts as well (such as sharing facilities and hosting joint professional development endeavors). It may be that the combined resources, as well as integrated governance structures for these two policies, gave the participating institutions multiple resources and strategies for planning K-14 workforce preparation, thus enabling them to be more coherent in broader educational development efforts (Orr, 1999).

In summary, whereas there are many similarities between community colleges and public schools that make them complementary educational institutions, there are structural and organizational factors that can either facilitate or interfere with K-14 system building. To address these factors, public policy seems to be instrumental in increasing the potential for implementation of successful K-14 collaborations.

## PUBLIC POLICY INCENTIVES AND IMPACT

From our review of federal and state school-to-work and education reform policies, we conclude that public policy and financial resources, often in the form of seed grants, can play a significant role in stimulating partnerships between community colleges and school districts. These policies and how states interpret them frame, in large part, how local community college and school districts gear up system building. By providing seed money for innovative development efforts and by endorsing and reinforcing common educational priorities, public policy can play a critical role in K-14 or K-16 system building (Orr, 1998). Illustrating this point, the U.S. Department of Education (USDE) recently instituted a new program called GEAR UP (for Gaining Early Awareness and Readiness for Undergraduate Programs) that is designed to encourage youths to hold high expectations while in school and prepare for college (USDE, 1999). GEAR UP grants are administered at either the local or state level, and they require partnerships between higher-education institutions, middle schools, and other organizations to encourage low-income middle-school students to begin to prepare themselves for college.

The role of public policy is also particularly clear in federal policies supporting Tech Prep, STWOA, and Goals 2000, although the extent to which secondary-to-postsecondary transition is presented as a central goal in each program has influenced how their implementation occurred. In Tech Prep, transition to the community college is explicitly defined through articulation agreements, but in Goals 2000, references to transition and articulation are more implicit. As a result, only some states fostered K-14 system building by stressing in their Tech Prep, STOWA, and Goals 2000 policies the fact that community colleges play a substantive role in local planning efforts. Whereas some states have used these policies in complementary ways, others have not, and the impact on formation of a system of student transition is likely to be influenced by the different levels of state commitment.

Several policy analysts point to state government as the impetus for further K-14 and K-16 system building for educational reform and improved student transition. According to Callan (1998), "The responsibility for public policy regarding both public schools and the public colleges and universities resides primarily at the state level" (p. 41). The state institutions are the only entities whose "interest, responsibility, and authority span public education from preschool through graduate education" (p. 41). Callan added, however, that past policies and processes thwart current reform efforts. He argued that "[n]ew links must be forged between the public schools and the colleges; standards for student performance are needed, ones that span the gap between the senior year in high school and the freshman year in college; school reform and teacher education must be linked in planning and implementation; and access to higher education must be maintained as a high priority" (p. 41).

Many state policies already promote a more seamless K-14 system to improve efficiency and promote cost savings. In the future, these types of capacity-building (i.e., system-building) policies will need to become more prevalent. In some cases, they need to be mandated to ensure that systemic policies and practices are developed, sustained, and rewarded. According to Tompkins (1999), state legislatures are pressuring public education and higher education institutions to "decrease the waste of time and money in transition . . . between high school and college" (p. 12). Several states are developing policies to award students dual credit for academic and vocational-technical courses taken during high school; these policies acknowledge and reward advanced college-level competencies that students acquire while still enrolled in high school.

Nonetheless, current state efforts to encourage K-14 and K-16 system building are insufficient to provide what Callan (1998) describes as collaboration "of the breadth and depth that will be required for the next century" (p. 44). To encourage further K-16 integration, Callan recommends that states set an agenda providing "fiscal and other incentives for collaboration and holding both public schools and colleges accountable for building the organizational bridges that are sorely needed" (p. 44). Thus, formation of a joint infrastructure, or bridge, is key in order for these objectives to take hold. In fact, the beginnings of a K-16 infrastructure are evident in states such as Illinois, where the three boards of education (K-12, community college, and higher education) have established a primary through "grade" 16 (P-16) alliance designating "shared responsibilities across the full continuum of education" (Illinois State Board of Education, Illinois Community College Board, & Illinois State Board of Education, 1999, p. 1). The three boards have committed to undertaking the following strategies, both separately and together: (1) clarify, focus, and align policies, priorities, and programs, (2) promote public awareness of the need for increased educational attainment, (3) leverage new resources and reallocate existing ones, (4) communicate consistently across educational levels, and (5) hold all partners (e.g., schools, colleges, agencies) accountable to specific benchmarks.

Despite pressure for, and encouragement of, secondary and postsecondary education collaboration, there is limited evidence of their prevalence or effectiveness. Research by Orr (1999) has shown that encouraging a K-14 system is a common policy strategy for the workforce preparation of youth, but national evaluations of Tech Prep and STWOA have yet to find many direct benefits for students.

Tech Prep, for example, was intended to create comprehensive and articulated programs for targeted "neglected majority" students through sequenced academic and technical training in secondary schools and community college, based on technical areas of study (Parnell, 1985). Yet, as a result of how Tech Prep has been implemented nationwide, Hershey, Silverberg, Owens, and Hulsey (1998) found that few students followed the intended 2+2 program sequence. Instead, while 58 percent of all Tech Prep students, as defined locally, started some type of postsecondary education or training after high school, only 19 percent actually entered articulated technical programs at community colleges. These results may be premature, however, since they were based on the early years of federal Tech Prep implementation, when little impact could have been expected at the community college level. More recent research by Bragg et al. (1999) on students in eight regional Tech Prep and School-to-Work systems showed higher matriculation rates but found that the percentage of students who continued in their 2+2 program sequence varied widely, depending on curricular, institutional, and system-wide factors.

STWOA has been more diffuse in its targets and strategies for school-to-work system building, and thus even less likely to have substantive impacts on K-14 collaborations and subsequent student experiences (Orr, 1998). According to Hershey and his colleagues (1998), STWOA was designed to amount to more than separate programs for different target groups. It was instead intended "to make it possible for a large number of students, with diverse backgrounds and abilities, to have coherently related experiences that help them to develop a career goal and begin preparing for it" (p. xxvi). As defined by STWOA, system building should be designed according to the level of student participation in a combination of activities, particularly comprehensive career development, a career major with integrated curricula, and a linked workplace activity. In the initial years of STWOA implementation, they found, however, that only in small, targeted (and usually selective) programs did local STWOA partnerships concentrate and combine a variety of integrated activities. Silverberg, Haimson, and Hershey (1998) confirmed that multi component STWOA implementation was rare, and that few students, most commonly vocational students, participated in all three major components (career development, career majors, and workplace activities). These studies concluded that, at least in the early stages of STWOA implementation, these programs could have an impact if they concentrated resources on a small number of students—certainly far fewer than was envisioned by either STWOA and Goals 2000, where all students were to be potential beneficiaries on some level.

Other research on K-14 collaboration for workforce preparation of youth generally identified a range of collaborative activities that varied in intensity and substance (Orr, 1999). These activities included (1) information-sharing strategies, particularly to encourage high school students to pursue technical careers and postsecondary education; (2) professional and curricular development to raise skill standards and improve student learning; (3) institutional bridging strategies for student transition through articulation agreements and assessments; and (4) shared, comprehensively organized, work-based learning for 2 + 2 educational experiences. Information-sharing strategies employed between community colleges and secondary schools were most common among these four types of activities, followed by professional and curriculum development strategies. Community college personnel often served as content and instructional experts and as information brokers with local business and industry. In these specific activities, secondary school students were encouraged to develop academic and career plans and to increase their readiness for postsecondary education.

Bridging strategies were helpful in formally linking the educational content of the two institutions. Articulation agreements facilitated student transition between the high schools and community colleges, and served to make explicit instructional goals and skills standards for courses of study at both educational levels. Several states, such as North Carolina and Texas, are developing statewide articulation agreements for these purposes and to increase the number of college-going students and save education costs and degree time. Orr (1999) found, however, that the primary benefits of articulation agreements depend on whether students take advantage of them by continuing their course of study at community colleges and applying the college credit earned in high school to their two-year degrees. Nonetheless, it appears from the state policy emphasis on articulation agreements that they are being used increasingly to help align the curricular content of high school and community college courses and programs.

Other research shows that much work can be done to improve articulation between high schools and community colleges for improved student readiness through interinstitutional communication, guidance, and shared assessment information. Nunley and Gemberling (1999) documented how the Maryland Partnership for Teaching and Learning made several recommendations for schools to better inform students and parents in order to improve the number of "college-ready" high school students. These included telling high school students their college-readiness standing, as based on college assessment tests and high school performance; providing guidance and intervention to help students plan better while in high school; and communicating college-level standards to parents. These recommendations led to several collaborative projects including data sharing between institutions to understand the high school course-taking patterns of college students enrolled in developmental courses at the community college. This information was then used for high school course-planning information for parents and students, to let them know the consequences of different high school course choices. The partnership also conducted a pilot project that allowed sophomores to take a high school version of the college assessment test in order to alert them and their parents about how they might be underprepared academically.

The Miami Valley Tech Prep Consortium in Dayton, Ohio, also uses this strategy, offering 10th grade Tech Prep students the opportunity to take the same academic assessments used for placement at Sinclair Community College. High school students are informed of their performance on mathematics, reading, and writing exams, which helps them to understand which courses they would be eligible to take at the community college if they were transitioning today. Often students learn they must take remedial courses before they can register for college-level work, which heightens the motivation of these young students to continue to more advanced academics while still enrolled in high school. Students are counseled as to the secondary courses they should take to ensure their readiness for a successful transition without remediation, into college-level academic courses (Bragg, 1999).

A fourth type of collaborative activity was identified by Orr (1999) in shared, comprehensive, work-based learning programs. These represent the most intensive form of joint action between high schools and community colleges engaged in the workforce development of youth. Although these programs are attractive for their potential to benefit students and employers, they seem to be the most difficult to undertake. Sometimes the 2+2 program of study did not materialize because of difficulties between the two institutions or insufficient planning. Many work-based learning programs found in Orr's study of four community colleges had standards-based secondary-level curricula but open-ended postsecondary education options. That is, students did not necessarily continue the same programmatic specialization in their two-year degree program that they had started in high school, the high schools were not necessarily explicit about the community college programs that complemented their programs of study, and the community colleges did not offer these students a unique program experience after they had transitioned there. Among the various comprehensive, work-based, learning program options available, Orr found that only youth apprenticeships and other similarly structured programs offered an articulated, sequenced, and standards-based course of study that included both a high school diploma and a two-year degree. However, these programs usually admitted only small numbers of students. This finding was consistent with the national Tech Prep evaluation research (Silverberg et al; 1998), which found comprehensive Tech Prep programs to be rare and those that included community college improvements even rarer.

Other research on K-14 and K-16 collaborations generally yielded similar findings. Typically, the role of higher-education institutions in these relationships has focused on K-12 system changes and interventions rather than changes in their own programs and processes (Callan, 1998; Grubb, Badway, Bell, & Kraskauskas, 1996). Grubb and his colleagues found several structural arrangements between community colleges and secondary schools designed to allow dual and concurrent enrollment (thereby shortening college degree time) and to improve, among all students, college preparation course taking in high school, college opportunity exposure, career and college planning, and labor market awareness among all students.

Many of these improvements could be gained through articulation agreements that are linked with more far-reaching education reform strategies rather than simply support credit accumulation. To achieve this broadened function, articulation agreements should establish program sequences between secondary and postsecondary education, with each sequence defined as a "seamless and increasingly rigorous program of study that has a logical progression from the secondary to the postsecondary level" (Bragg, 1999, p. 5). Bragg and her colleagues (1999) found some examples of jointly defined core curriculum that is sequential and rigorous, extending from secondary to postsecondary education. For example, Oklahoma City's Consortium to Restructure Education through Academic and Technological Excellence (CREATE) aligns curricula in grades 9 through 14 (Dornsife, 1997). Similarly, the Mt. Hood Educational Partnership of Gresham, Oregon, has developed curriculum competencies, specified desired outcomes, and developed sequential curricula throughout the high schools and community college.

## ORGANIZATIONAL CONSIDERATIONS FOR FUTURE POLICY DIRECTION

In analyzing public agency collaborations, Langman and McLaughlin (1993) found a range of collaboration, from least to most "coordination of services, sharing of services or resources, joint planning and joint action" (p. 150). Their analysis was useful because they distinguished between the nature of collaborative activities, on the one hand, and on the other, *structural relationships* between partners for achieving mutual goals, purposes, and activities. We would argue similarly that policy attention must be directed to the structural elements if substantive K-14 systems are to evolve.

In researching community college and secondary school collaboration, Orr (1999) found that the structure of collaborative relationships was associated with the scope and intensity of shared efforts. She found that the substance of this structure was dependent on three conditions: (1) the commitment of secondary schools and community colleges' commitment to develop a strong, shared educational transition system; (2) a mission priority on workforce development; and (3) a commitment to improving both the public schools' and community college's programs and services. Two factors facilitated change in the community colleges themselves—active business and industry interest and participation, and a formal, shared governance mechanism (Orr, 1999). Through extensive business input concerning training needs, community colleges learned about the gaps or inadequacies in their own programs for workforce preparation and, at times, became proactive by systemically assessing curricula through standardized review procedures. The active inclusion of a third party, specifically business and industry, with a vested interest in students as "products" of these two institutions seemed to stimulate more substantive and sustained collaborative planning and action. The role of business and industry in this planning seemed to add an accountability dimension that encouraged community colleges and their school district partners to design and offer more up-to-date and relevant vocational-technical degree programs. Moreover, the inclusion of this third constituency into the K-14 system dynamic may have helped to mediate interinstitutional turf problems that could potentially arise. Businesses in these communities, however, did not appear to be intent on limiting public education to skills training, although workforce development was a part of their interest. Instead, they seemed to have been active participants in, and sometimes leaders of, thought-provoking dialogues about the purpose of schooling, the use of academic and vocational-technical standards, how to further the academic and career goals of *all* students, and how to capitalize on the resources of high schools and community colleges for these purposes.

There are structural reasons that forging shared accountability strategies is difficult for school districts and community colleges. Tech Prep and STWOA initiatives are intended to foster K-14 collaboration. However, national evaluations revealed that the partnering institutions often have difficulty identifying program participants, defining curriculum elements, and sharing information (Bragg et al., 1997; Hershey et al., 1998). As of yet, there are no federal or state policies that define the mechanisms for shared accountability on goals, standards, student experiences, and assessment. Shared accountability for K-14 system building, we would argue, requires that (1) K-14 academic and vocational-technical standards be used to sequence K-12 and postsecondary education programs of study, (2) assessment criteria for K-12 promotion and graduation be linked to, and consistent with, admissions and graduation criteria for postsecondary education, (3) information on the use and outcomes of common standards would be shared among collaborating institutions and be the basis for the assessment criteria, and (4) governance and oversight mechanisms foster shared accountability and continuous improvement policies and practices in achieving these shared standards.

Stewart and Johanek (1998) drew similar conclusions when they argued for formation of an infrastructure to support substantive K-16 collaboration. They acknowledged that increased K-16 collaboration through better alignment and more coherent strategies would yield many benefits, not the least of which would be the development of more clarified and holistic local educational goals. Stewart and Johanek also thought that K-16 education reform should engage the intellectual vitality of teaching and learning across the two systems. They proposed looking beyond improving the administrative efficiencies in K-16 system building to fostering an "ecology of school-college connections" (p. 161) that would influence teaching and learning. As they explained, an ecological framework would

start from the qualities of interaction that constitute effective learning experiences, seeking to stimulate rich teaching/learning dynamics across institutions, linked by the principles and practices that underlie such processes. Primary linkages across academic levels would be based on research-informed principles of the teaching/learning process, and upon shared public pursuit of richer educational ecologies. (p. 161)

This shared framework would encourage school and college faculty to work collectively, thereby breaking down academic isolations and engaging their intellectual vitality, and to disseminate their ideas publicly for broader use.

While Stewart and Johanek's (1998) recommendations centered on academic skill reforms, such strategies already exist in some collaborations for the improved workforce development of youth. Some local communities, such as in Orange County, Florida, and Guilford County, North Carolina, used Tech Prep and STWOA policy opportunities to form interinstitutional curriculum teams, consisting of secondary school teachers and community college faculty, to establish shared technical skill standards and innovative teaching and learning practices, particularly through curriculum integration and work-based learning (Orr, 1998).

Institutional incentives and rewards are needed, however, to encourage teachers and faculty to work collaboratively on improving teaching and learning across institutions. Tompkins (1999) recommends that this collaborative work be defined as part of a college's responsibilities and rewards. This would include recognition of college faculty's participation in K-16 collaboration as a scholarly act and not simply service, and as a basis for institutional rewards through tenure, promotion, and merit (Tompkins, 1999). The Oklahoma City CREATE Partnership, for example, rewarded faculty who engaged in collaborative endeavors with special opportunities to attend workshops and conferences.

Building on Stewart and Johanek's (1998) ecological school-college framework, we would argue that there must be linkages formed at all levels of each system to enable all officials and staff to learn about their respective institutions, share information, and establish common goals and objectives. Shared planning opportunities, as evident in Florida, include holding joint college and school board meetings, establishing shared articulation and counseling strategies, and engaging college faculty in public school staff development (Rogers, 1996). Again, these partnership efforts require more than structural strategies. They must extend the ecological framework to a more holistic working relationships across all levels between schools and community colleges.

One way to foster a more ecological working relationship is for the collaborating institutions to use a problem-solving approach in tackling their common priorities and concerns, where they raise questions for joint inquiry, problem solving, pilot testing, and evaluation. Such an approach is illustrated by the Maryland Partnership for Teaching and Learning (Nunley & Gemberling, 1999), which wanted to improve collegiate readiness by raising academic standards K-16 and improving program articulation. The partnership, which included representatives from school districts, two and four-year colleges, and state education agencies, conducted a series of research studies on students' high school preparation experiences and a transcript analysis of students' high school course-taking patterns and college placement performance results. Using the results, they developed pilot efforts to give sophomores and seniors college assessment feedback and to improve college guidance. The partnership then evaluated its initiatives to determine their effectiveness and in order to make improvements or test alternatives. This problem-solving approach seems to help foster an equitable partnership rather than a dominant-subordinate one. Nunley and Gemberling (1999) drew similar conclusions, adding that this shared problem-solving approach creates more community support for education generally.

## CONCLUSIONS AND IMPLICATIONS

Given current trends and policy arguments for strengthened public school and community college linkages, we anticipate that the two educational systems will become more integrated. From our analysis of students' experiences in transitioning from high schools to community colleges and existing proposals for K-14 integration, we identified five objectives for public policies associated with K-14 educational system building. These are as follows:

- foster accessibility into and through rigorous programs of study across all levels of education;
- share and integrate preparation for academic and vocational-technical preparation at all levels;
- base integrated academic and vocational-technical preparation on recognized and agreed-upon standards (national, state, or local);

- foster a coherent educational experience across the systems, but pay particular attention to the transition points; and

- incorporate reciprocal accountability for student progress and completion, throughout the continuum of preparation.

Fiscal incentives, such as opportunities to reduce educational waste and improve high school preparation of students for college-level studies, can help to remove barriers to K-14 system building and simplify collaborative efforts. Interinstitutional commitments to other objectives, such as improving social equity and mobility opportunities for all students and improving workforce preparedness of youth, are more likely than fiscal incentives to stimulate deeper and more extensive forms of collaboration that challenge existing curriculum, program design, and student supports. Achieving more holistic K-14 system building requires greater attention to the structure to support these aims. This includes creating a combined mission, an appropriate interinstitutional infrastructure, a stronger commitment to reflect these priorities at both the secondary and postsecondary levels and enhanced accountability mechanisms that provide measures of progress on how well public schools and community colleges are progressing and achieving their shared mission and goals.

Federal and state policy remain the primary impetus for making K-14 system building a priority to meet the multiple goals. Such policy can also support future K-14 system development by encouraging creative solutions at both the institutional and staff levels. By providing seed grants and rewarding innovative partnerships, federal and state policies can create environments that support local system building, especially when state and local personnel are encouraged to think creatively about future opportunities. Entities from outside the system, especially business and industry, can have a positive impact on change when their goals are focused on enhancing education for all students and the entire community. Through shared governance mechanisms, enhanced accountability, and participatory problem solving approaches, K-14 system building can become a reality.

There are many advantages for students, institutions and society as a whole from improving the linkages between public schools and community colleges to form an educational continuum. There may be disadvantages as well when the tight coupling of the two educational systems results in tracking students and limiting their future opportunities. We believe, however, that a policy commitment to all three goals for K-14 system building—structural efficiencies, social equity, and workforce development—will prevent this from occurring. A combined commitment to social equity and workforce development will encourage interinstitutional efforts to maximize all students' career potentials, not narrow them prematurely by failing to help them be successful with college-level work or not encouraging them to pursue high skills–based technical programs of study. Moreover, given that many young people currently fail to achieve their college aspirations, we believe that their futures are actually far more restricted by the present incoherence among our educational institutions than they would be from a more coherent one.


## REFERENCES

American Association of Community Colleges (1999, February). [On-line]. Available: http://www.aacc.nche.edu/allaboutcc/

Baker, D. P., & Smith, T. (1997, Fall). Trend 3: A college education for all? *Teachers College Press, 99* (1), 57–61.

Bernhardt, A., Morris, M., Handcock, M., & Scott, M. (1998, February). *Work and opportunity in the post-industrial labor markets (Brief Number 19)*. New York: Teachers College, Institute for Education and the Economy.

Boesel, D., & Fredland, E. (1999, January). *College for all? Is there too much emphasis on getting a 4-year college degree?* Washington, DC: National Library of Education.

Boesel, D., & McFarland, L. (1994). *Final report to Congress: Vol. 1. Summary and recommendations*. Washington, DC: U.S. Department of Education, Office of Educational Research and Improvement.

Bragg, D. D. (1998, April). *How students assess their school to work opportunities*. Paper presented at the annual meeting of Council for the Study of Community Colleges, Miami Beach, FL.

Bragg, D. D. (1999, April). *Enhancing linkages to postsecondary education: Helping youths make a successful transition to college*. Paper presented at the annual meeting of the American Educational Research Association, Montreal, Canada.

Bragg, D. D., Dare, D. A., Reger, W., Ovaice, G., Layton, J., Zamani, E., Dornsife, C., Brown, C., & Orr, M. T. (1999). *The community college and beyond: Implementation and preliminary outcomes of eight local tech prep/school-to-work consortia*. Berkeley, University of California at Berkeley, National Center for Research in Vocational Education.

Bragg, D. D., & Griggs, M. B. (1997, Spring). Assessing the community college role in school-to-work systems. In E. J. Farmer and C. B. Key (Eds.), *The role of Community colleges in preparing students and facilitating transitions* (pp. 5–14). New Directions for Community Colleges, No. 97, San Francisco: Jossey-Bass.

Bragg, D. D., Puckett, P. A., Roger, W., Thomas, H. S., Ortman, J., & Dornsife, C. (1997, December). *Tech prep/school to work partnerships: More trends and challenges*. Berkeley: University of California at Berkeley, National Center for Research in Vocational Education.

Callan, P. (1998). The role of state policy systems in fostering separation or collaboration. In M. Timpane & L. White (Eds.), *Higher education and school reform* (pp. 41–56). San Francisco: Jossey-Bass.

Cohen, A. M., & Brawer, F. B. (1996). *The American community college* (3rd ed.). San Francisco: Jossey-Bass.

Conley, D. T. (1996, November). Oregon's Proficiency-based Admissions Standards System (PASS). In Education Commission of the States (Ed.), *Responding to school reform: Higher education defines new roles in Oregon, Wisconsin, and Florida*. Denver, CO: Author.

Dornsife, C. (1997). The postsecondary partner. In E. N. Andrew, C. Dornsife, M. M.

Flake, M. Hallihan, L. Jackson, M. Raby, & M. Steadman (Eds.), *Lessons learned: Five years in the urban schools network* (pp. 147–158). Berkeley: University of California at Berkeley, National Center for Research in Vocational Education.

Dougherty, K (1994). *The contradictory college.* Albany: State University of New York Press.

Farmer, E. I., & Key, C. B (1997). School-to-work systems and the community college (New Directions for Community Colleges, No. 97, pp. 97–106). San Francisco: Jossey-Bass.

Gray, K., & Herr, E. (1995). *Other ways to win: Creating alternatives for high school graduates.* Thousand Oaks, CA: Corwin Press.

Grubb, W. N (1996). *Working in the middle.* San Francisco: Jossey-Bass.

Grubb, W. N. (1998, September). *Learning and earning in the middle: The economic benefits of sub-baccalaureate education.* New York: Columbia University, Teachers College, Community College Research Center.

Grubb, W. N., Badway, N., Bell, D., & Kraskouskas, E. (1996). *Community college innovations in workforce preparation: Curriculum integration and Tech-Prep.* University of California at Berkeley: National Center for Research in Vocational Education.

Halperin, S. (1998). *The forgotten half revisited.* Washington, DC: American Youth Policy Forum.

Hamilton, S. F. (1990). *Apprenticeship for adulthood. Preparing youth for the future.* New York: Free Press.

Haycock, K. (1998). School and college partnership. In P. M. Timpane & L. S. White (Eds.), *Higher education and school reform* (pp. 57–82). San Francisco, CA: Jossey-Bass.

Hershey, A. M., Silverberg, M. K., Owens, T., & Hulsey, L. K. (1998). *Focus for the future. The final report of the national Tech-Prep evaluation.* Princeton, NJ: Mathematica Policy Research.

Horn, L., Berktold, J., & Malizio, A. (1998, May). *Profile of undergraduates in U.S. Postsecondary education institutions: 1995–96.* Washington, DC: U.S. Department of Education, Office of Education Research and Improvement.

Illinois Board of Education, Illinois Community College Board, & Illinois Board of Higher Education. (1999, March). *P-16 Partnership for educational excellence.* Springfield, IL: Authors.

Just, D. A., & Adams, D. A. (1997). The art of articulation: Connecting the dots (New Directions for Community Colleges, No. 97, pp. 29–39). San Francisco: Jossey-Bass.

Labaree, D. F. (1997, Spring). Public goods, private goods: The American struggle over educational goals. *American Educational Research Journal, 34*(1), 39–81.

Langman, J., & McLaughlin, M. W. (1993). *Collaborate or go it alone? Tough decisions for youth policy.* In S. B. Heath, & M. W. McLaughlin (Eds.) *Identity and inner-city youth* (pp. 147–175). New York: Teachers College Press.

Larson, J. C., Garies, R. S., & Campbell, W. E. (1996). *A profile of MCPS graduates and their performance at Montgomery College.* Montgomery, MD: Montgomery College/Montgomery County Public Schools.

Lewis, L., Farris, E., & Greene, B. (1996, October). *Remedial education at higher ed-*

*ucation institutions in fall 1995*. Washington, DC: U.S. Department of Education, Office of Educational Research and Improvement.

Marshall, R., & Tucker, M. (1992). *Thinking for a living*. New York: Basic Books.

Mayor's Advisory Task Force on the City University of New York. (1999, June 7). *The City University of New York: An institution adrift*. New York: Author.

McCabe, R. H., & Day, P. R. (1998). *Developmental education: A twenty-first century social and economic imperative*. Mission Viejo, CA: League for Innovation in the Community College.

McCabe, R. H., & Day, P. R. (1999). Can community colleges rescue America? *Community College Journal, 69,* (5), 20–23.

Nunley, C. & Gemberling, K. W. (1999, April/May). How high school/community college partnerships can boost academic achievement. *Community College Journal, 69*(5), 34–39.

Orr, M. T. (1998). Integrating secondary schools and community colleges through school-to-work transition and education reform. *Journal of Vocational Education Research, 23*(1), 93–111.

Orr, M. T. (1999, May). *Community college and secondary school collaboration on workforce development and educational reform: A close look at four community colleges*. New York: Columbia University, Teachers College, Community College Research Center.

Parnell, D. (1985). *The neglected majority*. Washington, DC: American Association of Community Colleges.

Parnell, D. (1994). The Tech Prep associate degree program revisited. In L. Falcone & R. Mundhenk (Eds.), *The Tech Prep associate degree challenge* (pp. 43–50). Washington, DC: American Association of Community Colleges.

Pauley, E., Kopp, H., & Haimson, J. (1995). *Home-grown lessons: Innovative programs linking school and work*. San Francisco: Jossey-Bass.

Projections of college enrollment, degrees conferred, and high-school graduates, 1998–2009, (1999, August 27). *The Chronicle of Higher Education,* p. 25.

Rogers, J. (1996, November). Education reform in Florida: The development of a K-12 system. In Education Commission of the States (Ed.), *Responding to school reform: Higher education defines new roles in Oregon, Wisconsin, and Florida* (pp. 29–38). Denver, CO: Author.

Rubin, L. (1996, November). The development of new approaches to college preparation and admissions in Wisconsin. In Education Commission of the States (Ed.), *Responding to school reform. Higher education defines new roles in Oregon, Wisconsin, and Florida* (pp. 19–27). Denver, CO: Author.

Sebring, A. S. (1996, November). Introduction and overview. In Education Commission of the States (Ed.), *Responding to school reform. Higher education defines new roles in Oregon, Wisconsin, and Florida* (pp. 1–6). Denver, CO: Author.

Silverberg, M. (1993). *Tech-Prep: A review of current literature*. Princeton, NJ: Mathematica Policy Research, Inc.

Silverberg, M. (1996). *The continuing development of local Tech-Prep initiatives*. Princeton, NJ: Mathematica Policy Research, Inc.

Silverberg, M., Haimson, J., & Hershey, A. M. (1998, July). *Building blocks for a future school-to-work system: Early national implementation results*. Princeton, NJ: Mathematica Policy Research.

Stewart, D. M., & Johanek, M. (1998). Enhanced academic connections. Deweyan waste, ecological pipelines, and intellectual vitality. In M. Timpane & L. White (Eds.), *Higher education and school reform* (pp. 141–186). San Francisco: Jossey-Bass.

Timpane, P. M., & White, L. S. (Eds.). (1998). *Higher education and school reform*. San Francisco, CA: Jossey-Bass.

Tinto, V. (1996). Persistence and the first-year experience at the community college: Teaching new students to survive, stay, and thrive. In J. Hankin (Ed.), *The community college: Opportunity and access for America's first-year students* (pp. 97–104). Columbia: University of South Carolina, National Resource Center for the Freshman Year Experience and Students in Transition.

Tompkins, D. (1999, February). Solving a "higher ed tough one." *AAHE Bulletin, 51*(6), 11–13.

U.S. Department of Education. (1998). *Digest of education statistics, 1997.* Washington, DC: Author.

U.S. Department of Education. (1999, September). Helping more students prepare for college through "GEAR UP" [On-line]. Available: http//www.ed.gov/gearup

Chapter 7 _____

# State Policies and the Community College's Role in Workforce Preparation

*Kevin J. Dougherty*

Community colleges and other sub-baccalaureate institutions are often ignored actors in the area of workforce preparation. Instead, four-year colleges and high school still command attention, depending on whether one is thinking of professional and managerial education, on the one hand, or vocational education, on the other. This myopic view of the community college shows up in various ways. Three-fifths of federal aid under the Perkins Act goes to secondary schools. Meanwhile, discussions about future needs for professional and managerial workers usually ignore community colleges, despite the fact that many baccalaureate degree holders start at community colleges.

Yet closer analysis soon discovers that community colleges play an absolutely crucial role in the total system of workforce preparation. A study of 1982 seniors in the High School and Beyond survey found that, of the 43 percent of the seniors who entered the labor force with subbaccalaureate college training, nearly half (48 percent) had begun at a community college (Grubb, 1996, pp. 54–56). Sometimes, community colleges are the main portals of entry to important occupations. For example, associate's degree holders—most of them graduated by community colleges—comprise 60 percent of graduates in registered nursing in 1996 (U.S. Bureau of the Census, 1998, p. 130). Moreover, community colleges play an active role in training current, and not just prospective, employees. Among private business establishments with over 50 employees that operated employee-training programs in 1995, 31 percent of those establishments used community colleges as one of their training suppliers (Frazis, Gittleman, Horrigan, & Joyce, 1997, p. 71). Finally, community colleges train, not just workers—whether prospective or current—but also managers, supervisors, and company owners, particularly of small firms.

This chapter examines how state policy shapes this plethora of workforce preparation activities on the part of community colleges. Distinguishing between preservice training, inservice training, and small business development, this chapter describes the structure and content of workforce training programs operated by community colleges, explains how state governments influence those programs, and then considers the problems and possible solutions to the current state of workforce training by the community college.

## PRESERVICE JOB TRAINING

### Structure and Content of Community College Programs

Community colleges are actively involved in providing preemployment training to a wide variety of students. These include both new entrants to the labor force who are fresh out of high school and labor force *reentrants*, whether unemployed workers, displaced homemakers, welfare recipients, or former prison inmates (Cohen & Brawer, 1996, chs. 8, 10; Grubb, 1996). This preemployment occupational training is often conceptualized as exclusively subbaccalaureate. But graduates of occupational programs are increasingly able to go on to pursue baccalaureate degrees. For example, in Florida, associate of science graduates of the auto technical program at Broward Community College can have virtually all of their courses—even the technical ones—credited toward a B.A. in professional management at nearby Nova Southeastern University (Derry, 1997).

Students who graduate from community college vocational programs receive substantially better wages than do high school graduates, although the payoffs are lower than for four-year college graduates. For example, community college students earning a vocational associate's degree earn 20 to 30 percent more than high school graduates who are similar in race and ethnicity, education of parents, marital status, and job experience. Students graduating from community colleges with one-year certificates outpace high school graduates in annual earnings by about 10 percent. And students who attend community college but do not receive a certificate or degree lead high school graduates by only about 5 to 10 percent in earnings for every year of community college. Meanwhile, college graduates with no advanced degrees on average earn about 40 percent more than high school graduates (Grubb, 1996, p. 90; 1998, pp. 10–11, Tables 6–9).

A word of caution, however: these estimates are average effects. The payoff to a given community college credential varies by the student's sex, social class background, and field of study. For example, women make more from associate's degrees and certificates than do men, but they make less when they have some college but no credential. The field of training also makes a big difference. The payoff is considerably higher for associate degrees in engineering and computers, business, and (for women) health than in education or humanities. Finally, community college students get much better returns if they find employment in fields related to their training (Grubb, 1996, pp. 95, 99, 102).

Clearly, the economic payoff to a community college degree can be quite significant. In fact, in several instances it can exceed that of a baccalaureate degree, if we are comparing, for example, an associate degree in engineering and a baccalaureate degree in humanities (Grubb, 1998, p. 16). However, we should not let this overlap in payoffs lead us—as it does some community college advocates—to state that a community college degree is as valuable as a bachelor's degree. This is only true in some instances. On average, looking across all fields of study, the baccalaureate degree is still significantly more valuable (Dougherty, 1994, p. 61; Grubb, 1998, p. 10).

### Existing State Policy toward Preservice Training

State governments encourage and shape the preservice training programs of community colleges through a variety of means, including exhortation, finance, regulation, and technical assistance. A typical location of exhortation to community colleges to engage in occupational preparation is in state master plans and mission statements, where community colleges are clearly told that they are to make workforce preparation a central mission (Dougherty, 1994, p. 220).

State financial incentives and penalties give muscle to these exhortations. States typically encourage community colleges to offer occupational education courses by offering more aid per full-time enrollment (FTE) than for academic programs (Dougherty, 1994, p. 220). For example, in fiscal year 1999 the state of Illinois rewarded enrollments in health care and technical courses at the rate of $65.10 and $43.61 per credit hour, respectively, while only providing $31.23 for baccalaureate preparation courses (Illinois Community College Board, 1998, p. 21). Meanwhile, the state of Texas in fiscal year 1999 contributed an average of $5.33 per contact hour for general vocational and technical programs, but an average of only $4.35 per contact hour for general academic programs (Texas Higher Education Coordinating Board, 1999). In addition, in the 1970s, states such as Washington and Illinois provided community colleges with more capital aid for building and equipping vocational facilities than for academic facilities.

States explain this differential in operating and capital appropriations as necessary to overcome the fact that occupational education programs, particularly in technical fields, are considerably more expensive to run than academic programs because of smaller classes and requirements for more expensive equipment. This cost differential certainly exists, but there is no doubt that differential aid has certainly spurred community colleges to expand their occupational education offerings (Dougherty, 1994, p. 220).

Usually, financial incentives carry regulatory requirements. Not surprisingly, states attach rules to state authorizations and appropriations for community colleges. But states also exercise considerable rulemaking discretion within federally authorized and financed programs as well, whether the reauthorized Perkins Vocational and Technical Education Act, the School to Work Act of 1994, the Personal Responsibility and Work Opportunities Act of 1996 (welfare reform legislation), or the Workforce Investment Act of 1998. State governments have considerable leeway in how they interpret federal program specifications and then in how rigorously they implement those specifications. The resultant interstate variation in interpretation and implementation results in considerable variation in how much funding community colleges get from federal programs and how they use that funding (Hershey, Silverberg, Owens, & Husely, 1998; Hershey, Silverberg, & Haimson, 1999, pp. 22–23; Orr, 1999).

Finally, states influence the vocational-education efforts of community colleges through capacity-building efforts such as technical assistance. States provide community colleges with help in developing new programs, particularly if they involve complex interorganizational alliances, as in the case of tech prep or school to work (Hershey et al., 1998, 1999, pp. 24–25).

### Problems and Possible Policy Solutions

Community college preservice education has a lot of room to improve, which means there is a major role for state policy in catalyzing such improvement. Let me enumerate both the needs and possible solutions.

*Vertical Integration and Transferability of Vocational Credentials.* Community college vocational students face a painful dilemma. Vocational associate degrees on average carry a greater economic payoff than terminal academic associate degrees that do not lead to a baccalaureate degree (Grubb, 1996, p. 95). Yet, academic associate recipients are much more likely than vocational associate recipients to pursue and attain baccalaureate degrees, which of course are much more valuable. Among 1980 community college entrants involved in the High School and Beyond survey, 49 percent of those completing academic associate degrees, but only 23 percent of those receiving vocational associate degrees, ended up transferring to a four-year college by spring 1984 (Grubb, 1991, pp. 200–201).[1] However, the dilemma—of whether to pursue a smaller, but more certain, payoff (in the case of a certificate or associate's degree) or instead to pursue a larger, but less certain, return (in the case of a bachelor's degree)—can be made less painful by state policy.

Not only is there still a strong divide within community colleges between largely terminal vocational programs and baccalaureate-oriented academic programs, there is also a deep fissure between the traditional vocational education programs and job-training programs focused on job reentry for dislocated workers, displaced homemakers, and welfare recipients. Often these programs provide quite short-term training in simple skills. Hence, they would benefit immensely from having the option of feeding into community college certificate and associate programs that provide greater skills and bring greater economic returns (Grubb, 1996, pp. 124–125).

In response, W. Norton Grubb has argued that training programs should be connected vertically, so that graduates of programs providing lesser skills or short-term training could later enter programs offering higher skills, longer training, and, typically, higher certificates or degrees. Moreover, training programs should be integrated horizontally, with trainees exposed, as needed, to various kinds of learning: technical skills, academic skills, adult basic (remedial) education, job search and career guidance skills, and so forth. In order to promote this integration, Grubb has suggested establishing state and local councils to oversee the development of a more integrated system, providing financial and regulatory incentives to community colleges and other training institutions to pursue program and institutional coordination, merging certain programs into the community college (such as the separate adult basic education system and the short-term training provided now by area vocational schools), and closing ineffective schools, particularly proprietary schools (Grubb, 1996, pp. 133–134).

While Grubb's vision of greater vertical and horizontal integration is eminently worth pursuing, three dangers should be noted. First, a much more structured system of workforce preparation may be considerably less able to rapidly and flexibly respond to sudden changes in the skill demands of the economy. While our now-loosely coordinated profusion of training providers and credentials does result in a lot of wasted effort, it also means that there is an abundance of training organizations to possibly respond to new economic needs. Also, those organizations can move more rapidly than if they were enmeshed in a system requiring consultation with many institutional partners.

Second, transferability is very hard to achieve, especially between dissimilar kinds of training rooted in different types of institutions. States have long pursued greater transferability of community college academic credits and degrees to four-year colleges with, at best, mixed success. Though real achievements have been made, some obstacles are persistent and new obstacles constantly emerge. These problems are even greater in the case of vocational degrees, which carry lower status and do not find any easy counterpart at four-year colleges (Dougherty, 1994, Chapters 4, 15).

Third, even if nearly full transferability were achieved, a new danger might appear: a major spiral of credentials inflation. As students who heretofore stayed put at a vocational certificate or associate degree now pursue higher degrees, middle and upper-class students are likely to respond by pursuing still higher credentials in order to preserve their edge in the labor market. The result would be to have less advantaged students paying much more for their education yet not improving their labor-market position. Meanwhile, society as a whole has to make enormous additional expenditures on education that are not called for by actual trends in the economy's skill requirements and thus unnecessarily divert resources from more pressing social demands.[2]

*Horizontal Integration.* The vision of creating a vocational education system that reduces obstacles to pursuing higher academic degrees clearly resonates with the frequent call in recent years for producing workers who are, not just technically competent, but also equipped with higher-order thinking skills, such as problem solving, decision making, and the ability to learn independently. Realizing this goal will require further efforts to overcome the horizontal divide between vocational and academic training in order to allow their fruitful integration (Grubb, 1996, pp. 136–157).

The federal and state governments have been pursuing this integration, most notably in the recent reauthorization of the Perkins Act. However, such integration is too often more a matter of word than of substance. A recent study found that many cases of supposedly extensive academic and vocational integration in community colleges were, on closer inspection, often specious. The supposed integration was quite minor or sometimes entirely missing (Perin, 1998). This argues that state legislation mandating such integration will need to be very attentive to issues of implementation.

*Student Awareness about Training Outcomes.* Regardless of whether a policy of greater transferability between credentials is pursued, students will need to know much better than they do now what are the varying returns to different community college programs and credentials. Students and, all too often, policy makers are unaware of the great variability by field of study in the returns to particular credentials, whether certificates, associate degrees, or bachelor's degrees (Grubb, 1996, p. 95; 1998, pp. 14–17). And while this is true of all students, working-class and nonwhite students particularly need more information, both because they are the least likely to receive adequate information to begin with and because they have fewer resources with which to cope with the consequences of poorly informed choices.

Some states are making notable efforts to improve students' ability to navigate the vocational education system. For example, the Florida community college and state university systems are developing a statewide system for computer-assisted student advising that can be expanded to include career advising (Florida State Board of Community Colleges, 1998, pp. 39–40). What remains to be seen, however, is whether such systems are as useful in reaching working-class, minority, and older students, as they must compete with recent high school graduates who are more computer literate and come from more advantaged backgrounds.

*Administrator Responsiveness to Labor Market Trends.* It is not only students, but also administrators, who face an information gap concerning vocational education. Community college preservice preparation programs too often lack up-to-date intelligence on the changing contours of the labor market. Today, the problem is less that courses are offered for which there is very little demand, though that continues to be an issue. The greater difficulty is that course contents and equipment are not keeping pace with the often rapidly changing skill demands of employers. Traditionally, community colleges have relied on a variety of devices to promote such alignment with the labor market, including business advisory committees and employer surveys. And more recently, they have used contract training as a way of identifying the cutting-edge skills needed by employers and then diffusing this knowledge to the noncontract-training side of the college (Dougherty & Bakia, 2000; Grubb, 1996, pp. 177–187, 189).

However, these information sources still need improvement. Until recently, community colleges have been funded almost exclusively on the basis of enrollments rather than outputs, so that their tracking of labor market trends has been a matter of choice more than necessity. While community colleges do close programs with low student enrollment, programs may be kept operating despite low employer demand because student enrollees have little knowledge about labor market conditions and continue to enroll in programs with poor job prospects (Grubb, 1996, pp. 187–190). Employers, meanwhile, have felt little pressure to clearly communicate their skills needs to community colleges because they often are hazy about what those needs really are, they draw on a wide variety of sources of skill training besides community colleges, and their hiring needs are unstable, varying greatly depending on the state of the business cycle (Grubb, 1996, pp. 196–198).

The community colleges' contribution to the lack of responsiveness to labor-market trends can be lessened by moving them toward funding formulas that emphasize outputs such as job placement. This would cause community colleges to actively track labor market requirements in order to ensure that students are able to secure jobs (Grubb, 1996, p. 198). As it happens, many states have been moving in the direction of performance-based funding, beginning with Tennessee in 1979 (Carnevale, Johnson, & Edwards, 1998). For example, in 1998, Florida passed legislation (SB1688) declaring that, in fiscal year 1999–2000, state aid for postsecondary vocational and adult general education (but not including continuing workforce education) would be partially based on institutional performance. Providers (community colleges and school districts) would be guaranteed only 85 percent of their 1998–1999 allocation, and additional funds would be dependent on their performance on measures of course completion, job placement, and service to particular categories of trainees (such as dislocated workers, welfare recipients, etc.). The course completion measure involves completion, not of an entire program, but of clusters of courses that contain a set of marketable skills. This is intended to reward community colleges for students who acquire skills that help them advance at work even if they do not complete all the requirements for a certificate or degree. This performance-funding mechanism makes community colleges concentrate on occupations that the Florida Education and Training Placement Information Program (FETPIP) deems as locally in demand by more heavily weighting the completion of courses for targeted occupations than courses for nontargeted occupations. With the advent of the state's performance based incentive funding system, occupational offerings by the community colleges are becoming more tightly connected to these targeted occupations (Florida State Board of Community Colleges, 1998, pp. 52–53; Florida State Department of Education, 1999a, 1999b).

Despite the attractions of performance-based accountability and funding, state governments should be wary because poorly conceptualized or inadequately measured outcomes can have quite negative outcomes. It is important that the outcomes not be defined simply in terms of such imprecise and uninformative measures of effective skills acquisition as employer or student satisfaction with the training. It is important to include more precise measures such as program completion, job placement, and, particularly important, long-term retention in the job. Meanwhile, poorly conceived outcome measures may trigger perverse consequences. Faced with demands for higher completion rates, community colleges will be very tempted to exclude students who are likely to have high dropout rates—such as high school dropouts and welfare recipients—even though such students particularly need effective workforce training or retraining. One solution is to follow states such as Florida in using composite measures of program completion that provide a bounty for completion by harder to teach students.

## INSERVICE TRAINING

Community colleges have long trained currently employed workers to upgrade their skills. Typically this training has been provided through the continuing education or community service division of a community college. Often trainees simply come on their own volition and bear the cost themselves. Other times, an employer pays the cost of attending a regular class that is not customized to that employer's requirements and enrolls a wide variety of students. But increasingly, employers have contracted directly with community colleges to provide training "customized" in one or another fashion to the employer's needs. When this happens, we talk of "contract" or "customized" training. Contract training has been quite variously defined (American Association of Community Colleges, 1993, p. 3; Bragg & Jacobs, 1991, pp. 18–21; Grubb, Badway, Bell, Bragg, & Russman, 1997, p. 5; Katsinas & Lacey, 1989). But in synthesizing these various definitions, one finds seven key features of contract training, of which the most important is that it is based on a contract between a community college and an outside organization. See Table 7.1 for these defining features.[3]

Although the content of contract courses is often adapted to the concerns of a particular contractor—with learning tasks, problems, terms, and so on being oriented to the concerns of the contractor—it is often the case as well that the course content is not adapted. Instead, the course is simply pulled out of the regular college curriculum or pulled off a shelf of already developed contract courses (Lynch, Palmer, & Grubb, 1991, pp. 24, 27). But in these cases, the program is usually customized in other ways: for example, through a nonstandard schedule (less than a semester long, given on weekends, or held every other week), location (at the contractor's premises); or student composition

**Table 7.1**
**Defining Features of Contract Training**

- an outside group (such as a firm, industry association, or government agency) contracts for a specific course or program
- the contractor is conceived of as the main client for the training. Students are secondary clients
- the community college receives payments from the contractor and/or public agencies providing third-party payments
- the contractor largely, if not entirely, determines who will receive the training
- the contractor has a significant or even decisive voice in framing training content
- the contractor has a significant or even decisive voice in defining measures of success
- the training program is usually customized in some fashion (content, schedule, etc.) to the contractor's requirements

(the trainees are restricted to the contractor's employees) (Grubb et al., 1997, pp. 4–5).

How extensive is contract training? Three nationwide surveys of community colleges, in 1989, 1992, and 1994, found that over 90 percent of community colleges offered contract training to firms, nonprofit organizations, and government agencies. At the typical community college offering contract training, enrollees in this program accounted for 17 to 18 percent of total (credit and noncredit) enrollments. However, these figures hide an enormous range, with one community college enrolling only 3 students in contract training and another enrolling 55,000 (Dougherty & Bakia, 2000).

## Existing State Policy toward Inservice Training

State governments encourage and regulate inservice training, whether contract training or ordinary continuing education, through a variety of means. Certainly, community colleges are exhorted—in state legislation, master plans, and mission statements for community colleges—to provide continuing education. In addition, financial inducements are provided. General, noncontractual inservice training is subsidized in many (but not all) states. For example, North Carolina runs a very extensive Occupational Continuing Education Program, which was budgeted at $31 million and trained over 285,000 people in 1997. The trainees may be enrolled in a general-purpose course or, if there are enough from one firm, they can be enrolled in a course customized to the desires of that firm (National Governors' Association, 1999, pp. 72–74, 141). Texas also underwrites the cost of noncredit continuing education vocational programs. In 1994, the state approved reimbursement for noncredit vocational and technical programs at the same rate as credit programs (National Governors' Association, 1999, p. 93).

Contract training, meanwhile, receives very wide support from states. A 1998 survey with 47 states responding found that nearly all operated programs to subsidize the costs of retraining current employees (Bosworth, 1999 National Governors' Association, 1999, p. 11); Community colleges were among the recipients of these funds in 30 out of 35 (86 percent) of the states for which we have figures on how they distributed aid among training providers. These 30 states ran a total of 43 programs to support contract education. Community colleges received, on average, 34 percent of the funds going through these state programs, but the range was quite high, varying from 0 going to community colleges in the case of seven state programs to 100% in the case of another six programs (Bosworth, 1999).

### Problems and Possible Policy Solutions

As with preservice vocational training, inservice training also has important deficiencies that should be addressed by state policy.

*Inadequate Integration of Technical Training and Other Necessary Services.* Inservice technical training is often poorly linked with other services that are of great importance for incumbent workers. A particularly important one is adult basic education, which is provided by a scattering of agencies with little connection to community colleges or, if provided by community colleges, often done so through a remedial division with little organizational interchange with the continuing education or contract education division (Grubb, 1996, pp. 210–211; National Governors' Association, 1999, pp. 12–13). This weakness of connection is worrisome because, as workers have to raise their technical skills, they frequently have to elevate as well their basic reading and math skills. As it is, a 1989 survey of contract training providers found that instruction in basic academic skills accounted for 12 percent of all contract courses (Lynch et al., 1991, p. 17). But it is likely that incumbent workers need far more exposure to instruction in basic academic skills than this. For example, in a 1995 survey of 2,473 firms served by community college workforce programs, 74 percent said their employees needed further training in basic communication skills and 54 percent said their workers needed more training in basic math skills (Zeiss et al., 1997, p. 43).

Grubb (1996, pp. 210–211) suggests that the federal government should push to have adult basic education merge into community colleges. But then states will have to ensure that, once within community colleges, adult education be closely integrated with other kinds of training services within the colleges. This integration is particularly necessary given mounting evidence that remediation is much more successful when it is not done by stand-alone divisions but rather is provided in immediate connection with technical training. This is important if only to bolster the motivation to learn of students who come to a community college seeking technical skills but instead are confronted by the need to receive extensive remedial education (Grubb, 1996, pp. 138–139, 158–163, Chapter 5; Perin, 1998).

*Inadequate Evaluation.* Despite its relative ubiquity, inservice training (particularly contract training) and the state programs financing it have been little evaluated (National Governors' Association, 1999, p. 13). To be sure, there are a few evaluations and these do find positive results of inservice training: trainees and their employer report high satisfaction with the training; and the trainees receive higher wages, are more often promoted, and get higher performance ratings than those not receiving training (Krueger and Rouse, 1996; National Governors' Association, 1999, p. 13; Van Horn, Fichtner, Dautrich, Hartley, & Hebbar, 1998, pp. 12–14).[4] Still, these evaluations are few and too often rely on small samples or subjective measures of satisfaction rather than large samples using carefully calibrated measures of skill acquisition, job placement, and job retention. Moreover, the evaluations shed little knowledge of what kinds of programs and training techniques work best, with what kinds of workers, and what kinds of firms. And if the aim is not just to train workers but also to make the entire firm more technologically sophisticated and economically competitive, it is quite unclear as to what kinds of training interventions produce such broad-gauged results.

But this knowledge gap extends further. Even if contract training definitively proves to be useful for trainees and employers, we do not know how good it is overall for the community colleges offering it. To be sure, such training apparently brings community colleges more revenues, students, and political clout (Dougherty & Bakia, 2000). At the same time, there is some evidence that contract training may undermine colleges' commitment to their more traditional educational tasks. The energetic pursuit of contract training leaves less administrative time, attention, and energy for such traditional missions as baccalaureate preparation, remedial education for underprepared students, and general education for citizenship. The transfer program may particularly feel the effects of a loss of administrative attention. It takes great administrative time and energy to construct and maintain effective articulation agreements with four-year colleges as new courses appear at community colleges and four-year colleges and as the signatories to the initial agreement pass on and new principal actors have to be socialized. The traditional missions of community colleges may also be threatened by the diffusion of a "business-like" ethos of operation, as these institutions try to attract and retain training contracts from business. Less emphasis may be placed on transfer and general education because business is not very interested in it and, as a result, community college administrators come to internalize this orientation (Dougherty & Bakia, 2000). Because these negative impacts are quite possible but we have no reliable data on their extent and depth, it is very important that states commission carefully evaluate the impact of contract training on the community college's entire mission.

***Unnecessary Corporate Welfare?*** Another topic meriting careful evaluation by state governments is whether state aid for contract training has substituted for firm spending, allowing firms to avoid paying their proper share of the costs of employee training. To be sure, states often do require firms to put up as much as half the cost of the training in order to receive grants (Bosworth, 1999). And an evaluation of New Jersey's state aid program found that firms receiving grants

**Table 7.2**
**Typical Services of Two-Year College Incubators**

| | |
|---|---|
| • office equipment and furniture | 78% |
| • office services | 89% |
| • accounting/tax assistance | 67% |
| • advice on business/strategic plan | 100% |
| • advice on financial management | 89% |
| • advice on sales/marketing | 89% |
| • advice on government procurement | 89% |
| • advice on securing government aid | 78% |

*Source*: National Business Incubation Association (1992), pp. 72–73.

stated that they planned to contribute $2 for every dollar they received in state aid (Van Horn et al., 1998, p. 11). Yet a study of the state aid program in New York State found that, when asked in 1987 what they would have done in the absence of state aid, 34 percent of recipient firms stated that they would have done the training with their own staff and 26 percent said they would have purchased training elsewhere (Winter & Fadale, 1990, p. 5). This raises the question of the degree to which state aid is unnecessarily subsidizing employee training efforts by firms. To date, there is little evidence that states have carefully examined this issue of unnecessary corporate welfare.

## SMALL BUSINESS ASSISTANCE

Beyond providing job training for current or prospective employees, community colleges also provide training for current and prospective managers and owners, especially of small businesses. This role has been clouded by the fact that it is described in various terms, partially overlapping and partially conflicting, which include small business assistance, business incubation, and technology transfer.[5]

Community colleges proffer small business assistance and incubation through a variety of institutional mechanisms. Sometimes they have formally designated small business centers or business incubators with their own facilities. Other times the assistance is provided in a very informal way, as when vocational teachers provide business advice to present and former students taking their courses.[6]

Small business development centers are sponsored by as many as one-third of community colleges, according to a national survey in 1989 (Lynch et al., 1991, pp. iv, 35, 41). As of 1993, between 25 and 75 business incubators were sponsored by two-year colleges, out of a total of at least 500 business incubators in the United States (Adkins, 1996, p. iii; Hernandez-Gantes, Sorenson, & Nieri, 1996: 5; Lynch et al., 1991, p. 41). These incubators at two-year colleges provide a variety of services, as listed in Table 7.2.

Community colleges also provide a lot of less formal assistance to small business. According to a national survey in 1989, 33 percent of community colleges held Small Business Administration training workshops, 18 percent helped businesses obtain financing, and 13 percent advised on contract procurement (Lynch et al., 1991, p. 41). In addition, vocational faculty in community colleges often consult informally with small firms, particularly those headed by students (current or former) of the community college.

### State Policy

Much of the development of small-business assistance and incubation has been driven by federal policy. For example, legislation (passed in 1980 and 1984 as PL 86–302 and PL 98–395) provided financial assistance for the establishment of Small Business Development Centers (Carmichael, 1991, p. 25). But small-business assistance efforts have also received independent and strong support from many state governments. New Jersey, Maryland, Illinois, Arizona, California, and Oregon, among other states, have established statewide networks of small business development centers (SBDCs) housed at community colleges (Carmichael, 1991, p. 29; Cutler, 1984, p. 30; Dozier, 1996, p. 18; Melville & Chmura, 1991, pp. 8–9). For example, the Illinois Department of Commerce and Community Affairs (DCCA) has provided grants to community colleges to start or expand business assistance and resource centers and has worked with community colleges to cosponsor small-business training workshops, run the state's Procurement Outreach Program, and promote industrial retention (Boyd-Beauman & Piland, 1983, p. 18; Burger, 1984, pp. 37–38).

### Problems and Possible Policy Solutions

There are virtually no data available on the impact on business firms and on community colleges of community college small-business development centers and incubators. What we have are a few studies on the impact on firms of incubators in general (most of them not sponsored by community colleges) (Adkins, 1996; National Business Incubation Association, 1992). And we have no data at all on the impact on community colleges of their efforts to provide small-business development assistance. As a result, a major goal for state policy should be to develop better information on the impact of the small-business assistance efforts of community colleges.

## SUMMARY AND CONCLUSIONS

The community college plays a major role in workforce preparation, both preservice and inservice. While this role has been strongly shaped by federal policy, it has also been powerfully molded by state policy, whether in the form of exhortation, financial inducements, regulations, or capacity building. This state policy has taken the form both of independent state initiatives and of the exercise of considerable state discretion in how to implement federal policy. In either case, state policy has had a powerful effect on the shape of the community college's role in workforce preparation.

Much remains to be done to perfect the workforce preparation efforts of community colleges. They are still fraught with major problems of program fragmentation, inadequate institutional accountability, and knowledge gaps on the part of students, community college officials, and state policy makers. To be sure, considerable corrective action is occurring under the aegis of recent federal legislation (particularly the Workforce Investment Act of 1988 and the reauthorization of the Perkins Act) and independent state initiatives. These acts may go a long way toward creating a workforce preparation system—with community colleges occupying a pivotal place—that is better coordinated, more transparent in its operations, and increasingly oriented toward defining success in terms of high rates of program completion and job placement rather than high numbers of enrollees. Nonetheless, much remains for state governments themselves to do, whether in deciding how to implement federal initiatives or how to address problems the federal initiatives fail to confront. In this chapter, we have particularly discussed the need to address deficiencies in program coordination and integration, institutional accountability, and informed choice available to trainees and their trainers.

The workforce training system suffers from great vertical and horizontal fragmentation. The passage of the Workforce Investment Act in 1998 catalyzed stronger efforts by state governments to tie together traditional pre-entry vocational training, retraining of dislocated workers and welfare recipients, and retraining of incumbent workers (National Governors Association, 1999, p. 12). So far, this push for greater integration does not seem to go far enough: it seems largely directed to coordinating still-separate programs through local one-stop centers and state workforce coordinating boards. As Norton Grubb has argued, what is needed is a more complete integration, involving the creation of a vertically and horizontally articulated system of workforce preparation, in which trainees may move easily from one kind of training to another. Training programs should be connected vertically, so that graduates of programs providing lesser skills can later enter programs offering higher skills and higher certificates or degrees. Moreover, training programs should be integrated horizontally, with trainees exposed, as needed, to various kinds of learning: technical skills, academic skills, adult basic (remedial) education, job search and career guidance skills, and so on. This integration would go a long way to resolving two important problems: the painful choice facing community college students between pursuing vocational training carrying more certain, but lower, reward and pursuing a less certain, but more remunerative, baccalaureate degree; and second, the divorce between vocational education, on the one hand and academic instruction or remedial education, on the other, which renders the latter two less effective than they would be if they were more closely integrated with vocational education. But while commending this goal of greater vertical and horizontal integration of programs, this chapter has also raised the warning that such integration will be very hard to pursue, might make the workforce-training system less responsive to changing labor market demands, and also might trigger an inflationary spiral in the demand for educational credentials.

A key component of creating a workforce training system that is more responsive to the dynamics of the economy is to change the formula for state aid from one based solely on input measures, such as enrollments, to one giving considerable weight to output measures, such as program completion and job placement. This is a major concern of the Workforce Investment Act (1998) and the recent reauthorization of the Carl Perkins Vocational and Technical Education Act. And already, many states are rapidly moving in the direction of performance-based funding. However, despite the attractions of performance-based accountability and funding, states need to be very wary of the distorting effect of poorly conceptualized or poorly measured outcomes. The first may catalyze perverse consequences, such as excluding harder-to-teach students, who make the community college look bad on outcome measures, and the second might lead to rewarding the wrong kinds of programs.

Finally, a major problem with the current system of community college workforce preparation is lack of knowledge, whether by trainees, about what programs to choose, or trainers, about what kinds of programs to offer. In the case of students, much needs to be done to provide them much more extensive, up-to-date, and clearly stated information about the economic payoffs to different kinds of training programs and degrees, both vocational and academic. In the case of trainers, major efforts are being made by states and the federal government to better determine what occupations are in demand and how well training programs are meeting that demand. Yet even the more sophisticated evaluations are still too rare and too limited in scope. In particular, there is a great need for careful evaluation of the impact of small business development programs. Moreover, in the case of contract training programs, states need much more information on their impact, both on trainees and firms and on community colleges themselves. We should not assume that the strong expansion of the community college's workforce preparation role under the impetus of state and federal policy has been an unalloyed good for the community college. In fact, there is some evidence of significant harm from contract training.

## NOTES

The research reported here was partially supported by the Community College Research Center, Teachers College, Columbia, University with funds from the Sloan Foundation. I wish to thank the numerous state officials who sent me reports and answered my question. I also with to thank Joshua Haimson of Mathematica Policy Research for his very thorough critique of an earlier draft of this chapter.

1. Similar figures turn up in studies by state coordinating bodies. In Illinois, 14 percent of 1983–1985 occupational program graduates in Illinois went on to four-year colleges

(Illinois Community College Board, 1987). In Maryland, the comparable figure was 27 percent (Maryland State Board for Community Colleges, 1988). Meanwhile, a longitudinal study of students entering nearly 20 California community colleges in fall 1978 found that three years later 16.1 percent of the "technical transfers" (those who were judged to have baccalaureate aspirations but largely took vocational courses) had transferred to a four-year school. This figure compared favorably with the 19.7 percent of academic transfer aspirations who also transferred within three years (Sheldon, 1982, pp. 1–21, 3–29, 4–26, 2–48).

2. For excellent discussions of the general phenomenon of credentials inflation, see Brown (1995) and Collins (1979).

3. Contract training is often seen as restricted to the training of current employees (Grubb, 1996, p. 185). However, the features of contract training described in Table 7.1 apply as well to many programs designed for prospective employees: a notable case is the auto service technician programs run by the major auto companies (Dougherty & Bakia, 2000).

4. The findings are buttressed by data from other studies of inservice job training, but not of contract training specifically. Several studies—using the Employment Opportunities Pilot Project Survey of Firms (EOPP), the National Longitudinal Survey of Youth (NLSY), and company-specific data—have found that on-the-job training has a positive and significant impact on wages, despite controls for a variety of employee and labor market characteristics. However, these studies are not of community college–provided contract training, so there is a limit to the applicability (Dougherty & Bakia, 1999).

5. Small business *assistance* involves providing owners and managers of small and medium-sized businesses with advice and training in such areas as management and personnel practices, marketing, finance, government contract procurement, introduction of new production technologies and work practices, compliance with new government regulations, and training of employees (Grubb et al., 1997, pp. 6–7; Hernandez-Gantes et al., 1996; Katsinas & Lacey, 1989, pp. 34–35; Lynch et al., 1991, pp. 35, 41; Palmer, 1990, pp. 14–15). Small business *incubation*, meanwhile, encompasses all the business services already mentioned but focuses on firms that are just emerging or even still in gestation. Besides providing business advice, business incubators often also provide low-cost space and administrative support for the first few months or years of a new firm's life (Hernandez-Gantes et al., 1996, pp. 4–5, 20, 31, 36; National Business Incubation Association, 1992, pp. 1, 59, 72–74). Finally, *technology transfer* both overlaps with, and diverges from, assistance and incubation efforts. While including the provision of advice on new production techniques to owners and managers of new firms, it also comprises the training of line employees.

6. In addition, in the early 1990s, about 7 percent of community colleges were operating advanced technology centers (ATCs), helping small and medium-sized firms keep track of new production technologies and work practices, trying the innovations in factory-like facilities on the community college campus, and then introducing them into the workplace (Ernst & Johnson, 1991, p. 24; Hinckley, 1997, p. 1; Lynch et al., 1991, pp. 35, 41; Smith, 1991, p. 20). Since the early 1990s, however, ATC's apparently have been losing their function of demonstrating and testing new production techniques for small business. Community colleges found that the costs of keeping ATCs equipped with up-to-date equipment was prohibitive and that small business people were primarily interested in advice on finance, marketing, and similar topics.

# REFERENCES

Adkins, D. (1996). *A decade of success: 10th anniversary survey of business incubators.* Athens, OH: National Business Incubation Association.

American Association of Community Colleges. (1993). *The workforce training imperative: Meeting the training needs of the nation.* Washington, DC: Author. (ERIC Document Reproduction Service No. ED 358 878)

Bosworth, B. (1999). *Unpublished tabulations from the 1998 survey of state-funded, employer-focused job training programs.* Belmont, MA: Regional Technology Strategies.

Boyd-Beauman, F., & Piland, W. E. (1983, November). Illinois, Arizona find great resources in colleges. *Community College Journal, 54,* 18–20.

Bragg, D. D., & Jacobs, J. (1991). *A conceptual framework for evaluating community college customized training programs* (MDS-175). Berkeley, CA: National Center for Research in Vocational Education.

Brown, D. K. (1995). *Degrees of control: A sociology of educational expansion and occupational credentialism,* New York: Teachers College Press.

Burger, L. T. (1984, November). The progress of partners. *Community College Journal, 55,* 36–39.

California State Job Training Coordinating Council. (1998). *Road atlas for preparing California's workforce.* Sacramento: Author.

Carmichael, J. B. (1991). Meeting small business needs through Small Business Development Centers. In G. Waddell (Ed.), *Economic and workforce development* (New Directions for Community Colleges, No. 75, pp. 25–30). San Francisco: Jossey-Bass.

Carnevale, A. P., Johnson, N. C., & Edwards, A. R., (1998, April 10). Performance-based appropriations: Fad or wave of the future? *Chronicle of Higher Education,* p. B6.

Cohen, A. M., & Brawer, F. B. (1996). *The American community college* (3rd ed.). San Francisco: Jossey-Bass.

Collins, R. (1979). *The credential society.* New York: Academic Press.

Cutler, E. (1984). Open for business. *Community College Journal, 55,* 28–30.

Derry, W. (1997). Interview by Kevin Dougherty with Auto Tech Coordinator, Broward Community College. Ft. Lauderdale, FL.

Dougherty, K. J. (1994). *The contradictory college: The conflicting origins, outcomes, and futures of the community college.* Albany: State University of New York Press.

Dougherty, K. J., with the assistance of Bakia, M. F. (1999). *The new economic-development role of the community college: Final report to the Sloan Foundation.* New York: Columbia University, Teacher's College Community College Research Center.

Dougherty, K. J., & Bakia, M. F. (2000). Community colleges and contract training: Content, origins, and impacts. *Teachers College Record, 102* 197–243.

Dozier, K. E. (1996, June/July). Ed>Net: The California community college approach to economic development. *Community College Journal, 66,* 15–18.

Ernst, C., & Johnson, R. (1991, October/November). Planning and developing and ATC. *Community College Journal, 61,* 22–25.

Florida State Board of Community Colleges. (1998). *The Florida community college system: A strategic plan for the millennium, 1998–2003.* Tallahassee: Author.

Florida State Department of Education. (1999a). *Workforce development education funding formula system.* Tallahassee, FL: Author. URL: www.firn.edu/doe/fetpip/funding.htm

Florida State Department of Education. (1999b). *Workforce education and outcome information services.* Tallahassee, FL: Author. URL: www.firn.edu/doc/fetpip/weois.htm

Frazis, H. J., Gittleman, M, Horrigan, M., & Joyce, M. (1997). Formal and informal training: Evidence from a matched employee-employer survey. *Advances in the Study of Entrepreneurship, Innovation, and Economic Growth, 9,* 47–82.

Grubb W. N. (1991). The decline of community college transfer rates: Evidence from national longitudinal surveys. *Journal of Higher Education, 62*(2), 194–217.

Grubb, W. N. (1996). *Working in the middle.* San Francisco: Jossey-Bass.

Grubb, W. N. (1998). *Learning and earning in the middle: The economic benefits of subbaccalaureate education.* New York: Columbia University, Teachers College, Community College Research Center.

Grubb, W. N., Badway, N., Bell, D., Bragg, D., & Russman, M. (1997). *Workforce, economic, and community development: The changing landscape of the "entrepreneurial" community college.* Berkeley: University of California, National Center for Research in Vocational Education.

Hernandez-Gantes, V. M., Sorensen, R. P., & Nieri, A. H. (1996). *Fostering entrepreneurship through business incubation: The role and prospects of postsecondary vocational-technical education: Report 1. Survey of business incubator clients and managers* (MDS-893). Berkeley: University of California, National Center for Research in Vocational Education.

Hershey, A. M., Silverberg, M. K., & Haimson, J. (1999). *Expanding options for students: Report to Congress on the national evaluation of school-to-work implementation.* Princeton, NJ: Mathematica Policy Research.

Hershey, A. M., Silverberg, M. K., Owens, T., & Husely, L. K. (1998). *Focus for the future: The final report of the national tech-prep evaluation.* Princeton, NJ: Mathematica Policy Research.

Hinckley, R. C. (1997). *Planning and developing the advanced technology center.* Waco, TX: National Coalition of Advanced Technology Centers.

Illinois Community College Board. (1987). *Follow-up study of students who completed community occupational programs during fiscal years 1983–1985.* Springfield, IL: Author. ERIC . . . ED 282 614

Illinois Community College Board. (1998). *Operating budget appropriation and supporting technical data for the Illinois public community college system, fiscal year 1999.* Springfield, IL: Author.

Katsinas, S. G., & Lacey, V. A. (1989). *Community colleges and economic development: Models of institutional effectiveness.* Washington, DC: American Association of Community Colleges.

Krueger, A., & Rouse, C. (1996). *The effect of workplace education on earnings, turnover, and job performance.* Princeton, NJ: Princeton University, Center for Economic Policy Studies.

Lynch, R., Palmer, J. C., & Grubb, W. N. (1991). *Community college involvement in contract training and other economic development activities* (MDS-379). Berkeley: University of California, National Center for Research in Vocational Education.

Maryland State Board for Community Colleges. (1988). *Maryland community colleges: 1987 Program Evaluations*. Annapolis: Author. ERIC ED 295 699

Melville, J. G., & Chmura, T. J. (1991). Strategic alignment of community colleges and state economic development. In G. Waddell (Ed.), *Economic and Workforce Development* (New Directions for Community Colleges, No. 75, pp. 7–15). San Francisco: Jossey-Bass.

National Business Incubation Association. (1992). *The state of the business incubation industry, 1991*. Athens, OH: Author.

National Governors' Association. (1999). *A comprehensive look at state-funded, employer-focused job training programs*. Washington, DC: Author.

Orr, M. T. (1999). *Community college and secondary school collaboration on workforce development and educational reform: A close look at four community colleges*. Unpublished paper, Columbia University, Teachers College.

Palmer, J. C. (1990). *How do community colleges serve business and industry? A review of issues discussed in the literature*. Washington, DC: American Association of Community Colleges Document Reproduction Service. (ERIC ED 319 443)

Perin, D. P. (1998). *Curriculum and pedagogy to integrate occupational and academic instruction in the community college*. New York: Columbia University, Teachers College, Community College Research Center.

Shavit, Y., & Mueller, W. (1999). *Vocational secondary education: Where diversion and where safety net?* Paper presented to the 1999 annual meeting of the American Sociological Association, Chicago, IL.

Sheldon, M. S. (1982). *Statewide longitudinal study: Report on academic year 1978–1981, Part 5*. Los Angeles: Pierce College. ERIC ED 217 917

Silverberg, M. K., Haimson, J., & Hershey, A. M. (1998). *Building blocks for a future school-to-work system: Early national implementation results*. Princeton, NJ: Mathematical Policy Research.

Silverberg, M. K., & Hershey, A. M. (1995). *The emergence of tech-prep at the state and local levels*. Princeton, NJ: Mathematical Policy Research.

Smith, E. B. (1991, October/November). Responding to industry demands: Advanced technology centers. *Community College Journal, 61*, 18–21.

Texas Higher Education Coordinating Board. (1999). *Public junior colleges 1998–1999 biennium, basis of legislative appropriations*. Austin: Author. URL: www.thecd.state.tx.us/divisions/finance/jrcolrates.htm

US Bureau of the Census. (1998). *Statistical abstract of the United States, 1998*. Washington, DC: U.S. Government Printing Office.

Van Horn, C., Fichtner, A., Dautrich, K., Hartley, T, & Hebbar, L. (1998). *First-year interim report, evaluation of the workforce development partnership program: Executive summary*. New Brunswick, NJ: Rutgers University, Heldrich Center for Workforce Development.

Winter, G. M., & Fadale, L. (1990). Impact of economic development programs in SUNY community colleges: A study of contract courses. *Community Services Catalyst, 20*(2), 3–7.

Zeiss, T., et al. (1997). *Developing the world's best workforce*. Washington, DC: American Association of Community Colleges, Community College Press.

## Chapter 8

# State Dual Credit Policy and Its Implications for Community Colleges: Lessons from Missouri for the 21st Century

*Anthony G. Girardi and Robert B. Stein*

For many observers, the late 20th century has been a time for rethinking and revising many long-established and indispensable institutions. Yet the form and characteristics of such fundamental institutions as family and civic life, government and religion, work, and education have resisted adaptation in the face of sweeping technological and economic transitions. Their controversial nature notwithstanding, such observations are particularly piercing to the world of education because the American educational system seems resistant to comprehensive reform efforts (Tyack & Cuban, 1995). Perennial reform efforts and constant critiques seem to only reinforce education's sheer immutability. As Boyer argued: "Though the lockstep has loosened a bit, the patterns of the past remain entrenched. . . . Society pays homage to habit, and, in education, habits are perhaps most pervasive. The rhythm of the academic pattern stirs the soul for a lifetime; people have trouble envisioning education in any form other than that which it has always taken" (cited in Maeroff, 1983, p. viii).

This intransigence is partly due to the common impression that the structure of the educational system constitutes a consistent and rational whole. Nevertheless, despite outward appearances, neither the evolution nor the organization of the American educational system has ever been wholly coherent or systematic. The structure of the contemporary American educational system, premised on an age-based segregation of students, is a piecemeal amalgam of curricular elements. The modern American educational framework consists of a series of stages, from preschool through the elementary and middle grades to high school and beyond, which do not constitute a meaningful whole (Hodgkinson, 1985, 1999). Boundaries between traditional sets of grades or levels are nowhere more pronounced than between graduation from high school and matriculation into college. Until recently, any meaningful relationship between high school and college occurred more by chance than design.

The K-16 movement has sought to redress these structural discontinuities by promoting high standards of achievement for all students. These standards will result in a seamless transition between high school and college. The movement itself is an acknowledgment of the barriers between elementary, secondary, and postsecondary levels. K-16 initiatives in a number of states have identified, as did, for example, the California Education Round Table, the following priorities: "aligning high school graduation standards with expectations of college freshmen . . . [intensifying] the delivery of services designed to prepare students, . . . [and strengthening] the transfer process among and within higher education sectors" (Edgert & Polkinghorn, 1999). Among the reasons for secondary-postsecondary collaboration is the recognition that too few recent high school graduates are ready for college or work (Tafel & Eberhart, 1999, p. 5). At the same time many students are ready to advance to college work before high school graduation. K-16 initiatives have emerged to address the reality that students proceed at different paces through the educational system. These efforts have emphasized high school and college collaboration, encouraging increased connectivity between the two levels and allowing students to advance through the system in a more sensible and appropriate way.

Partly in response to such priorities, colleges and universities throughout the nation are providing students with increased opportunities to earn college credit while still in high school. They do this by a variety of means. The College Board's Advanced Placement (AP) and College Level Examination Program (CLEP) programs and the International Baccalaureate (IB) degree program are national programs that provide high school students with advanced college credit opportunities. AP and CLEP offer credit by examination that is accepted at many colleges and universities. After matriculation to a college, students who score high enough on a national AP or CLEP examination are granted college credit based on each college's acceptance policies. Like the AP program, the IB program offers students a complete educational program, including uniform curriculum and teacher preparation, leading to a standardized examination (available on-line at http://www.ibo.org/ibo/english/diploma.htm). In the case of dual credit or concurrent enrollment programs, by contrast, there is no national model or standardized examination. Rather, high school students enroll in a single class and, on successful completion, receive both high school and transcripted college credit.

The broad category of "programs whose anticipated outcomes are articulation, and enhanced student achievement through taking college classes while still in high school" is known as concurrent enrollment (Harkins, 1998, p. 56). Harkins (1998) succinctly stated the range of possibilities in configuring concurrent enrollment programs: "There are various ways of structuring such partnerships. The high school student may go to a campus, the college faculty may go to the high school or the high school students may be taught by their high school teacher in the high school" (p. 56). According to Greenberg (1989), "[T]here are currently a variety of concurrent enrollment models, each with its own student selection criteria, ranging from open access to all students to more restrictive requirements negotiated between local school boards and cooperating colleges" (p. 12). For this reason, the nomenclature of concurrent enrollment programs is not uniform or ubiquitous. Concurrent enrollment programs go by different names, exhibit some variation in program characteristics, and are intended to serve various purposes. Moreover, the distinctions between such terms as *dual credit* and *concurrent enrollment* are thus not everywhere consistent. Generally speaking, concurrent enrollment is a genus of programs that include dual credit, and dual credit itself is sometimes also referred to as "dual enrollment" and "college in the high school." As a matter of convenience and clarity in this essay, the term *dual credit* refers to the delivery to high school students of a single course that, on successful completion, results in both high school and college credit. Moreover, as the term is used in this chapter, dual credit courses are normally offered at the high school during the schoolday, with the help of high school faculty who have adjunct faculty status with the postsecondary institution offering the collegiate credit.

The particular form of concurrent enrollment programs known as dual credit programs or dual credit partnerships is of particular interest in the policy context because of the unique characteristics that distinguish it from other forms of concurrent enrollment. Because dual credit courses are typically taught in the high school and by high school teachers, the potential exists for programs to bear little resemblance to on-campus offerings and to retain little connection to the on-campus departmental administrative structure. As dual credit partnership programs proliferate, state policy can either enhance or weaken quality, access, and credit transferability; policy can either widen or close the gaps experienced by high school students in the transition to college. Furthermore, even though dual credit has existed for many years, the escalated impact of dual credit programs demands that state and system policy makers evaluate and develop dual credit policy. One reason is that more and more dual credit students are earning credit from one college and seeking to transfer it to another. Given the capacity for heterogeneity in program quality, many states are seeking to develop an appropriate policy framework supporting dual credit in transfer. Such a framework can help policy makers, administrators, and program directors to address many of the apparent anomalies that dual credit presents to a higher-education system.

While dual credit's philosophical origins lie in its value in creating a seamless transition between high school and college—such as by motivating high school students to continue on to college and by bridging the differences between the cultures and curricula of secondary and higher education—programs also have the following benefits (Stein & Girardi, 1999, p. 87):

• Enhancement of the high school curriculum
• Provision to teachers of professional development opportunities

- An increase in access to college-level resources
- Integration of high school and collegiate-level experiences
- Reinforcement of the need to be adequately prepared for college
- Utilization of a familiar environment
- Shortening of time to degree

Because community colleges address the need for a transitional sequence from high school to college, the development of these institutions can be seen as a consequence of the same impulse that spurred the development of dual credit programs. Considered in these terms, not only the history, but also the future, of community colleges and the development of dual credit programs are intimately linked. According to Cohen and Brawer (1996), most community colleges began as "upward extensions of secondary schools" (p. 8). In a manner reminiscent of modern justifications for dual credit programs, turn-of-the-century educators looked on community colleges as a way to shift early postsecondary education away from the universities (p. 6). These earlier educators envisioned doing away with the rigid barriers between high school and college and allowing students to proceed at their own pace through the array of credit requirements for admission to universities (see for example, Storr, 1966, p. 120).

While the proposals to fully relegate the function of instruction in the first two years of college to junior colleges never fully materialized, community colleges nevertheless formed as a result of the hopes they expressed. Since many contemporary dual credit initiatives mirror these earlier arguments, the philosophical origins of dual credit date at least to the beginnings of community colleges. Moreover, community colleges fill many roles, a reality that makes them particularly apt providers of dual credit. Community college missions are shaped by basic commitments, including "a commitment to serving all segments of society through an open-access admissions policy that offers equal and fair treatment to all students; a commitment to a comprehensive educational program; a commitment to serving its community as a community-based institution of higher education; and, a commitment to teaching" (Vaughan, 1995, p. 3). Each of these basic commitments affects the development of dual credit programs within the two-year sector.

As community colleges have evolved into comprehensive institutions, the delivery of general education and other lower-division coursework for the purposes of transfer to four-year colleges and universities has remained a major element of their missions. Inasmuch as community colleges formed as a result of an awareness of the need for a meaningful and effective transition from high school to college, dual credit programs have exhibited a similar development. Moreover, it is against the backdrop of community colleges as providers of general education that the rise of dual credit programs among community colleges should be seen, because, like community colleges themselves, dual credit programs arose in part to provide general education credit in preparation for college.

Such programs were well suited to the community colleges, which saw in them a suitable instrument for fulfilling a foundational and highly traditional mission.

## CHARACTERISTICS AND ORIGINS OF DUAL CREDIT PROGRAMS

The structure of dual credit programs is not uniform beyond being institutionally centered and based on some form of agreement with school districts or schools. Dual credit programs are not broadly systematic. Throughout the nation, it appears, practices mirror the diversity of structural and administrative practices, which, for instance, Vogt (1991) found in her study of dual enrollment articulation practices among Virginia community colleges and public schools. Vogt found diversity on a number of dimensions of program administration: responsibility for program administration was assigned to a wide range of community college positions; faculty at different institutions participated in course-related planning to varying degrees; written guidelines were usually, though not necessarily, developed; and enrollment admissions criteria were often the sole domain of the high schools (pp. 137–138).

The very beginnings of dual credit programs were spontaneous and sporadic and cut across educational sectors. Individual programs arose in response to perceived needs for innovative partnerships. According to a report by Edmonds, Mercurio, and Bonesteel (1998), Syracuse University's Project Advance "originated 25 years ago at the behest of seven Syracuse area high school principals and superintendents who met with Syracuse University staff to explore the possibility of developing a program to challenge high school seniors, many of whom had completed all of the requirements for high school graduation . . . by the end of the eleventh grade" (p. 1). Project Advance now serves 120 high schools in five states. Thus, it began as a program separate from state sponsorship and oversight yet is prolific and "regional in scope" (p. 1).

Dual credit also has a long tradition in Missouri. According to its director (Pam Mueller, personal communication, August 12, 1999), St. Louis University's "1818" program dates to 1959, when it was piloted with St. Louis University High School to provide college English credit. At its outset, the express purpose of this program was to encourage high school students to graduate from high school. At the same time, the program was intended to shorten students' time in school: the original name of the program, "1-8-1-8," was an attempt to convey the intent that the program should subtract one year from the first eight years of (elementary) school and one year from the next eight years of schooling. Because of this broad vision, the program can be seen as part of the larger K-16 movement.

Though a number of institutions throughout the country have provided dual credit continuously for the past several decades, the 1980s witnessed a conspicuous proliferation in dual credit partnership programs. This proliferation has been partially attributed to the work of the Carnegie Foundation for the Advancement of Teaching and the Carnegie Commission on Higher Education. In 1971, the commission published the report, *Less Time, More Options: Education beyond the High School*, which urged educators to reevaluate the lockstep mode of educational advancement to higher education (Postsecondary Education Planning Commission, 1997, p. 12). In 1982, the Carnegie Foundation for the Advancement of Teaching helped to organize the first national conference of state school superintendents and college and university presidents, and in 1983 it published a report highlighting some of the dual credit partnerships then in progress (Maeroff, 1983, p. vii).

In Missouri, two of the largest dual credit providers are four-year institutions that began their programs in the 1980s. The University of Missouri-St. Louis's Advanced Credit Program began in 1986 and by 1999 had grown to serve 60 high schools (University of Missouri–St. Louis, 1999). University of Missouri-Kansas City's (UMKC) High School/College Program began in 1979 as a partnership with five high schools in two districts; it continued to grow throughout its history, and by 1997 UMKC's program included more than 55 high schools in 42 districts (University of Missouri–Kansas City, 1998, p. 3).

Andrews and Marshall (1991) document the beginnings of a program at an Illinois community college. The program exists on a very local level, beginning in 1986 when the "administration at Marquette High School in Ottawa, Illinois, decided to experiment by offering its honor students a challenge seldom offered to high school students in the state. Sophomores and juniors were given the opportunity to enroll in college courses offered by nearby Illinois Valley Community College during their junior and senior years" (p. 47).

Other illustrations of early community college dual credit programs include Kingsborough Community College's (in Brooklyn, New York) College Now Program, which began in 1984 in four high schools (Wilbur et al., 1988, p. 22). The Florida dual enrollment program is a state-mandated program in which "[a]ll state-funded community colleges in Florida are required by legislative act to develop a plan with local school districts that allows high school students to enroll concurrently in college courses. The legislation mandates that the courses be taught at the high school site" (Greenberg 1989, p. 32).

Kiger and Johnson (1997), citing the Ohio Board of Regents (1994), argue that dual credit programs are "fundamental to the functional mission of the community college's mission and have become a mandated service expectation of some community colleges in the United States" (p. 687). Even so, such programs, particularly those based in the community college sector, exhibit a wide range of explicit purposes. For example, the National School-College Partnership (NSCP) Database (1995) is a database of college–high school partnerships. Though by no means exhaustive and only most recently updated in 1995, the database contains information on concurrent enrollment programs, namely, "programs which offer college courses for high school students as a primary focus of the program," at community colleges in a number of states. The purposes reported by community colleges for their concurrent enrollment programs are strikingly varied. These purposes range from giving students "an opportunity to explore fields of study before making a financial commitment to them," to providing students with the "opportunity to experience college classes and have access to the recreational and cultural activities of the college" to targeting, "moderately achieving junior and senior high school students . . . , encouraging and motivating them to complete high school and attend college." The NSCP Database also affords a rough picture of the scope of typical community college programs: all but 3 of the 92 recorded programs serve less than 30 students. For this reason, and because of the limited number of high schools reported as partner high schools, the database also suggests that the local nature of school college partnerships is especially emblematic of those which include community colleges.

Clearly then, there is a precedent for dual credit activity among two-year and four-year, public and independent institutions. Dual credit program delivery cuts across sectors. Nevertheless, institutions are motivated to provide dual credit for different reasons. The variety of purposes ascribed to dual credit is the basis for a good deal of the tensions that dual credit engenders, particularly those which exist between the two- and four-year sectors.

An examination of dual credit is particularly germane to community colleges because it is in partial fulfillment of their unique missions that dual credit has become an important program among community colleges and community college systems. Dual credit programs provide an effective means for community colleges to perform a variety of traditional missions. Nevertheless, dual credit programs can be difficult to harmonize with the complexities of community college administration and politics. This has as much to do with dual credit's challenge to traditional boundaries—between secondary and postsecondary levels of education, between cultures, between curricula—as it does with its popularity and desirability among so many constituencies. Dual credit programs not only challenge traditional boundaries between various educational sectors but also challenge the boundaries between the diverse roles within community colleges.

Although the very beginnings of dual credit programs are attributable to innovations which occurred at the institutional level, encouraged in part by the work of the Carnegie Foundation for the Advancement of Teaching and the Carnegie Commission on Higher Education, the pronounced expansion of dual credit programs across the country is a consequence of a number of impulses. For one, as we have seen, dual credit assists community colleges in fulfilling many important missions. At the same time, declining community college enrollments, low test scores and high dropout rates in secondary schools, were among the factors contributing to the "growing recognition among community college leaders that they must not only actively recruit high school students, but also collaborate with high schools to prepare students to succeed in college" (Mabry, 1989, p. 48). The most typical manner of collaboration between community colleges and high schools has been dual credit programs (p. 49). Thus, "the number of articulated programs continues to increase and the breadth of collaboration and cooperation continues to expand" in recognition of the benefits of community college-high school partnerships (p. 53).

Though dual credit programs are typically institution based, a number of states have policies or legislation that support or encourage dual credit activity. The pronounced expansion and recent prominence of dual credit programs are also largely a consequence of legislated funding incentives. State funding of dual credit programs typically takes one or a combination of two basic forms. In one form, legislation simply allows dual credit students to be counted for state aid purposes both as full-time secondary students and for their hours enrolled as college students. Such an arrangement allows multiple source or duplicative state funding for individual students, with public colleges and high school districts receiving state allocations for students' high school enrollment. Under such circumstances, students are responsible for paying discounted tuition. For instance, in Florida, "students enrolled in community college or university dual enrollment instruction . . . may be included in calculations of full-time equivalent student memberships for basic programs for grades 9 through 12 by a district school board. Such students may also be calculated as the proportional shares of full-time equivalent enrollments they generate for the community college or university conducting the dual enrollment instruction" (Sherry, 1998, pp. 6–7). This form of funding for dual credit, of course, takes place only in states that use some form of enrollment-based formula for funding postsecondary institutions. In a second form, state funding supports dual credit programs by reimbursing students for college tuition, either directly or via the institution or school district.

The assortment of motives behind dual credit program expansion suggests that it is a response to broader forces affecting both higher education generally, as well as community colleges specifically. A 1997 report on trends facing California community colleges highlights some of the economic issues facing dual credit programs in community colleges nationally in the 21st century. The report suggests that community colleges will have to intensify outsourcing efforts as well as face decreased funding and increased accountability and state-level controls (McIntyre, 1997). If dual credit programs are understood as a means of outsourcing—both for labor and for facilities—then program expansion and states' concomitant attempts to enhance program accountability emerge as part of larger trends confronting community colleges. Furthermore, dual credit programs thus seem to have arisen as a means for colleges to acquire state resources in an environment characterized by Cohen and Brawer (1996) as one of increased complexity of state reimbursement patterns accompanied by an increased proportion of funds coming from the state (p. 141). In other words, since a number of states provide funding incentives for dual credit programs, dual credit has spread partly as a result of what Cohen and Brawer describe as a shifting of major support for community colleges from local to state tax revenues (p. 150).

Dual credit programs not only potentially reduce instructional costs, they reduce costs associated with student services and physical plant operation and maintenance. In his critique of dual credit courses in English composition, Schwalm (1991) notes the compelling financial incentives—for institutions, for states, for students—associated with dual credit programs:

> Especially for tax-supported institutions, the financial incentives are enormous. The co-operating college (public or private) receives tuition and credit hours for doing virtually nothing: no classrooms, no supplies, no clerical support, and often no instructor's stipend. . . . The state subsidizes one year of literacy education rather than two. The financial incentives are complemented by many students' delight with this strategy for avoiding freshman composition. (p. 52)

Thus market forces themselves are behind dual credit's growth: it is simply less expensive to provide than on-campus instruction. These pressures have far reaching implications for community colleges, affecting missions, programs, and fundamental objectives. A recent report (Cohen, Rifkin, Lee, McKinney, & Yamasaki, 1998) outlines these pressures:

> [D]windling revenues combined with rising operational costs, and a student population that seeks an ever-greater variety of institutionally based services and programs . . . exert exceptional pressure on community colleges to rethink complex and multifaceted institutional missions and alter the way they do business. . . . The pressures for accountability and assurances of a quality educational product are also tied to the economic forces at work on the community college. . . . The multiple missions of community colleges make it difficult to cope with apprehension about economic challenges, for example, by reassessing priorities, downsizing, outsourcing, or borrowing other tactics from the business world. The ramifications of such actions go straight to the heart of a fundamental objective of most community colleges: open access. (p. 36)

Faced with multiple and often contradictory missions, then, many community colleges struggle to maintain a coherent identity. This identity crisis is perhaps most pronounced in the tension between providing both collegiate-level general education while at the same time providing remediation for students ill-prepared to do collegiate-level work. Such identity crises are also characteristic of dual credit programs, and perhaps the most damaging of the unintended consequences of allowing dual credit to flourish outside of an effective policy context. Maintaining the distinctness of separate missions, when desirable, can be problematic. The challenge for administrators and policy makers in designing effective dual credit programs is to clearly define in policy and program structures the diverse purposes associated with collegiate-level instruction in contrast to remediation.

Dual credit programs have the potential both to enhance community colleges' efforts to fulfill their mission of providing access and to effect substantial cost savings by shortening time to degree and reducing tuition. Its potential benefits, however, fail to be realized when dual credit is impossible to transfer or does not fit into a coherent academic program on campus and effectively reduce time to degree.

## STATE POLICY APPROACHES

While continuously running institution-centered dual credit programs date as far back as the late 1950s, enabling legislation and state-level or system-level programs are a more recent phenomenon. The development of state concurrent enrollment programs and policies, inclusive of more specifically dual credit programs, has been undertaken by the states in distinct and diverse ways. A 1997 survey by the State Higher Education Executive Officers suggests the wide range of approaches to concurrent enrollment policy taken by states (cited in Russell, 1998, p. 90). The report indicates that while some states are highly engaged in the process of concurrent enrollment delivery, including dual credit, others set forth only broad-based parameters for what is viewed as fundamentally an institution-school district relationship. Policy makers in some states have no interest in dual credit and other concurrent enrollment activity. In still other states, dual credit is just beginning to capture the interest of policy makers.

States' approaches to dual credit policy are distinguished from one another along a variety of dimensions, including for instance, financial incentives for offering programs, course location, student eligibility criteria, faculty qualifications, and program administration and evaluation. Because of the plethora of approaches, its variety of purposes, and the diversity of environments in which it exists, there are very few consistent characteristics of dual credit. Programs exist in most states, yet comparatively few have substantial policies to govern them. Nevertheless, states provide the context for the development of dual credit policy.

A study by the Education Commission of the States (1997) identified 11 states (Colorado, Florida, Georgia, Maine, Massachusetts, Minnesota, New Jersey, Ohio, Utah, Washington, and Wisconsin) as having "comprehensive" programs defined as follows: "Minimal or no cost to students, credit received applies towards high school graduation and postsecondary institutions, few course restrictions"; and 5 states (Arizona, Arkansas, Indiana, Kansas, and Louisiana) with limited programs in which "[s]tudents pay tuition costs of postsecondary classes, more academic credit restrictions, stringent criteria on eligible courses." The Oregon Early Options study (Oregon University System, 1998) provides another prominent and relatively recent discursive survey of states' dual credit policies, statutes, and funding mechanisms. With 31 state higher-education executive officers responding, 23 states indicated having "programs involving dual (high school/college) enrollment, concurrent enrollment, and/or dual credit programs" (p. 22). Reisberg (1998) estimates that colleges in at least 38 states have formal "dual enrollment" programs which allow high school students to take college courses while accumulating credits toward high school graduation.

State and system boards, then, are in various stages of dual credit policy development. In a number of states, dual credit is not perceived as an issue worthy of attention by state or system boards; in other states, boards and representative bodies are meeting to iron out and formulate policy. Aside from error attributable to differential response rates, the range of estimates of states' involvement arises from the distinctions in operational definitions of "concurrent enrollment" programs. This variety is a function of the diverse approaches states have taken vis-à-vis dual credit, the variety of approaches that have flourished independently of state involvement, and the reality that dual credit policy emanates from the state, system, and institutional levels. Even so, it is clear that dual credit is something in which many states are involved, to whatever extent. Nevertheless, though definitional distinctions convey some sense of states' policy postures respecting dual credit, they provide no information concerning the magnitude of a state's dual credit activity, as expressed in such quantitative terms as number of students involved or credit hours generated. Indeed, magnitude is not necessarily a function of the comprehensiveness of state policy or legislative intervention; dual credit programs exist in a number of states that have no state or system dual credit policies. Thus, while state legislatures and policy makers have adopted a variety of stances with respect to dual credit, the prevalence of dual credit programs in a state is not solely a function of state-level attention. As we have seen, institution-based dual credit activity may advance quite independently of state, or even system, policy involvement.

Nevertheless, though state legislation and policy may not specifically address dual credit, the distinctive development of practices and policies related to concurrent enrollment is largely a function of the unique policy environments and educational landscapes of individual states. Indeed, the phenomenon of dual credit is so oriented to states that semantic distinctions between models of concurrent enrollment correspond to state boundaries. Thus, for example, what is known as "dual credit" in Missouri is typically called "college in the high school" in other states, such as Minnesota.

In a context in which dual credit partnership programs can flourish independently of effective oversight and broad state or system-wide quality control, there is vast potential, not only for inconsistencies in dual credit program quality, but also for a range of problems associated with such fundamental matters as access and transfer. This potential is only magnified when state incentives augment the host of impulses driving the proliferation of dual credit. When considered as a public policy issue, then, the most fundamental question to ask about dual credit is, "What is its purpose?" If state, system, or institutional policy makers can clearly establish the purposes for dual credit programs, they can sidestep much of the controversy over its credibility, portability, and accessibility.

Clearly, dual credit has numerous interwoven purposes and responds to a variety of perceived needs. Yet embedded in this diversity of purposes and benefits are some basic tensions. Indeed, many of the objectives advanced for dual credit programs are mutually incompatible. In light of dual credit's variance from education's traditional organizational structure and its divergence from more traditional modes of curriculum, instruction, and program administration, this incompatibility only reinforces the central importance of recognizing and defining the purpose of any state, system, or institutional level dual credit program. The tensions between dual credit's purposes emerge because institutions necessarily engage in dual credit for many reasons beyond the academic purposes of the programs: it is easy; it has the potential to generate considerable income with very little investment; it is a way to recruit students; it is popular among colleges' local constituencies.

Particularly as it has evolved in Missouri, the most fundamental tension in dual credit's multiple purposes involves a philosophical controversy over which students should participate in dual credit programs. On one hand, the notion that dual credit can motivate students to persist to college suggests that dual credit programs should include students of various academic skill levels, such as an average or marginally superior students, or students who may not otherwise choose to attend college. As we have seen, many programs located at community colleges exist for the express purpose of providing encouragement and motivation to low and moderately achieving high school students. At the same time, other prominent rationales for dual credit suggest that dual credit opportunities are more appropriate for college bound or otherwise higher achieving students only.

Because the collegiate nature of the dual credit programming can be associated with the college readiness of the students in dual credit courses, and because course quality—conceived in terms of the extent to which courses match on-campus offerings—constitutes a touchstone of course transferability, this tension can be framed as a dispute over access and transferability. As such, it is one which is especially salient for community colleges. Not only does it point up the reality that community college programs can be philosophically distinct from programs at other institutions; it also highlights the fact that points of view with respect to this debate are typically demarcated along sector boundaries. The tension between dual credit as a means of enhancing access on one hand, and the need to support dual credit in transfer through state policy on the other, constitutes one of the core problems associated with allowing different models of dual credit to exist within a single policy framework. Lambert and Mercurio (1986) articulate the key problem:

Currently there are no explicitly defined criteria to help distinguish programs that are well-administered from those that may be haphazard. Thus, as high school-college cooperative programs proliferate, college deans, admissions officers, registrars and faculty advisers face the problem of evaluating fairly the college credits earned by high school students. They must decide whether to award students academic credit, exempt students from required courses, place students in advanced courses, or give students no recognition whatsoever. (p. 28)

Though this problem can be meaningfully addressed through state policy, access and transferability are at odds when restrictions on program entrance are used as indicators of program quality. Because some dual credit programs, particularly many located at the community colleges, target poorly and moderately achieving high school students, state initiatives to support quality by restricting access to students meeting certain, relatively high, eligibility requirements are perceived as both restricting access to college resources from whole categories of students and disproportionately penalizing community colleges.

Higher education policy makers in Missouri have recently reviewed and comprehensively revised the state's dual credit policy. Because other states are similar to Missouri in their experiences with dual credit and because many are just beginning to address potential problems through state policy, we offer Missouri as a case study of dual credit policy development.

## MISSOURI AS A CASE STUDY

### Background

Missouri's diverse higher education system balances the promotion of state policy with a rich tradition of local autonomy. The state is home to 18 public two-year campuses, 13 public four-year campuses, and 26 major independent institutions. In fall 1998, the number of Missouri's full-time undergraduate, graduate, and professional enrollments was over 198,000. While separate boards exist for each institution, the Missouri Coordinating Board for Higher Education (CBHE) serves as the state's planning agency, assuming major responsibility for the development of state policy for higher education, the recommendation of budgets for public institutions, and the distribution of regular reports to its general assembly, the governor, and the public concerning questions of access, efficiency, and quality.

Though dual credit programs had existed in Missouri institutions for decades, in 1990 Missouri's General Assembly passed legislation permitting high school students both to enroll in college-credit courses and, at the same time, to be counted as attending high school for state-aid purposes. At the time, dual credit was perceived to be an important vehicle by which adequately prepared students could make an efficient and effective transition from high school to college. Immediately, institutional interest and activity in dual credit increased and Missouri found itself in a policy void—with enabling legislation but no prior identification of dual credit in previous policies.

In the immediate wake of Missouri's 1990 legislation, the CBHE recognized the need for policy to ensure the quality and collegiate caliber of dual credit courses. Although general policies concerning off-campus instruction had been adopted by the board several years earlier, dual credit courses had never been addressed as a specific category. Initial policy discussions held by the CBHE in the early 1990s emphasized that dual credit course offerings were not meant to short-circuit the high school experience or to redress resource problems in secondary education. Rather, the board saw the awarding of high school and college credit as an administrative convenience, allowing students to meet high school graduation requirements and school districts to avoid the loss of funding based on average daily-attendance figures. Nevertheless, Missouri's initial board policy, approved in 1992, avoided the delineation of a clear purpose for dual credit.

During the discussions leading up to this policy, extensive debate centered around the degree to which policy should restrict, assess, and otherwise control dual credit programs. In the end, responding to institutional recommendations, the CBHE purposefully determined to set few explicit restrictions on the delivery of dual credit courses as well as to include no provisions for institutional accountability in its initial policy beyond putting institutions on notice that reports could be requested as needed. Consequently, the board chose to allow a laissez-faire environment, predicated on the goodwill and professionalism of institutions involved in dual credit program delivery. Thus, the broad-based 1992 guidelines focused exclusively on assuring program quality, mainly by calling for dual credit programs to duplicate on-campus programs in as many respects as possible. Missouri's first dual credit policy thus identified dual credit program quality in terms of its similarity to on-campus course work. The policy focused on the collegiate nature of course curriculum and assessment, faculty qualifications, and administrative and structural issues.

In Missouri equivalency to on-campus courses not only arose as the benchmark of dual credit program quality; it has also come to serve as the rationale for dual credit's transferability. Coordinating an environment in which more and more students enter college with transcripted dual credit, often seeking to transfer it later, many of Missouri's institutions became concerned not only with the quality of dual credit courses per se but also with ways to demonstrate dual credit's equivalency to on-campus course work. Yet throughout the decade of the 1990s, the question of dual credit occupied only a part of the larger transfer landscape. As the question of transfer came to the fore of state policy attention, Missouri's Coordinating Board for Higher Education began to sponsor annual state transfer conferences. Through the years, the subject of dual credit kindled abundant and increasingly heated debate at these conferences. While arguments were impassioned, they were driven primarily by emotion and speculation. Thus, with the intention of gaining a handle on the scope, magnitude, and programmatic aspects of dual credit, the board staff, working through chief academic officers of public and independent institutions, designed and distributed a survey of programs delivered during fiscal year (FY) 1996.

While the survey indicated forcefully the far-reaching extent of dual credit in the state, it also suggested that many institutions had only a weak grasp on quality control in their dual credit programs. Despite the 1992 dual credit policy, systemic incentives and Missouri's tolerant policy environment allowed casual and mediocre program practices. In many instances dual credit programs operated more as weapons of institutional competition than as instructional programs. The 1996 survey indicated that most dual credit students had no access to college resources, that dual credit courses often did not use the same syllabi as on-campus courses, and that many instructors were not qualified based on standards recommended by Missouri's regional accrediting body, the North Central Association.

By 1997–1998 a second state survey of dual credit programs at Missouri's two-year and four-year, public and independent institutions indicated that 34 Missouri institutions offered dual credit in high schools to an estimated (duplicated headcount) 41,000 students—an enrollment estimate representing approximately a 64 percent increase over that of only two years prior. The state's 1997–1998 survey of dual credit programs also indicated that while most activity was accounted for by the state's three largest programs, all of which are located at four-year institutions, Missouri's public two-year sector is prominent in the overall scheme of dual credit in the state.

Community colleges not only participate in dual credit provision and serve a sizable portion of Missouri students; community colleges in Missouri also fill a particular mission with respect to dual credit. Preliminary analysis of data collected in the Enhanced Missouri Student Achievement Study suggests that in the 1996–1996 academic year, about 56 percent of students receiving dual credit delivered by community colleges transferred that credit to a different institution upon graduation from high school. At the same time, this figure was about 79 percent for students receiving dual credit from a four-year institution. Community college dual credit programs, then, do not exist in a vacuum since overall (in 1996–1997), only about 33 percent of Missouri's dual credit students went on as first-time, full-time degree-seeking students to the same institution that initially awarded them dual credit. Community colleges are vital components of a network of higher education in the state in which dual credit programs perform a prominent role.

The 1997–1998 state survey confirmed that most dual credit in Missouri was taught in high schools by high school faculty with variable degrees of connection to on-campus programs; programs were often administered through continuing education departments. Over half the courses were taught in "mixed classes"—classes in which only some students take the course for college credit. Furthermore, there was considerable variability in such matters as the extent to which institutions established student eligibility requirements, required minimal teaching credentials, provided orientation programs for adjunct faculty, and afforded student access to college resources. In short, the inclusion of traditional quality assurance practices was variable. Because of their often tenuous connection to on-campus academic structures, and with 1,700 high school faculty serving as adjunct instructors, dual credit programs threatened to develop as "shadow operations."

In the late 1990s, the proliferation of programs, the awareness of imperfect compliance with Missouri's 1992 dual credit policy, and dangers of allowing dual credit programs to continue to exist outside the traditional structure of state higher education brought dual credit to the forefront of the state policy-making process. Missouri's policy framework permitted an overall disparity between policy and practice. As dual credit programs generated an ever greater number of credit hours, they emerged as a source of controversy both within and between institutional sectors.

For three years, Missouri policymakers sought to enhance dual credit as one form of advanced credit through a formal process of policy revision, working with institutional representatives in reconsidering the board's 1992 policy. Throughout this period, the board and its staff were at the center of an emotional debate between dual credit's enthusiastic promoters and vehement detractors. Open dialogue included discussions at statewide conferences and an iterative process of drafting and redrafting exploratory versions of a new policy. Contributions to and critiques of early drafts were sought from the state's secondary and postsecondary educational community. During this intense review process, strong opinions were expressed, symbolic of the great variability in the approaches of particular institutions and in the perceptions of the purposes of dual credit. Debate centered around the proper degree of comprehensiveness of a revised policy as the state struggled to identify ways of operationalizing program quality. Missouri's experience of a frank and open review process also exposed many of the anomalies and difficult issues presented by dual credit to a system of higher education.

## Some Salient Issues in Missouri

Even though dual credit in many states is transferred without controversy, in Missouri it has arisen as a vexing transfer issue. In spite of recent strides in state policy supporting transferability and the comprehensive portability of regular on-campus credit among public institutions, dual credit emerged as an obstacle to transferability and a threat to existing transfer agreements: the transfer of dual credit was not always seamless and supported by articulation. At least one of Missouri's most prominent independent institutions refused to accept dual credit in transfer. In Missouri, the uncertain transferability of dual credit reached the pinnacle of irony when it became clear that some students had transcripted dual credit from institutions to which they were refused admission upon graduation from high school. Quite apart from the ethics of not accepting one's own dual credit students as full-time students on campus, such cases point out how dual credit programs and on-campus programs might bear no necessary relationship to one another. The divergence between dual credit and on-campus admissions standards is one example of the often-anomalous nature of dual credit.

In spite of the continued efforts in Missouri higher education to ease transfer and to move toward a more thorough statewide "system" of higher education, questions persisted as to the extent to which the learning experiences in dual credit courses are equivalent to those of similar courses offered on college campuses. Primarily because many institutions viewed program quality as the litmus test for dual credit portability and transferability, Missouri sought to develop a uniform policy which would both embrace the diversity of approaches to dual credit as well as assert underlying principles of program quality. Though from the beginning of the process of policy revision, policy makers conceived of program quality in terms of program inputs, such as student eligibility and faculty qualifications, they were also eager to incorporate some guarantees of program quality in terms of assessable outputs. This approach to policy revision, emphasizing uniformity of inputs and measurability of outputs, proved a sizable challenge in light of the generally differing admissions selectivity of Missouri's two- and four-year sectors and the amount of dual credit transferred between them. Missouri's four-year institutions were anxious to see a policy specifically and comprehensively addressing the quality of measurable program inputs and outputs. On the other hand, Missouri's community college sector believed that dual credit should be viewed, and treated, no differently from any other credit originating at their institutions. This tension most often manifested itself in a dispute over whether or not to codify a distinction between dual credit and on-campus credit in the context of transfer.

Transcripted dual credit courses are not universally accepted as college credit. Moreover dual credit challenges transfer because, though it ostensibly facilitates student entrance, credit earned as dual credit may not bear a necessary relation to a coherent program on campus. In other words, dual credit may result neither in advanced standing in an academic program nor in a shortened time to degree. While dual credit programs provide great potential for minimizing the disconnect between the high school and college experience, in such cases dual credit represents simply another obstacle to credit transfer. Missouri focused attention on program quality because of quality's instrumental role in assuring dual credit transferability. Yet a crucial challenge to policy makers, of course, was in operationalizing quality. As with many educational programs, officials were constrained to use proxies for quality indicators and, by and large, relied on measures of inputs as measures of program quality. At the same time, state policy makers had to caution themselves against cavalierly judging program quality on the basis of image or stereotype.

Dual credit in Missouri has been largely framed as a transfer issue. But dual credit has important consequences for access. For one, this is because Missouri's efforts to enhance program quality have been seen as at odds with commitments to open access. Predictably, concerns about accountability and ideas for enforcing it were often in conflict with ideas for achieving increased access. For instance, in Missouri as in other states, policy makers have sought to assure a uniform level of program quality by controlling program inputs such as requiring a minimum grade point average (GPA) for dual credit courses. This mode of quality assurance has the potential to limit access to dual credit programs. Arguably, however, dual credit programs do not enhance access to college experiences if they do not deliver collegiate-level courses. Furthermore, a state's commitment to universal college access does not require abrogating high school academic requirements nor necessarily entitle all high school students an opportunity to earn college credit.

## The 1999 Policy

Dual credit is a phenomenon with important consequences for access and transfer because of the anomalies it raises in the framing of an equitable and consistent policy framework. In June 1999, Missouri's CBHE 1999 adopted new comprehensive dual credit policy guidelines in order to more adequately address these anomalies. These guidelines centered on a set of key interrelated issues: (1) purposes for dual credit, (2) appropriate quality standards, (3) transferability, and (4) policy enforcement.

*Purposes for dual credit.* The intent of the policy is to ensure quality and to promote the educational goals and values common to institutions of higher education. The policy provides institutions with parameters for designing dual credit programs in high schools that mirror on-campus delivery and that support access, quality, and efficiency. Because these parameters allow individualized program characteristics, the CBHE also called for a "principles of good practice" statement to accompany the new policy. The "principles of good practice" statement, offered as a guide to the day-to-day implementation of the dual credit policy, reflects the awareness that no single policy tool can embrace the broad range of approaches to dual credit delivery. Nevertheless, while flexibility in services according to student and institutional needs is acknowledged, each institution has the responsibility to provide evidence of program quality.

The CBHE's policy outlines a few central and overarching precepts which drive the rest of the policy. The most important of these is the assertion that dual credit is appropriate for high achieving students, who have mastered or nearly mastered the high school curriculum. While multiple purposes are served by dual credit, the policy clarifies that its primary aim is to provide students with opportunities for collegiate-level academic challenges and for avoiding unnecessary duplication in coursework. Dual credit experiences should supplement, not take the place of, high school graduation requirements. Second, the policy emphasizes the importance of academic over pecuniary considerations in implementing dual credit programs. Both of these assertions undergird the policy's continued emphasis on program quality and transferability.

*Appropriate Quality Standards.* Missouri's policy embeds its statements on appropriate quality standards in underlying principles of quality expressed by Missouri's regional accrediting body, the North Central Association of Schools and Colleges, Commission on Institutions of Higher Education. Clear, uniform, and specific expectations concerning student eligibility, program structure and administration, faculty qualifications and support, assessment of student performance, and transferability of credit are outlined for the academic community. By vesting responsibility for course quality within the on-campus academic department, the policy asserts the central role of an institution's full-time faculty in the design and delivery of the curricula. Because courses must be approved by on-campus faculty, the responsibility of the full-time faculty for the quality of dual credit programs is affirmed.

As a matter of program structure and content, Missouri's policy requires that dual credit courses duplicate on-campus, numbered, courses and that these dual credit courses should be administered by the appropriate on-campus academic department. Instructors must be approved by on-campus faculty. On-campus faculty have responsibility for assessment and evaluation measures. Academic departments of the respective disciplines are responsible for orientation and evaluation of dual credit instructors. Access to student and academic support must be comparable to that available to students taking the identical course on campus. Chief academic officers are responsible for assuring the academic quality and for demonstrating accountability for policy implementation. These requirements are intended to do away with dual credit programs operating at the periphery of the institution, with no connection to the on-campus departmental administrative structure.

The policy imposes statewide student eligibility requirements including a minimum high school overall GPA of 3.0 and adequate performance on state tests. These state tests are performance based and discipline specific. By tying eligibility to performance on these tests, the policy aims to align dual credit minimum requirements with standards of mastery developed for Missouri K-12 education. The policy also sets up uniform dual credit admission and thus addresses some of the tension between the two- and four-year sectors.

*Transferability.* The goal of Missouri's 1999 dual credit policy is to promote high quality of courses, while maintaining institutional autonomy. The policy thus assures that students who receive dual credit from institutions that are in compliance with the proposed policy can expect to transfer up to five dual credit courses. Transferability of additional courses would not be guaranteed; rather, it would be subject to institutional discretion. The policy's guarantee of five dual credit courses in transfer represented a compromise among state policymakers at the same time that it reflected the policy's espoused philosophical rationale for dual credit. While Missouri's two-year sector forcefully argued against any minimum guarantee of transferable credit hours, viewing such a guarantee more as a limit, Missouri's state board saw five courses, or about 15 to 20 credit hours, as the upper limit of an "introduction" to college. The five-course minimum emanates from the assumption that dual credit should smooth the transition between high school and college, not replace a substantial segment of the on-campus collegiate experience. The guarantee is also intended to encourage students to consider the match between their dual credit experiences and their on-campus programs. The policy represents an advance over the 1992 policy by assertively promoting compliance with agreed-upon standards and assurance of transferability for a limited number of dual credit hours. By tying institutional policy compliance to the transferability of dual credit hours delivered by a given institution and directing all institutions to publish their policies concerning receipt of dual credit courses in transfer, the policy incorporates meaningful incentives for broad-based policy compliance.

These elements related to transferability have several prominent implications. By demanding that dual credit courses be comparable to on-campus, collegiate-level experiences, they assure dual credit's transferability among all of Missouri's public institutions and those independent/proprietary institutions agreeing to comply with the policy. Moreover, these aspects of the policy provide systemic incentives for policy compliance. Given the capacity for variety in program quality, the policy aims to ensure the caliber of dual credit courses and to ensure that dual credit students receive truly accelerated and enriching learning experiences. In this way, the policy is intended to enhance students' access to college-level coursework, as well as the transferability of the credit they earn. Far from restricting transferability, the new guidelines not only ensure the transferability of credit earned via competent programs, but advance the interests of students by augmenting coursework's conformity to coherent on-campus programs. Lastly, the policy's provisions on transferability are intended to support and empower students in their roles as consumers: not only does the policy set up structural inducements for students to use dual credit to fit into coherent on-campus degree programs, the policy also aims to enhance students' capacity to make informed choices regarding the benefits of dual credit programs.

*Policy Enforcement.* By requiring institutions to submit annual reports and calling for public dissemination of a list of policy-compliant institutions, the policy aims to reinforce accountability. One primary incentive for institutional policy compliance is that consumers will become better informed about institutions in good standing. The policy requires institutions conducting dual credit programs to submit annual reports and calls on the Missouri Coordinating Board for Higher Education to publicly disseminate a list of policy-compliant institutions. Each institution has the responsibility to provide evidence of dual credit quality and implementation of the policy guidelines. Based on this evidence, the CBHE will maintain an updated list of dual credit programs that are in compliance with policy and share this list of compliant programs with the state's Department of Elementary and Secondary Education and other interested constituents. By setting up this "seal of approval," the policy is intended to enable students in their roles as consumers and thereby establishing an effective incentive for policy compliance.

## CONCLUSION

Any effort to develop state- or system-level dual credit policy must begin with the acknowledgment that dual credit programs have existed for some time, often being quite removed from any effective policy context. But there are consequences to allowing dual credit to flourish outside a policy context. A crucial challenge for state policy makers is that of developing and implementing state policy on top of an existing tradition of dual credit provision. Throughout the country, many unique approaches to dual credit have arisen; at the same time, so have strikingly imaginative ways of subverting dual credit's most laudable purposes. Nevertheless state policy can be used as a tool to promote quality and consistency across institutions, ensuring the portability of college credit earned by high school students through dual credit programs. Inasmuch as dual credit overcomes traditional boundaries, it has the potential both to threaten and to enhance the broader goals of education. The challenge for policy makers is to structure dual credit policy to reverse the negative consequences of allowing dual credit programs to exist outside of a policy context, but in a way that builds on their existing and potential strengths.

Community college dual credit programs constitute an arena in which questions about the proper balance between admissions standards and access continue to be addressed. Among the primary challenges to policy makers and programs directors is that of balancing the aims of dual credit with the multiple roles of the community college. Dual credit programs can appropriately and effectively fit into the broader complex of the community college missions. Yet dual credit raises challenges to balancing these multiple roles to the extent that assuring quality can mean the imposition of restrictions, eligibility requirements, and other standards. Moreover, the quality of dual credit programs affects, not only its transferability from one institution to another, but also, given a context of broad transfer, the overall quality of a state higher-education system. Community colleges are exceptionally well positioned to be primary deliverers of dual credit because of their connections to local communities. But because of their commitments to open enrollment and comprehensive access, they must carefully examine their extensive programming in high schools. In any event, community college leaders and state policy makers are well advised to clearly distinguish between the general imperative for college access, on one hand, and questions surrounding access to dual credit courses, on the other.

When dual credit resists transfer, it controverts one of its primary reasons for existence, namely, supporting the transition from high school to college. In spite of arguments that dual credit should be treated as on-campus credit (i.e., that it should be treated as homogenous with on-campus credit), Missouri chose to bracket dual credit with a comprehensive state policy. In an environment that is increasingly receptive to, and dependent on, transfer, it is crucial that dual credit programs be able to demonstrate quality, subject to the standards of accreditation that guide on-campus course delivery. Transferability can function as an incentive to support quality dual credit programs. The challenge in developing a comprehensive state policy is to embrace quality control and the credibility of dual credit courses. In Missouri this was done by framing dual credit as a transfer issue and using transferability as a lever to raise quality standards of dual credit programs. Policy makers have to resolve the lingering questions surrounding program inputs and restrictions and arrange a context that supports the development of vital and valuable college-high school partnerships. Missouri's experience suggests that, absent a reasoned and forceful policy, the seductiveness and continued expansion of dual credit programs threaten to undermine the value and efficacy of a state's overall system of higher education. Even so, such partnerships have the potential to raise the overall quality of high school instruction and genuinely address the needs of high school students.

State legislatures are applying pressure for early enrollment and advanced credit opportunities, and market forces are pushing for their expansion. In light of the multitude of forces pressing for the expansion of dual credit, it promises to continue as an ever more prevalent phenomenon. For this reason, moreover, it will become a still more controversial issue. The provision of dual credit on an unlimited scale, without quality controls, can threaten the overall integrity of a state system. State and system policy makers will have to respond. Yet dual credit cannot be regarded solely as a matter for higher education policy makers. Its value and its reason for being lie in its ability to ease the transition from high school to college. State policy affecting the K-12 system as well as higher education can either widen or close the gap experienced by students during this transition. By promoting a consistent and coherent dual credit policy in both K-12 and higher-education sectors, states can approach a true comprehensive K-16 system. Dual credit that takes place in high school settings and is taught by high school teachers can produce a ready-made cadre of partners in a comprehensive rethinking of the high school–college transition. Furthermore, the potential for technology to penetrate the physical boundaries between high schools and colleges holds out the opportunity to reevaluate dual credit in terms of a broader, student-centered K-16 agenda in which both colleges and high schools are genuine and active partners. Community colleges are well suited to begin shaping this agenda.

## REFERENCES

Andrews, H. A., & Marshall, R. P. (1991). Challenging high school honor students with community college courses. *Community College Review, 19*(1), 47–51.

Carnegie Commission on Higher Education. (1971). *Less time, more options: Education beyond the high school* (A special report and recommendations by the Carnegie Commission on Higher Education). New York: McGraw-Hill.

Cohen, A. M., & Brawer, F. B. (1996). *The American community college* (3rd ed.). San Francisco: Jossey-Bass.

Cohen, A. M., Rifkin, T., Lee, L., McKinney, K., & Yamasaki, E. (1998). *New expeditions—Vision and direction for the nation's community colleges: Topical bibliographies and analyses*. Los Angeles: ERIC Clearinghouse for Community Colleges. (ERIC Document Reproduction Service No. 423 002)

Edgert, P., & Polkinghorn Jr., R. (1999, Fall). California's collaboration to improve education. *Metropolitan Universities, 10*, 41–48.

Edmonds, G. S., Mercurio, J., & Bonesteel, M. (1998). *Research Report: Syracuse University Project Advance and the Advanced Placement Program: Comparing Two National Models for Curricular Articulation and Academic Challenges.* Syracuse University, Syracuse, NY.

Education Commission of the States. ECS Clearinghouse. (1997). *Postsecondary options/ Dual enrollment* [On-line]. Available: http://www.ecs.org/ECS/ECSWeb.nsf

Greenberg, A. R. (1989). *Concurrent enrollment programs: College credit for high school students.* Bloomington, IN: Phi Delta Kappa Educational Foundation.

Harkins, S. C. (1998). *Concurrent enrollment partnerships: Structure, relationships and success elements of programs offering college courses at the high school taught by the high school teacher.* Doctoral dissertation, University of Pittsburgh.

Hodgkinson, H. L. (1985). *All one system: Demographics of education—Kindergarten through graduate school.* Washington, DC: Institute for Educational Leadership.

Hodgkinson, H. L. (1999). *All one system: A second look.* Washington, DC: Institute for Educational Leadership.

International Baccalaureate Organisation. (1999). *The diploma programme* [On-line]. Available: http://www.ibo.org/ibo/english/diploma.htm

Kiger, D. M., & Johnson, J. A. (1997). Marketing the perceptions of a community college's postsecondary enrollment options program. *Community College Journal of Research and Practice, 21*(8), 687–693.

Lambert, L. M., & Mercurio, J. A. (1986, Spring). Making decisions: College credits earned in high school. *The Journal of College Admissions, 111,* 28–32.

Mabry, T. (1989). The high school/community college connection: An ERIC review. *Community College Review, 16*(3), 48–55.

Maeroff, G. I. (1983). *School and college: Partnerships in education.* Lawrenceville, NJ: Princeton University Press and The Carnegie Foundation for the Advancement of Teaching.

McIntyre, C. (1997). *Trends important to the California Community Colleges: A technical paper for the 2005 Task Force of the Chancellor's Consultation Council.* Sacramento: California Community Colleges Office of the Chancellor. (ERIC Document Reproduction Service No. 413 029)

The National School-College Partnership Database [Electronic database]. (1995). Syracuse, NY: Center for Research and Information on School-College Partnerships, 111 Waverly Avenue, Suite 200, Syracuse NY 13244–2320 [Producer and Distributor].

Ohio Board of Regents. (1994, June 17). Regents adopt performance measures for two-year colleges (News Release), 1–8.

Oregon University System (1998). *Oregon early options study.* Prepared for the Joint Boards of Education by the Office of Academic Affairs, Oregon University System, in cooperation with the Oregon Department of Education Office of Community College Services. Available: http://www.osshe.edu/aca/earlyoptions.htm

Postsecondary Education Planning Commission. (1997). *A review of acceleration mechanisms in Florida public education: Report and recommendations of the Florida Postsecondary Education Planning Commission.* Tallahassee: Florida State Department of Education.

Reisburg, L. (1998, June 26). Some professors question programs that allow high-school students to earn college credits. *The Chronicle of Higher Education*, pp. A39–A40.

Russell, A. B. (1998). *Statewide college admissions, student preparation, and remediation policies and programs: Summary of a 1997 SHEEO survey.* Available: http://www.sheeo.org/pubs/pubs-list.htm#access

Schwalm, D. E. (1991). High school/college dual enrollment. *WPA: Writing Program Administration, 15* (1–2), 51–54.

Sherry, H. R. (1998). *Interim report on dual enrollment.* Tallahassee: Florida State Department of Education.

Stein, R. B., & Girardi, A. G. (1999). Mending the disconnect: Establishing quality and portability of dual credit courses through state policy. In S. E. Van Kollenburg (Ed.), *A collection of papers on self-study and institutional improvement* (pp. 87–92). Chicago: North Central Association of Colleges and Schools, Commission on Institutions of Higher Education.

Storr, R. J. (1966). *Harper's university: The beginnings; a history of the University of Chicago.* Chicago: University of Chicago Press.

Tafel, J., & Eberhart, N. (1999). *Statewide school-college (K-16) partnerships to improve student performance.* Available: http://www.sheeo.org/pubs/pubs-list.htm#access

Tyack, D., & Cuban, L. (1995). *Tinkering toward Utopia: A century of public school reform.* Cambridge, MA: Harvard University Press.

University of Missouri–Kansas City College of Arts and Sciences. (1998). *College of Arts and Sciences high school/college program* [Brochure]. Kansas City: Author.

University of Missouri–St. Louis. (1999). *Advanced credit program* [On-line]. Available: http://www.umsl.edu/~asp

Vaughan, G. B. (1995). *The community college story: A tale of American innovation.* Washington, DC: American Association of Community Colleges.

Vogt, J. W. (1991). *Dual enrollment articulation practices between Virginia's community colleges and public schools (1989–90).* Doctoral dissertation, University of Virginia.

Wilbur, F. P., et al. (1988). *School-college partnerships—A look at the major national models.* Reston, VA: National Association of Secondary School Principals, in cooperation with the American Association for Higher Education and Syracuse University Project Advance. (ERIC Document Reproduction Service Number 291 320)

*Chapter 9* ──────────────────────────────

# Statewide Transfer and Articulation Policies: Current Practices and Emerging Issues

*Jan M. Ignash and Barbara K. Townsend*

As we enter the 21st century, it may be difficult to imagine that transfer and articulation are still key policy issues in higher education. After all, the literature on higher education has been occupied with these issues since at least 1956, when Bird's chapter in *The Public Junior College* discussed the concept of *transfer shock* (although he did not call it that) and provided evidence that the grades of transfer students were approximately the same as those of native students and of students transferring from other four-year institutions (cited in Kintzer, 1996, p. 5). So why are transfer and articulation still major policy issues in most states? Why don't all states have statewide articulation agreements? Are two-year and four-year colleges fundamentally incapable of developing strong transfer policies and articulation agreements unless they are pushed to do so by legislative mandate or governing board action? In those states that have managed to implement strong transfer policies and articulation agreements, what are the components of their policies and agreements?

This chapter takes a national perspective in examining the major policy issues still facing states as they attempt to build better articulation agreements for all undergraduates at public and private institutions, including students transferring among multiple institutions (called *swirling*) and those transferring from four-year to two-year colleges (called *reverse transfers*). Most of the implications and recommendations presented in this chapter draw upon the results of a survey of statewide articulation agreements conducted during spring 1999. This survey was designed to provide current (1999) information on how many states have statewide articulation agreements and, of those that do, to assess how strong those agreements are.

The purpose of this chapter is threefold: to describe the history and current status of state-level transfer and articulation agreements, to identify a core of principles that mark strong agreements, and to project emerging trends and policy issues that states will need to address as they work on articulation. The chapter is divided into four sections. The first section reviews pertinent literature in the field relating to articulation and transfer policy issues. The second section presents the research questions and the methodology of the national study of state-level articulation agreements. Results of the survey of 43 responding states are presented in the third section. Some emerging trends and policy implications are presented in the final section, with recommendations for states interested in improving existing articulation agreements.

The terms *transfer* and *articulation* are used frequently throughout this chapter. The difference between these two terms is perhaps most easily perceived as one between the "who" and the "what." Transfer refers to student flow among institutions and programs—the "who." When we talk about *transfer rates*, for example, we are concerned with the percentage of students that transfer among institutions or sectors. Articulation refers to courses and programs—the "what." Cohen and Brawer (1996) define articulation as the movement of "students' academic credits from one point to another" (p. 205). Articulation agreements can be developed for individual courses, or chunks of a program such as a block of integrated and sequenced nursing courses, or an entire degree. Articulation encompasses transfer and is "the entire range of processes and relationships involved in the systematic movement of students interinstitutionally and inter-segmentally throughout postsecondary education" (Kintzer & Wattenbarger, 1985, p. iii).

## STATE-LEVEL INTEREST IN DEVELOPING TRANSFER POLICIES AND ARTICULATION AGREEMENTS: PAST AND PRESENT

While it may seem that the state role in promoting transfer of students and articulation of programs has always been important, in the mid-1980s, the role was less evident. A monograph published by Kintzer and Wattenbarger in 1985 provided a comprehensive look at articulation as a state-level phenomenon (Kintzer & Wattenbarger, 1985). The authors described four basic patterns of articulation and transfer within the 50 states: (1) formal and legally based guidelines and policies mandated by law or a higher education master plan (8 states at the time of Kintzer and Wattenbarger's study); (2) policies within a state system that provide general direction for the transfer process and less so for articulation services (25 states); (3) voluntary cooperation among institutions (28 states); and (4) special agreements for the transfer of vocational and technical course credit (just a few states) (Kintzer, in 1996, p. 8).

Dorothy Knoell's 1990 monograph, *Transfer, Articulation, and Collaboration: 25 Years Later*, published five years after Kintzer and Wattenbarger's analysis, compared the differences in articulation and transfer conditions in the early 1960s to the mid-1980s. Knoell examined four general dimensions of two-year to four-year transfer and articulation issues: (1) the role of state legislatures and agencies in all aspects of facilitating transfer and articulation, including funding; (2) the feasibility of voluntary statewide transfer and articulation compared to agreements developed by groups or pairs of two- and four-year colleges; (3) the involvement of faculty compared to other college administrators and advisors in articulation; and (4) the incidence of special funding for transfer and articulation activities (Knoell, 1990, p. 11). Because state governing or coordinating boards for higher education were not established in most states in the early 1960s, it is not surprising that Knoell found that most efforts to promote transfer and artic-ulation were institution-driven. By the mid-1980s, the emphasis shifted to system-wide transfer and articulation policies that were often directed by legislatures or state boards of higher education.

This state-level interest in articulation and transfer has only become stronger since the mid-1980s, largely because of increasing perceptions, held by our nation's leaders as well as the general public, that a better educated populace is a necessity for everyone. Several recent surveys of opinion leaders and the general public have indicated an increasing belief in the importance of higher education and an affirmation of the U.S. tradition of broad access to higher education. In a February 1998 survey of 700 Americans, Immerwahr (1998) found that "a college education has taken on the status that a high school di-ploma had a number of years ago" and that the importance of higher education had increased in the last five years (p. 3). The general public also believes that a college education is not only beneficial for the individual, in helping to achieve a middle-class lifestyle, but also for the local economy, in helping to provide employers with educated workers (Immerwahr, 1998, pp. 3–4). These results were corroborated in a state-level survey of 654 Illinois residents and 40 opinion leaders during fall 1998, in which 94 percent of the residents and 98 percent of opinion leaders who participated in the survey agreed that "[g]etting a college education is more important than it was 10 years ago" (Parsons, DeGrush, & Johnson, 1998, Table 12). Another study, conducted by Immerwahr (1999) for the National Center for Public Policy and Higher Education, surveyed 601 of the nation's leaders in government, business, and education and found that 64 percent believed that the nation can never have too many college graduates. Even more of the leaders (73 percent) believed that their own state needed more college-educated workers to attract more high-tech business (p. 2). The report quoted one survey respondent who said: "The purpose of higher education has really changed. We are no longer educating an elite population, but instead building a usable body of skills for the society as a whole" (p. 2). Further, the study found that the leaders believed that it was "essential to insure that higher education is accessible to every qualified and motivated student" (p. 5).

Results of several other national and state surveys also indicate that the gen-eral public and opinion leaders also feel that access to an undergraduate, four-year education is a public need and a social good, as opposed to graduate education, which is viewed as more of an individual need and a privilege. In a series of telephone surveys conducted in Illinois during fall 1998, researchers found that 71 percent of residents supported investing any new state dollars in undergraduate education, rather than graduate or professional education. Moreover, 93 percent of the opinion leaders agreed. Several opinion leaders stated that graduate education benefits the individual and is discretionary, whereas undergraduate education is more fundamental and necessary to the state's well-being (Illinois Board of Higher Education [IBHE], 1998, pp. 3, 7; see also Harvey & Immerwahr, 1995, pp. 4–8, 13–16). In another study, Immerwahr (1998) found that only 49 percent of the 700 respondents in his survey believed that the vast majority of people who are qualified to go to college have the opportunity to do so (p. 7). While this percentage is an improvement from the 37 percent of respondents in 1993 who believed that qualified Americans have access to college, these results indicate that half of Immerwahr's respondents were still concerned about access. And the greatest concern was about students from low-income families, those students most likely to begin their collegiate careers at community colleges and then transfer to four-year institutions. Immerwahr (1998) also reported that "when people are feeling better about access, their overall attitudes about higher education are more positive," but when people are worried about access, educators are likely to hear the calls for more radical reform efforts (p. 6).

These studies point out the intense interest by the nation's leaders and the general public in promoting access to four-year undergraduate degree programs. These findings are consistent with the growing impatience of many states with the slow progress in addressing the barriers that impede student flow between two- and four-year degree programs. No better evidence of this is needed than the fact that 15 states have developed or improved statewide articulation agreements since 1995.

## PRINCIPLES FOR A STUDY OF STATE-LEVEL ARTICULATION

In assessing national progress in improving transfer and articulation, it is important to identify a core of common principles that seem to be critical in developing strong state-level articulation agreements. We drew on the literature on transfer and articulation as well as some existing state policies to develop seven principles we believe to form a basis for what constitutes good articulation. As a group, these principles provide a core of indicators on which to assess the strength of a particular state's articulation agreement.

*Principle #1: Associate and baccalaureate degree-granting institutions are equal partners in providing the first two years of baccalaureate degree programs.* Transfer has traditionally been thought of as going in one direction, upwardly vertical, whereby students flow from the community colleges to four-

year colleges and universities. However, there are several other possible transfers, and these patterns are becoming increasingly common. For example, in
May 1997, the Illinois Board of Higher Education reported that little more than
half (54 percent) of in-state transfer students followed the traditional pattern
from community colleges to four-year institutions. Almost one in five (19 percent) were "reverse transfers," that is, students who transferred from either a
public or private four-year institution to a community college (IBHE, 1997b,
p. 1). About 13 percent of undergraduate students nationwide are reverse transfers (Townsend, 1999). Over one quarter (27 percent) of the Illinois in-state
transfer students transferred from a two-year college to another two-year college,
from one private institution to another, or from a public four-year college or
university to another (IBHE, 1997b, p. 1).

Illinois is not unusual among states in documenting an increase in nontraditional transfer patterns. Cohen and Brawer (1996) noted that "Articulation
... covers students going from high school to college; from two-year colleges
to universities and vice versa; double-reverse transfer students, who go from the
two-year college to the university and then back again; and people seeking credit
for experiential learning as a basis for college or university credit" (pp. 205–
206).

In short, four-year colleges are not just receiving transfers from two-year
colleges. Four-year colleges are also sending transfers to two-year colleges and,
sometimes, later receiving back these same transfers. Thus it is just as important
for the four-year sector to have strong articulation agreements in place as it is
for the two-year sector.

*Principle #2: Transfer students should be treated comparably to "native"
students by the receiving institution.* In their 1985 study, Kintzer and Wattenbarger found that policies at four-year institutions discriminated against transfer
students. Problems typically arose from the kinds of courses that were counted
in transfer, students being "shut out" of the majors they wanted, and university
staff evaluating the community college courses for credit-worthiness without
input from the community college staff (pp. 40–41).

A number of states have policies stipulating that transfer and native students
be treated the same. In Texas, for example, although no statewide articulation
agreement exists per se, state agency regulations do provide fairly explicit directions for transfer agreements and note that a college or university can adopt
its own admission standards or grading policies "so long as it treats transfer
students and native students in the same manner" (Texas Higher Education Coordinating Board, THECB Rules and Regulations, Section 5. 401, [on-line]
Available: http://www.thecb.state.tx.us/rules/rulemain.htm. In Illinois, the Board
of Higher Education policy on undergraduate education stated, "Any student
admitted in transfer to an Illinois baccalaureate degree-granting institution
should be granted standing comparable to current students who have completed
the same number of baccalaureate-level credit hours and should be able to progress toward baccalaureate degree completion at a rate comparable to that of

students who entered the baccalaureate institution as first-time freshmen" (Illinois Board of Higher Education, 1994, p. 19). The Missouri Coordinating Board of Higher Education (1998) recently published its *Principles of Good Practice for Transfer and Articulation*, which included this statement: "The transfer process should treat both native and transfer students equally" (p. 1).

*Principle #3: Faculty from both two-year and four-year institutions have primary responsibility for developing and maintaining statewide articulation agreements.* As the content area experts, faculty should develop articulation agreements. In her comparative study of transfer and articulation in 11 states, Knoell (1990) found that "[i]ncreasing faculty participation in articulation activities at the state, regional, and local levels is having positive effects on the transfer process in ways that go beyond the agreements that are reached" (p. 72). Cohen and Brawer (1996) note that since the beginning of the 20th century, the predominant view in higher education has been that the faculty, "as independently functioning practitioners, should have the power to define the curriculum" (p. 324). They also stress that "All curriculum must, in the end, be based on knowledge" (p. 327). Who better than the faculty, then, to develop statewide articulation agreements? Legislators, state agency staff members, and college and university administrators do not have the same depth and breadth of knowledge in a field as do the content area experts in that field. A number of states support this principle. Florida, for example, has established a process that uses the Articulation Coordinating Committee to bring together faculty within a field to review courses for the state's common course numbering system. Over 600 faculty from Florida's public community colleges and universities have been involved in the initial development of articulation agreements for their respective subjects. Faculty also participate in course review committees to ensure that any course submitted by an institution for inclusion into the statewide agreement is an 80 percent match to the statewide course outline (Connie Graunke, personal communication, June 24, 1999). Hawaii's policies include the statement that faculty will be directly involved in developing the articulation agreement "since they are the most knowledgeable as to what constitutes degree-level competencies and comparable coursework" (University of Hawaii, 1998, p. 3).

*Principle #4: Statewide articulation agreements should accommodate those students who complete a significant block of coursework (such as the general education requirements) but who transfer before completing the associate's degree.* Many students today transfer before completing their associate's degree, at least in states where regulations do not prohibit them from doing so. In their 13-state study, Palmer, Ludwig, and Stapleton (1994) found that only 37 percent of community college transfer students completed their associate's degree before transferring. State-level articulation agreements need to be crafted with students' actual transfer patterns in mind. For example, Illinois Board of Higher Education policies expect institutions in that state to consider that "[s]tudents admitted in transfer who have satisfactorily completed the Illinois General Education Core Curriculum at any regionally accredited Illinois college or university prior to transfer should be granted credit in lieu of the receiving institution's all campus, lower-division general education requirement for an associate or baccalaureate degree" (IBHE, 1997a).

*Principle #5: Articulation agreements should be developed for specific program majors.* The general education portion of an Associate of Arts degree normally comprises 12 to 13 courses, approximately 40 semester credit hours. For students who are completing an associate degree to transfer as juniors, they need to have completed some of the coursework in their program major. Programmatic articulation agreements among institutions for students who are majoring in the liberal arts and sciences have been commonly developed for several decades. Less common are agreements developed in the more occupationally-oriented fields, although a few states are beginning to tackle program articulation here as well. Idaho, in particular, has made progress in achieving Associate in Applied Science (A.A.S.) degree articulation. Recently, the Idaho State Board of Education redesigned the A.A.S. degree to include 16 credits of general education from the academic campus. Efforts are also underway in Idaho to identify the transfer of complete and partial A.A.S. degrees, as well as the transfer of the general education portion of A.A.S. degrees. In Florida, in 1998 the legislature passed Senate Bill 1124, requiring statewide articulation of the Associate in Science (A.S.) degree (called an A.A.S. degree in other states) to bachelor's degrees. Agreements have been developed for *career ladders* in the more technical fields of electronic engineering technology, radiologic sciences, and hospitality management, with discussions still continuing for agreements in nursing, business, and computer sciences.

*Principle #6: A state's private institutions should be included in statewide articulation agreements.* In states with a strong history of private higher education, private colleges and universities need to be included in any statewide articulation agreement. At the very least, in all states the largest private institutions should be included in statewide articulation agreements. For example, 15 out of over 100 private four-year institutions in Illinois enroll over 75 percent of all the undergraduates who attend private institutions in that state. For Illinois's articulation initiative to be strong, these institutions must be included.

*Principle #7: A statewide evaluation system should monitor the progress and completion of transfer students.* Most statewide articulation efforts are both time-consuming and costly. Legislatures and the public can logically be expected to ask, "How are we better off now that we have a statewide articulation agreement?" Also, for states to improve upon existing agreements, officials need to conduct systematic evaluations of how well these agreements are functioning. At a minimum, the system should provide the number of transfer students by sector and by program major, the percentage of students who transferred without loss of credit, and the time-to-degree of transfer students, compared to native students, by program major. If results indicate that there are problems, qualitative studies should be conducted to discover why.

## SURVEY OF STATE-LEVEL ARTICULATION
## AGREEMENTS

These seven principles provide the framework for our study of current state-level articulation agreements. We wished to answer the question, "Of those states with statewide articulation agreements, how many have developed strong articulation agreements?" We rated the strength of a state's articulation agreement by evaluating it in terms of the seven principles, as follows. Strong statewide articulation agreements should include various transfer patterns (two-year to four-year, two-year to two-year, four-year to four-year, and four-year to two-year) between two- and four-year public and private institutions (Principles 1, 2, and 6), require considerable faculty involvement from both two- and four-year sectors (Principle 3), include both general education and program major transfer components (Principles 4 and 5), and have a systematic method of evaluating the effectiveness of the articulation agreement plan (Principle 7).

In spring 1999 we sent a brief survey questionnaire that asked states whether they had a statewide articulation agreement, when the agreement was developed, what the agreement included, which students and institutions the agreement covered, what sort of communication methods were used to inform students, and what evaluation mechanisms were used to assess the effectiveness of the agreement. The survey was sent via E-mail to the executive directors of state higher education agencies listed in the 1999 SHEEO (State Higher Education Executive Officers) directory and also to directors of community college state agencies.

Forty-four states responded, although one of these (Minnesota) did not answer enough of the survey for the results to be usable and is thus classified as a nonresponding state. The other nonresponding states were Alaska, Nebraska, New Hampshire, New Jersey, North Carolina, and Vermont.

### THE RESULTS

Of the 43 states fully responding to the survey, 34 (79 percent) reported that they had developed a statewide articulation agreement. The 9 states without a statewide agreement were Delaware, Maine, Michigan, New York (both the City University of New York [CUNY] and the State University of New York [SUNY] systems), Pennsylvania, South Carolina, Tennessee, Texas, and Wisconsin.

Among the remaining 34 states with statewide articulation agreements, there was considerable variation in the types of transfer, the types of institutions, and the percentage of undergraduates covered by the agreements (see Table 9.1). If a state's agreement reflects Principle 1, "Associate and baccalaureate degree-granting institutions are equal partners in providing the first two years of undergraduate education," one would expect to see transfer patterns that included reverse transfers as well as the more traditional two-year to four-year transfer pattern. If a state's agreement reflects Principle 6, one would expect a sizable

**Table 9.1**
**Institutions, Sectors, and Percent of Undergraduates Included in Statewide Articulation Agreements ($n = 34$)**

| State* | Type of transfer covered by state policy | | | | | | | Percent of Undergraduate students covered by statewide articulation agreement? | |
|---|---|---|---|---|---|---|---|---|---|
|  | 2- to 4-year | 2 to 2 | 4 to 4 | 4 to 2 (reverse transfers) | Publics only? | Publics & private, non-profits? | Publics & private, for profits? | Publics? | Privates? |
| Alabama | X | X | X | X | X |  |  | 100% | 0% |
| Arizona | X |  |  |  |  |  |  | 100% |  |
| Arkansas | X | X | X | X | X |  |  | 100% | 0% |
| California | X | X | X |  |  | X | X | 100% | 75%* |
| Colorado | X |  |  |  | X |  |  | 31% | 0% |
| Connecticut | X | X | X | X |  | X |  |  |  |
| Florida | X | X | X |  |  | X | X | 100% | 5% |
| Georgia | X | X | X | X | X |  |  | 100% | 0% |
| Hawaii | X | X | X | X | X |  |  | 100% | 0% |
| Idaho | X | X | X | X |  | X |  | 100% | 50% |
| Illinois | X | X | X | X |  | X | X | 100% | 60-65% |
| Indiana |  |  |  |  |  |  |  | 100% | 0% |
| Iowa | X |  |  |  |  |  |  | 100% | 0% |
| Kansas | X |  |  |  | X |  |  | 100% | 0% |
| Kentucky | X | X | X | X | X |  |  | 100% | 0% |
| Louisiana | X | X | X | X | X |  |  | 100% | 0% |
| Maryland | X | X | X | X | X |  |  | 100% | 0% |
| Massachusetts | X |  |  |  | X |  |  |  |  |
| Mississippi | X | X |  |  | X |  |  | 100% | 0% |
| Missouri | X | X | X | X | X |  |  | 100% |  |
| Montana | X | X | X | X | X |  |  |  |  |
| Nevada | X |  |  |  | X |  |  | 98% |  |
| New Mexico | X | X | X | X | X |  |  | 100% | 0% |
| North Dakota | X | X | X | X |  | X | X | 100% | 60% |
| Ohio | X | X | X | X | X |  |  | 100% | 0% |
| Oklahoma | X | X | X | X | X |  |  | 100% | 0% |
| Oregon | X |  |  |  | X |  |  | 100% |  |
| Rhode Island | X |  | X | X | X |  |  | 100% | 0% |
| South Dakota | X |  | X |  |  |  |  | 100% |  |
| Utah | X | X | X | X | X |  | (X**) |  |  |
| Virginia | X |  |  |  | X |  |  | 100% |  |
| Washington | X |  |  |  |  | X |  |  |  |
| West Virginia | X | X | X | X | X |  |  | 100% |  |
| Wyoming | X |  |  |  | X |  |  | 100% |  |
| Total "Yes" | 33 | 21 | 22 | 19 | 23 | 7 | 4 |  |  |

*Percentage includes regionally accredited private institutions only.
**Utah reported some voluntary compliance among the major, for-profit private institutions.

portion of the private institutions to be participating in the agreement and a substantial portion of private college undergraduates to be covered in the statewide agreements. Table 9.1 shows that the traditional pattern of public community college to public four-year college or university is still the dominant one. Substantially fewer states addressed articulation among two-year colleges ($n = 21$), among four-year colleges ($n = 22$), or in a reverse pattern from four-year colleges to community colleges ($n = 19$). In addition, most states had crafted agreements for the public sector only. Just 7 of the 34 states with state-wide articulation agreements included (in-state) private, nonprofit colleges. Four of these 7 also included private, for-profit institutions. Of the states with agreements with private institutions, only 4 states (California, Idaho, Illinois, and North Dakota) reported that a substantial portion of the undergraduate student population enrolled in private institutions were covered.

The second measure of the strength of statewide articulation agreements, as stated in Principle 3, concerns the extent to which faculty are involved in developing the agreements. On the survey questionnaire, respondents were asked to rate how extensively faculty were involved in developing the statewide agreement. Options included "very involved," "somewhat involved," "not very involved," and "not at all involved." Table 9.2 shows that 20 of the 32 states (63 %) responding to this question reported that faculty were "very" involved in developing these agreements.

Principle #4 addresses the need for articulation to allow students who transfer before completing the associate's degree to do so without losing credits. Conversely, students who wish to complete an associate degree in a specific major should be able to know what courses in their associate degree program will transfer to ensure they can transfer without loss of credit. Principle 5 addresses the need for articulation agreements in specific program majors. Table 9.3 shows the number of states in which statewide articulation agreements address one or several of the "chunks" of a program that students can complete before transferring. Of the 34 states reporting a statewide agreement 23 indicated there was one or more associate degrees designated as a degree that would automatically transfer to all four-year public state institutions. In a few states this degree was the Associate in Arts (A.A.) degree only. Other states designated additional degrees, with the A.S. being the most typical. Only two states (Louisiana, Virginia) have designated the A.A.S. degree, which is usually explicitly identified as a nontransfer degree (e.g., Tennessee). Twenty-two states have statewide requirements for general education, which means the state stipulates either the number of credit hours without suggesting subjects or stipulates that a student needs a specified number of credits in some suggested subjects. Twenty-four states have developed a common core of general education for all state schools. In almost all these states, the general education core follows the distribution model, whereby students have to complete a certain number of credits in specified areas distributed among the arts and sciences. Only 7 states have agreements specifying statewide requirements for program majors, and 13 have common course numbering or a similar system to identifying equivalent courses across sectors. Only 3 states, Florida, Georgia, and Oklahoma, have agreements specifying any kind of achievement testing, and only Florida and Georgia use the achievement tests as "rising junior" examinations. Before students, both transfer and native, can be admitted to junior class standing, they must pass this exam.

The final measure on which states were asked to provide information about

**Table 9.2**
**Extent of Faculty Involvement in Statewide Articulation Agreements ($n = 32*$)**

| State | Faculty involvement? | | | |
|---|---|---|---|---|
| | Very Involved | Somewhat Involved | Not Very Involved | Not At All Involved |
| Alabama | | | X | |
| Arizona | X | | | |
| Arkansas | | X | | |
| California | X | | | |
| Colorado | X | | | |
| Connecticut | X | | | |
| Florida | X | | | |
| Georgia | X | | | |
| Hawaii** | X (programs) | X (overall) | | |
| Idaho | | X | | |
| Illinois | X | | | |
| Iowa | | X | | |
| Kansas | | X | | |
| Kentucky | X | | | |
| Louisiana** | X | X | | |
| Maryland** | X (gen. ed.) | X (B.S. Tech.) | | |
| Massachusetts | | X | | |
| Mississippi | | X | | |
| Missouri | X | | | |
| Nevada | | | X | |
| New Mexico | X | | | |
| North Dakota | X | | | |
| Ohio | X | | | |
| Oklahoma | X | | | |
| Oregon | | | X | |
| Rhode Island | X | | | |
| South Dakota | | X | | |
| Utah | X | | | |
| Virginia | | X | | |
| Washington | | | X | |
| West Virginia | X | | | |
| Wyoming | X | | | |
| Total | 20 | 11 | 4 | |

*Thirty-two of the 34 states with statewide articulation agreements responded to this question.
**Three respondents gave two answers ("Very" and "Somewhat Involved"), depending on the component being articulated.

the strength of their statewide articulation agreements concerned evaluation. Principle 7 addresses the need for evaluation of statewide articulation agreements in order to assess how well the agreements are working and to remedy any weaknesses. Table 9.4 lists the states and the type of evaluation activity underway. States are not listed if they did not respond, did not know, or (in two cases) if the response was unintelligible. Only 13 states reported any type of evaluation, although 6 indicated that data-driven efforts were being planned. Of those states conducting evaluations, 6 had data-driven, systematic evaluation efforts, such as Georgia's statewide follow-up reports on transfer students, California's intersegmental computer program that evaluates transfer activity, and Colorado's accountability indicators, set by the Colorado Commission on Higher

## Table 9.3
### Transfer Components Included in Statewide Articulation Agreements ($n = 34$)

| State | Transfer Components Specified in Statewide Articulation Agreements | | | | | | | |
|---|---|---|---|---|---|---|---|---|
| | Associate degrees (names) | Requirements for general education | Common general education core[1] | Require-ments for majors | Common course numbering—or equivalent | Achieve-ment testing program | "Rising Junior" exam for transfer students | "Rising Junior" exam for native students |
| Alabama | | X | X | | | | | |
| Arizona | X (AA, AS, ABus.) | X | X | X | | | | |
| Arkansas | | X | X | | | | | |
| California | | X | X | | X | | | |
| Colorado | X (AA, AS) | X | X | | X | | | |
| Connecticut | X | X | X | | | | | |
| Florida | X (AA) | X[2] | | X | X | X | X | X |
| Georgia | X (AA,AS) | X | X | X | X | X | X | X |
| Hawaii | X (AA) | | | | | | | |
| Idaho | X (AA,AS) | X | X | | X | | | |
| Illinois | | | X | X | X | | | |
| Indiana | | | X (other) | | | | | |
| Iowa | X (AA) | | | | | | | |
| Kansas | X (AA,AS) | X | X | | | | | |
| Kentucky | | | X | | X | | | |
| Louisiana | | X | X | | X | | | |
| Maryland | X (AA,AS, & AAS for BS Tech.) | X | X | X (BS Tech. only) | | | | |
| Massachusetts | X | | X | | | | | |
| Mississippi | X | | | X | | | | |
| Missouri | X (AA) | X | X | | | | | |
| Montana | | X | X | | | | | |
| Nevada | X (AA,AS,AB) | X | | | | | | |
| New Mexico | X[2] | | X | | | | | |
| North Dakota | X[3] | X | X | | X | | | |
| Ohio | X (AA,AS) | X | X | X | | | | |
| Oklahoma | X (AA,AS) | X | X | | X | X | | |
| Oregon | X (AA Transfer) | X[4] | | | | | | |
| Rhode Island[5] | | | | | | | | |
| South Dakota | (slated for 1999-2000) | X | | | X | | | |
| (Texas[6]) | | | | | | | | |
| Utah | X | X | X | | X | | | |
| Virginia | X (AA, AS, AA&S) | | | | | | | |
| Washington | X (AA) | X | X | | | | | |
| West Virginia | X | | X | | | | | |
| Wyoming | | | | | X | | | |
| Total | 23 | 22 | 24 | 7 | 13 | 3 | 2 | 2 |

[1]All general education requirements are "distribution requirements" (e.g., specified number of credits in English, humanities, natural sciences, social sciences, sciences), unless otherwise indicated.

[2]Other general education transfer arrangements: Florida specifies that 36 credit hours of general education are transferable but does not dictate in which subjects. New Mexico specifies transfer modules in broad areas of 64 credit hours, but not associate degrees.

[3]North Dakota has transfer agreements for nursing ladders and degrees in construction and industrial technologies.

[4]In Oregon completion of the general education program at the sending institution satisfies the general education component at the receiving institution.

[5]Rhode Island publishes a Transfer Guide for students that is distributed annually to academic advisors at all public institutions.

[6]While Texas does not have a statewide articulation agreement per se, the state agency in Texas does identify subject matter parameters for 36 of the 42 general education credit hours in communication, math, social sciences, natural sciences, and humanities. The state agency then asks institutions to identify the courses that are equivalent to the state's transfer guide and leaves it up to the institutions to comply.

**Table 9.4**
**Type of Evaluation of Statewide Articulation Agreements ($n = 17*$)**

| Type of Evaluation of Statewide Articulation Agreements | | |
|---|---|---|
| Data driven efforts underway ($n = 6$) | Data driven efforts planned ($n = 6$) | Anecdotal evaluation ($n = 7$) |
| California | Arizona | Mississippi |
| Colorado | Illinois | Missouri** |
| Florida | Kentucky | North Dakota |
| Georgia | Missouri** | Oklahoma** |
| Hawaii | Oklahoma** | Rhode Island |
| New Mexico | Utah | Virginia |
| | | Wyoming |

*Seven states did not answer the survey and 10 states reported that they do not have statewide articulation agreements. Of the remaining 34 states, half (17 states) reported that no evaluation efforts were underway or did not answer the question.
**Missouri and Oklahoma's responses fit two categories.

Education for the state legislature, to measure the effectiveness of the articulation agreements. The other 7 states used anecdotal information through feedback from students on the state's Web site or telephone hot line or comments at deans' or academic advisors' meetings to assess the effectiveness of articulation, but they did not use systematic statewide evaluation.

Considered together, summary Tables 9.1 through 9.4 provide the basis for deriving subscores to measure the overall strength of state's articulation agreement (see Table 9.5). Using a technique recommended in Miles and Huberman (1984) for cross-site analysis, we developed a format that allows for a rapid evaluation of each case and for comparison between cases (p. 163). Each subscore for each state on the five variables of transfer directions, sectors, transfer components, faculty involvement, and evaluation is derived from the richer description of summary Tables 9.1 through 9.4.

Each variable is assessed on its strength using a 5-point scale, from "strong" (●), to "fairly strong," (◕), to "moderate" (◑), to "fairly weak" (◔), to "weak" (○). Rather than use a numerical scale of 1 to 5, the authors chose to use the symbols. Using a numerical scale might imply that one can average the numbers to come up with a final numerical score and then rank order all 50 states. Using symbols, however, allowed us to group states according to strength of their articulation agreements, without implying a precise individual ordering.

The first column of the sub-score, labeled "Transfer Directions" in Table 9.5, shows how many transfer patterns were included in the state's articulation agreement. If a statewide agreement only covered transfers between two-year colleges, the agreement is considered weak (○). If an agreement covered two- to four-year college transfers, it is considered "traditional" or normal (◑). If a state included two-year to two-year, four-year to four-year, and traditional two-year to four-year transfers, it is considered above average on transfer (◕). States in which articulation agreements covered both traditional and reverse transfers are considered strong (●).

# Table 9.5
## Site-Ordered Descriptive Meta-Matrix: Summary of Strength of State-Level Articulation ($n$ = 43 states)

| State | Articulation Agreement Sub-Scores | | | | | Overall Score |
|---|---|---|---|---|---|---|
| | Transfer Directions | Sectors | Transfer Components | Faculty Involvement | Evaluation[1] | |
| Alabama | ● | ◐ | ◐ | ○ | ○ | ◐ |
| Arizona | ◐ | ◐ | ● | ● | ◐ | ◑ |
| Arkansas | ● | ◐ | ◐ | ◐ | | ◐ |
| California | ◑ | ● | ◑ | ● | ● | ● |
| Colorado | ◐ | ◐ | ◑ | ● | ● | ◐ |
| Connecticut | ● | ◐ | ◐ | ● | ○ | ◑ |
| Delaware* | ○ | ○ | ○ | ○ | ○ | ○ |
| Florida | ◑ | ◐ | ● | ● | ● | ◑ |
| Georgia | ● | ◐ | ● | ● | ● | ● |
| Hawaii | ● | ◐ | ◑ | ◐ | ● | ◐ |
| Idaho | ● | ● | ◑ | ◐ | | ◑ |
| Illinois | ● | ● | ● | ● | ◐ | ● |
| Indiana | ○ | ◐ | ◑ | ○ | ○ | ◑ |
| Iowa | ◐ | ◐ | ◑ | ◐ | | ◐ |
| Kansas | ◐ | ◐ | ◐ | ◐ | | ◐ |
| Kentucky | ● | ◐ | ◑ | ● | ◐ | ◑ |
| Louisiana | ● | ◐ | ◑ | ● | | ◑ |
| Maine* | ○ | ○ | ○ | ○ | ○ | ○ |
| Maryland | ● | ◐ | ◑ | ● | | ◑ |
| Massachusetts | ◐ | ◐ | ◐ | ◐ | | ◐ |
| Michigan* | ○ | ○ | ○ | ○ | ○ | ○ |
| Mississippi | ◐ | ◐ | ◐ | ◐ | ◑ | ◐ |
| Missouri | ● | ◐ | ◐ | ● | ◐ | ◑ |
| Montana | ● | ◐ | ◐ | | | ◐ |
| Nevada | ◐ | ◐ | ◐ | ○ | | ◐ |
| New Mexico | ● | ◐ | ◐ | ● | ● | ◑ |
| New York* | ○ | ○ | ○ | ○ | ○ | ○ |
| North Dakota | ● | ● | ◑ | ● | ◑ | ● |
| Ohio | ● | ◐ | ● | ● | | ● |
| Oklahoma | ● | ◐ | ◑ | ● | ◐ | ◑ |
| Oregon | ◑ | ◐ | ◐ | ○ | | ◐ |
| Pennsylvania* | ○ | ○ | ○ | ○ | ○ | ○ |
| Rhode Island | ● | ◐ | ○ | ● | ◑ | ◐ |
| South Carolina* | ○ | ○ | ○ | ○ | ○ | ○ |
| South Dakota | ◐ | ◐ | ◐ | ◐ | | ◐ |
| Tennessee* | ○ | ○ | ○ | ○ | ○ | ○ |
| Texas* | ○ | ○ | ○ | ○ | ○ | ○ |
| Utah | ● | ◐ | ◑ | ● | ◐ | ◑ |
| Virginia | ◐ | ◐ | ◑ | ◐ | ◑ | ◐ |
| Washington | ◐ | ◐ | ◐ | ○ | | ◐ |
| West Virginia | ● | ◐ | ◐ | ● | ○ | ◑ |
| Wisconsin* | ○ | ○ | ○ | ○ | ○ | ○ |
| Wyoming | ◐ | ◐ | ◑ | ● | ◑ | ◐ |

[1]Blank cells indicate that the state representative did not answer this question or did not know the answer.

*These 9 states do not have statewide articulation agreements. They do have voluntary agreements between two or more institutions. Seven other states did not respond to the survey: Alaska, Minnesota, Nebraska, New Hampshire, New Jersey, North Carolina, and Vermont.

The second column of the subscore, labeled "Sectors," refers to whether the statewide agreement covered both public and private sectors of higher education (see Table 9.1). States that included only public institutions or covered undergraduates enrolled only in the public sector are considered normal or "moderate," (◐), while states that included at least half of the undergraduates enrolled in the private sector are considered "strong" (●).

The "Transfer Components" column uses the results in Table 9.3 to measure whether the state's articulation agreement covered only degrees, which was the most restrictive type of agreement (○), or covered general education requirements and/or a general education common core in the agreement (◐). This latter type of statewide agreement is considered stronger than agreements based solely on receipt of the associate degree because so many community college students transfer before earning that degree. Agreements that address general education components are more flexible and inclusive. If a common course numbering (CCN) system was also part of the statewide agreement, the agreement is considered stronger yet (◑); this is because CCN systems allow even greater flexibility in transfer since students can transfer courses, rather than entire components or degrees. Finally, if the state's agreement included specific agreements for many individual program majors as well as general education, that agreement is considered strong (●).

The fourth column in the subscore, "Faculty Involvement," shows ratings from weak to strong, based on whether the state responded that the faculty was "very involved" (●), "somewhat involved" (◐), or either "not very involved" or "not at all involved" (○).

The last measure to be included in the subscore, "Evaluation," shows whether the state used systematic, data-driven evaluation to monitor and improve statewide articulation (●), whether such data-driven efforts were planned (◐), whether the state relied on anecdotal information from students or the campuses to assess how well articulation was proceeding (◑), or whether no evaluation efforts were underway or planned (○). In cases where state officials gave two responses to a question, the stronger of the two responses was chosen.

In order to illustrate clearly which states have strong statewide articulation agreements, Table 9.6 groups them in clusters according to the strength of their overall articulation agreements, rather than alphabetically, as in Table 9.5. For a state to be considered "strong" in its statewide articulation agreement, it needed to show that it was "strong" (●) in at least three categories and no weaker than "moderate" (◐) in a fourth category or "strong" in two categories and no weaker than "fairly strong" in the other two. (The fifth category "Evaluation," while vitally important, is not included in assessing the strength of a state's current articulation agreement because so many states have developed or refined statewide articulation agreements since 1995 and are just now beginning to discuss the need for effective evaluation.) Of the 43 responding states, 5 (California, Georgia, Illinois, North Dakota, and Ohio) are revealed to have developed

**Table 9.6**
**Strength of Statewide Articulation Agreements ($n$ = 43 states)**

| Strength of Statewide Articulation Agreement | |
|---|---|
| **Strength of Articulation** | **States** |
| Strong (●) | California |
|  | Georgia |
|  | Illinois |
|  | Ohio |
|  | North Dakota |
| Fairly Strong (●) | Arizona |
|  | Connecticut |
|  | Florida |
|  | Idaho |
|  | Kentucky |
|  | Louisiana |
|  | Maryland |
|  | Missouri |
|  | New Mexico |
|  | Oklahoma |
|  | Utah |
|  | West Virginia |
| Moderate (◐) | Alabama |
|  | Arkansas |
|  | Colorado |
|  | Hawaii |
|  | Iowa |
|  | Kansas |
|  | Massachusetts |
|  | Mississippi |
|  | Montana |
|  | Nevada |
|  | Oregon |
|  | Rhode Island |
|  | South Dakota |
|  | Virginia |
|  | Washington |
|  | Wyoming |
| Fairly Weak (◓) | Indiana |
| Weak or No Articulation (○) | Delaware* |
|  | Maine* |
|  | Michigan* |
|  | New York* |
|  | Pennsylvania* |
|  | South Carolina* |
|  | Tennessee* |
|  | Texas* |
|  | Wisconsin* |

*These states do not have a statewide articulation agreement.

"strong" statewide agreements that pay attention to all or most of these principles.

For a state to be considered "fairly strong," the state needed to show that it was "strong" (●) in at least two categories and no weaker than "moderate," (◐) in the other two categories. Twelve states have "fairly strong" agreements (Arizona, Connecticut, Florida, Idaho, Kentucky, Louisiana, Maryland, Missouri, New Mexico, Oklahoma, Utah, and West Virginia).

In the next group, states that had "moderate" agreements were at least "moderate" (◐) in three of the first four categories. The 16 states in this category were Alabama, Arkansas, Colorado, Hawaii, Iowa, Kansas, Massachusetts, Mississippi, Montana, Nevada, Oregon, Rhode Island, South Dakota, Virginia, Washington, and Wyoming.

Only one state, Indiana, had a "fairly weak" (ɔ) articulation agreement. The state agency in Indiana sets policies for the different campuses of the seven public institutions, including recommendations for a 30-credit transferable general-education core, but these recommendations do not apply cleanly across the entire state. At three public institutions (Indiana University, Purdue University, and Ball State University), the core general education requirements are program specific. At the other four public institutions, the core general education requirements are campus specific.

Finally, nine states did not have a statewide articulation agreement, although they did have voluntary agreements between two or more institutions. These states (Delaware, Maine, Michigan, New York, Pennsylvania, South Carolina, Tennessee, Texas, Wisconsin) were considered "weak" (o) in articulation.

## RECOMMENDATIONS FOR STATE-LEVEL IMPROVEMENT OF TRANSFER AND ARTICULATION

We conclude our examination of state-level articulation agreements with some recommendations for policy makers to consider if they wish to improve transfer and articulation in their states.

1. States without a state-level policy need to assess whether one is needed. Students who have transferred or are considering transferring should be a primary source of data in making this assessment. If the decision is made not to pursue having a state-level articulation agreement, the rationale for this decision needs to be made available to citizens of the state as well as to those interested in studying transfer and articulation.

2. In states with articulation agreements, policy makers need to ensure that the agreements take into account students' "transfer swirl." A limitation of a number of these policies is that they seem based upon a dated assumption about student transfer, namely that it occurs in one direction only—upwardly vertical or from the two-year college to the four-year college. However, the reality is that transfer occurs in several directions and is not just upwardly vertical. Therefore, policies should address not just transfer from the two-year to the four-year sector, but also transfer within sectors and from the four-year to the two-year sector (reverse transfer).

3. Similarly, tying transfer to completion of the associate degree(s), designated as the transfer degree(s), may be unrealistic, given that many community college students transfer to another institution (which could be a two-year or a four-year school) before they complete the A.A. degree (Cohen & Brawer, 1996). Statewide articulation agreements need to facilitate student transfer with an agreed-upon general education core and at other appropriate points *before* completion of the associate's degree.

4. Private (nonprofit) institutions need to be included in statewide articulation agreements, especially in states with a strong private sector.

5. Given the growth of the for-profit (proprietary) sector of higher education,

policy makers need to consider including for-profit institutions (at least the degree-granting ones) in state-level articulation agreements.

6. Faculty need to be involved, not only in the development of statewide articulation agreements, but also in their maintenance. Several states (e.g., Hawaii) have clearly stated that the faculty are the most knowledgeable about curriculum and need to be directly involved in developing articulation agreements.

7. Ongoing, formal evaluation of the overall effectiveness of a state's articulation agreement is vital. The evaluation should have a two-pronged purpose: formative, so as to improve existing agreements, and summative, to indicate how well the policy is working. Again, students should be consulted as part of the evaluation process.

## EMERGING ISSUES

Additionally, we see several emerging curricular developments that merit policy makers' consideration in developing or revising state-level articulation agreements: (1) interdisciplinary courses, (2) a competency-based approach to general education, and (3) dual credit programs.

Interdisciplinary general-education courses have existed since the beginning of the 20th century, with Columbia's survey courses in contemporary civilization as prime examples (Levine, 1978). They continue in popularity today, especially with the growth of interdisciplinary studies during the 1960s and 1970s. Interdisciplinary courses most commonly combine subject categories in the arts and sciences, such as history and literature or political science and economics. Less frequently, interdisciplinary courses will combine liberal arts and sciences subject matter with more applied or occupational subject matter, as in a building construction class that includes strong components of art appreciation and history. There is a risk that articulation, at both the state and institutional levels, may become overly prescriptive and thus discourage interdisciplinary courses. Articulation agreements need to accommodate interdisciplinary courses. For example, an integrated undergraduate music course that is a two-semester sequence carrying 12 credits each semester and that incorporates theory, harmony and keyboard skills, and aural skills could be given its own course number designation that would allow for transfer credit for what typically amounts to three 4-credit-hour courses.

The creation of interdisciplinary courses would be encouraged by the development of a statewide, competency-based general-education program. All the states with a common general education core follow the distribution model, which tends to preclude interdisciplinary courses because they are hard to fit into what is essentially a discipline-based model. However, as of 1999, Missouri is developing general education goals and competencies for its public colleges, as part of its revision of the general-education component of its transfer and articulation policy. Once the goals and competencies are agreed upon, each college is to develop a 45-hour general block addressing these goals and competencies. Institutional distinctiveness and autonomy can be manifested in each block because each college is directed to respect another institution's general education block and accept it in toto. If a student transfers before completing one institution's general education block, the receiving institution will determine which competencies the student still needs to fulfill.

A primary assumption behind the development of this approach to general education is that most students will complete the general education block before they transfer since doing so is to their advantage. If this assumption proves erroneous, Missouri may find that a competency-based approach to general education undermines student transfer because of institutional disagreements about which competencies students have achieved if they have not completed the entire block. Missouri's pioneer efforts bear watching and evaluating.

A more established curricular trend than competency-based general education is the development of dual credit or dual enrollment programs. As Girardi and Stein indicated in Chapter 8, states have permitted the development of these programs during the past two decades in order to facilitate a seamless student transition from high school to college. Dual credit programs involve a partnership between a high school and a higher-education institution (two-year or four-year) to offer courses for which high school students can receive both high school and college credit. Upon graduation from high school, students with dual credit may choose to enroll in the partnership college with some or all of the credits counting toward their college degree. Alternatively, students may "transfer" these credits to another college.

Some colleges have been reluctant to accept dual credit courses offered by other higher-education institutions. In particular, some four-year colleges have been reluctant to accept two-year college dual credit courses. It may be that dual credit courses also need to be addressed in state-level articulation policies.

In sum, the results of our national survey regarding state-level articulation policies show that across the United States, states have indeed made progress in facilitating student transfer, especially among public institutions. Development of these policies is an important step in a state ensuring a seamless transition between and within its higher-education sectors, a transition that can ultimately lead to more state citizens obtaining the baccalaureate. But in no state is the job done. The need for articulation never ends, since curriculum is constantly changing to reflect new knowledge. Policy makers and institutional leaders must continue to work together to develop even better statewide articulation policies.

## REFERENCES

Cohen, A. M., & Brawer, F. B. (1996). *The American community college* (3rd ed.). San Francisco: Jossey-Bass.

Harvey, J., & Immerwahr, J. (1995). *Goodwill and growing worry: Public perceptions of American higher education. A report for the American Council on Education.* Washington, DC: American Council on Education.

Illinois Board of Higher Education. (May 13, 1994). *Undergraduate education: Transfer and articulation reexamined.* Springfield, IL: Author.

Illinois Board of Higher Education (1997a, May). *Board of Higher Education policies on undergraduate education. Transfer and articulation. Adopted September 1990. Amended September 1994 and May 1997.* Springfield: Author.

Illinois Board of Higher Education (1997b, May 6). *Transfer and articulation. Item #4A.* Springfield: Author.

Illinois Board of Higher Education. (1998, December 15). *Results and implications of the statewide surveys of residents, employers, and opinion leaders in Illinois. Item #61.* Springfield: Author.

Immerwahr, J. (January 1999). *Taking responsibility: Leaders' expectations of higher education.* San Jose, CA: National Center for Public Policy and Higher Education and the Public Agenda.

Immerwahr, J. (1998). *The price of admission: The growing importance of higher education.* San Jose, CA: National Center for Public Policy and Higher Education and the Public Agenda.

Kintzer, F. C. (1996). A historical and futuristic perspective of articulation and transfer in the United States. In T. Rifkin (Ed.), *Transfer and articulation: Improving policies to meet new needs* (New Directions for Community Colleges, No. 96, pp. 3–13). San Francisco: Jossey-Bass.

Kintzer, F. C., & Wattenbarger, J. L. (1985). *The articulation/transfer phenomenon: Patterns and directions.* Washington, DC: American Association of Community and Junior Colleges. (ERIC Document Reproduction Service ED 257 539)

Knoell, D. (1990). *Transfer, articulation, and collaboration: Twenty-five years later.* Washington, DC: The American Association of Community and Junior Colleges.

Levine, A. (1978). *Handbook on undergraduate curriculum.* San Francisco: Jossey-Bass.

Miles, M. B., & Huberman, A. M. (1984). *Qualitative data analysis: A sourcebook of new methods.* Newbury Park, CA: Sage Publications.

Missouri Coordinating Board for Higher Education. (1998, June 11). *Principles of good practice for transfer and articulation.* Jefferson City: The Missouri Coordinating Board for Higher Education.

Palmer, J. C., Ludwig, M., & Stapleton, L. (1994). *At what point do community college students transfer to baccalaureate-granting institutions? Evidence from a 13-state study.* Washington, DC: American Council on Education. (ERIC Document Reproduction Service ED 373 844)

Parsons, J., DeGrush, A., & Johnson, T. (1998, October 30). *Higher education in Illinois: A survey of residents and opinion leaders in the state* (Unpublished report to the Illinois Board of Higher Education). University of Illinois at Chicago, Survey Research Laboratory.

Texas Higher Education Coordinating Board. *Chapter 5, Program development; Subchapter S, Core curriculum transfer and field of study curricula.* Austin: The Texas Higher Education Coordinating Board. [On-line]. Available: http://www.thecb.state.tx.us/rulesrulemain.htm

Townsend, B. (Ed.). (1999). *Understanding the impact of reverse transfer students on community colleges* (New Directions for Community Colleges, No. 106). San Francisco: Jossey-Bass.

University of Hawai'i. (June 23, 1998). *University of Hawai'i system student transfer and articulation.* E5.209. [on-line]. Available: http://www.advising.hawaii.edu

## Chapter 10

# Reframing Remediation as a Systemic Phenomenon: A Comparative Analysis of Remediation in Two States

*Kathleen M. Shaw*

In the past several years, remedial education has emerged at the center of heated debates regarding the purpose and function of higher education. Articles in the national media point to an "epidemic" of remedial education "stretching from the Ivy League to public community colleges" ("Remedial Education," 1996), and multi-part series on remediation have been printed in several prominent newspapers, such as the *Boston Globe* and the *Washington Times*, to name but two. *City on a Hill* (1995), by journalist James Traub, paints a dismal picture of the open admissions policies of the City University of New York (CUNY) and the resulting remediation that the university offers. It makes a strong argument for removing remediation from the four-year sector and reinstating higher and, presumably, more objective entrance requirements, such as performance on standardized tests. In contrast, Lavin and Hyllegard's 1996 longitudinal study of CUNY's open admissions policies suggests that remediation plays a critical role in the long-term life chances of poor and minority students.

Most recently, these debates have erupted as a task force report charges that CUNY has "plunged into a spiral of decline," fueled in no small part by the prominence of its remedial education programs ("City Panel," 1999). Spirited and often histrionic letters to the editor regarding remediation splash across the pages of the *New York Times* and the *Daily News* in response to editorial or opinion pieces about the relative worth of CUNY and its graduates (e.g., "In America," 1998; "Open Admissions," 1998). Indeed, unlike most debates about educational practice which remain in the esoteric journals of career academics or policy makers, debates about remediation have entered the public domain.

That remediation has entered the public-debate arena with such intensity is precisely because our approaches to it reflect deeper beliefs about the purpose of higher education in general. Should colleges and universities function as democratizing institutions that provide access and opportunity for students who have traditionally been shut out of this experience? Should we create and maintain an educational hierarchy based on meritocratic principles that only allow an elite few to enter the halls of four-year colleges and universities? And, ultimately, what role should a college education play in the life chances of American citizens?

Despite the rhetoric that accompanies (and contributes to) the recent surge in policies designed to alter or control remedial education, little research has been done on the process by which such policies are developed at the state level, nor on the ways in which remediation is implemented at the institutional level. Moreover, most considerations of remediation are limited to the postsecondary sector and fail to examine the ways in which postsecondary remediation policy relates to all facets of the educational system, from K to 16.

In an attempt to develop a fuller understanding of this critically important form of educational policy and its potential to affect access to education throughout the educational pipeline, in this chapter I examine two states with markedly different approaches to remediation. In doing so, I uncover significant variation not only between the states, but among sectors and institutions within each state. These data suggest that a broader, more inclusive model which spans educational sectors is needed to study remediation and its effects on educational attainment.

## DEFINING REMEDIAL EDUCATION

Despite the fact that the phrase "remedial education" is bandied about with increasing frequency in both the popular and academic press, there is considerable confusion regarding the definition of this term. In the simplest of definitions, remedial education generally refers to courses that are offered at the postsecondary level and whose content is generally considered "precollege." Yet since there is such a wide variation in the content and pedagogy of such courses, those who devote their lives to practicing or studying the delivery of precollege courses draw distinctions between approaches to teaching this type of course.

In the past 30 years, "developmental education" has emerged as a legitimate field of both practice and scholarship. This field draws a sharp distinction between developmental and remedial education. Whereas remediation is defined as a narrowly focused effort to "compensate for deficiencies in prior learning" (Boylan, 1995 p. 1), developmental educators have taken on a much broader mission. In addition to providing basic skills, developmental education addresses the needs of the "whole person" by integrating personal and academic development. Its proponents maintain that "it is a far more sophisticated concept involving a combination of theoretical approaches drawn from cognitive and developmental psychology" (Boylan, 1995 p. 1). In addition to content-based coursework, developmental education programs may also offer tutoring, study skills courses, and counseling. While remedial education is seen as one element of developmental education, it is viewed as a small subset of a much broader and comprehensive arsenal of services available under the developmental education umbrella.

There are further definitional problems. *Remediation* is, in essence, a relative term. While nearly all postsecondary institutions offer some type of remediation, a skill level termed remedial in one institution may be considered college level in another. For example, students who place into remedial courses at an elite private institution are very different indeed from the average community college remedial student.

This inconsistency is exacerbated by forms of assessment and placement which can vary enormously—in some states, even by institution. In a 1986 study conducted by the Southern Regional Education Board (SREB), a survey of the organization's fourteen member states revealed that nearly 100 combinations of 70 different tests in reading, writing, and mathematics were used in assessing students' college-readiness (SREB, 1986, p. 1). Moreover, individual states and institutions utilize such a wide range of cutoff scores on these examinations that there is no clear consensus regarding what constitutes even a minimal competence level.

Clearly, there is considerable confusion surrounding both the identification and teaching of students who are not deemed college ready. Yet regardless of distinctions made between developmental and remedial education in scholarly journals, current debates utilize *remedial education* as an umbrella term that encompasses all precollege coursework. Since both development and remedial education are generally considered precollege, and since students are most often placed in them when it is determined that they are deficient in some skill or knowledge area, I will refer to them in the aggregate as *remedial education*. While the use of this term masks the wide variation seen in the delivery of precollege courses and in the definition of what constitutes precollege work itself, it allows me to enter into current debates regarding the policy and practice of this fundamentally important function of postsecondary education.

## THE DEMOGRAPHICS OF REMEDIAL EDUCATION

The demographics of remediation provide a crucial context within which to analyze current and emerging remediation policies and practices. The University of Wisconsin developed the first college preparatory department in 1849. Since then, remedial education has proliferated across all sectors of higher education. Nearly all community colleges offer some form of remediation, and in the 1992–1993 academic year, 78 percent of public four-year colleges and 66 percent of private four-year colleges offered remedial instruction (National Center for Educational Statistics, 1994). Such courses exist even in the hallowed halls of Harvard where, according to Harvard Education Professor Charles Willie, courses that help to develop students' academic skills have existed since just after World War II (Hawkins & Phillip, 1993).

According to a 1996 report issued by the American Council on Education, about 13 percent of all undergraduates took at least one remedial course in the 1992–1993 school year (ACE, 1996). On its face, this figure does not appear to warrant the growing furor surrounding remedial education and its place in the postsecondary sector. While most colleges offer remedial courses of some sort, a relatively small proportion of students nationally enroll in them. Moreover, the vast majority of students enrolled in remedial courses are white. According to the American Council on Education (1996), 65 percent of those participating in remediation of some sort are white. As Hunter Boylan states, "These programs are not targeted for minority students, but for those who are first generation college students. . . . Those whose admission to college may have resulted from a philosophy of educational opportunity may be non-traditional but they are not, necessarily, minorities" (as quoted in Hawkins & Phillip, 1993, p. 33). However, ethnic and racial minorities are disproportionately represented in remedial courses. For example, while blacks make up only 10 percent of the college student population, they comprise 15 percent of those enrolled in remedial courses. In total, though, minorities account for only 35 percent of remedial students (U.S. Department of Education, 1996).

Yet perception is often more potent than reality. As is evidenced by an analysis of the debates surrounding remediation analyzed elsewhere (Shaw, 1997), the rhetoric surrounding remediation is charged by issues regarding access and equity—particularly for poor and minority students. These debates may be fueled in part by the fact that remediation tends to be an extremely common and visible component of the educational enterprise at institutions that enroll large numbers of ethnic and racial minorities. A look at several educational systems that serve these populations is instructive. In 1986, the California State University system provided remedial courses to 60 percent of its incoming freshmen ("Ready or Not," 1995). At CUNY, the proportion of students needing remediation in 1999 rose to nearly 90 percent of its community college students and 72 percent of its four-year college freshmen ("City panel," 1999). Historically Black Colleges and Universities (HBCUs) have a proud tradition of providing broad-based remediation (Hawkins and Phillip, 1993). At community colleges, which as a sector serve a disproportionate number of ethnic and racial minorities, remediation is an integral part of the curriculum. As a result, remediation is, in the minds of many policymakers and pundits, inextricably linked to race. As Bruno Manno stated in a recent article in *Change*, "Today, access to postsecondary institutions is afforded those who are prepared to do college-level work as well as those who are not. We undermine the promise of American life and do neither group a service when we use race or class or some other substitute rather than academic criteria to determine college admission" (Manno, 1995, p. 49).

## ASSESSING THE EFFECTIVENESS OF REMEDIATION

Very little rigorous empirical research has been conducted on either the short- or long-term effects of remedial education. While proponents of remediation argue that such courses prepare students for "college-level" work, statistical evidence is ambiguous. A transcript study conducted in the early 1990s by the National Center for Developmental Education revealed that 77 percent of students who passed developmental math courses went on to earn passing grades in college-level courses. The same was true of 91 percent of students passing developmental English courses (Boylan, 1992). Yet the National Center for Educational Statistics reports that the failure rate in remedial courses is much higher than that for college-level courses. While 7.3 percent of students enrolled in college-level courses failed, 23 percent of students enrolled in remedial reading courses failed; 27 percent failed writing courses; and fully 33 percent failed math courses (1994). Hence, while students who successfully emerge from remedial courses are likely to continue to be successful in their college-level courses, the failure rate in remedial courses is disproportionately high.

Yet there is very little research available on the long-term effects of remedial education on students' ultimate level of educational attainment. However, Lavin and Hyllegard's 1996 follow-up study of CUNY graduates from 1970 and 1980 is suggestive. As the proportion of students enrolled in remedial courses grew between these two time periods, so did the rate of dropout. In addition, the number of credits earned per semester, grade point average and transfer to four-year institutions dropped considerably (pp. 226–227). Yet they also found that, in tracking these students over a five-year period, the influence of remediation on credit accumulation shrunk, while other factors, such as full-time employment, grew (p. 228). Again, we are presented with a somewhat muddled picture of the effects of remediation on students' long-term academic success.

## CURRENT APPROACHES TO SOLVING THE REMEDIATION "PROBLEM"

As a result of the public and contentious debates that are occurring without the benefit of empirical data to back them up, a number of state and large urban public educational systems are changing, sometimes dramatically, the nature of remedial education. These emerging policies vary dramatically, offering solutions ranging from the elimination of remediation altogether to relegating its delivery to the private sector. Next, I provide a brief overview of some of the more dominant or innovative emerging remediation policies. The first two approaches to remediation are relatively rare. The second two are becoming increasingly common in terms of their prominence in debates about remediation, and in emerging remediation policy itself.

## "Mainstreaming" Remedial Education

This is a concept that is currently being advanced by Henry Levin and associates at the National Center for Postsecondary Improvement (NCPI) at Stanford University. Based on the Accelerated Schools model, which has proven successful in the K-12 sector, Levin advocates an approach to postsecondary education which incorporates basic skills acquisition into an exhilarating, challenging, and supportive educational environment (Levin et al., 1999). Rather than segregating remedial education and those students enrolled in it, Levin suggests that the remediation process can be infused into the broader educational enterprise. As a large-scale approach to reforming remedial education, this concept is still in its infancy. However, Levin's work is currently focused on identifying and analyzing approaches to remediation that seem to be crossing traditional boundaries which separate remediation from other, more mainstream approaches to education. In all instances, he focuses on the particulars of an individual program rather than broader, state-level policy.

Levin highlighted many of these innovative programs at a 1998 conference sponsored by NCPI and the Ford Foundation entitled *Replacing Remediation in Higher Education*. For example, LaGuardia College, a community college in the CUNY system, has developed a creative and critical thinking program that focuses on incorporating higher-order thinking skills into remedial courses (Chaffee, 1998). Individuals from Georgia State University described their use of adjunct courses to supplement traditional college-level courses (Commander & Stratton, 1998). Tinto reported on his study of learning communities and their potential for providing rigorous, high-quality educational experiences for students of all academic abilities (Tinto, 1998). In each of these examples, the acquisition of basic skills is enmeshed with higher-order skills and activities.

## "Outsourcing" Remediation to the Private or K-12 Sector

The question of where remediation should be offered is a bitterly disputed one. However, there is a small but vocal minority that is clamoring to relegate remedial education entirely outside the system of public postsecondary education altogether. Although few states or educational systems have implemented such a plan, several are actively debating this issue.

One of the foremost proponents of such a strategy is New York City mayor Rudolph Guiliani, who sees a shift to private tutoring companies as a viable strategy (Schrag, 1999). As Guiliani asserts, such a policy could certainly do no harm; "It cannot get worse; it can only get better" (Barry, 1998). Although the CUNY trustees have failed to explicitly endorse the privatization of remediation, the mayor's appointed task force on CUNY, headed by Benno Schmidt, did ("City Panel," 1999).

Yet several proprietary educational companies have actually begun to enter the remedial education business. Kaplan Education Centers and Sylvan Learning

Systems are designing and, in some cases, teaching such courses in several colleges. Dozens more in a variety of states are considering hiring one of these companies to deliver remedial courses (Gose, 1997). While there is very little evidence of success and the price for their services is often quite high, such commercial ventures are becoming increasingly palatable to colleges and universities that are being held accountable for the efficiency and success of their remedial programs.

Others maintain that remediation, or at least its cost, should be borne by the system that is perceived to have caused it—namely, the public K-12 sector. Underlying this solution is a concern for the financial cost of remediation, which is portrayed as an unjust burden on the taxpayer. George Luffey, the chairman of the Louisiana Board of Regents in 1993, articulated this concern well when he stated, "When they get remediation at four-year institutions, we're having to pay college teachers to teach courses that should have been taught in high school" ("States Step Up," 1993). Ironically, to many who champion this solution to remediation, the failure of the K-12 system is due to educational "fads" that are "unproven" (Mulcahy, 1997).

Some states, such as Massachusetts and Georgia, have developed proposals that would force school districts whose graduates are enrolled in remedial courses to pay for them. When a superintendent receives "an invoice for $14,000 from the university system for the cost of these classes, that's going to raise some eyebrows," according to the chair of the Massachusetts Board of Higher Education, James Carlin (quoted in Sandham, 1998). To date, however, no states have passed such legislation.

## Raising Standards in the K-12 Sector

One of the underlying factors that fuels the remediation debate is the perceived link between performance in the K-12 sector and performance in the postsecondary sector. This relationship is a complex one, and contradictory arguments about cause and effect abound. Some critics assert that public schools' failure to adequately educate students has resulted in the proliferation of remediation that currently characterizes American postsecondary education (e.g., "Race to the Botton," 1995; Reising, 1997). The 1999 CUNY task force report illustrates this perspective, stating that "New York City's public schools are extremely uneven in educational quality, passing on to CUNY large numbers of students whom the schools have failed" ("City Panel," 1999). Others maintain that low high school performance can only be remedied by increasing standards at the postsecondary level. In this way, colleges and universities can send a "clear message" to high schools regarding the level of rigor required to succeed in college ("Remedial Education," 1996).

In response to these debates, some statewide departments of education and large urban public school systems have developed K-12 educational reform efforts that dovetail with emerging postsecondary remediation policies. In many instances, these reforms are focused on increasing performance and graduation standards in public schools. For example, Texan high school students must pass an exit exam before receiving their diploma. In addition, the Texas Higher Education Coordinating Board instituted the Texas Academic Skills Program (TASP), a standardized exam required of all high school graduates who wish to enroll in college courses. Those students who do not pass all portions of the exam are relegated to remedial courses (Texas Higher Education Coordinating Board, 1997).

### Relegating Remedial Education to the Community College Sector

By far the most common response to the remediation "problem" is to relegate these courses solely to the two-year sector. Many states are moving toward shifting, or have already shifted, all or most remediation to the community college sector. The most prominent current example of this strategy is CUNY, which is in the process of limiting remedial education to the two-year colleges in the system. This policy was adopted by the CUNY board of trustees in 1998 and endorsed by the mayor's task force. Other states, such as Florida, California, Massachusetts, Georgia, Texas, and Virginia, are considering delivering, or have already begun to deliver, most or all of their remedial classes in the two-year sector.

This trend has the potential to seriously reduce access to four-year institutions (and, ultimately, the baccalaureate degree) for those students designated remedial. Although it is too soon to gauge the long-term effects of such policy, related research is suggestive. Sociologists and a small but important group of other educational researchers have long been quite critical of community colleges. Brint and Karabel (1988), Rhoads and Valadez (1996), London (1978) and Weis (1985) furnish compelling evidence that community colleges provide the illusion of educational opportunity, but ultimately serve to prevent or minimize the upward mobility of their poor, working class, and/or minority students. Others point to the dwindling proportion of community college liberal arts graduates (McGrath & Spear, 1991), and to evidence that the most these students can achieve is maintenance of their relative socioeconomic status in the face of a changing occupational structure.

Within the general structure of these arguments, remedial education can be seen as one of the mechanisms with which these institutions "cool out" their students. Studies conducted by Dougherty (1994), Grubb (1991), and others have consistently shown that the chances of attaining a baccalaureate degree have always been significantly reduced when students begin their postsecondary education at a community college. This is particularly true for poor and minority students, who are disproportionately represented in both the community college sector and in remedial education courses (National Center for Educational Statistics, 1994). Nationally, community college transfer rates average 22 percent, but they drop to 11 percent in the urban community colleges, in which most poor and minority students enroll (Cohen, 1992).[1] However, as the concentration of those students who are most at risk for dropout—namely, remedial students— increases in community colleges, transfer rates may well dip significantly below the averages reported by Cohen. Moreover, poor and minority students stand to be disproportionately affected by this possibility. CUNY estimates that placing remedial education in its two-year colleges will sharply reduce enrollment in its four-year colleges for all groups. While the projected drop in enrollment for whites is estimated to be 38 percent, for blacks it is 46 percent, and for Hispanics, 55 percent ("Ending Remediation," 1998). It is unclear at this point whether these students will enroll in community colleges or decide to walk away from postsecondary education altogether. Either way, their chances of obtaining a baccalaureate degree would appear to be much slimmer.

## Coordination as a Critical Variable

The most prominent emerging remedial education policies share a common characteristic: they are occurring in states or large city-wide educational systems that are highly coordinated. While these high levels of coordination are designed to increase educational quality throughout the K-16 system by raising standards and better targeting needed services to students, they could also result in a reduction in the experimentation and innovation that could improve actual remedial education practice.

In states that do not exhibit high levels of coordination within their educational systems, the picture of remediation which emerges is quite different. Rather than developing a unified policy or even philosophy regarding remediation and its role in various postsecondary education sectors, both two and four-year institutions develop their own remediation policies, often in response to concerns about the quality of local public school systems or pressures about replication of services. In Philadelphia, Pennsylvania, for example, the local state-affiliated university raised admissions standards and decreased the amount of remediation available to incoming students, choosing instead to direct such students to local community colleges. These community colleges have responded by increasing their remedial services, and several small, private four-year colleges in the area have quietly increased their remedial offerings in an attempt to attract those students turned away by the large state university. While articulation agreements between the state university and these institutions have been developed to improve the transfer process, the ways in which these shifts in policy have affected students' progress through the educational pipeline remains unclear. In states with low levels of coordination, institutional-specific policies regarding remediation may make movement through the educational pipeline difficult and confusing, and the diversity of approaches to remediation which develop may vary significantly along a number of dimensions.

## EXAMINING REMEDIATION FROM A SYSTEMS PERSPECTIVE

When taken together, the evidence suggests that some types of emerging remedial education policy could well result in real reductions in educational opportunity for disadvantaged populations. Yet to draw such a blanket conclusion would be foolhardy, given the complexities and variation of current remedial education policy. Clearly, remedial education is an issue that spans educational sectors. In both the debates surrounding remediation and the policy that is being developed, the four-year sector, the K-12 public schools, and community colleges all figure prominently. These interconnections among and between educational sectors require us to examine remediation from a systems perspective.

In the broadest sense, I use the term *system* to denote the relationships among the various sectors of public education offered within a defined geographical area, including K-12, community college, and four-year colleges and universities. The educational system that exists within a particular city, for example, may be tightly coordinated, loosely coupled, or simply a set of essentially unrelated sectors; and while the nature of the system is likely to distinctly affect the implementation of remediation policy and students' progress through the educational pipeline, the process by which such phenomena occur is unknown. Yet variations in these factors and others may significantly affect, in either positive or negative ways, access to postsecondary education. Hence, a critical element of an educational system is the degree to which it is coordinated.

However, there is virtually no research that either examines the development of remedial education practice within varying policy contexts or examines the effects of official remediation policy throughout educational "systems." To begin to explore the degree to which variation in remedial education policy exists both within and across states and their educational systems, I compare in this chapter two states: Massachusetts and Maryland. Each embodies sharply different approaches to formulating and implementing remedial education policy and practice. Yet they are roughly similar in terms of size, geographical location, and demographics (see Table 10.1).

As will be described in more detail, Massachusetts displays a highly coordinated state-wide system of higher education, while Maryland is noted for its lack of coordination. Moreover, each state has a major urban center, with a complex educational system that encompasses K-12, community colleges, and four-year colleges and universities. The wide array of approaches to remediation represented by these states provides a rich opportunity to conduct descriptive and comparative analyses of varied remediation policies and practices.

Data were collected from two major sources. First, I interviewed five state-level policy makers (three from one state, two from the other) who have been involved in debates about remediation and the development of remediation policy. I also interviewed four mid-level administrators employed at specific post-secondary institutions (two in each state). Second, I examined a variety of documents describing state-level remediation policy, state and institutional data collection capacity, and institutional-level remediation policy and practices.

## THE STATES

### Massachusetts: A Highly Coordinated Educational System

In the past several years, Massachusetts has made significant strides in developing a statewide coordinated strategy for addressing remediation. As can be seen in Table 10.2, in 1996, the Massachusetts Board of Higher Education (MBHE) adopted a statewide policy that does not allow more than 5 percent of first-time freshmen to be enrolled in remedial reading, writing, and math courses in any public four-year institution by fall 1998. In a distinct shift in the state's remedial education policy, which had formerly mandated that institutions across the system offer remediation (Massachusetts Board of Higher Education, 1998, p. 10), community colleges have now been designated as the sole deliverers of such courses.

To achieve this goal, MBHE, which governs all public two and four-year postsecondary institutions in the state, adopted a highly coordinated strategy that includes a mandatory placement examination, financial incentives for state colleges and universities to develop collaborative arrangements with local community colleges for the delivery of remedial education, mandatory submission of information about remedial education policy to the MBHE, and the establishment of a multisector Developmental Education Advisory Group (MBHE, 1998).

To support and assess the success of this new remedial education policy, MBHE has developed an extensive database which tracks the performance of high school graduates during their freshman year. Reported measures include GPA, number of remedial courses taken, number of credits earned, and whether students return their sophomore year. Plans are underway to expand this database to continue to collect longitudinal data (MBHE, 1998, p. 14). This database is designed in part to encourage partnerships between high schools and public colleges, which are seen as "[a] win-win situation for students, taxpayers, and participating institutions" (p. 14).

The state is also working toward developing an array of policies designed to mitigate the potentially negative effects on access that these remedial education policies might pose. For example, both the University of Massachusetts and the state college systems have adopted a Joint Admissions Agreement which guarantees university admission to community college students who meet certain standards (MBHE, 1986, p. 1, p. 3). In addition, the board has adopted a joint admissions tuition advantage program, in which any student enrolled at a com-

**Table 10.1**
**Summary of Pertinent Descriptive Statistics: Maryland and Massachusetts (1997)**

| | Maryland | Massachusetts |
|---|---|---|
| State Population | 5,094,000 | 6,118,000 |
| Racial and Ethnic Distribution: | | |
| White | 71% | 89.8% |
| Black | 25% | 5.0% |
| Hispanic | 2.6% | 5.0% |
| Asian | 3.0% | 2.5% |
| 1997 Per Capita Income | $28,969 | $31,524 |
| Poverty Rate | 10.2% | 10.6% |
| Number of Public Postsecondary Institutions: | | |
| 2-year | 20 | 18 |
| 4-year | 15 | 15 |
| Proportion of Adults with Bachelor's Degree | 15.6% | 16.6% |
| # Enrolled in Postsecondary Education: | | |
| 2-year | 104,118 | 72,030 |
| 4-year | 113,159 | 101,824 |
| Proportion of Enrollments Made Up of Minority | | |
| Students: 2-year | 33.3% | 19.6% |
| 4-year | 36.3% | 13.5% |
| Overall: | 32.2% | 17.7% |
| Population of City | **Baltimore:** 703,000 | |

**Table 10.1 (*Continued*)**

| | Maryland | Massachusetts |
|---|---|---|
| Minority Population of City | 59% Black<br>1% Hispanic<br>1% Asian/Pacific Islander<br>(40% White) | 26% Black<br>11% Hispanic<br>5% Asian/Pacific Islander<br>(58% White) |
| Public Four-Year Colleges in City | Univ. of Maryland, Baltimore County<br>University of Baltimore<br>Coppin State<br>Morgan State | University of Massachusetts-Boston |
| Public Two-Year Colleges in City | Baltimore City Community College | Bunker Hill Community College<br>Roxbury Community College |

205

**Table 10.2**
**Summary of Remediation Practices and Policies: State Level**

| State | Coordination/ Governance of Four-Year Institutions | Coordination/ Governance of Two-Year Institutions | State Remediation Policies: Four-Year Institutions | State Remediation Policies: Community Colleges | Degree of Variation Among Sectors | Data Collection Practices |
|---|---|---|---|---|---|---|
| Massachusetts | State-level: MA Board of Higher Education, a coordinating board with significant authority in areas of budget and broad policy | State Level: MA Board of Higher Education<br><br>All community colleges under jurisdiction of MA Board of Higher Education | By Fall 1998: No more than 5% of first-time frosh in 4-year institutions may be in remedial courses<br><br>Mandatory statewide placement exam<br><br>Strong incentives for sectors to collaborate | Nearly all remediation to be offered in two-year sector<br><br>Specifics of remediation in two-year sector left to individual institutions? | Very little. Remediation essentially eliminated in four-year sector. However, 2-year institutions vary in their approach to remediation. | In 1996, MBHE hired a national accounting firm to upgrade their databases. Since then, the state has been issuing its annual College-to-School Report. The Report breaks down data by both high school and postsecondary institution, and reports as well the percentage of students who were enrolled in remedial education during their first year of college that returned to college the following year. |
| Maryland | Maryland Higher Education Commission. Coordinating body with no jurisdiction over individual schools. Primary responsibility is policy analysis. | All community colleges have independent governing boards. | Only 1 stipulation: colleges not to give college credit for remedial courses | Only one stipulation: colleges not to give college credit for remedial courses | Extreme. Evidence of a pilot project to privatize remediation; no uniformity within or across sectors in remediation practice | Statewide Student Outcome and Achievement Report (SOAR), which includes performance of high school graduates in first year public postsecondary institutions, % of students receiving remediation in each public institution. Also tracks retention and graduation rates by high schools and colleges. |

munity college under a joint admissions program agreement will be eligible for a 33 percent tuition waiver during her or his two years of enrollment at a four-year institution (MBHE, 1998).

*The Educational System in Boston.* As Table 10.3 illustrates, Boston is the home of several public state colleges and universities, but only one is a four-year institution, University of Massachusetts–Boston (UMB). The other two, Bunker Hill Community College and Roxbury Community College, are two-year institutions. As can be seen in Table 4, only 5 percent of UMB's students are enrolled in remedial courses, per the state's requirements. The vast majority of remedial students are therefore enrolled in the city's two community colleges.

According to MBHE, collaborative arrangements among these institutions and between these institutions and the city's public high school system have emerged as a result of the increased coordination of remediation practice. For example, an Urban Collaborative Enhancement Project includes all three of the institutions listed above, plus several other area community colleges. Also, MBHE recently awarded $124,000 to UMB and an area community college to collaborate on a joint assessment, placement, and advising program (MBHE, 1998, p. 13). In addition, UMB participates in multiple partnerships with urban high schools. While it is difficult to assess at this juncture the degree to which interaction among the sectors of education within the Boston system is the result of the state's emerging remedial education policies, it is quite evident that much of its current activity is directed toward addressing the implications of these policies.

At the same time, the state is implementing a statewide testing program for grades 4, 8, and 10. By 1999 all students will be tested in English, mathematics, science and technology, and history. Beginning in the year 2001, students will be required to pass the 10th grade test in order to graduate. However, support for students who perform poorly will be a local responsibility (Massachusetts Department of Education, 1998b, pp. 1–5). Boston's public school system, under the direction of Superintendent Thomas Payzant, has, for the last several years, been undergoing significant reform.

## Maryland: A State with Little Coordination in Educational Policy

In contrast to Massachusetts, Maryland's Higher Education Commission (MHEC) has very little direct authority over public postsecondary institutions (Table 10.2). Rather, the primary mission of MHEC is to conduct broad, state-wide planning and policy analysis in the postsecondary education arena. While MHEC does use its office to issue various policy recommendations, individual postsecondary institutions retain a high degree of autonomy.

Partly as a result of this low level of coordination, the state does not have a coordinated policy regarding remedial education. Moreover, the Maryland state

**Table 10.3**
**Summary of Educational Systems: Baltimore, MD, and Boston, MA**

| | BALTIMORE | BOSTON |
|---|---|---|
| Size of K-12 Public School System | 111,891 | 98,000 |
| Current K-12 Reform Efforts | Standards-Based Reform, including a new Master Plan that requires performance standards for both teachers and students | Standards-Based Reform, which aligns with requirements of the 1993 Massachusetts Education Reform Act. |
| Amount, Type of State Control of K-12 System | State abolished school board and has established alternative governance structure that includes an advisory board.<br><br>Management of district seen to be in complete disarray. | Standardized K-12 exams state-instituted and controlled |
| Standardized Exams | Participates in statewide standards-based exams. Has performed poorly | Exams in grades 4, 8, and 10<br><br>By 2001, cannot graduate without passing 10th grade exam |
| Public Postsecondary Institutions: | | |
| Four-Year: | University of Baltimore (upper level only)<br>Undergrad enrollment: 1,795<br>Minority enrollment: 25% Black<br> 1% Hispanic<br> 3% API<br> 71% White<br><br>Coppin State (Historically Black Institution)<br>Undergrad enrollment: 3,540<br>Minority enrollment: 95% Black<br> 5% Other | University of Massachusetts, Boston<br>Undergrad enrollment: 7,804<br>Minority enrollment:<br> 13% Black<br> 5% Hispanic<br> 9% API<br> 73% White |

Table 10.3 (*Continued*)

|  | BALTIMORE | BOSTON |
|---|---|---|
|  | University of Maryland, Baltimore County<br>Undergrad enrollment: 8,014<br>Minority enrollment: 16% Black<br>2% Hispanic<br>14% API<br>68% White |  |
|  | Morgan State<br>Undergrad enrollment: 6,299<br>Minority enrollment: 95% Black<br>5% Other |  |
| Two-Year: | Baltimore City Community College<br>Undergrad enrollment: 5,970<br>Minority enrollment: 74% Black<br>1% Hispanic<br>2% API<br>24% White | Roxbury Community College<br>Undergrad enrollment: 2,600<br>Minority enrollment: 62% Black<br>26% Hispanic<br>2% AP<br>10% White |
|  |  | Bunker Hill Community College<br>Undergrad enrollment: 5,695<br>Minority enrollment: 21% Black<br>12% Hispanic<br>13% API<br>54% White |

legislature has displayed little interest in this topic, as is evidenced by the fact that no bills regarding remediation have been introduced to date (Michael J. Keller, personal communication, August/September 1998). The state's lack of coordination in the postsecondary arena has resulted in remarkably diverse approaches to remediation across institutions. They vary along the dimensions of amount and type of remediation offered, placement exams, and limits on remedial courses. The only uniformity in remediation policy that exists is the requirement that no college-level credit be offered for remedial courses.

Yet there is some movement toward increased coordination of remediation policy. In 1996, the MHEC issued a report on remediation practice and policy at all state-affiliated postsecondary institutions. In large part due to the prodding of the Maryland Department of Education (the K-12 governing entity) and MHEC, the instructional deans of all Maryland community colleges have voluntarily convened to develop a set of more standardized procedures regarding remedial testing and placement. While these plans are tentatively scheduled to be implemented in the year 2000, participation is voluntary and extends only to formal placement and examination procedures. Moreover, there is some doubt that the plans will go into effect by the scheduled date (Michael J. Keller, personal communication, August/September 1998).

*The Educational System in Baltimore.* Unlike Boston, which houses only one public four-year institution, Baltimore is home to four, including two HBCUs (Coppin State and Morgan State). However, the city has only one community college, which enrolls a relatively small number of students (under 6,000). As can be seen in Table 10.3, these institutions vary significantly with regard to size and demographics; just as importantly, they vary in their approaches to remediation as well.

In fact, these institutions display a remarkable array of remediation policies and practices. As Table 10.4 illustrates, the city's only community college enrolls the highest proportion of its students in remedial education—84 percent. However, the proportion of students enrolled in Baltimore's four-year institutions varies dramatically. The University of Baltimore, which offers only the last two years of a college education, enrolls less than 1 percent of its students in remedial classes, and offers only remediation in math only. In contrast, 66 percent of Coppin State's students require remediation, and the college's offerings are far more extensive, including courses in math, writing, and reading, as well as skills labs.

The vast majority of students who graduate from Baltimore City public schools and attend college do so at one of the five public institutions in Baltimore. As Table 10.2 suggests, the Baltimore public school system is currently in disarray; as a result of a long-standing lawsuit regarding its Special Education practices, the state in 1996 terminated the city's superintendent, and appointed an advisory board to govern the system. An interim superintendent has been appointed to develop a short and long-term reform plan, and the system is in the process of finalizing a master plan for reform, which includes performance standards for teachers and students. The state of Maryland, which has long been at the forefront of the standards movement in the K-12 sector, has developed a statewide, mandatory testing plan in which the Baltimore public schools participate. Nearly 80 percent of the schools in the state identified as "low performance" on these exams are located in the city of Baltimore ("State Vows to Improve Readiness," 1997).

## Comparing the States

As can be discerned from the narrative description of each state and city above along with the summary information provided in Tables 10.2 through 10.4, Massachusetts and Maryland display strikingly different approaches to educational policymaking in general, and remediation in particular, at the state level. Massachusetts is a more highly coordinated state at all levels, and across sectors as well. Remediation is controlled in both the four-year and the two-year sectors, and students enrolled in the K-12 system will soon be unable to successfully graduate without passing a state-wide exam. Moreover, the state can now successfully track the movement of its students from one sector to another by virtue of its upgraded databases.

Maryland, in contrast, displays a distinctly "hands-off" approach to educational policy making at nearly all levels. Policies and practices related to remedial education vary significantly both within and across sectors; and in contrast to Massachusetts' reliance on a single placement exam, Maryland's colleges and universities utilize 18 separate tests, along with a myriad of locally developed instruments. Students need only pass a remedial course in Maryland to move on to college-level courses; in Massachusetts, they must pass both the course and a standardized exit exam. And while the state has placed a cap of no more than 5 percent of four-year college students enrolled in remedial courses in Massachusetts, the four-year institutions in Baltimore vary wildly in the percentage of their students enrolled in remedial courses, from a low of 1 percent to a high of 66 percent.

Differences in policy at the state level result in profoundly different practice at the institutional level. Moreover, as may be inferred by a system-wide review of remediation practices across Boston and Baltimore, students who test into remedial courses in these two cities have extremely different experiences. Whereas Boston's two community colleges are currently using locally developed tests for remedial placement, the state is moving towards implementing a standardized assessment procedure. Each institution both tests for and offers courses in three areas—reading, writing, and mathematics. Also, students must successfully pass an exit exam before moving into college-level courses. In short, the remedial experiences in Boston are fast becoming increasingly standardized, and increasingly rigorous as well.

In contrast, underprepared students entering the postsecondary arena in Bal-

**Table 10.4**
**Summary of Remediation by Postsecondary Institutions in Each System: Baltimore, MD, and Boston, MA**

| INSTITUTION | % Students Taking at Least 1 Remedial Course | Placement in Remedial Courses Determined by: | Type of Remediation Offered | Requirements for Leaving Remedial Courses | Limitations on Taking Remedial Courses |
|---|---|---|---|---|---|
| University of Maryland, Baltimore County | 13% | Locally developed norms* | Math, writing and reading courses | Satisfactory completion of course | Limit of 3 times |
| University of Baltimore | <1% | Locally developed norms | Math course only | Satisfactory completion of course | None |
| Coppin State | 66% | Locally developed norms | Math, writing, and reading classes; Skills lab | Satisfactory completion of course; Passing exit exam | None |
| Morgan State | 27% | Locally developed norms | Summer program for incoming students needing remediation; students must pass exit exam to enroll in college-level courses in fall; Program includes math, writing, and reading courses | Satisfactory completion of summer remediation program | None |
| Baltimore City Community College | 84% | Locally developed norms | Math, writing and reading courses | Satisfactory completion of course | Limit of 2 times |

**Table 10.4 (Continued)**

| INSTITUTION | % Students Taking at Least 1 Remedial Course | Placement in Remedial Courses Determined by: | Type of Remediation Offered | Requirements for Leaving Remedial Courses | Limitations on Taking Remedial Courses |
|---|---|---|---|---|---|
| University of Massachusetts, Boston | 5% (required as of 9/1/98) | Currently locally-developed norms, but state task force just completed plan to Standardized assessment practices | Math, writing and reading courses | Satisfactory completion of course; Passing exit exam | No limit |
| Bunker Hill Community College | 60% | Currently locally-developed norms, but state task force just completed plan to standardize assessment practices | Math, writing and reading courses | Satisfactory completion of course; Passing exit exam | No limit |
| Roxbury Community College | 81% | Currently locally-developed norms, but state task force just completed plan to standardize assessment practices | Math, writing and reading courses | Satisfactory completion of course; Passing exit exam | No limit |

*Each institution uses a placement test; however, there is wide variation in the types of placement tests used across the state, including over 18 standardized tests as well as a myriad of locally developed instruments.

213

timore are confronted with a dizzying array of options, none of which presents a clear-cut advantage over the other. While the vast majority of students at some institutions enroll in remedial courses, very few are placed in such courses at other colleges. Unlike Boston's movement toward standardized placement and testing procedures, Baltimore's postsecondary institutions utilize a wide variety of placement procedures. The extent and content of courses varies significantly as well, ranging from one math course at University of Baltimore, to math, writing and reading classes plus skills labs at Coppin State. Morgan State even offers a summer program for incoming students. And whereas some institutions require students to pass an exit exam in addition to receiving a passing grade in remedial courses, the city's community college has no such requirement.

However, it is important to note a critical contextual factor that may also affect students' experiences of remediation: namely, the relative number of two-year versus four-year institutions in each city. In Boston, most students who are designated remedial attend one of the two community colleges in that city; at least at the community college level, they have a limited choice. However, if they successfully make it through remediation, the only public four-year institution that is available to them is the University of Massachusetts–Boston. As a result, the policies and practices of UMB are profoundly important to their ability to obtain a baccalaureate degree. The clear and consistent messages that the state's highly coordinated remedial education policy sends provide a clear roadmap both for individual students, and for the city's K-12 public education sector as well.

Baltimore's top-heavy configuration of postsecondary institutions provides a distinctly different context for remediation practice and policy. Because the city has only one community college (and a small one at that), a state-wide policy that would locate all remediation in the community college sector might well be a logistical nightmare for the city as well as for Baltimore City Community College. However, the wildly varying remediation practices that exist in the city's five postsecondary institutions are inherently confusing. In the absence of a uniform set of remediation policies, how do students determine which institution provides them with the best chances of success? And, just as importantly, what cues does the Baltimore public school system take from the disorganization of the rest of the educational system in the city?

## A SYSTEMS-BASED RESEARCH AGENDA ON REMEDIATION

Obviously, such questions demand a more thorough and detailed analysis of remediation policy and practice. When taken as a whole, this initial overview of remediation policies and practices in two states suggests that remedial education cannot be understood as a monolithic, uniform approach to dealing with issues of preparation and "college readiness." Indeed, despite the ideologically inspired rhetoric surrounding remediation, which I have documented elsewhere

(Shaw, 1997), the effects of remedial education on movement through the educational pipeline are likely to be dependent upon a number of factors occurring at various levels of educational policy making and practice, including state level, system level, and institutional level. It is simply impossible to determine whether remediation, in all of its variations, is wholly good or wholly bad on a global level.

It is for these reasons that studies that continue to explore the ways in which remediation affects, and is affected by, the various educational sectors are critically important. Unless we first understand the specific context in which remediation policy emerges and the specific ways in which this policy plays out in the K-12, community college, and four-year sectors, we cannot reasonably assess the effects of these policies on students' educational success. In the field of evaluation, these issues are often framed in terms of getting into the "black box" of an intervention, so as to understand first whether a particular model was implemented in the way it was intended. Only after establishing a thick description of how that intervention operates at all levels can we then assess its effectiveness. This is the case, as well, for remediation.

To that end, I pose a set of specific research questions that are designed to uncover the context in which remediation policy emerges, the ways in which these policies are functioning at the state, institutional, and classroom level, and ultimately, what their effects on student mobility might be. These questions include the following:

**State Level**

1. How does each state approach remediation? How is remedial education defined? Do coordinated remediation policies exist? Why or why not? What is the history behind the coordination (or lack thereof) of the state's postsecondary education sector? How do they interrelate within each level of the postsecondary system, and the governing board for the state's public education?

2. What types of political, ideological, or financial concerns led to each state's current postsecondary education system? How do these concerns affect each state's current approach to remedial education policy?

**System Level**

1. What are the remedial education policies that exist in the major postsecondary institutions in each system? How do the remedial education policies and practices that exist within the system relate to each other? How does K-12 educational policy, particularly with regard to standards and graduation requirements, relate to remediation policy at the postsecondary level? To what degree do standards and remediation policy complement or contradict each other across each system? How is this practice influenced by policy emerging at the state level?

2. How do the remedial education policies that exist in each system affect the retention

of students throughout the K-16 educational pipeline? Are the effects evenly distributed among ethnic and racial groups?

**Institutional Level**

1. In what ways do institutions from each sector in the system (high schools, community colleges and four-year institutions) differ in their responses to remediation philosophy, policy, and practice?
2. How is this practice influenced by emerging policies at the state level? At other institutions within the system?
3. How do the interactions between students and faculty engaged in remedial activity vary across these institutions?

## POLICY IMPLICATIONS FOR THE 21ST CENTURY

Remediation has the potential to profoundly affect the purpose and functioning of every sector of public education. Hence, as we continue to debate the merits and purposes of remediation, we debate as well the role that education will play in this country as we enter the new millennium. One thing is certain, however: unless we creatively address the underlying issues that have made remedial education a necessary component of the postsecondary educational landscape, access to meaningful higher education will continue to elude large portions of our population.

Like many, I would argue that, ultimately, our goal should be to eliminate the need for remedial education in our postsecondary institutions. There are, however, several different strategies that can be adopted to achieve this goal. On the one hand, we can devote our energies toward developing a more highly stratified and structured postsecondary education system, the better with which to sort students into varying levels of educational access. This certainly seems to be the most common approach to addressing the remediation problem as we head into the 21st century. Many states and educational systems see community colleges as the only logical place in which to offer remediation; others are toying with the idea of locating remediation outside of the public postsecondary sector altogether, to be offered by for-profit entities such as Sylvan Learning Centers. In this scenario, students will literally never darken the doorstep of a public college—either four-year or two-year—unless, and until, they have adequately demonstrated their proficiency in reading, writing and mathematics. As a result, remediation will indeed be eliminated from the postsecondary sector.

Yet locating remediation wholly outside the four-year sector erects barriers to the baccalaureate that are extremely difficult to overcome. In addition to the obvious access and equity issues such policies pose, this type of approach to remediation may well be ultimately untenable, in large part because four-year institutions cannot afford to lose substantial portions of their current student populations to community colleges or entrepreneurial enterprises. Undoubtedly, student enrollment in four-year colleges and universities will begin to shrink (in many, it already has); and with the decline, the need for large portions of tenured faculty and those who give administrative support to the postsecondary educational enterprise will also shrink. As a result, the external pressure to increase "quality" and "standards" that has fueled recent changes in remediation policy may ultimately be supplanted by far more pragmatic concerns emerging from within the academy, such as job stability and financial resources. Already, we have begun to hear "underground" stories about the ways in which some four-year institutions "get around" their states' remedial education restrictions in order to continue to enroll this portion of the student body; such stories will probably continue to emerge as public four-year institutions face the implications of sharply decreasing enrollments brought on by these policies.

The movement toward removing remedial education from the four-year sector can, however, result in creative and meaningful agreements between community colleges and four-year institutions, such as joint admissions agreements, core courses with common syllabi, and other innovative approaches designed to reduce the disparities between the two- and four-year experience. While it will probably always be more difficult for students in pursuit of a baccalaureate degree to achieve their goals by first attending a community college, postsecondary educational systems are capable of significantly reducing the barriers to transfer that have traditionally existed—particularly when receiving institutions are motivated by financial necessity.

Yet to look for future solutions to the remediation issue solely in the postsecondary sector is to miss a critical contributing factor. Talk of "forcing" the K-12 sector to deal with remediation before students enter the hallways of academe is becoming increasingly common. Although there is almost no evidence of any educational policy that places real (e.g., financial) pressure on public education to actually "remediate" its graduates that do not pass postsecondary entrance examinations, standards-based educational reform often does carry with it a financial incentive for schools to increase the number of students that pass standardized achievement or graduation tests. As we move into the 21st century, we should pay careful attention to the degree to which such K-12 policies affect the proportion of students entering postsecondary education who require remediation.

While the emphasis on outcomes, which is a prominent component of the standards-based K-12 educational reform movement, may improve academic performance for some, it does not provide a systematic, comprehensive approach for addressing the needs of those students most at risk for failure: poor and/or minority students in large urban areas. Certainly, students who place into remedial courses come from all different racial and ethnic backgrounds. Yet they are disproportionately from low-income households, a fact that has a critical bearing on the quality of education that they receive. It has been amply documented that there is an enormous disparity in the per-pupil expenditure across school districts, a variable that is largely explained by the property taxes on which so much of so many school districts' budgets are based (Kozol, 1987). As our housing patterns become increasingly segregated by race and ethnicity (Massey and Denton, 1996), such disparities promise to grow. Recent efforts by New Jersey, Massachusetts, and other states to redistribute educational resources in a more equitable manner are encouraging, but they are being met by strong resistance on many fronts. As a result, we are unlikely to see anything approaching an adequate level of funding for those students most in need of a quality K-12 education as we enter the next millenium. Stark differences in the quality of preparation that public school students receive will continue to insure that the playing field is anything but level.

Yet the need for postsecondary education continues to grow in this postindustrial economy. Employment options for those without a college degree are shrinking particularly in urban areas. Meanwhile, options are increasing for college graduates—particularly those with well-honed technical skills. As a result, our economy is producing a bifurcated population that consists of those with the skills and credentials necessary to make a living wage, and those without. Within this context, college attendance promises to become ever more critical to an individual's economic well-being. Thus, regardless of how poorly prepared students may be, they will nevertheless continue to seek access to the baccalaureate degree.

Clearly, the K-12 and postsecondary sectors of education will continue to be intricately entwined, regardless of whether we perceive and act on their relationship to each other. Indeed, the current remediation rhetoric which pits one sector of education against another does little for those students who must successfully navigate their way through the entire K-16 pipeline. As we begin a new century, it is therefore incumbent upon us as educators, as parents, and as citizens to reconceptualize our thinking about the educational system as one that encompasses all elements of public education—from kindergarten through the baccalaureate degree. Only by taking a systems perspective can we begin to think about the ways in which weaknesses in one sector contribute to weaknesses in another. In doing so, we can ultimately begin to envision as well ways to build strength into each sector that will benefit all of them.

Will we expend the resources that will enable us to construct educational systems that provide an adequate education at all levels for all students—thus eliminating the need for remediation? And if not, will changes in remedial education policy facilitate movement through the educational pipeline, or hinder it? Ultimately, the answers to these questions will determine whether access to higher education and its prize, the baccalaureate degree, will again become a fading dream to large portions of our population that have traditionally been disenfranchised from higher education in this country.

## NOTE

1. These figures are based on research conducted by Arthur Cohen, who calculates transfer in the following manner: among students who are enrolled in a community

college for the first time and have completed at least 12 credits, the percentage of these that transfer successfully to a four-year college within four years.

## REFERENCES

American Council on Education. (1996). *Remedial education: An undergraduate student profile*. Washington, DC: Author.

Astin, A. (1998). *Evaluating remedial programs is not just a methodological issue*. Paper presented at the Conference on Replacing Remediation in Higher Education, Stanford, CA.

Barry, D. (1998, January 30). The Guiliani budget: The Politics. *New York Times*, pp. 43, 48.

Boylan, H. (1992). *The impact of developmental education programs*. Paper presented at the First National Conference on Research in Developmental Education, Charlotte, NC.

Boylan, H. (1995). Making the case for developmental education. *Research in Developmental Education, 12* (2), 57–61.

Brint, S., & Karabel, J. (1988). *The diverted dream: Community colleges and the promise of educational opportunity in America*. New York: Oxford University Press.

Chaffee, J. (1998). *Critical thinking: The cornerstone of remedial education*. Paper presented at the Conference on Replacing Remediation in Higher Education, Stanford, CA.

City panel rips decline at CUNY. (1999, June 5). *New York Daily News*, p. 7.

Clark, B. (1960). *The open door college*. New York: McGraw-Hill.

Cohen, A. (1992). *Defining and tracking transfer in community colleges*. Report to the Ford Foundation. Unpublished ms.

Commander, N. E., & Stratton, C. B. (1998). *Beyond remediation: Adjunct courses as a new direction for academic assistance*. Paper presented at the Conference on Replacing Remediation in Higher Education, Stanford, CA.

Dougherty, K. (1994). *The contradictory college*. Albany: State University of New York Press.

Ending remediation. (1993, June 5). *Change*, p. A26.

From remediation to acceleration: Raising the bar in developmental education. (1999). *Change Magazine, 31* (1) 57–60.

Gose, B. (1997, September 19). Tutoring companies take over remedial teaching at some colleges. *Chronicle of Higher Education*, p. A44.

Grubb, W. N. (1991). The decline of transfer rates: Evidence from national longitudinal surveys. *Journal of Higher Education, 62* (2), 194–217.

Grubb, W. N. (1998). *From black box to Pandora's box: Evaluating remedial/developmental education*. Paper presented at the Conference on Replacing Remediation in Higher Education, Stanford, CA.

Hawkins, B. D., & Phillip, M. C. (1993, January 28). Calls to raise admissions standards open Pandora's box of issues for campuses, students. *Black Issues in Higher Education*, pp. 32–34.

Healy, P. (1998, June 5). CUNY; 4-year colleges ordered to phased out remedial education. *Chronicle of Higher Education*, A 26.

Hull, G. (1998). *Alternatives to remedial writing: Lessons from theory, from history, and a case in point*. Paper presented at the Conference on Replacing Remediation in Higher Education, Stanford, CA.

In America: Cleansing CUNY. (1998, May 29). *New York Times*, p. A29.

Lavin, D., & Hyllegard, D. (1996). *Changing the odds: Open admissions and the life chances of the disadvantaged.* New Haven, CT: Yale University Press.

Levin, H. (1999). *Remediation in the community college.* Paper presented at the Workshop on the Multiple and Changing Roles of the Community College. Social Science Research Council, New York.

London, H. B. (1978). *The culture of a community college.* New York: Praeger Press.

Manno, B. (1995). Remedial education: Replacing the double standard with real standards. *Change,* 27 (3) pp. 47–59.

Martin, D. C., & Arendale, D. R. (1998). *Mainstreaming of developmental education: Supplemental instruction and video-based supplemental instruction.* Paper presented at the Conference for Replacing Remediation in Higher Education, Stanford, CA.

Maryland Higher Education Commission. (1996). *Study of remedial education at Maryland public campuses.* Annapolis: Author.

Maryland Higher Education Commission. (1997). *Relationship between high school and college performance by Maryland students.* Annapolis: Author.

Massachusetts Board of Higher Education. (n.d.). *Implementation guide for Massachusetts Board of higher education developmental education policy for the Commonwealth's public colleges and university.* Boston,: Author.

Massachusetts Board of Higher Education. (1997a). *College-to-school report for Massachusetts high school graduates: Second annual report.* Boston: Author.

Massachusetts Board of Higher Education. (1997b). *Mindpower in Massachusetts: The Commonwealth's natural resource.* Boston: Author.

Massachusetts Board of Higher Education. (1997c). *New admissions standards for the Massachusetts state colleges and universities: Implementation guide for high school guidance counselors.* Boston: Author.

Massachusetts Board of Higher Education. (1998). *Joint admissions agreements.* Boston: Author.

Massachusetts Department of Education. (1998a). *Guide to the Massachusetts comprehensive assessment system: Science and technology.* Boston: Author.

Massachusetts Department of Education. (1998b). *The Massachusetts test for students: Read all about it!* Available: http://www.doe.mass.edu/mcag/ganda98

McGrath, D., & Spear, M. (1991). *The academic crisis of the community college.* Albany: State University of New York Press.

Mulcahy, R. (1997). Should school districts pay for college remediation? *American Teacher, 82*(4), 4.

National Center for Educational Statistics. (1994). *Report on the state of remedial education, 1992–1993.* Washington, DC: U.S. Department of Education.

Open admissions cheats best students. (1998, May 29). *New York Times*, p. A20.

Race to the bottom: The remedial crisis. (1995, June 18). *Washington Times*, pp. B1, B3.

Ready or not: California plans to cut down remedial courses at four-year colleges. (1995, March 31). *The Chronicle of Higher Education*, p. A23.

Reising, R. W. (1997). Postsecondary remediation. *The Clearing House, 70,* 172–173.

Remedial education: The high cost of catching up. (1996, March 17). *Boston Globe*, p. 26.

Remedial education: The responsibility of high schools? (1996, March 31). *Chicago Tribune*, pp. 4, 12.

Rhoads, R. A., & Valadez, J. R. (1996). *Democracy, multiculturalism, and the community college*. New York: Garland Press.

Rouche, J. E., & Rouche, S. D. (1993). *Between a rock and a hard place: The at-risk student in the open door college*. Washington, DC: The Community College Press.

Sandham, J. L. (1998, February 18). Mass. plan would make districts pay for remediation. *Education Week*, p. 23.

Schrag, P. (1999). End of the second chance? The crusade against remedial education. *American Prospect, 44*, 68–74.

Shaw, K. M. (1997). Remedial education as ideological battleground: Emerging remedial education policies and their implications for community college student mobility. *Educational Evaluation and Policy Analysis*, 284–296.

Southern Regional Education Board. (1986). College-level study: What is it? *Issues in Higher Education, 22*, 1–4.

State vows to improve readiness for college. (1997, June 29). *Baltimore Sun*, p. 15B.

States step up efforts to end remedial courses at four-year colleges. (1993, January 24). *The Chronicle of Higher Education*, p. A28.

Students who want extra help: One-year limit on remedial work at CUNY dismays many. (1995), July 1). *New York Times*, p. 21.

Texas Higher Education Coordinating Board. (1997). *TASP: FYI*. Austin: Author.

Tinto, V. (1998). *Learning communities and the reconstruction of remedial education in higher education*. Paper presented at Conference on Replacing Remediation in Higher Education, Stanford, CA.

Traub, J. (1995). *City on a hill: Testing the American dream at city college*. Reading, MA: Addison-Wesley.

Weis, L. (1985). *Between two worlds*. New York: Routledge.

## Chapter 11

# Teaching and Learning in the New Information Age: State-System Policies for Technology

*Rosa Cintrón, Connie Dillon,*
*and Tammy Boyd*

Technology is a driving force for change throughout all sectors of our society. Within this context, higher education is often criticized for moving too slowly and even accused of resisting technological change. Among higher-education institutions, the community college, with its reputation for innovation and entrepreneurial solutions, is uniquely positioned to provide leadership in applying technology to improve teaching and learning in the 21st century. However, community colleges do not exist within a vacuum; rather, they are subject to a variety of political pressures from within and outside the higher-education community. State policies reflect these pressures and can serve either as a force for, or a barrier to, significant change. For example, during the 1990s, statewide coordinating and governing boards continued to be involved with community colleges through public policies dealing with issues of access, cost, quality, development, and utilization of classroom technology (Epper, 1997, p. 553).

To be successful and effective, the integration of technology into the classroom must move from marginal usage to the day-to-day practices of higher education. This change will not happen in a policy vacuum. Public policy must be a force for change if such change is to be institutionalized. If this change becomes a desirable goal, the relationship among technology, public policy, and the traditional mission of the community college will become clear.

We have come to realize that the adoption of distance education in higher education depends not upon a rational system . . . but rather upon a political system. . . . Issues of policy rather than issues of effectiveness will ultimately determine the place of distance education in higher education. . . . If distance education requires us to transform our vision of teaching and learning, that vision will be largely defined by the community college. (Dillon & Cintrón, 1997, pp. 1–2)

A recent review of literature examining research pertaining to technology in the community college identified four recurring themes: (1) access and equality, (2) teaching and learning, (3) quality, and (4) technological infrastructure (Dillon & Cintrón, 1997). In this chapter we explore the congruity between what the literature suggests we know about technology in the community college and how states are responding to technological change. For each theme we identified the following questions:

1. *Access and Equality*: What policies, if any, direct the access to instructional technologies in teaching and learning?
2. *Teaching and Learning*: What policies, if any, direct the use of instructional technologies in teaching and learning? What do these policies indicate, if anything, about the role(s) of faculty and students as teachers and learners?
3. *Quality*: What are the criteria defining quality in the use of instructional technologies in teaching and learning?
4. *Technology Infrastructure*: Who controls the infrastructure to technologies? Who has (has no) access to the infrastructure?

We began with an analysis of seven current research studies that focused on some facet of technology and state higher-education policies. Then we examined seven states' actual higher-education policy documents relating to technology for teaching and learning. The states are those of the Big 12 institutions: Colorado, Iowa, Kansas, Missouri, Nebraska, Oklahoma, and Texas. The policies' governing authority varies from state to state, with some state policies governing all higher-education institutions and others governing all public education (Tellefson & Fountain, 1994). In some of the seven states, community colleges are governed as part of the higher-education system (Oklahoma, Texas, Nebraska, Missouri); in others they are governed as part of the Vocational-Technical system (Colorado); in still others they are governed as part of the public education system, which includes K-12 (Iowa and Kansas).

## TECHNOLOGY AND HIGHER EDUCATION: POLICY STUDIES

A review of the seven current policy studies analyzed the evolution of telecommunications in several states. Some states were studied by more than one researcher: Colorado, Minnesota, and Maine (Epper, 1996); Utah, Oregon, and Colorado (Ketcheson, 1996); and Minnesota, Hawaii, and Oregon, (Orozco, 1991). Two studies focused on educational telecommunications systems (Epper, 1996; Ketcheson, 1996), while the third examined state government infrastructure (Orozco, 1991). Last, two of the five policies studied provided state-by-state analyses of educational telecommunications policies, either at a regional or national level (Hezel Associates, 1998; Southern Regional Education Board, 1997).

## Access and Equality

The review revealed that educational access and economic development for rural areas serve as the driving force behind the development of telecommunications systems. For example, in Maine the use of telecommunications in higher education is aimed at increasing the employability of the general population (Epper, 1996). In most states, the use of the telecommunications infrastructure for stimulating economic development focuses on its educational applications and other economic and governmental services. It is important to note that there is very little discussion about the use of technology to address educational inequities of the legally defined protected classes.

Another issue related to access and equality is that of funding policies. Telecommunications is assumed by policy makers to be an efficient way to reduce the cost of education, while cost recovery is a goal often cited and planned to be achieved through charges to institutional users, that is, students. Institutional charges vary among the states, with some states charging all users equal rates and others having a system of differential charges, generally based on the nature of use, usage, or distance. One similarity among these policies is the lack of clarity as to how institutions will recover these costs, whether through operating funds, tuition, or usage fees passed on to the students. The relationship between technology and educational equality remains unclear, if not problematic, as these policies do not address an equation whereby full-cost recovery, access, and equality are offered to an increasingly diverse student population. One of the most powerful assumptions behind these policies (that telecommunications can reduce educational costs) may be erroneous, unfounded and insufficiently based on empirical research because there is an absence of data equating the implementation of technology to lower costs.

## Teaching and Learning

In general, the investment in the technological infrastructure is much greater than the investment in the educational infrastructure. There is very little written guidance in these policies or in the general policy literature about support for the effective utilization of these technologies. One exception is the state of Utah, where annualized funding for faculty development is provided. The quality of teaching and learning generally lies within the institutional reward structure, as opposed to being a state-mandated responsibility. It is unclear how any given institution (within the systems of the states analyzed in these studies) will be able to formulate, implement, and evaluate the integration of technology in teaching and learning without some push from the state level. These studies identified policies that are, also, almost silent regarding the state or institutions that have the responsibility of providing student support services (e.g., libraries, financial aid, articulation with four-year colleges, admission, and advising).

The scholarly literature about faculty perceptions of classroom technology indicates that the faculty perceive technology as an enhancement of teaching, as opposed to a vehicle for changing teaching. Additionally, how and how much faculty will use technology as an instructional tool will be determined by the leadership provided through institutional policy (Parisot, 1997). Dallet and Opper (1997) suggest that the most difficult aspect in the adoption of technology in teaching and learning will be addressing the culture(s) of higher education and changing faculty duties so that teaching no longer depends on the physical proximity of the student and teacher for 15-week semesters.

## Quality

In the policy studies, the issues of quality are discussed in terms of jurisdiction. In other words, the impetus for developing an educational telecommunications infrastructure in many states is the threat of competition from educational providers in other states. Yet Kovel-Jarboe (1997) indicates that although geographic service areas have impacted much of the policy relating to institutional missions, these documents have often been more about differentiating among types of institutions in a specific locale and less about duplication of programs. The same author cautions policy makers that, as it has become feasible to deliver courses, programs, and whole degrees without regard to the location of the learner, the educational mission may be acquiring a new meaning. Therefore, notions of duplication, overlap, and uniqueness shift dramatically with permeable geographic boundaries (Kovel-Jarboe, 1997, p. 28). Thus, at the state level, the debate is between fostering "intrastate competition" versus "intrastate cooperation," thus resulting in the elimination of duplicate programs. It was also observed that most states are transferring regulatory authority to regional accrediting agencies while contemporaneously making significant changes in quality measures.

Some authors have argued that traditionally, the strategies for assuring quality have been primarily regulatory (e.g., accreditation). However, "distance education forces us to alter our understanding of the purpose of and audience for education and policies must reflect that shift. . . . [In other words,] seat time or contact hours [might become] meaningless in the distributed learning environment" (Kovel-Jarboe, 1997, p. 25).

## Technological Infrastructure

The issues with respect to higher education relate to its role in the priorities established for access to state-level technological infrastructure. Questions emerge in relation to the role that higher education should play along with other governmental agencies in establishing priorities and the ability of the educational sector to compete, at the same level, with many other agencies (e.g., hospitals, K-12). Higher education often participates as only one member of many among advisory councils that oversee these services. This situation becomes more difficult for colleges and universities as the increasing variety and complexity of the telecommunication technologies cannot be easily managed by existing policies and structures (Zeller, 1995).

Issues of access, priorities, and the role of higher education in the infrastructure of technology will continue to be challenged by the transition from technologies that lend themselves to centralization (e.g., satellite and broadcast technologies) to technologies that are more decentralized in nature (e.g., the Internet and the World Wide Web).

Another important issue related to technological infrastructure is that of control. Who will control the infrastructure? Most of the states identified in the policy studies have opted for state-controlled telecommunications systems. It remains unclear whether some states will lease services from private telecommunications providers and how much the regulation of the infrastructure will be controlled by a public utility commission.

In summary, we can note some discrepancy between the scholarly literature and the policy studies we reviewed. Whether or not this is another example of the chasm between academic research and policy making is unclear. Nonetheless, these studies suggest that state policies are not informed by, or at least fail to integrate, empirical findings in the following areas: the relationship between cost recovery, access, and equality; ways to teach and learn with technology; leadership; and student support services.

## BIG-12 POLICIES

Our analysis of state-level polices used the framework proposed by Anderson (1994), who stated, "Policy formulation involves developing pertinent and acceptable proposed courses of action (often called alternatives, proposals, or options) for dealing with public problems" (p. 102). This study does not analyze the implementation or evaluation of the policies under scrutiny. Rather, it treats these policies as independent variables so that the analysis discusses various means by which these policies address teaching and learning with technologies in the listed states' community colleges. According to the American Association of Community Colleges (1999), there are a total of 158 public community colleges in the states under analysis: Colorado (16); Iowa (17); Kansas (20); Missouri (13); Nebraska (7); Oklahoma (17); and Texas (68).

### Data Collection

For each state, the coordinating board for the community college sector was contacted through phone or E-mail. The nature of the study was explained and all policies regarding teaching with technology were solicited. These documents included statewide plans, legislation, web sites, annual reports, conference presentations, contracted technical reports, coordinating board rules, administrative codes, and surveys. This material was supplemented by additional documentation including phone interviews, analysis of documents pertaining to other states, and perusal of the *Chronicle of Higher Education*. Five of the seven states contacted submitted their policies. A one-page policy statement was received from Kansas and Iowa, both of which did not further respond to the requests presented.

### Data Analysis

Themes and categories were developed based upon a prior review of the literature (Dillon & Cintrón, 1997). These themes were used to reduce the information in the various documents to a manageable and meaningful matrix where the similarities and differences were illustrated providing data for interstate analysis.

## RESULTS

### Definition of Instructional Technologies

Given the rapidly changing telecommunications environment, these states are struggling to define instructional technologies. As technologies move from centralized to distributed systems, a clear demarcation between traditional and distance education is becoming increasingly impossible. However, most of the state policies analyzed attempted to classify distance education as something different from traditional, campus-based education (see Table 11.1).

Five of the states provided some definition of distance education. The key concepts addressed in these definitions included the following:

1. the delivery system
2. asynchronous versus synchronous communication
3. location of learning
4. separation of teachers and learners

Focusing on educational concepts rather than technology-driven concepts, Missouri's description of distance education offers the broadest approach. Emphasis is given to instruction that is learner centered, faculty supported, and compatible with institutional mission. Thus it appears that the state of Missouri makes no attempt to define distance education as something separate and unique. While most states include both group-based and individualized instruction, Nebraska's definition includes only instruction that is delivered to groups of students who

**Table 11.1**
**Definition of Distance Education**

| State | Definition of Distance Education |
|---|---|
| Missouri | • Distance education is not explicitly defined, but some of the "desirable characteristics" are: emphasize access, be learner-centered, be faculty-supported, provide high-quality instruction, support institutional missions, emphasize educational partnerships and use integrated evaluation and improvement strategies. |
| Oklahoma | • Distance education is defined as all arrangements for providing instruction through print and electronic communications media to persons engaged in planned learning in a place or time different from that of the instructor(s). |
| Colorado | • Distance education is defined as implementing telecommunications technologies to provide asynchronous, learner-centered degrees and certificates; it integrates educational technologies and best practices for curriculum and instruction. |
| Texas | • Distance education is defined as instruction in which the majority of instruction occurs when the student and instructor are not in the same physical setting, may be synchronous or asynchronous, delivered to any single or multiple location(s); offered at other than the main campus, outside taxing district of community/junior college district or via instructional telecommunications. |
| Nebraska | • Distance education is defined as telecommunications-based instruction of college-level courses offered where any number of students are assembled at a receiving site by a postsecondary institution for the purpose of engaging in instruction by means of telecommunications regularly emanating from a sending institution; it excludes instruction provided to personal residences, courses which use telecommunications primarily to enhance or supplement instruction, but includes instruction delivered via terrestrial or satellite installations including television, radio, telephone and/or computer communications. |
| Kansas | No information |
| Iowa | No information |

meet at specific sites. Distance education and telecommunications technologies are frequently synonymous. Oklahoma's policy and the Electronic Community College of Colorado's policy include both print and electronic technology. The Electronic Community College of Colorado defines distance education as asynchronous, and thus appears to exclude real-time, group-based learning.

## Access and Equality

Issues of access and equality are primarily discussed in terms of specific locale or area of a state, economic development and funding (see Table 11.2). For instance, Missouri addresses the importance of geographic access with particular emphasis on the Northeast portion of the state. In Oklahoma, access is aimed

**Table 11.2**
**Access and Equality**

| State | Access and Equality |
|-------|---------------------|
| Missouri | • Access is defined as reaching all geographic areas of the state<br>• Equality has been defined as outreach to rural/underserviced areas<br>• Access is paid for by the students and the state<br>• Student support services for library and financial aid are provided by the state |
| Oklahoma | • Access is aimed at reaching all geographic areas, particularly rural<br>• Equality is geared toward reducing in-state educational disparity<br>• Access is paid for by institutions through their use of the existing student fee structure<br>• Student support services are the institutions' responsibility |
| Colorado | • Access is understood to be open admissions<br>• Equality is open admissions<br>• Access is paid for through tuition and grants<br>• Electronic Community College of Colorado provides student support services |
| Texas | • Access is defined as meeting residents' needs<br>• Equality not mentioned<br>• Student support services are the institutions' responsibility |
| Nebraska | • Access is defined as meeting demonstrated need and demand for courses and programs<br>• Equality is not mentioned<br>• Student support services are the institutions' responsibility |
| Iowa | No information |
| Kansas | No information |

at reaching all geographic areas, particularly the rural communities. Texas and Nebraska focus less upon geographic access and more on meeting the needs of students and employers in the state. The Electronic Community College of Colorado does not address geography, but rather addresses access in terms of an open admission policy.

Economic development is discussed as part of the efforts that provide access to job-specific education through the new technologies. Missouri's policy addresses the need to meet the state's industrial employment needs. Oklahoma's policy addresses improving its ranking on national economic indicators that surpass the national average. Nebraska, Texas, and Oklahoma address meeting the perceived needs of students and employers; however, no needs assessment mechanism is proposed.

Funding issues include the cost of access to and programming of the infrastructure. These costs include capital and operating expenses. It is interesting to note that none of the policy documents address funding policies of any kind.

Although several states provided information about current appropriations, none addressed long-term funding policies.

While the policy documents do not address funding, an analysis provided by Hezel (1998) based on a state-by-state survey of educational telecommunications, does provide some description of the funding mechanisms employed by these states. In 1998, the state of Colorado appropriated funds from the general fund for a technology learning grant and revolving loan program targeting higher education. Institutions interested in receiving these funds must apply for funding. While these funds address programming issues, infrastructure issues are largely supported at the institutional level. In Iowa state general funds subsidize the Iowa communications network, the state's telecommunications infrastructure. In addition to providing funding for capital expenses, in FY1998, $3.135 million was allocated from the general fund to support operations. Participating institutions then leased connections to the backbone, paying for a seven-year lease for each drop. The state of Kansas has several telecommunications systems operated and funded by a variety of agencies. In 1998 the Kansas legislature appropriated funding to allow educational institutions to purchase equipment and provide educational programming, including $1 million for use by community colleges and one urban university. In Missouri institutions can request funds that target technologically strategic initiatives. Funds have also been allocated to establish a telecommunications-based delivery system, including a common library platform. In addition, community colleges received funding to deliver programs to unserved geographic areas outside their taxing districts' geographical boundaries. The state of Nebraska uses lottery funds and a universal services fund to support innovation and technology development for the K-12 sector. In Oklahoma, OneNet (the state's telecommunications infrastructure) receives an annual appropriation to supplement funds generated by institutional users. No information was provided about technology-related funding sources for higher education in the state of Texas. In this state, colleges and universities have historically developed and funded both capital and operating expenses in their own telecommunications infrastructure (Hezel Associates, 1998).

## Teaching and Learning

While states have many issues to resolve surrounding the technological infrastructure, it is the educational infrastructure that is so critical to successful use of these technologies. The educational infrastructure includes all systems necessary to support teaching and learning. For instance, faculty must be retrained on how to effectively utilize these new technological tools.

While many documents referred to the importance of faculty development and training for telecommunications, only Oklahoma and Colorado make specific reference to funding faculty training and support at the state level (see Table 11.3). Both states provided funding during FY1998 for institutional fac-

**Table 11.3**
**Teaching and Learning**

| State | Teaching and Learning |
|---|---|
| Missouri | • Institutions are responsible for recruitment of faculty with expertise and/or retraining of current faculty |
| Oklahoma | • Institutions responsible for faculty development |
| Colorado | • Electronic Community College of Colorado draws qualified faculty from existing community colleges |
| Texas | • Institutions are responsible for training and support |
| Nebraska | • Institutions are responsible for training and support |
| Iowa | No information |
| Kansas | No information |

ulty development initiatives. However, there was no discussion about a long-term commitment to the faculty development.

Another often-overlooked support system is in the area of student services. Students need technology support and advice, access to library services, and financial aid information (among many other services). In addition, the staff providing these services requires training. While these policy documents discuss the importance of educational infrastructure, few states have policies articulating these issues. Historically, many of these concerns have been institutional issues or domains; however, the distributive nature of the telecommunications environment may push states toward greater involvement with these traditionally institutional prerogatives.

Only Missouri's policy addresses student support issues. Missouri has established MOBIUS, a common library platform. In addition, Missouri Student Assistance Resources Services (MORSTARS), a one-stop shop for state and federal aid, provides information and resources related to funding in higher education. The Electronic Community College of Colorado has contracted with a sister institution (Arapaho Community College) for the provision of certain student services. Students access library services through any community college in the state or through the Colorado Area Resource Library Services (CARL), which provides electronic access to public library holdings.

### Quality

Quality criteria for distance education offerings are addressed in all the policy documents provided (see Table 11.4). Most states' quality criteria mention that

**Table 11.4**
**Quality**

| State | Quality |
|---|---|
| Missouri | • Quality includes planning, assessment, accountability, content, support of institutional mission, meeting state and institutional criteria and addressing state employment needs<br>• Courses must meet or exceed state standards |
| Oklahoma | • Quality consists of transferable credit hours and instruction to improve the quality of life and national economic ranking<br>• Courses must meet or exceed state and/or regional accreditation standards |
| Colorado | • Quality is defined as compatible with institutional mission statement and general education core guidelines<br>• Courses are outcome-based and students are evaluated on stated outcomes |
| Texas | • Quality is defined as meeting on-campus standards and being accredited<br>• Courses must meet on-campus and accreditation standards |
| Nebraska | • Quality of courses consists of sufficient breadth, depth and rigor for degree completion and comparable to on-campus instruction<br>• Courses must meet on-campus standards |
| Iowa | No information |
| Kansas | No information |

distance education offerings must be as good as, or better than, existing institutional standards as established by professional accreditation bodies. Quality standards in Oklahoma are also linked to quality-of-life and national economic ranking. The policy provided by the Electronic Community College of Colorado is the only one that addresses student outcomes as a measure of quality. For Missouri and Colorado, one additional factor used to assess quality is compatibility with the institutional mission.

Jurisdictional issues emerged as a quality concern. Most state policies appear to be moving away from the concept of geographic service areas as the primary determinant of institutional mission. Rather, policies discuss the need to make institutional missions compatible with their programmatic strengths while minimizing duplication. Texas community colleges can offer programs outside their taxing districts if approved by the state board in the institutional plan. One primary consideration for approval is whether the existing college in that district currently offers that program.

Kansas has some of the more restrictive policies for community colleges. A community college cannot offer courses in an area already served by a four-year institution. In addition, community colleges are prevented from offering programs out-of-state. According to Hezel Associates (1998), these policies are currently under review.

Missouri has 12 regional technical education councils, one in each community college district. These councils were established to direct planning and delivery of technical education throughout the state. One primary purpose is to work with business, education, and community leaders to identify needs and coordinate program delivery. The community colleges also participate in consortia with vocational-technical schools, colleges, and universities.

### Technology Infrastructure

Most states rely upon more than one telecommunications system to meet a variety of state government needs. These often evolve as separate entities and involve many differing technologies. There appears to be little cooperative efforts within private telecommunications interests and more state control. Telecommunications systems are frequently administered and operated by an existing agency, such as a department of administration within the state government.

Only Missouri addresses technological infrastructure in its higher-education policy documents. MoreNet is the Missouri Research and Education Network, which provides Internet access and offers other technology-related services (Hezel Associates, 1998). A telecommunications advisory group representing the colleges and universities in the state was appointed by the coordinating board in 1996 to guide the implementation of recommendations and set funding priorities.

Iowa operates the Iowa Communications Network (ICN), which is governed by a six-member commission that sets policy and makes legislative recommendations. Educational interests are represented by the Educational Telecommunications Council, which advises the commission. No information was provided about the role of higher education or the community colleges in this council.

In Colorado and Texas, colleges and universities have established independent systems. Community colleges in Colorado cooperated on a grass-roots level and, in 1986, formed the Techcommunications Cooperative of Colorado (Telecoop) (Epper, 1996). In Texas the Dallas County Community College District is a major national telecourse producer and also involved in a variety of state and district telecommunications systems.

Among the states studied, Oklahoma is the only one in which the state's telecommunications infrastructure is operated by the state higher-education governing board. This system, OneNet, provides voice, video, and data services to over 1,000 sites throughout the state and serves a variety of state agencies, including K-12 and the state's Vocational-Technical System (Hezel Associates, 1998).

Kansas has two information networks that provide services to the higher education community. The Kansas Board of Regents operates TELENET2, a videoconference system that provides video-conferencing services with courses offered by three 4-year institutions. While many community colleges offer distance learning, they are limited by geographic service area regulations (Hezel Associates, 1998).

Nebraska operates a variety of well-coordinated telecommunications networks (Hezel Associates, 1998). Using satellite and fiber optics systems, the Nebraska Educational Telecommunications System (NET) provides services to the educational community. In addition, the Nebraska Information Technology Commission (NITC) was formed to provide statewide telecommunications planning.

## SUMMARY AND CONCLUSIONS

While access is stated as a goal of these policies, access is generally conceived of as access to regions rather than access for students or the general citizenry of the state. Even though many policies address access as a goal, there is little direction regarding who should pay and who should benefit. None of the policies address funding, except to encourage full-cost recovery. The potential discrepancy between the goal of access and the goal of full-cost recovery is not addressed. Until who should pay and who should benefit are clearly defined, technology may reduce rather than increase access for certain sectors of the student population, especially those who cannot afford to pay (Zeller, 1995). We need to be concerned that technology will increase, rather than reduce, the gap between the "haves" and the "have-nots." For those sectors of the population traditionally served by the community college, educational access is certainly at risk in an increasingly costly technological environment. Community college leaders must ensure educational access to all, regardless of their income or expertise.

The state role in regulation and coordination of educational planning may be declining. The states studied appear to be deferring quality control issues to the regional accrediting bodies at a time in which these accrediting bodies are in a state of flux (Gellman-Danley, 1997). As states no longer define institutional mission within the concept of geographic service areas, the state's role in determining institutional mission may be diminished. States are struggling with the differentiation between "open markets" and the duplication of programs. In response, states appear to be encouraging more grass-roots institutional coordination initiatives. While states may be moving away from the strict regulation of quality and institutional mission, they may, in turn, be moving toward greater involvement in areas traditionally under the purview of institutions—such as student personnel services.

The rapid changes in the technological environment will demand more systematic approaches to faculty development, training, and technological compatibility, as well as student support systems, in order to control costs and provide seamless educational opportunities. Historically, community colleges have attempted to be "all to all" for their students, taking on some of the role of a social service agency. As many of these services move from the purview of the institution to that of the state, community college leaders must be able to clarify priorities—whether to provide social services on campus, to make these services available statewide, or to use technology to become a center of referral to students who need special services.

The role of higher education in prioritizing the state's telecommunications resources is largely unaddressed. Discussions on telecommunication infrastructure are absent in most of the policies provided. The competition for access to infrastructure will continue to increase. Unless higher education offers a clear vision concerning its role in statewide telecommunications, its role may be diminished. Community college leaders will have to determine whether to join forces with the rest of the higher education community, or to secure access to the infrastructure as an independent sector and go it alone. An important factor identified by Epper (1997) and Ketcheson (1996) was the presence of a visionary leader who was able to articulate higher education's unique role in the telecommunications environment and develop alliances within the higher-education and political sectors. This point was also emphasized by Lape and Hart (1997) in discussing the strong tie between policy and leadership. These authors have stated that the faculty's adoption of distance education will require a new way of formulating institutional policy. In other words, if public policy is a designated behavior developed by a governmental body (Anderson, 1994), then leadership is the ability to achieve the goals through the people in the organization. This is important because "[a] key factor in the acceptance of distance education is the recognition among leadership groups that changes in teaching patterns required by distance education must be accompanied by institutional incentives and support for planning and development of courses" (Lape & Hart, 1997, p. 19).

Many states attempt to define distance education as a function of technology and treat distance education as separate and unique from on-campus instruction. However, given the trend toward technological convergence, it will likely become increasingly difficult to distinguish between distance and traditional education. By defining quality in terms of "traditional education," we may be failing to realize technology's potential to improve all kinds of learning, regardless of its location. It is proposed that part of the conceptualization required in the area of educational technology is the need to refer to technologies—in plural. This is not a trivial detail. The distinction is based on the concept of distributed learning, in which all technologies are integrated within a learning system. Instructional technologies, too, challenge the tendency to reduce the complexity of the media to simple concepts defined by one or two tools (e.g., television, books, or E-mail). Under the reconceptualization of the vocabulary used in the discourse of technology, the blackboard as well as the overhead (and for that matter, a computer and VCR) become part of the toolbox available for teaching and learning.

In the states we analyzed, community colleges are part of a comprehensive system of postsecondary education. While these documents might mention specific tasks for community colleges (e.g., Missouri uses community colleges for industrial training), there is no discussion of what differentiates community colleges from the four-year institutions with regard to teaching and learning with technology. The distinction Missouri makes is that community colleges are associate degree–granting institutions that specialize in workforce development. This distinction still fails to specifically address how community colleges will use the new technologies in teaching and learning. In the literature, however, community colleges are noted for their fast, continuous ability to adapt, adopt, and diffuse new technologies, as compared to four-year institutions. If technology is intended to maximize resources and efficiency, it then seems counterproductive on the state's part to ignore or underestimate the long-established expertise that community colleges have maintained in teaching and learning with the new technologies.

Last, we agree with Ruppert (1997), who acknowledges that the impact of new technologies in our lives is already being felt in colleges and universities. Thus, there is little doubt that "educational technology holds enormous potential to expand and enhance teaching and learning at all educational levels. And perhaps nowhere is the responsibility greater for realizing this potential than at the state level" (p. 5).

## REFERENCES

American Association of Community Colleges. (1999). *Number of community colleges, 1998* [On-line]. Available:http://www.aacc.nche.edu

Anderson, J. (1994). *Public policymaking.* Boston, MA: Houghton Mifflin.

Coordinating Commission for Postsecondary Education (1993, December 10). *Rules and regulations concerning authorization for out-of-state institutions to offer courses and programs in the state of Nebraska* [On-line]. Available:http://www.nol.org/ NEpostsecondaryed/rules&regs.htm

Coordinating Commission for Postsecondary Education (1994, July 26). *Rules and regulations concerning off-campus programs in the state of Nebraska* [On-line]. Available:http://www.cape.state.he.us/

Dallet, P., & Opper, J. (1997). Reducing time-to-degree with distance education. In C. Dillon & R. Cintrón (Eds.), *Building a working policy for distance education* (New Directions for Community Colleges, No. 99, pp. 43–52). San Francisco: Jossey-Bass.

Dillon, C., & Cintrón, R. (1997). (Eds.). *Building a working policy for distance education: A comparative case study of statewide policies* (New Directions for Community Colleges, No. 99) San Francisco: Jossey-Bass.

Epper, R. (1996). *Coordination and competition in postsecondary distance education: A comparative case study of statewide policies.* Unpublished doctoral dissertation, University of Denver.

Epper, R. (1997). Coordination and competition in postsecondary distance education. *The Journal of Higher Education, 68,* 551–587.

Gellman-Danley, B. (1997). Who sets the standards? In C. Dillon & R. Cintrón, (Eds.),

*Building a working policy for distance education* (New Directions for Community Colleges, No. 99, pp. 73–82). San Francisco: Jossey-Bass.

Hezel Associates. (1998). *Educational telecommunications and distance learning: The state-by-state analysis 1998–1999.* Syracuse, NY: Author.

Kansas State Department of Education. (n.d.). *Policy for distance learning courses offered by Kansas community colleges, technical colleges, and area vocational schools.* Topeka, KS: Author.

Ketcheson, K. (1996). *Organizational responses to educational telecommunications policy in three states: Oregon, Colorado and Utah.* Doctoral dissertation, Portland State University. (University Microfilms International, 9627253)

Kovel-Jarboe, P. (1997). From the margin to the mainstream. In C. Dillon, & R. Cintrón, (Eds). *Building a working policy for distance education* (New Directions for Community Colleges, No. 99 pp. 23–32. San Francisco: Jossey-Bass.

Lape, D., & Hart, P. (1997). Changing the way we teach by changing the college. In C. Dillon & R. Cintrón (Eds.), *Building a working policy for distance education* (New Directions for Community Colleges, No. 99, pp. 15–22). San Francisco: Jossey-Bass.

Missouri Coordinating Board for Higher Education. (n.d.). *2020 vision—The hyperlink: Higher education in Missouri.* Jefferson City: Author.

Missouri Coordinating Board for Higher Education. (1996, December 12). *Missouri's plan for postsecondary technical education: Summary of plans, regional technical education councils.* Jefferson City: Author.

Missouri Coordinating Board for Higher Education. (1997, June). *2020 vision: Focus on the blueprint (1996 annual report).* Jefferson City: Author.

Missouri Coordinating Board for Higher Education. (1998, April 16). *Blueprint for Missouri higher education: 1998 report on progress toward the statewide public policy initiatives and goals for Missouri higher education.* Jefferson City: Author.

Missouri Coordinating Board for Higher Education. (1999, February 22). *Maintaining Missouri's tradition of affordable higher education: Prepared for the Missouri Commission on the Affordability of Higher Education.* Jefferson City: Author.

Missouri Department of Higher Education. (n.d.). *Show-me higher education: Results of the blueprint (1997 annual report).* Jefferson City: Missouri Coordinating Board for Higher Education.

National Center for Higher Education Management Systems. (1998, October 20). *Oklahoma learning site policy: Prepared for the Oklahoma State Regents for Higher Education.* Boulder, CO: Author.

Oklahoma State Regents for Higher Education. (n.d.). *Survey of faculty instructional development activities.* Oklahoma City: Author.

Oklahoma State Regents for Higher Education. (1997a, September). *Policy statement on program approval.* Oklahoma City: Author.

Oklahoma State Regents for Higher Education. (1997b, September). *Policy statement on program review.* Oklahoma City: Author.

Oklahoma State Regents for Higher Education. (1998a, June). *Chapter 2 Division of Academic Affairs: Purpose of the Division of Academic Affairs.* Oklahoma City: Author.

Oklahoma State Regents for Higher Education (1998b, June). *Policies and procedures pertaining to the electronic delivery of courses and programs.* Oklahoma City: Author.

Oklahoma State Regents for Higher Education. (1999, January 14). *Oklahoma learning site policies and procedures*. Oklahoma City: Author.

Orozco, L. (1991). *State telecommunications policy*. Doctoral dissertation, University of Minnesota. (University Microfilms International, 9134530.)

Parisot, A. (1997). Distance education as a catalyst for changing teaching in the community college. In C. Dillon & R. Cintrón (Eds.), *Building a working policy for distance education* (New Directions for Community Colleges, No. 99, pp. 5–14). San Francisco: Jossey-Bass.

Resource Group for a Telecommunications-Based Delivery System. (1996, June 13). *Recommendations for a telecommunications-based delivery system*. Paper presented to the Coordinating Board for Higher Education. Maryville, MO: Author.

Ruppert, S. (1997). *Going the distance*. Washington, DC: National Education Association.

Southern Regional Education Board. (1997). *Telecommunications status, trends and issues in SREB states*. Atlanta, GA: Author.

Task Force on Critical Choices for Higher Education. (1992, June 5). *Suggested statewide public policy initiatives and goals: Report to the Coordinating Board for Higher Education*. Jefferson City: Missouri Coordinating Board for Higher Education.

Tellefson, T., & Fountain, B. (1994). A quarter century of change in state-level coordinating structures for community colleges. In J. Ratcliff, S. Schwarz, & L. Ebbers, (Eds.), *Community colleges*. (ASHE Reader Series, pp. 105–114). Needham Heights, MA: Simon & Schuster Custom Publishing.

Texas Higher Education Coordinating Board. (n.d.). *Chapter 5, Subchapter H: Approval of distance learning for public colleges and universities* [On-line]. Available: http.www.the.cb.state.tx.us/

Zeller, N. (1995). Distance education and public policy. *The Review of Higher Education, 18* (2), 123–148.

# PART III

## INSTITUTIONAL LEVEL

Chapter 12 _____

# SUNY General Education Reform and the Community Colleges: A Case Study of Cross-Purposes

*George H. Higginbottom and*
*Richard M. Romano*

On December 15, 1998, without public deliberation or justification, the Board of Trustees of the State University of New York (SUNY) promulgated a system-wide, 30-credit-hour general-education core requirement. The new curriculum included new requirements in foreign languages, Western Civilization, and U.S. history, and it proposed to supersede all existing campus-based general-education programs. The new program is a mixture of knowledge and skills requirements common to many general-education curricula elsewhere. What is different has less to do with the curriculum itself (although it does bear the unmistakable imprint of a conservative, Western culture preservationism) than the bold assertion that a publicly appointed body of citizens has the authority to enact, rather than simply ensure, the quality of the higher-education curriculum. The trustees, in effect, challenged the intellectual authority of the faculty over an important element of the collegiate course of study, breaking an ancient academic tradition and signaling, perhaps, a portent of things to come.

Almost immediately, faculty governance bodies across the state, as well as many campus administrations, condemned the action, and some faculty groups vowed to resist implementation of the plan. Although the trustees' action was aimed primarily at the four-year colleges within the system, the community colleges clearly had a large stake in the process. Having carefully crafted general-education programs designed to achieve curricular coherence and community among diverse interests, community colleges could scarcely ignore the implicit message to "get in line." Of greatest concern was the effect upon transfer students. Some would likely be facing a costly extension of their baccalaureate studies, and graduates of technical A.A.S programs would be even further behind as baccalaureate transfers.

While most community college personnel applaud greater curricular uniformity within SUNY, few are comfortable with this sort of heavy-handed intervention. Cynical readings of the trustees' action elicited varied appraisals from the campuses: many decried the ideological context of the new curriculum; all found the intrusion illegitimate and wrong-headed; some, especially the community colleges, suspected an ulterior, downsizing motive; and all agreed that the future would be contentious.

This chapter is the story of how one New York community college, Broome Community College, is reacting to this abrupt change in state university education policy. It also reviews institutional policy on general education curricular reform and the ongoing dispute over aims and interests in a time of searching redefinition of the community college mission and its niche in American postsecondary education.

## BROOME COMMUNITY COLLEGE AND THE STATE UNIVERSITY OF NEW YORK

Broome Community College (BCC) is a two-year unit of the State University of New York located in the south central area of the state about 200 miles from New York City. The college has one campus with approximately 6,000 students 4,000 FTEs enrolled in credit courses, 75 percent of whom come from the local county of Broome.

Founded in 1946 as a technical college, BCC added programs in liberal arts and business in the 1960s. Of its matriculated student population, approximately 60 percent are in university-parallel, transfer-oriented programs and 40 percent are enrolled in technical-occupational programs in business, engineering technology, health sciences, and human services. In addition to its degree programs, the standard array of corporate service and non-credit courses is offered for the local community. Over the past eight years, the college has lost about 1,000 FTEs due to local corporate downsizing and out-migration.

The State University of New York (SUNY) is the largest integrated public university system in the United States, with 370,000 students, 200,000 of whom are enrolled at its community colleges. The 4 graduate campuses, 12 specialized centers, 13 liberal arts colleges (formerly teachers colleges), and 6 two-year technical colleges are referred to as state-operated campuses because the state provides 70 percent of their revenue and the system administration has more direct control over their budgets than do other colleges and universities. The 30 community colleges, relying on the state for roughly 40 percent of their operating revenues, have greater fiscal autonomy. Sponsoring counties supply approximately 20 percent of community college budgets, with the balance coming from tuition and other sources.

While technically part of the SUNY system, the community college and its complex mission are poorly understood by central administration, according to the community college presidents. Among the complaints usually cited are fiscal, transfer, and curriculum control issues. System administration at the state capital in Albany is headed by a chancellor and a provost who report to a 15-member board of trustees appointed by the governor. Within this organizational structure the community colleges are represented by a vice-provost, a position that is widely regarded as powerless.

Because of their dissatisfaction with the budget process, the community college presidents have discussed the possibility of separating from the SUNY system and, in 1998, the first steps were taken to study this option. Separatist sentiment is driven more by fiscal and mission considerations than by curriculum issues, such as forced compliance with the trustees' new general-education plan. If separation and noncompliance did occur, however, it would very likely make baccalaureate transfer more difficult. Depending upon its makeup—whether broad-based skills and knowledge objectives, or discrete, prescribed courses— a core general education curriculum could contribute, respectively, to system unity or rupture. A legally difficult and fiscally risky undertaking, separation at this point seems unlikely.

## CURRICULUM OVERSIGHT: SUNY AND THE STATE EDUCATION DEPARTMENT

Curriculum at the community college level is regulated by a variety of state agencies, including the State University of New York and the state education department, which set broad requirements for both public and private education. College degree programs, as elsewhere, are distinguished by their liberal arts and sciences content: three-quarters of the 60-hour minimum credit requirement for the Associate in Arts (A.A.) degree; one-half for the Associate in Science (A.S.); and one-third for the Associate in Applied Science (A.A.S.) degree. The state also specifies that the liberal arts and sciences component of each degree program must strike a balanced distribution among the conventionally partitioned disciplinary groupings of humanities, natural science (including mathematics), and social science. Subject to state approval and accreditation standards, each campus decides what specific courses will be required and what constitutes a "reasonable balance" in the distribution of liberal arts courses within each degree program. Community colleges also award Associate in Occupational Studies (A.O.S.) degrees; these are vocational programs without a requisite liberal arts component.

For all units of the State University of New York, state education law does, in fact, vest curricular authority in the university trustees. Until recently, however, trustees understood the tacit injunction against encroaching on traditional faculty prerogatives. What led the SUNY trustees to preempt this faculty prerogative is owing to several strong currents in the stream of contemporary higher education reform. These currents include the standards and quality movement;

the collateral, political expectation for greater fiscal accountability; and the out-
fall of the postmodern "culture wars."

## STANDARDS, ACCOUNTABILITY, AND CULTURAL POLITICS

These aforenoted initiatives and issues have taken on powerful political over-
tones in New York since the 1994 election, which replaced the liberal governor,
Mario Cuomo, with a conservative Republican, George Pataki. As the Cuomo
appointees left the university board, Governor Pataki replaced them with more
conservative and interventionist trustees, some with strong ideas as to how the
quality of higher education can be improved and what kind of learning students
should be exposed to, others with deep commitments to competitive and entrepreneurial notions of public education at all levels, and all committed to greater
public accountability.

Quality and accountability initiatives endorsed by the trustees are similar to
those enacted in recent years throughout public higher education—greater fiscal
oversight, funding tied more closely to performance, and public and private
sector pressure for higher standards. While college administrators struggle to
comply with new fiscal measures, entire college communities, under the insistent
pressures of regional accrediting agencies, have reluctantly come to take up the
standards and quality improvement agenda. These measures seem to most fair-
minded educators to be legitimate areas of oversight and policy; trustees are,
after all, guardians of the public trust. But the SUNY board's curricular imposition, especially in the absence of vigorous intellectual debate, is judged by
most among the academic community to be both meddlesome and imprudent.

Curriculum mandates tend quickly to unite faculty in opposition because they
violate several revered academic dicta and practices, such as the democratic
virtue of broad participation, procedural attention to reasons and arguments
(public justification), and the locus of intellectual authority. The imposition of
a general-education curriculum from above, and by people who are presumed
to lack the appropriate credentials, is objectionable for other reasons as well.
Not only has general-education reform on each college campus been lengthy
and difficult, but the curricular products, for the most part, have been thought-
fully wrought and hard-won. As a result, each of these curricula incorporate
unique features that reflect local compromises, the variety of campus missions
and student needs, and the creative initiatives of faculty. Each curriculum also
reflects sincere concerns for the quality and efficacy of student learning.

The struggles for general education reform that have taken place campus by
campus throughout the 1980s and 1990s have tended to reinforce campus and
faculty curricular autonomy because these initiatives were not driven by SUNY
system leadership—neither by the chancellor, the provost, nor the trustees. Aside
from occasional, system-sponsored general-education conferences, individual
campuses have produced their reform curricula independently, informed by their

own missions, as well as the national debate triggered by the Harvard "core" curriculum in 1979, and usually taking into account the impact of proposed changes upon community college transfers. Community colleges also have diligently crafted general education goals and curricula with an eye, both to the requirements of senior colleges, and to the perceived needs of a diverse group of students—concerns that cannot always, nor easily, be harmonized. Broome Community College's experience is instructive in this case.

## GENERAL EDUCATION AT BROOME COMMUNITY COLLEGE

Before the late 1980s, BCC's general-education program was defined strictly in terms of the liberal arts and sciences distribution requirements specified by the state. The campus interpreted "reasonable balance" for the A.A.S. degree, for instance, to be a minimum of 6 credits in English, 6 credits in social science, and the remaining 8 of the required 20 liberal arts credits in math and science. Arts and Sciences credits for the A.A. and A.S. degrees were increased proportionally to meet the three-quarter and one-half percentage requirements (of 60 total) specified by the state. From its founding in 1946 to about 1980, BCC's course requirements were changed from time to time, but the conception of general education as arts and sciences distribution, as elsewhere in higher education, remained unchallenged.

Within BCC's distribution curriculum, however, one significant trend was the increasing vocationalization of the liberal arts requirement. Technical-occupational faculty sought to replace the more academic courses, for example composition and literature, with ones presumed to have greater vocational utility, such as technical writing, speech and applied social science. Particularly in the 1970s, the liberal arts component of the A.A.S. curriculum drifted away from the conventional ideals of broad-based intellectual inquiry, or preparation for lifelong learning and democratic citizenship, and toward a set of more narrowly defined skills having clearer connection to the work place. Professional accrediting and licensing organizations also contributed to this narrowing of the liberal arts component of the A.A.S. degree. In short, the workforce training orientation of technical-occupational faculty was a serious obstacle to those seeking greater coherence and purpose in arts and sciences distribution, and to the intellectual authority of liberal arts faculty who claimed custodial responsibility over that component of all curricula.

Concurrently, labor market shifts and the prevailing antiestablishment influence of popular culture had the effect of diverting students from study in technical fields and toward the human services and liberal arts transfer programs. Questions concerning the role of education in a world threatened by nuclear annihilation and environmental degradation and a democratic society sorely afflicted by a virulent racism led inexorably to inquiry into the subjects—humanities, history, and social science—having useful things to say about these crises.

At BCC the time was ripe for a thorough review of general education, and a challenge to the weakly coherent distribution curriculum and the workplace utility ethos was mounted from within.

Buoyed by philosophical statements from the state education department and the SUNY system affirming the intellectual, nonvocational purposes of liberal and general education, as well as an evolving literature on the higher-education curriculum, a small group of faculty within the liberal arts area opened a dialogue. The works which most informed their understanding were the *Harvard Report on the Core Curriculum* (Harvard Committee, 1978), Boyer and Levine's *A Quest for Common Learning* (1981), and the innovative curricula at Miami-Dade Community College (Luckenbill & McCabe, 1978) and Los Medanos Community College (Los Medanos College, 1976). Following lengthy deliberation, a general consensus emerged that the distribution requirement at BCC lacked coherence and clarity of purpose and that it needed to be replaced by something better.

The college administration, somewhat fearful of alienating the technical faculty, nonetheless agreed, in 1981, to form a campus-wide task force to study the curriculum. After six years of debate, the administration gave its full support to a proposal to change the focus of the general education program and a full campus vote on the compromise proposal passed. While the final vote on the new program passed by a narrow majority, with more technical faculty in opposition than in favor, a good deal of cooperation came from all areas, as the campus moved to change the core requirements. Along with curriculum implementation in fall 1987, faculty were provided incentives to help them meet the new standards; professional development efforts, aided by a U.S. Department of Education (USDE) Title VI grant to internationalize the curriculum, were mounted; and the plan became an institutional priority.

The BCC general education program soon became a model for others in the state university system. Without elaborating on the details of the new program here (see Romano, 1995), it is important to note that it owes less to political compromise among departments (the trade-offs of the old distribution requirement) than to a collective resolve to upgrade students' skill and knowledge base and to prepare graduates to be competent citizens, independent thinkers, and lifelong learners. Such goals have become a commonplace of general education curricula among both two- and four-year colleges.

The 1987 plan set up seven new goals common to all degree programs; henceforth, associate degree graduates would be expected to (1) communicate effectively, (2) acquire civic competence, (3) develop global and cross-cultural perspectives, (4) think critically, (5) reason ethically, (6) apply mathematical and scientific concepts and methods and understand technology, and (7) maintain good health and fitness. These goals were to be attained by requiring certain courses of all students and by infusing all of the goals into as many courses as possible. Thus, two redesigned English courses and two "W" (writing emphasis) courses were required for all degree programs. Additionally, of two required courses in social science, at least one was to be selected from a small group of designated courses aimed at promoting civic competence.

The 1987 plan represented the culmination of the internal reform of the general education program at BCC. Meanwhile, the state-operated, four-year campuses were developing their own general education curricula. The potential for system-wide articulation chaos was ameliorated substantially by a SUNY administration directive requiring baccalaureate campuses to honor community college general education curricula in A.A. and A.S. programs. With one or two exceptions the accommodation was working well, despite the lack of curricular uniformity or coherence. But the political winds in Albany changed and increased velocity, once the Pataki-appointed trustees began to complain publicly about the quality of education within the system and, especially, about the absence of a system-wide core (Board of Trustees of State University of New York, 1995).

## CONTESTING THE CURRICULUM

In 1995, at the urging of the trustees, the provost took a proactive stance by seeking to improve the quality and uniformity of general education within SUNY. Beginning with a system-wide conference in fall 1996 on the status of general education nationally and within SUNY, a Joint Task Force of the University Senate and the Faculty Council of Community Colleges was formed to review and make recommendations on a range of issues which the assembled faculty identified. After more than a year of deliberation, which included information sharing and consensus building processes involving leadership across the system, a general education plan endorsed by faculty, provosts, and presidents of the various campuses was presented to the chancellor.

The joint task force report (Joint Task Force on General Education, 1998) urged the adoption of a plan that incorporated learning goals in four skill areas, three knowledge and inquiry domains, and four integrative, thematic studies. A year following submission of the report, in early December, 1998, the chancellor made a recommendation to the Trustees based substantially upon the report of the provost (Salins, 1998), but that also favorably referenced the joint task force report. Subsequently, on December 15, 1998, the trustees promulgated a new general education curriculum quite unlike the plan submitted on behalf of the whole SUNY faculty, chief academic officers, and presidents—or, for that matter, the provost's.

More than a routine disagreement over central authority and local autonomy, this dispute challenged other long-standing prerogatives and injected a powerful, authoritarian presence into the midst of what previously had been a consultative process. The reaction of the SUNY faculty was predictable. Faculty Senates across the system condemned the trustees' action. In the midst of a bitter backlash, the university provost appointed a 15-member committee (including 5 members from two-year colleges) to make recommendations on program implementation. At BCC, as elsewhere, confusion reigned. Now the college had three general-education programs to consider: the 1987 homegrown plan, the Joint Task Force plan, and the new trustees' plan. Suddenly, the college's autonomy was sharply restricted, its intellectual and curricular integrity subverted, and the quality and coherence of its own program subject to revision by an external authority.

## COMMUNITY COLLEGE GENERAL EDUCATION

With so diverse a constituency, mission, and program mix, community college general-education programs that propose to establish common requirements across the curriculum are constrained both by credit limitations and the institution's technical-practical education discourse. Meeting the workforce needs of local employers is a key mission of the community college, ever more so in view of the Secretary of Labor Robert Reich, President Bill Clinton, and Vice President Al Gore's celebration of the community college role as the preeminent workforce trainer in the information age. Community college administrators seek autonomy in order to respond more creatively and quickly to these local needs, while state education bureaucracies, embodying more traditional academic conceptions of higher education's goals and makeup, rein in the community college's entrepreneurial inclinations. Uniform degree requirements, specified and differentiated by their liberal arts and sciences content, is one means of maintaining system control and, some would argue, quality as well.

Despite rather mechanistic distinctions among degree programs, faculty have produced serious and well thought out curricular justifications based on the putative value of liberal learning. The justifications typically reference consensual goods: good lives, good character, good citizenship, good judgment, the capacity for independent learning, employability, and so on. These outcomes of liberal learning give strong direction to the objectives of general education, which can be thought of, in part, as the skills, knowledge, and dispositions needed to realize liberal education's loftier goals (Schneider & Shoenburg, 1998). While it was not always the case, general-education learning goals are increasingly specified as competencies, or proficiencies, as the accumulation of positive knowledge has ceded primacy to intellectual skills and experience with systematic inquiry and analysis (Gaff, 1991).

Community colleges that aspire to create college-wide general-education curricula find it easier to specify learning goals, rather than required core courses, because goals can be attached variously to discrete courses, entire curricula, and/or courses across the curriculum. Typically, most general-education learning outcomes—written and oral communication, critical thinking, moral reasoning, for example—become "infusion" objectives taught across the curriculum (Higginbottom & Romano, 1995). Predicating common general education learning goals for A.A., A.S., and A.A.S. degree curricula requires some reconceptualization of liberal learning to accommodate both the structural constraints of the degree programs and the utilitarian outlook of community college faculty, as well as system-wide articulation. Community colleges, far more than other higher education institutions, confront the challenge of blending more traditionally academic notions of liberal education with the utilitarian functionalist inclinations of their faculty, students, and external constituencies (Higginbottom, 1994).

The task has been made more difficult as a consequence of the aggressive curricular intervention of the SUNY trustees on behalf of a more content specific and doctrinal general education which, to critics, reflects the cultural disquietudes of those who find the sources of both national unity and academic excellence in jeopardy, but remediable through a health-restoring dose of traditional studies (Levine, 1996). While the curriculum recently enacted specifically exempts community colleges, they have been urged to adopt these general education standards; the consequences for transfer students from institutions outside the fold ensure early compliance.

Not only are local campus interests frequently in conflict with centralized, system rules on curricular content, program registration, and accreditation, but they are also buffeted by contending intellectual and political factions advocating beliefs that many community college faculty and administrators regard as inchoate and irrelevant to their more pragmatic concerns and missions. But, as members of a huge higher-education apparatus, community colleges are profoundly affected by the outcomes of these mainly external conflicts.

For many community college faculty, general-education requirements, and even the liberal arts degree requirements, pose unwelcome curricular intrusions into the more serious and legitimate task of preparing students for the workplace. For the most part, however, the liberal arts and sciences component of A.A., A.S., and A.A.S. programs has been easily accommodated and, because these requirements were in place when the community college system was inaugurated, they have the legitimacy of permanence and familiarity. General education, on the other hand, is a less familiar concept, and insofar as it requires across-the-campus agreements and collaboration, it collides with the narrower, technical, or training foci of many faculty.

The diversity of institutional interests moves general education inexorably in the direction of learning goals that can be specified as proficiencies, or competencies, because they interfere least with the composition of established curricula. Broome Community College's general-education program has moved in this direction both for reasons relating to institutional culture and the assessment movement in higher education. It is also the case that throughout higher education, general education itself has, since the 1980s, moved away from the core curriculum concept and toward more skills-centered goals linked to multidimensional features (Gaff, 1994, 1999). General education schemes now are as likely to include co-curricular programming and linkages to teaching and learning theories as specific courses or fields of study (Ratcliff, 1997). Learning community arrangements originating in contemporary epistemic and pedagogical concepts, as well as student development theories, have come to be integrated with general education, further deemphasizing the centrality of positivist knowledge in favor of constructivist notions and featuring problem-focused collaborative inquiry.

Against these inquiry-oriented, pragmatic conceptions of collegiate general education, the SUNY Trustees' core course concept seems poorly informed and regressive. It is out of step with contemporary epistemology, learning theory and, arguably, the needs of students (Parker, 1998). What is more, it threatens to undo hard-won gains in collegiality and cross-disciplinary collaboration, not to mention the frontal assault upon what the faculty have determined to be the most appropriate goals of a common learning.

## SPECULATIONS ON THE FUTURE OF GENERAL EDUCATION AT BCC

During the last 20 years on this campus, the general education debate has been dominated by internal concerns over the appropriateness and coherence of the curriculum. Changes made to that curriculum, such as the 1987 reform, were faculty-led initiatives and were not imposed by forces from outside the campus. However, even if a new election should replace the Pataki trustees with a group more friendly to faculty autonomy, other powerful forces in the external environment have the capacity to produce diverse scenarios in the general education curriculum over the next two decades. These forces include accountability and performance based funding; the displacement downward of remedial education; the continuing culture wars; the workforce training movement; and changing conceptions of liberal arts education.

### Accountability and Performance-Based Funding

Community colleges are increasingly pressured to be accountable, and if they are not, their funding is frequently jeopardized. Most colleges are working with outcomes-based competencies as a means of meeting these demands, but many of the goals of liberal learning are not easily adapted to the outcomes format. Assessing for value-added in critical thinking, for example, is a lot more difficult than testing for competencies in, say, accounting, engineering, or nursing. Evaluating learning through performance criteria is difficult at best in areas like literature, where student-constructed meaning is the paramount goal (Eisner, 1999); however, it is unlikely that community colleges will have the time or the expertise to develop good assessment methods for general education. Instead, they are likely to respond to the accountability challenge with hastily developed instruments that will focus on things most easily measured.

Along with the workforce development movement, the drive for accountability will push liberal education into the background and a narrow functionalist outlook will prevail. Consider the following statements from an AACC white paper looking toward *The New Curriculum* in the 21st century as evidence of the trend:

community colleges must also address the growing needs of a workforce constantly seeking skills upgrade, retraining and lifelong learning. . . . What we currently call the core curriculum . . . also needs transformation. . . . The core curriculum is not learning centered nor outcomes based. . . . To design a true core curriculum, faculty should define collectively what program graduates should know and be able to do and design learning experiences to achieve those ends. . . . A curriculum based on outcomes gives learners the knowledge, skills and attitudes that are valued by employers. (cited in Flynn, 1998, pp. 11–12)

## Remediating and Downsizing

Many within the SUNY system feel that the hidden agenda behind the trustees' action is a desire to downsize the university system and shift remedial education to the community colleges. This approach would follow the lead of the second largest public system within the state, the City University of New York (CUNY). The CUNY trustees, a board separate from SUNY but of a similar mind, is in the process of closing the remedial programs within the CUNY four-year units and shifting all such education to the six CUNY community colleges. Under this plan, the two-year colleges will do most, or all, of the teaching of English as a second language (ESL) and remedial education and training. Liberal education will be left to the four-year units, which will drop their open admissions policies and become smaller, but more selective.

A similar policy could occur within SUNY. In such an environment the broader, liberalizing goals of community college general education could be supplanted by a concept of general education as basic skills instruction. A more selective admission policy at the baccalaureate colleges would accompany the new core curriculum's inherent bias against A.A.S. transfers, and also drive prospective transfers in university parallel associate degree programs out of the system.

## Continuing Culture Wars

Intellectual forces largely generated outside the campus will continue to influence the curriculum. For the moment the Western culture restorationists, as represented by the SUNY trustees' core requirements, have the upper hand. Their cultural restoration program will be implemented in some form within the SUNY system and will impact the community college curriculum negatively.

Their perspective is best exemplified in the backlash against the abandonment of the Western civilization requirement (Stanford's being the most celebrated case), and its alleged displacement by the agendas of ideological multiculturalists (Carnochan, 1993). Against the presumed socially unifying powers of Western institutions, philosophy, and literature, the National Association of Scholars study (1996) and that of its New York affiliate, the New York Association of Scholars (1996), arrayed the insidious, socially disintegrative contemporary absorptions with race, ethnicity, gender, and sexual orientation in the college curriculum. The reassertion of a Western civilization core, together with the absence of a diversity requirement, aims to recenter the European heritage in the higher education curriculum. It does not, of course, proscribe diversity offerings in the general-education curriculum (campuses are free to add other requirements), but it moves multicultural goals and their advocates to the periphery and, where general education faces credit constraints, as in the community colleges, the trustees' new requirements will displace local ones.

In direct opposition to the restorationists are the postmodernists, multiculturalists, and critical theorists. With a deep skepticism toward positive truth and knowledge claims and a profound suspiciousness of hidden ideologies and master narratives, humanities scholars especially will be overtly hostile to the trustees' plan. Universal claims about truth, knowledge, and prescriptive learning will be deconstructed and shown to be false, subjective, self-referential, and hegemonic. While it is difficult at this juncture to divine the outcome of this contemporary update of the curricular struggles between the "ancients" and "moderns," which have periodically shaken up higher education (Levine, 1996; Carnochan, 1993), the resolution of the dispute is likely to favor the postmoderns, who typically are unfriendly toward any type of general education.

To be aware of these recurring curricular struggles, however, does little to quell the stridency of the debate between rival positions, each of which advances, with equal certainty, its mutually exclusive intellectual claims. What is at stake at the community college, beyond the transfer issue, are curricular coherence and relevance, concerns that the conservatives are only partially responsive to and that the postmoderns are more inclined to deconstruct than accept as legitimate goals of general education. Many community college faculty and administrators favor a general education that seeks direct engagement with the more urgent matters of the day—diversity, democratic citizenship, global understanding. These matters, arguably, are better met head-on, as explicit learning goals and as not accidental outcomes of survey courses or "great books" discussions.

The diversity of the community college's student body, as well as the growing demand for teaching prospective workers so-called "soft skills" (attitudes and strategies for getting along with fellow workers), underscores the logic of multicultural general education. This practical intention is in sharp contrast to the conservative fears of social and cultural balkanization through preoccupation with racial and ethnic difference (Salins, 1997) and the paranoia that seeks simplistic solutions in curricular nostrums—quick doses of Western civilization, great books, and the like. Granted the reasonableness of genuine alarm over the most radical expressions of racial and ethnic particularism (Ravitch, 1990), deliberate strategies to bridge the pessimistic "binary logic of multiculturalism—

forced assimilation or genocide" (Duster, 1997, p. 264) need to, and can successfully, be mounted through pragmatic learning and innovative pedagogy, by adherence to the basic political rules of our democratic system (Glazer, 1997), and by seeing "polyethnic claims as demands for inclusion," not separation (Kymlicka, 1995, p. 176).

The legacy of New York's culture wars and the memory of divisive battles (memories that are strong among the state's political leadership and SUNY's academic leadership) suggest that conflict born of polarizing ideologies will continue. In light of the SUNY faculty's moral, intellectual, and curricular commitment to diversity and multiculturalism, the university's campuses will continue to be sharply at odds with system leadership for the foreseeable future. We predict, however, that in the end, the multiculturalists will prevail and the general education curriculum will surely reflect the diversity of American society and culture, as it is indeed doing, without the collapse of democratic institutions or racial and ethnic separatism.

### Workforce Training

Community colleges promote themselves as the workforce training centers of the 21st century. Increasingly this is taken to mean short-term training of job-related skills, as opposed to the broader goals of general education. These job-related skills also happen to be the easiest ones to measure and are readily accommodated to the competency-based education that is an important force within higher education. The workforce-training mentality has the potential of compromising the goals of general education, either by co-opting it altogether (Higginbottom, 1994) or by weakening it through diverting college resources away from it.

Such a curricular rupture is not necessary. Bridging education and training goals has been an historic strength of the community college. The latter are valued for their job-directed practicality, while the former keep students in touch with higher education and provide opportunities for life-long learning (Grubb, 1999). At Broome Community College, and most other SUNY two-year institutions, faculty continue to seek reconciliation of these goals through the general education curriculum. High baccalaureate transfer rates among technical-occupational degree earners, together with concerns for the adequate preparation of democratic citizens and life-long learners, have kept the debate alive until now. But the internal dialogue faces new realities and unfamiliar constraints.

The mainstream of workforce trainers, both on and off campus, and their corporate allies will no doubt object strongly to the SUNY Trustees' mandate for foreign language study, Western civilization, and the like. Defenders of AAS programs will refuse to adapt, or will seek waivers, but prospective transfers will suffer when the four-year SUNY institutions enforce their requirements on students lacking the appropriate general-education course work. Pushed to adapt their curricula to workplace needs, faculty in A.A.S. programs will come to focus on a narrow band of learning goals, such as reading, writing, and speaking skills; critical thinking and problem-solving abilities; and the capacity to work successfully in teams. Wanting so little of a liberal arts education, but if forced by the trustees' general-education curriculum to include far more, BCC could easily follow the lead of local and national workforce trainers and develop a mentality that ignores the new baccalaureate standards. Doing so would destroy the bridge that heretofore has so effectively spanned the divide between education and training. In short, A.A. and A.S. programs will become more transfer-oriented, but A.A.S. programs and faculty are likely to become more alienated from higher education.

## Cosmopolitan Pragmatism and the New Liberal Arts

Grounded in the ideas of American pragmatism, one recent effort to revision liberal and general education will be of interest to community college faculty, and it may well become the authoritative curricular philosophy for the next millennium. According to its advocates (Kimball, 1986, 1995, 1997; Orrill, 1997); a "cosmopolitan" (Kloppenberg, 1997), neopragmatist liberal and general education comprises an ensemble of intellectual, practical, and dispositional goals that, arguably, could overcome the toxic confrontation between the conservative, culture restorationists and the liberal postmodernists. Neopragmatists insist on the rootedness of educational goals in our present circumstances, as well as the obligation of a clear, consensual specification of curricular purpose. Liberal and general education here would have students do the following: (1) acquire the capacity and motivation to pose edifying questions and to make sense of personal and collective experience; (2) develop critical frames of mind and independent judgment with which to confront the power of managed information and ideas; (3) hone their discursive skills and abilities in the context of substantive knowledge and the conceptual ecology of what Minnich (1997) terms "the American tradition of aspirational democracy"; and (4) acquire global and multicultural perspectives and negotiating skills and environmental awareness.

Given historical and theoretical justification by various scholars (Miller, 1998; Orrill, 1995, 1997), the gathering consensus proposes to resolve ideological conflict by aligning the liberal arts with the epistemologial realism of William James and John Dewey. A pragmatist liberal and general education will be problem focused, experiential, historicist, ethically centered, cooperative and collaborative, multicultural, intellectually plural, and experimental. Like other pragmatists, Astin (1997), contends that this conception of general and liberal education must begin with the problems of the contemporary society and polity. Its exemplars are social activists who combine theory with practice, like Jane Addams (Lagemann, 1997), and here general education has, above all, a civic purpose. Ehrlich (1997) sharply contrasts the experimental, applied approach with its traditional nemesis, the abstract, deductive metaphysic espoused by the resto-rationists, the former being concerned with the skills and knowledge students need to solve problems and the intellectual power and flexibility to deal with contingent truth and knowledge and with diverse values and perspectives and the latter being focused (unproductively) on the so-called reality of transcendent and universal truth.

Anderson (1997) notes, ironically, that both conservatives and postmodernists share a (relativist) epistemology that regards knowledge as a cultural artifact and mind as epiphenomenon, whereas pragmatists actively construct knowledge to, among other things, transcend culture. Against these culturalist theories, An-derson endorses pragmatism as "the best opportunity to reopen the basic ques-tions of truth, excellence, and the good," and "the strongest philosophy we have for countering the dominant skepticism, iconoclasm, and pessimism of the mod-ern university" (p. 123).

It is no accident, of course, that these ideas and curricular goals closely par-allel both the SUNY joint task force proposal and most community college general-education aims, and the reason should be obvious. Where there exists thoughtful, engaged conversation on the purposes of general education, refer-encing both the status of knowledge and student needs, faculty tend to agree. They agree on student needs, and they also tend to agree that both backward-looking, class-permeated social and cultural ideals and esoteric theories of lan-guage and ideology that gainsay concrete experience are not useful.

If utility is the dominant curricular screen at community colleges, an enriched meaning, such as found in cosmopolitan pragmatism, holds the dual promise of satisfying the demand for relevance while also providing an adequate intellectual justification for liberal arts and general education. As ever, in the absence of clear external direction, community college faculty will continue to contest the curriculum, agreeing on the suitability of a pragmatic turn in the general-education program yet remaining sharply divided over the specific implications for learning goals.

## CONCLUSION

The remaining question concerns which of these five scenarios seems most likely to prevail in the first quarter of the 21st century. It is pretty easy to predict that, for the next few years, the trustees' new core will dominate discussion of the general education curriculum within the SUNY system. It is not yet clear just how this requirement will be implemented, nor whether the trustees will insist on a strict interpretation or be comfortable with more flexible renderings. However, it is clear that the community colleges will not take the lead in im-plementing the new core; they will stand back and watch the four-year units fight it out. In the unlikely case that a strict interpretation of the requirements prevails and the funding can be secured for implementation, the new core will

likely split the community college by producing two general-education programs—one for occupational students and another for university-parallel students.

Over the next ten years, however, it seems unlikely that the new core will
survive in the form that the trustees first envisioned. Given the total lack of
faculty support and the substantial funding requirements for full implementation,
it might well collapse. The complexity of the task of managing it on a system-
wide basis and the numerous opportunities for faculty to sabotage both the letter
and intent of the requirement at so many levels seem to ensure this result. This
may, in fact, happen even before the community colleges find it necessary to
implement the requirement.

What will happen if the trustees' plan collapses? What will become of the
general education requirement at BCC? Will it revert to the 1987 plan in its
original form, or will a new system-wide dialogue on general education lead to
the intellectually rich cosmopolitan pragmatism thematized in Orrill (1995)? We
conclude on the slightly pessimistic note that a more likely scenario is a gradual
drift into a narrow curricular functionalism driven by workforce training goals
and reinforced by the demands for easily measured standards of accountability.
In any case, it is clear that the external forces that we have identified will keep
the pot boiling well into the 21st century.

## REFERENCES

Anderson, C. W. (1997). Pragmatism, idealism, and the aims of liberal education. In R.
    Orrill (Ed.), *Education and democracy: Re-imagining liberal learning in America*
    (pp. 111–130). New York: College Entrance Examination Board.
Astin, A. W. (1997). Liberal education and democracy: The case for pragmatism. In R.
    Orrill (Ed.), *Education and democracy: Re-imagining liberal learning in America*
    (pp. 207–224). New York: College Entrance Examination Board.
Board of Trustees of the State University of New York. (1995). *Rethinking SUNY*. Al-
    bany: SUNY.
Boyer, E., & Levine, A. (1981). *A quest for common learning*. Washington, DC: The
    Carnegie Foundation for the Advancement of Teaching.
Carnochan, W. B. (1993). *The battleground of the curriculum: Liberal education and
    American experience*. Stanford, CA: Stanford University Press.
Duster, T. (1997). The stratification of cultures as the barrier to democratic pluralism. In
    R. Orrill (Ed.), *Education and democracy: Re-imagining liberal learning in Amer-
    ica* (pp. 263–286). New York: College Entrance Examination Board.
Ehrlich, T. (1997). Dewey versus Hutchins: The next round. In R. Orrill (Ed.), *Education
    and democracy: Re-imagining liberal learning in America* (pp. 225–262). New
    York: College Entrance Examination Board.
Eisner, E. W. (May, 1999). The uses and limits of performance assessment. *Phi Delta
    Kappan*, pp. 658–660.
Flynn, W. J. (1998). *New expeditions: The search for the learning centered college*
    (AACC White Paper on Teaching and Learning). Available: http://www.
    aacc.neche.edu/initiatives/newexpeditions/learning white.htm

Gaff, J. G. (1991). *New life for the college curriculum.* San Francisco, CA: Jossey-Bass.

Gaff, J. G. (1994). Project on strong foundations for general education. In his *Strong foundations: Twelve principles for effective general education programs.* Washington, DC: Association of American Colleges and Universities.

Gaff, J. G. (1999). *The academy in transition.* Washington, DC: Association of American Colleges and Universities.

Glazer, N. (1997). *We are all multiculturalists now.* Cambridge, MA: Harvard University Press.

Grubb, W. N. (1999). *From isolation to integration: Occupational education and the emerging systems of workforce development* (CenterPoint, No. 3). Berkeley, CA: National Center for Research in Vocational Education.

Harvard Committee. (1978). *Harvard report on the core curriculum.* Cambridge, MA: Harvard University, Office of the Dean, Faculty of Arts and Sciences.

Higginbottom, G. (1994). Workforce utility and the humanities: General and occupational education in the community college. *Journal of General Education, 43*(4), 273–289.

Higginbottom, G., & Romano, R. M. (Eds.). (1995). *Curriculum models for general education* (New Directions for Community Colleges, No. 92). San Francisco: Jossey-Bass.

Joint Task Force on General Education. (1998). *Final report on general education.* State University of New York University Senate and Faculty Council of Community Colleges, Albany.

Kimball, B. A. (1986). *Orators and philosophers: A history of the idea of liberal education.* New York: Teacher's College Press.

Kimball, B. A. (1995). *The condition of American liberal education.* New York: College Entrance Examination Board.

Kimball, B. A. (1997). Naming pragmatic liberal education. In R. Orrill (Ed.), *Education and democracy: Re-imagining liberal learning in America* (pp. 45–68). New York: College Entrance Examination Board.

Kloppenberg, J. T. (1997). Cosmopolitan pragmatism: Deliberative democracy and higher education. In R. Orrill (Ed.), *Education and democracy: Re-imagining liberal learning in America* (pp. 69–110). New York: College Entrance Examination Board.

Kymlicka, W. (1995). *Multicultural citizenship.* New York: Oxford University Press.

Lagemann, E. C. (1997). From discipline-based to problem-centered learning. In R. Orrill (Ed.), *Education and democracy: Re-imagining liberal learning in America* (pp. 21–44). New York: College Entrance Examination Board.

Levine, L. (1996). *The opening of the American mind: Canons, culture and history.* Boston, MA: Beacon Press.

Los Medanos College. (1976). *The education plan.* Pittsburgh, CA: Community College Press.

Lukenbill, J. D., & McCabe, R. H. (1978). *General education in a changing society.* Dubuque, IA: Kendall/Hunt.

Miller, G. (1998). *The meaning of general education: The emergence of a curriculum paradigm.* New York: Columbia University Press.

Minnich, E. K. (1997). The American tradition of aspirational democracy. In R. Orrill (Ed.), *Education and democracy: Re-imagining liberal learning in America* (pp. 175–206). New York: College Entrance Examination Board.

National Association of Scholars. (1996). *The dissolution of general education: 1914–1993*. Princeton, NJ: Author.

New York Association of Scholars. (1996). *SUNY's core curricula: The failure to set consistent and high academic standards*. Albany, NY: Empire Foundation for Policy Research.

Orrill, R. (Ed.). (1995). *The condition of American liberal education*. New York: College Entrance Examination Board.

Orrill, R. (Ed.). (1997). *Education and democracy: Re-imagining liberal learning in America*. New York: College Entrance Examination Board.

Parker, M. C. (1998). General education in fin de siècle America: Toward a postmodern approach. *Journal of General Education, 47*(1, 2, 3,) 1–18, 87–116, 195–224.

Ratcliff, J. L. (1997). Quality and coherence in general education. In J. G. Gaff & J. L. Ratcliff (Eds.), *Handbook of the undergraduate curriculum* (pp. 141–170). San Francisco, CA: Jossey-Bass.

Ravitch, D. (1990, Summer). Multiculturalism: E pluribus plures. *The American Scholar*, pp. 337–354.

Romano, R. M. (1995). General education at Broome Community College: Coherence and purpose. In G. Higginbottom & R. M. Romano (Eds.), *Curriculum models for general education* (New Directions for Community Colleges, No. 92, pp. 11–20), San Francisco: Jossey-Bass.

Salins, P. D. (1997). *Assimilation American style*. New York: Basic Books.

Salins, P. D. (1998). *General education: Overview and recommendations* (Report of the Provost to the Chancellor). Albany, New York.

Schlesinger Jr., A. M. (1992). *The disuniting of America: Reflections on a multicultural society*. New York: W. W. Norton.

Schneider, C. G., & Shoenburg, R. (1998). *Contemporary understanding of liberal education*. American Association of Colleges and Universities.

*Chapter 13*

# Institutional Policies That Promote Persistence among First-Year Community College Students

*Romero Jalomo Jr.*

Campus policy makers agree that a student's success in college largely is determined during the first year of enrollment. Specifically, the initial weeks of college are the most critical for first-year students in terms of developing attitudes and impressions about campus life, including their overall adjustment to college (Noel, Levitz, & Saluri, 1985; Upcraft & Gardner, 1989). During the first weeks of their college enrollment, students will have socializing experiences with faculty, administrative staff, counselors, and peers that will influence their satisfaction with campus life and success in college (Tinto, 1993). In order to influence positive academic outcomes for first-year students, campus policy makers have implemented a variety of programmatic and curricular intervention strategies. In the past 30 years many institutional policies were designed with a consideration of prevailing student demographics in order to identify the characteristics of those most likely to leave college (Brawer, 1996).

Over a decade ago Upcraft and Gardner (1989) estimated that approximately 4 million students would arrive on college campuses throughout the United States seeking postsecondary education. In the period that followed their publication of *The Freshman Year Experience*, their estimations of future first-year student cohorts that "will be increasingly diverse and substantially different from the freshmen who preceded them" (p. 1) appear both insightful and accurate. As the 21st century dawns, community colleges in the United States continue to enroll large percentages of first-year students from diverse backgrounds and with diverse interest (Cohen & Brawer, 1996).

In this chapter attention will be directed to the growing diversity among first-year community college students. There will be a special focus on student transitions to college and issues surrounding first-year attrition, along with current institutional policies designed to facilitate student persistence. Among those persistence policies that will be examined are transitional bridge programs, orientation programs, freshman-year seminars, mentoring programs, and multifaceted approaches that include a combination of interventions. The chapter concludes with recommendations for campus policy makers that have proven useful for increasing persistence among first-year students.

## STUDENT DIVERSITY IN COMMUNITY COLLEGES

Today at most community colleges one finds a mosaic of first-year students from diverse backgrounds, with varied academic preparation and multiple educational goals. Demographic forecasts for the next decade suggest that student diversity in community colleges will continue to be more reflective of local demographic patterns than will student diversity in neighboring four-year colleges and universities. The wealth of experiences and expectations that community college students bring to higher education often distinguish them from more traditional students who enroll at universities immediately on graduation from high school (Rhoads & Valadez, 1996). Cohen and Brawer (1996) contend that were it not for the open-access mission of community colleges, many of its students would not be eligible to pursue a higher education. Student diversity in community colleges is an attribute that can be strengthened when a successful transition to college is assured.

During the second half of the 20th century, community colleges enrolled perhaps the most diverse student clientele in higher education in terms of academic preparation. Today's profile of community college students is broad and can include one or more of the following attributes: full-time or part-time employees; first-generation college students; nontraditional-age and returning adults; immigrant, non–native English speakers; middle-, lower-, and working-class backgrounds; ethnic and racial minorities; general equivalency diploma (GED) graduates; and the academically underprepared (Zwerling, 1992). While some community college students come from backgrounds that fit the profile of traditional college students, many are considered nontraditional or first-generation college students. During the first decade of the 21st century, community college policy makers will be challenged to provide a meaningful, substantive, and conducive learning experience for these students.

According to recent figures published by the Department of Education, during the 1996–97 academic year approximately 5.6 million students attended two-year colleges in the United States (U.S. Department of Education, 1998). This figure constitutes approximately 46 percent of the 12.3 million undergraduate students enrolled in colleges and universities across the country. However, certain student populations, such as Hispanics and American Indians, continue to enroll as a majority of their groups's undergraduate population in two-year colleges. In 1996, over one-half million (657,400) Hispanic students could be found on public and private two-year college campuses. The total number of Hispanic students who attended two-year colleges represented approximately 61 percent of the group's total undergraduate enrollment in higher education during the 1996–1997 academic year. In the same year a majority (56 percent, or 70,200) of American Indian undergraduate students in higher education were enrolled in two-year colleges. Nearly half of all African-American (47 percent, or 636,000) and Asian (46 percent, or 327,100) undergraduate students also were enrolled in two-year colleges compared to 43 percent (3,780,800) of Caucasian students during the same year (U.S. Department of Education, 1998). At the turn of the century, rising numbers of ethnic and racial minority students are expected to enroll in community colleges. Their enrollment will require campus policy makers to ensure a successful transition to college and provide intervention strategies to combat attrition.

### The Importance of a Successful Transition to College

Community colleges continue to face challenges in retaining first-year students possessing a variety of academic skills, social interests, and life experiences. It is imperative that campus policy makers channel these skills, interests, and experiences toward achieving academic success during the students' first year in college, particularly since research suggests that a student's experience during the first year of college is crucial to future academic success (Noel et al., 1985; Terenzini et al., 1994; Tinto, 1993; Upcraft & Gardner, 1989). Academic success may be contingent on how well first-year students negotiate the transition to college and encounter affirming experiences in college. However, a positive and successful transition from high school or work to college remains a challenge for many first-year community college students (Jalomo, 1995; Rendon, 1994; Terenzini et al., 1994; Upcraft & Gardner, 1989).

In a study of first-year college students, Terenzini and others (1994) found that the transition from high school or work to college is a complex process that varies according to several important influences: a student's social, family, and educational background; the nature and mission of the institution attended; the student's educational aspirations; the people encountered in college; and the complex interaction of these influences. These findings support Nora's (1993) assertion that community college students bring diverse socioeconomic, academic and social characteristics to college, factors that continuously will influence their academic progress. For many first-year students with little or no family experience with college-going behaviors and practices, these factors become magnified as many students can become overwhelmed, confused, and discouraged with their first-year college experience (Jalomo, 1995; Rendon, 1994; Terenzini et al., 1994; Zwerling, 1992). The dilemma of an overwhelming first-year experience can eventually lead some students to consider leaving college altogether.

## Student Attrition in Community Colleges

The National Center of Education Statistics estimated that since 1990, almost 50 percent of all students who entered college, left before earning an associate or baccalaureate degree (Ting, 1998). High rates of institutional departure continue to fuel a debate on whether community colleges function as open or revolving doors for nontraditional student populations, who tend to view these colleges as their best and, often, only opportunity to obtain a higher education (Dougherty, 1994; Valadez, 1993). According to Tinto (1993), first-year attrition represents a very sizable part of all institutional attrition, "leaving little wonder that institutional concern with attrition centers on the freshman year" (p. 15).

For particular student populations the issue of attrition has become severely acute. For instance, Brown and Robinson Kurpius (1997) reported that although American Indian students earned higher Scholastic Achievement Test (SAT) scores than either African-American or Hispanic students, their college attrition rates were higher than any ethnic or racial minority student group. Citing national survey results, the researchers reported that American Indian students experience college attrition rates of as high as 75 to 93 percent. President Clinton's 1996 Commission on Educational Excellence for Hispanic Americans reported that Hispanics have the highest high school dropout rate; moreover, few seek a postsecondary education and still fewer graduate from college (cited in Rodriquez, 1996). Hispanic students also were reported as the least likely among the major racial and ethnic minority student groups to persist in college (Santiago, 1996).

First-year student attrition is a problem that affects many community colleges. Efforts to identify the sources of the problem and create interventions to curb potential dropouts have risen over the past decade (Brawer, 1996). Simultaneously, increasing numbers of nontraditional and first-generation college students continue to enroll in community colleges. Because community colleges continue to be the initial college choice for most of these students (Cohen & Brawer, 1996), the problems of high student attrition during the first year, and subsequently low educational attainment and persistence rates have led campus policy makers to employ a variety of strategic interventions. The following section highlights some of the most widely implemented institutional policies employed to increase first-year student persistence in community colleges at the end of the 20th century.

## POLICIES DESIGNED TO INCREASE FIRST-YEAR STUDENT PERSISTENCE

The consistently high attrition rate among first-year community college students has prompted campus policy makers to search for answers to solve the departure puzzle. Focusing on intervention strategies to help first-year students persist in college represents an alternative approach to exploration into why students leave. In the long run, this approach may have a greater impact for community colleges (Brawer, 1996). Current research suggests the most widely implemented and effective campus policies designed to improve persistence among first-year students are transitional bridge programs, orientation programs, freshman seminars, mentoring programs, and multifaceted approaches. The following section provides a description of each institutional policy.

## Transitional Bridge Programs

Transitional bridge programs typically are designed for high-risk students who enter college lacking basic study skills or adequate academic preparation or are undecided on a career or life goal. In describing high-risk students who participate in bridge programs, Hardy and Karathanos (1992) found that often they are first in their family to attend college, graduated in the lower third high school senior class, have marginal grade point averages, tested into either developmental English or math, or come from low socioeconomic backgrounds. Transitional bridge programs are usually preenrollment programs that begin during the summer prior to a student's enrollment in college and may last upward to the entire first year. Most bridge programs aim to help students develop academic skills and social networks; navigate the campus geography; become familiar with campus resources and services, including advising systems; and examine values and academic goals. Bridge programs also help students with personal growth and adjustment to college by helping them develop strategies to achieve academic success and personal development.

Santa Rita and Bacote (1997) reported that bridge programs have become more popular as efforts to keep and graduate high-risk students from college increase. Advocates of bridge programs argue that by enrolling in these programs, students learn how to access vital academic resources, develop study and time management skills, gain self-confidence, and develop social networks (Terenzini et. al., 1994). For students who enter college academically unprepared, transitional bridge programs appear to make a positive difference in their persistence and academic outcomes.

Research studies evaluating the effectiveness of transitional bridge programs indicated that they have helped to ease students' transition and adjustment to college, improve students academic performance, and influence their persistence in college (Santa Rita & Bacote, 1997). In a study of college student persistence, Forster, Swallow, and Fodor (1999) found that success in college for at-risk students was related to the development and use of effective study skills derived from participation in a college study skills course. Hardy and Karathanos (1992) found that students who had low academic self-concept prior to their enrollment in a semester-long bridge course recorded a significant gain in academic self-concept upon completion of the course and met the goal of enhancing their likelihood of future academic success.

In a study of summer bridge programs in two-year and four-year colleges,

Santa Rita and Bacote (1997) found that transitional bridge programs primarily consisted of intensive instruction, academic support, study-skill workshops, and peer counseling. Students also met with counseling psychologists who helped them develop problem-solving skills and shared information about academic support services. The study found that summer bridge programs for high-risk and low-income, minority students can help facilitate their transition and adjustment to college and improve their persistence rates. Particular bridge programs like Bronx Community College's College Discovery Prefreshman Summer Program demonstrated that offering a strong curricular and counseling component in a transitional program can help first-year students adapt to campus life and succeed in college (Santa Rita & Bacote, 1997).

## Orientation Programs

Orientation programs demonstrate another campus intervention policy designed to enhance the opportunity for community college students to succeed in college. Brawer (1996) suggests that orientation programs in community colleges are perhaps the most popular intervention policy to facilitate student persistence. Perigo and Upcraft (1989) described orientation efforts as those activities, programs, and courses designed to help first-year students make the transition from their previous environments to the collegiate environment with a goal of enhancing their success in college. Despite varying in purpose, content, and scheduling, most community colleges offer some form of student orientation that contains information regarding academic programs and provides advice about utilizing campus resources and student services. Orientation programs also allow first-year students to collaborate with faculty, administrative staff, and their peers.

Community colleges have realized the multiple benefits of offering orientation programs to help ease students transitions to college (Santa Rita, 1992). Successful orientation programs have positive influences on first-year student academic and social involvement and have demonstrated a significant effect on student persistence and educational attainment (Perigo & Upcraft, 1989). Research confirms substantial and significant effects of orientation programs on both the level of social integration and that of commitment to campus attended (Robinson, Burns & Gaw, 1996).

Helping students to become aware of campus resources and mechanisms through which to become involved on campus is an important aspect of most orientation programs. A well-developed orientation and advising policy that seeks and requires students' academic involvement often achieves satisfaction among students and positively influences student retention (Young, Backer, & Rogers, 1989). In a study of four North Carolina community colleges, Glass and Garrett (1995) found that completion of an orientation course during the first semester of enrollment promoted and significantly improved student performance despite differences in age, gender, race, major, placement exam scores, or employment status.

Orientation programs are typically one to three days in duration and are important for disseminating information regarding campus resources, student life opportunities, and the establishment of peer networks. Generally, placement tests, class registration, and campus tours occur during the two-and three-day formats. Coll and VonSerggern (1991) found that most orientation programs contained the following elements:

- Descriptions of college program offerings;
- Statement of the college's expectations for students;
- Information about assistance and services for examining interests, values, and abilities;
- Encouragement to establish working relationships with faculty;
- Information about services that help with adjustment to college; and
- Financial aid information.

Gordon (1989) suggested that orientation programs should also include explanation of campus services; opportunities to meet key campus personnel, establish friendships with peers, and develop a relationship with advising; early career planning; development of study and time management skills; goal setting; and outstanding peer role models. First-year student orientation must appropriately be timed and sequenced from preenrollment, during the entering period, and throughout the first year (Perigo & Upcraft, 1989). Orientation programs must also demonstrate a sustained and coordinated effort by the entire campus community to provide first-year students with "anything and everything they need to know during the first few days of enrollment" (Perigo & Upcraft, 1989, p. 85).

In a study that measured the impact of an orientation course at Valencia Community College in Orlando, Florida, Nelson (1993) found that between 1987 and 1992, 81 percent of students who enrolled in the course passed their first semester courses, as compared to 67 percent of those students who did not participate in any additional preparatory coursework and 56 percent of students who enrolled in other college preparatory courses. After four terms, 65 percent of the students who enrolled in the orientation course still were enrolled at the college. The study's findings cited the orientation course as a powerful tool for developing academic skills and improving retention among first-year students.

Queensborough Community College in Bayside, New York, developed an "Introduction to College" course that combines a four-week orientation seminar with a writing-across-the-curriculum initiative. The four seminar sessions focus on intellectual, vocational, emotional, and social development. The course prepares students to address the academic and personal demands of being a first-year college student. A study conducted in 1980 found that 85 percent of first-year students who enrolled in the "Introduction to College" seminar registered for courses the following spring term (Papier, 1990). In a follow-up study ten years later, Papier (1990) found a positively correlated relationship between academic progress and retention at the campus, while suggesting that participation in the ongoing orientation seminar contributed to a successful college experience and promoted student retention at the college.

### Freshman Year Seminars

A student retention initiative that continues to grow in popularity in community colleges is the Freshman Year Seminar. Originally freshman courses were referred to as orientation courses but today the term seminar is more widely used (Gordon, 1989). Freshman seminars have a specific focus in helping first-year students adjust to college, navigate their new environment, and develop academic skills for their future success. Freshman seminars typically combine academic, social, personal and career components in an attempt to increase the odds of students persisting beyond their first year of college.

Beal and Noel (1980) noted almost two decades ago that the most effective approach for improving retention among community college freshmen was offering a course during the first semester of study. Research has since indicated that first-year programs, such as college survival skill courses, have a positive effect on the persistence rate of entering students (Barefoot & Gardner, 1996; Fidler, 1991). In addition, when academic advising is incorporated in tandem with freshman seminars, research documents that persistence rates increase along with students' self-concept (Hardy & Karathanos, 1992).

Barefoot and Gardner (1996) reported that in fall 1994, the National Resource Center for the Freshman Year Experience and Students in Transition administered a national survey of freshman seminar programming to determine characteristics and variations of seminars at regionally accredited colleges and universities. Of the 1,001 institutions that responded to the survey, 72 percent (720) reported that they offered a special course for first-year students called a freshman seminar, colloquium or student success course. The different types of freshman seminars included extended orientation (72.2%) that offered a blend of topics essential for student success; an academic seminar with uniform content (11.3%) focusing on a single topic or an interdisciplinary course that addressed a single theme from a variety of disciplinary perspectives; an academic freshman seminar (7.8%) where content was determined by the instructor; or a class categorized as either a basic skills course or professional seminar (9%).

Community colleges have recognized the value of Freshman Seminar courses in improving retention rates. Course goals for a typical freshman seminar include developing academic skills; providing an orientation to campus resources and facilities; and easing the transition and adjustment of students to college (Fidler & Fidler, 1991). Barefoot and Gardner (1996) report that the most common course topics include academic skills, time management, campus facilities, career planning, and diversity. Empirical studies conducted at Bronx Community

College (New York), Phillips Community College (Arkansas), and Miami-Dade Community College (Florida) document that freshman orientation courses effectively foster retention (Santa Rita & Bacote, 1997).

According to findings derived from the 1994 National Survey of Freshman Seminar Programs (Barefoot & Gardner, 1996), the characteristics of freshman seminar courses for reporting colleges included the following:

- 75 percent of seminars were graded by a letter grade;
- 43 percent were required for all first-year students; 29 percent were required for high-risk students; and 29 percent were elective courses for new students;
- 86 percent of seminars carried academic credit toward graduation;
- 50 percent carried one semester/quarter hour of credit; 16 percent carried two hours of credit; 24 percent carried three hours of credit; 10 percent carried more than three hours of credit;
- 50 percent of seminars carried elective credit; 26 percent carried general education credit; 19 percent carried credit toward core requirements; 2 percent carried credit toward major requirements;
- In 33.5 percent of institutions, the freshman seminar instructor was the academic advisor for all seminar students (Barefoot & Gardner, 1996).

In an attempt to reduce the attrition rate among first-year students, Miami-Dade Community College developed a one-credit "College Survival Seminar" covering topics such as time management, study skills, memory and reading techniques, test preparation and stress management. In an attempt to measure the effectiveness of the course, Belcher (1987) found that completing the seminar in the first semester significantly reduced the attrition rate and improved students' grade point average. The participants of the study consisted of 1,145 first-year students who completed the survival skills course and 863 first-year students who did not. The study's findings revealed that the attrition rate for students who completed the course was significantly lower than for students who did not. In addition, students who completed the course had a higher grade point average after their first semester than students who had not taken the course.

## Mentoring Programs

While most community colleges employ transitional bridge programs, orientation programs, or freshmen year experience courses to help improve persistence rates among first-year students, others have found that integrating academic advising, linked courses and mentoring promotes persistence of the most "at-risk" first-year students. An intervention strategy growing in popularity on community college campuses is mentoring programs. Mentoring initiatives have involved faculty, administrative staff, and student peers. Santa Rita (1992) noted that student emotional attachments to campus can strongly be encouraged by support systems carefully designed to converge during a student's initial contact with the institution. Bronx Community College of the City University of New York sponsors a Student Assistant Program in which enrolled students are recruited each year and trained to familiarize new students to campus prior to the first day of classes. The primary goal of the program is to train currently enrolled students to provide individual assistance to entering students with registration, campus resources, the academic demands of college, student services offerings, student life opportunities, and the like (Santa Rita, 1992). Student assistants in some cases serve as mentors to high-risk students.

Valencia Community College in Orlando, Florida, employed faculty mentoring in combination with its orientation course to form the MORE (Mentors and Orientation Reinforce Education) program to address attrition among its first-year student population. The MORE program targets high-risk students into a "Student Success Course" and utilizes faculty to serve as academic mentors. A study of the program's effectiveness found that first-year student retention increased 10 percent when adding the faculty mentoring dimension than by merely offering the orientation program (Nelson, 1993).

Mentoring is the foundation of the Puente Project, a community college retention program created in 1981 at Chabot College in Hayward, California. The Puente Project was originally designed to increase the number of Mexican American/Latino community college students transferring to four-year colleges and universities (McGrath & Galaviz, 1996). The success of the program in getting a high percentage of students (many of whom are first-generation college students) to complete community college and successfully transfer to, and graduate from, senior institutions has prompted replication of the program in 38 community colleges throughout the state. To date, over 9,000 students have enrolled in Puente's Community College Program. Of the students who complete the one-year program, 48 percent transfer to four colleges and universities, as compared with less than 7 percent of non-Puente students (McGrath & Galaviz, 1996). Puente's Community College Program combines innovative teaching and counseling methods with community involvement. It provides community college students with academic counseling, a two-course, accelerated writing-class sequence, and mentors from the professional community. College counselors match students with mentors and Puente teachers to augment the classroom learning experience with community resources. Among its recent outcomes the program has reported the following:

- Among Puente students who have transferred to the University of California (UC), 95.6% graduate within four years, as compared with 73% for all transfer students at UC and 62% of Chicano transfer students at UC.

- Results from a survey of students who entered Puente in 1987 and 1989 found that 56% of students completing the program transfer within three years, compared to only

7% of firsttime freshmen who enter community college with the goal of transfer (McGrath & Galaviz, 1996, pp. 28–30).

In Miami-Dade Community College (MDCC) a mentoring program was established for high school students identified as "high risk." The program employed high school teachers to provide mentoring to promote college entrance and orientation prior to students' graduation from high school. A key feature of the program is the professional development of high school teachers to provide mentoring to students; the program also establishes linkages between college and high school staff in an effort to promote enrollment and persistence prior to the freshman year. MDCC has implemented additional mentoring programs targeting specific student groups, such as the Black Student Recruitment Program, which involves training counselors and administrators to mentor black students in their feeder high schools. The college continues to support students as they enter college by offering survival courses that provide assistance and tutorial services to targeted "at-risk" students. At MDCC, faculty members who teach the freshman year seminar course also serve as mentors. The mentorship component of the survival course was designed to provide entering students with academic and social support (Padron, 1992).

Research reveals that freshman orientation programs with a mentoring component have helped reduce the first-year student attrition rate (Brawer, 1996). In those community colleges where students are required to enroll in an orientation course during their first semester, mentoring has shown to make a positive impact on first-year student persistence.

## The Multifaceted Approach

Brawer (1996) noted that first-year students require different intervention approaches to insure their persistence in college. As a result, community colleges have taken a multifaceted approach in an attempt to increase persistence among this student group. A multifaceted approach is one that utilizes a combination of academic, student services, and in some instances, community resources. A multifaceted approach also may be mandated by district policy or system-wide initiative. In those cases, resources are normally allocated to community colleges to augment their efforts (Chavez & Maestas-Flores, 1991; McGrath & Galaviz, 1996, Padron, 1992; Santiago, 1996). Examples of multifaceted initiatives include using learning communities with first-year student programs at LaGuardia Community College in New York and Seattle Central Community College in Washington (Tinto, Goodsell, & Russo, 1994); creating a cadre of academic advisors, counselors, and peer-student mentors to assist students throughout their first year at Leeward Community College in Hawaii (Tinto, 1998) and Bronx Community College in New York (Santa Rita, 1992); and linking community mentors and organizations with a collaborative campus effort to retain high-risk students at Evergreen Valley College in San Jose, California (Chavez &

Maestas-Flores, 1991) and in over 30 other community colleges in California (McGrath & Galaviz, 1996). The following section briefly describes three community college approaches.

***Learning Communities in LaGuardia Community College.*** As part of its Coordinated Freshman Program, LaGuardia Community College in Long Island City, New York, offers a learning community environment to support its basic skills course offerings for first-year students. Learning communities allow first-year students to coregister in courses together or schedule courses in blocks so that students can register for two or more of the same courses (Tinto, 1998). Among the features of LaGuardia's Coordinated Freshman Program are:

• Programs offered during summer and intersession to allow students to refine academic skills;

• Paired courses and course clusters linked together by common themes, assignments or techniques taught by instructors who have collaborated in the design of the curriculum;

• Special study groups where students work together to master difficult course content (LaGuardia Community College (Tinto et al., 1994).

The New Student House at LaGuardia is a learning community designed for first-year students who required basic skill development. The New Student House allows groups of first-year students to enroll in thematically linked basic skill courses where they make up the only members of the classes. In addition, students are required to enroll in an Integrated Seminar that includes academic advising, problem solving, study skills seminars, and test-taking strategies (Tinto et al., 1994). Research findings derived from a multimethod study that measured the impact of learning communities at Seattle Central Community College, the University of Washington, and LaGuardia Community College indicated the following:

• Participation in a first-year learning community enabled students to develop a network of supportive peers that helped them make a successful transition to college;

• The impact of learning communities on both social and academic life at LaGuardia and Seattle Central was more noticeable than at the University of Washington;

• Remedial students benefited from participation in a learning community;

• Students participating in the New Student House at LaGuardia were more positive in their views and more involved in learning activities than were their nonremedial peers, and they persisted at comparable rates (Tinto et al., 1994).

***The Freshman Year Initiative Program at Bronx Community College.*** The Freshman Year Initiative Program (FYIP) was established at Bronx Community College in 1991 to assist first-year students who require remediation in mathematics, reading, or writing. The primary goal of FYIP is to provide a comprehensive academic foundation with applied counseling to enhance academic achievement among these students (Baron, 1997). Participants register for three 5-week modules (or two remedial courses and one college-level course) and attend an orientation and career development course which meets for one hour per week during the entire 15-week semester. A counselor teaches the freshman orientation course and also is responsible for meeting with students throughout their first semester to provide academic, career, financial, and personal counseling. The central components of the FYIP are as follows:

- Creation of a holistic counseling center;
- Administration of the Noel-Levitz Retention Management System (RMS), Myers-Briggs Type Indicator (MBTI), and the California Occupational Preference Survey (COPS) to enable students to learn more about themselves;
- Establishment of peer counseling programs;
- Creation of a rapid counseling system (RCS); and
- Inclusion of student development, problem-solving, and coping skill development into the campus orientation and career development courses (Baron, 1997).

Preliminary results have highlighted the effectiveness of the Freshman Year Initiative Program. For example, the retention rate from fall 1993 to fall 1994 for first-year students not participating in the program was 59.3 percent, compared to 76.5 percent for those who completed the program (Baron, 1997). Students who participated in FYIP also achieved higher grades in their developmental and college-level courses when compared to their counterparts who were not in the program. FYIP students also withdrew from classes less frequently and were less likely to receive incomplete grades.

*The ENLACE Program at Evergreen Valley College.* Since the creation of the Puente Project in 1981, particular community colleges in California have employed Puente's innovative model to create their own individualized campus and community-based approach to meeting both student and community needs. One such program, developed in 1989 at Evergreen Valley College in San Jose, California, is ENLACE, "a program signifying a community's investment in education" (Chavez & Maestas-Flores, 1991, p. 64). ENLACE was designed to serve educationally disadvantaged and underrepresented Hispanic students at Evergreen Valley College by linking college faculty, counselors, administrative staff, students and student organizations, community mentors and organizations, and corporate community in an attempt to increase Hispanic student persistence in college. Reporting on data collected from a three-year study of ENLACE students, Chavez and Maestas-Flores (1991) discovered the following:

- The ENLACE instructional/counseling/mentor model improves the academic achievement of Hispanic students.
- The structure serves to move more successfully "developmental English/math" Hispanic students into the general education curricula.

• ENLACE students have significantly higher retention levels than their non-ENLACE Hispanic counterparts at Evergreen Valley College.

• The potential to transfer to four-year institutions, as well as to complete requirements for the A.A./A.S. degree, is significantly improved. ENLACE maximizes the opportunity for Hispanic students to meet the matriculation goals of the college district. (p. 67)

### Summary

Insuring that students successfully transition to college and experience a rewarding first year is a concern shared by community college policymakers. During the past 30 years campus policy makers have enacted institutional policies that continue to affirm the diversity that students bring to college by actively engaging them prior to, and during, their enrollment in college. Research demonstrates that persistence in college improves when a variety of intervention strategies are enacted to enable first-year students to become active participants in a campus learning community. Particular campus policies that were cited as positively influencing first-year student persistence included transitional bridge programs, orientation programs, freshman seminars, mentoring programs, and multifaceted approaches.

## RECOMMENDATIONS FOR CAMPUS POLICY MAKERS

To help ensure that students experience a meaningful and rewarding first year in community colleges, campus policy makers and practitioners can intervene in several critical areas. First, campus policies should be initiated to help ease the transition to college. As Terenzini and colleagues (1994) noted, "If the transition from high school or work to college can be negotiated successfully—the likelihood of student change, educational growth, and persistence are significantly increased" (p. 69). Second, campus policies should be established to create proactive, hospitable environments that invite students to campus, and involve them in collaborative academic and social programs and activities. Here are five recommendations designed to accomplish these goals.

1. *Create transitional bridge programs that begin prior to students' enrollment in college and extend into the first year of enrollment.* As community colleges strive to address the needs of first-year students, the colleges must also confront complex issues relating to "high-risk" students. This issue is critical for campus policymakers because the increasing enrollment of high-risk students is expected to continue into the 21st century (Roueche & Roueche, 1993). Terenzini and colleagues (1994) suggest that campus policy makers and practitioners be aware of the varying character of the transition process for different types of students. Because high-risk students require more attention than their traditional peers, the use of transitional bridge programs should be considered prior to students' enrollment in college. Summer bridge or intersession programs can

help high-risk students prepare for their first-year college experience by informing them about campus support services, helping students develop friendships, and assisting students in making connections with faculty and administrators. It is often an outcome of these programs that students later develop a support network. Bridge programs that are offered prior to students' enrollment in a community college, usually during the summer or intersession, have been shown to be effective in the persistence of students especially when they include faculty, counselors, administrative staff, and peer mentors (Santa Rita & Bacote, 1997). These programs should provide student assistance in the development of college-level study skills, social skills, peer networks, and resource acquisition.

Upcraft (1989) suggests that successful bridge programs should address the development of academic and intellectual competence; the establishment and maintenance of personal relationships; identity development; career and lifestyle exploration; personal health maintenance and wellness; and formulation of an integrated philosophy of life. In order to develop an orientation program that will provide the most support for first-year students, campus policymakers should vary orientation programs in format and length.

2. *Require students to complete an orientation program prior to their enrollment, during the initial weeks of their first term, or in an extended format during the first year.* Orientation programs should be required or highly encouraged for entering students. The options for scheduling a campus orientation are holding it during the senior year in high school, the summer prior to a student's enrollment, the beginning of each term, or continuously throughout the academic year. The most effective orientation programs are those that link advising, placement testing, and registration with orientation activities (Perigo & Upcraft, 1989). Orientation must integrate students intellectually and socially by exposing them to campus academic and student services.

In order to plan for an effective orientation program, campus policy makers must make available to the orientation programming staff information about first-year students, including their backgrounds, academic abilities, interests, and needs. Upcraft (1989) suggests that campus policy makers integrate six important components when designing an effective campus orientation program. The required components include leadership commitment; incorporation of student development theory; meeting of the diverse needs of first-year students; implementation of the program at the appropriate time; program evaluation; and involvement of the entire campus community. Subsequently, faculty, and staff development programs should be offered that address student background characteristics, including their cultural traits and the multiple contexts from which they come (Padron, 1992) as well as suggestions for designing curriculum and developing teaching and counseling styles that are sensitive to the diverse nature of first-year students (Rendon, 1994).

Campus policy makers who are concerned about offering an extended orientation program may consider replicating many of the elements of the freshman orientation course at Bronx Community College. Bronx's freshman orientation enables students to develop basic college survival skills in areas of academic life: set career goals, managing time, analyze classroom behavior, assess instructor demands, and utilize library and other resources. Emphasis is placed on students' understanding of an academic environment and its demands on their developing successful coping and achievement behavior (Santa Rita and Bacote, 1997).

3. *Require first-year students to complete a for-credit freshman seminar.*

Fidler and Fidler (1991) provided evidence demonstrating the effectiveness of freshman seminars offered for credit. In addition, the researchers found that persistence rates of first-year students who returned for their sophomore year increased after participation in freshman seminars. There is little doubt that freshman-year seminars can help first-year students familiarize themselves with the campus learning community and acquire the necessary academic and social skills needed to succeed in college.

The format of freshman seminars will differ in community colleges. While some will offer intensive workshops at the beginning of a term, others will offer weekly meetings during the initial weeks and most will offer a for-credit semester-long seminar (Barefoot & Gardner, 1996). An important consideration for campus personnel to address in freshman seminars is the determination of academic goals for first-year students. Academic goals have both institutional and student implications. An institutional concern is that student academic goals often are used to determine college transfer and persistence rates. A student consideration is that they meet with faculty and advisors to review these goals and create a plan on how to accomplish them.

4. *Establish mentoring programs for first-year students that create a sense of community and involve faculty, counselors, advisors, administrative staff, and student peers.* Because of the important role self-perception plays in the academic, social, and cultural aspects of the transition to college, first-year students in need of mentoring should be afforded the opportunity to participate in programs offered in a variety of formats (Terenzini et al., 1994). Mentoring programs should be sensitive to the diverse nature of students and offer services in a comprehensive and collaborative manner. Campus policy makers should seek to pool resources from academic units and student services in order to establish a sense of community when designing mentoring programs.

Gardner (1996) suggests that in order to help first-year students, especially those who are the first in their family to attend college, appropriate counseling and mentoring programs must be offered because many will require help in managing stress and sorting out their feelings. Academic advisors, counselors, faculty, and administrative staff can facilitate the mentoring process by providing a sort of corrective feedback that will help first-year students mediate the stress associated with the transition to college (Jalomo, 1995).

Institutions interested in establishing student peer mentoring groups can begin by identifying student representatives from various student organizations, student government, or those students interested in helping new students on campus to become familiar with institutional processes and offerings (Santa Rita, 1992). College students selected to participate as peer mentors should be those identified as having already successfully negotiated the transition to college and are academically in good standing.

5. *Employ a multifaceted approach that utilizes a combination of academic, student services, community resources.* As the 20th century was drawing to a close, Roueche and Roueche (1993) observed that at-risk student populations were becoming the majority in many community colleges. The difficulty of at-risk students in persisting in college and attaining their educational goals continues to confound campus policy makers, who have designed numerous interventions over the years to increase their retention rates. Among the influences that hinder at-risk student participation and persistence in college is lack of academic preparation. Inadequate academic preparation in secondary school is an acute problem that plagues many high-risk students. Romo (1998) found poor academic preparation to be a crucial reason for low college enrollments among economically disadvantaged students. Nora (1993) argued that academic preparation must be studied as a factor that influences at-risk students' access to, and persistence in, college.

Without sufficient academic preparation, many at-risk students will chance their academic achievement and educational goal attainment in college solely on institutional policies. In the 21st century the challenge for community college policy makers will be to design collaborations with their educational partners—namely, secondary schools and senior institutions,—in a mutual effort to increase the level of academic preparation for at-risk students at each segment of the educational pipeline.

Campus policy makers who are interested in pursing a multifaceted approach to increase first-year student persistence should consider the model employed at LaGuardia Community College. LaGuardia's Coordinated Freshman Program includes a strategic combination of new student orientation, a summer preparatory program, new student seminar, individual counseling, first-year student workshops, counseling groups, and academic support interventions (Tinto et al., 1994). The primary goal of such an effort should be to offer students programmatic, curricular, and counseling interventions in a collaborative manner before, during, and at the end of their first year in college.

Creating learning communities that promote connected learning environments in and out of class is a strategy than can be linked to most first-year student initiatives. Research demonstrates that students who participate in learning communities, taking their courses together and in sequence, develop close friendships, and establish academic support networks, which help foster their transition to college and future academic success (Terenzini et al., 1994; Tinto et al., 1994).

Campus policy makers should consider employing resources from both academic units and student services when designing learning communities on campus, similar to the Puente Project and ENLACE programs in California (Chavez

& Maestas-Flores, 1991; McGrath & Galaviz, 1996). Multifaceted learning communities can provide opportunities for collaborative faculty and student interaction in and out of class while meeting the transitional and learning needs of first-year students.

## CONCLUSION

Earning a higher education often serves as the best means of social mobility available to our nation's youth. Graduating from college is associated with more stable patterns of employment and higher earnings. Completing a successful first year in college is often the first step towards determining an academic major that is congruent with skills and competencies required by a complex and specialized labor market in the 21st century.

New and innovative strategies to promote persistence and high academic achievement among first-year students must continue to be developed on a number of levels. First-year students must be taught academic and social skills as well as be challenged to develop competencies necessary for their success in college. At an institutional level, faculty, administrative staff, and counselors must continue to provide proactive intervention strategies to insure persistence among first-year students.

First-year students will continue to be a vital asset to community colleges in the 21st century and beyond. Their enrollment will continue to significantly impact community colleges in the areas of funding, facilities planning, curriculum development, student services, campus culture, and their overall well-being. It is imperative that community college leaders continue to address the needs of their first-year students and promote efforts to increase their persistence.

## REFERENCES

Barefoot, B. O., & Gardner, J. N. (1996, March 17). *Early interventions that make a difference.* Presentation at the National Conference on Higher Education, American Association for Higher Education, Columbia, SC.

Baron, W. (1997). *The problem of student retention: The Bronx Community College solution—The freshman year initiative program.* (ERIC Documentation Reproduction Service No. ED 409 971)

Beal, P. E., & Noel, L. (1980). *What works in student retention.* Iowa City: American College Testing Service.

Belcher, M. (1987). *Addressing retention through an orientation course: Results from a North Campus study.* Miami-Dade, FL, Community College, Miami Office of Institutional Research.

Brawer, F. B. (1996). *Retention-attrition in the nineties.* Los Angeles, CA: ERIC Clearinghouse for Community Colleges. (ERIC Document Reproduction Service No. ED 393 510)

Bronx Community College. Office of Institutional Research. (1996). *Institutional research report.* New York: City University of New York.

Brown, L. L., & Robinson Kurpius, S. E. (1997). Psychosocial factors influencing academic persistence of American Indian college students. *Journal of College Student Development, 38* (1), 3–11.

Chavez, M., & Maestas-Flores, M. (1991). Minority student retention: ENLACE. In D. Angel & A. Barrera (Eds.), *Rekindling minority enrollment* (New Directions for Community Colleges, No. 74, pp. 63–67). San Francisco: Jossey-Bass.

City University of New York. Office of Institutional Research and Analysis. (1997). *CUNY Student Data Book, Fall 1996* (Vol. 1). New York: Author.

Cohen, A., & Brawer, F. (1996). *The American community college* (3rd ed.). San Francisco: Jossey-Bass.

Coll, K. M., & VonSerggern, D. J. (1991). *Community college student retention: Some procedural and programmatic suggestions.* (ERIC Document Reproduction Service No. ED 345 816)

Curtis, S. M., & Harte, J. (1991). *A freshman retention project at Borough of Manhattan Community College.* (ERIC Documentation Reproduction Service No. ED 348 096)

Dougherty, K. J. (1994). *The contradictory college: The conflicting origins, impacts, and futures of the community college.* Albany: State University of New York Press.

Fidler, P. (1991). Relationship of freshman orientation seminars to sophomore return rates. *Journal of the Freshman Year Experience, 3* (1), 7–38.

Fidler, P., & Fidler, D. (1991). *First national survey of a freshman seminar program: Findings, conclusions, and recommendations* (Monograph No. #6). Columbia, SC: National Resource Center for the Freshman Year Experience.

Forster, B., Swallow, C., & Fodor, J. H. (1999). Effects of a college study skills course on at-risk students. *National Association of Student Personnel Administrators Journal, 36,* 120–132.

Gardner, J. N. (1996, November/December). Bottom line: Helping America's first-generation college students. *About Campus, 1* (5), 31–32. San Francisco: American College Personnel Association and Jossey-Bass.

Glass, J. C., & Garrett, M. S. (1995). Student participation in a college orientation course, retention, and grade point average. *Community College Journal of Research and Practice, 19* (2), 117–132.

Gordon, V. P. (1989). Origins and purposes of the freshman seminar. In M. L. Upcraft & J. N. Gardner (Eds.), *The freshman year experience* (pp. 183–197). San Francisco: Jossey-Bass.

Hardy, C. D., & Karathanos, D. (1992). A bridge course for the high-risk freshmen: Evaluating outcomes. *National Association of Student Personnel Administrators Journal, 29,* 213–222.

Jalomo, R. (1995). *Latino students in transition: An analysis of the first-year experience in the community college.* Unpublished doctoral dissertation, Arizona State University, Tempe.

McGrath, P., & Galaviz, F. (1996, November/December). In practice: The puente project. *About Campus, 1*(5), 27–30. San Francisco: American College Personnel Association and Jossey-Bass.

Nelson, R. (1993). *The effect of SLS 1122 and faculty mentors on student performance.* Orlando, FL: Valencia Community College. (ERIC Document Reproduction Service No. ED 371 778)

Noel, L., Levitz, R., & Saluri, D. (1985). *Increasing student retention: Effective programs and practices for reducing the dropout rate.* San Francisco: Jossey-Bass.

Nora, A. (1993). Two-year colleges and minority students' educational aspirations: Help or hindrance? In J. Smart (Ed.), *Higher Education: Handbook of Theory and Research,* (Vol. 9, 212–247). New York: Agatha Press.

Padron, E. (1992). The challenge of first-generation college students: A Miami-Dade perspective. In L. S. Zwerling & H. B. London (Eds.), *First-generation students: Confronting the cultural issues* (New Directions for Community Colleges, No. 80, pp. 71–80). San Francisco: Jossey-Bass.

Papier, S. (1990). *Joining freshman orientation concepts with writing-across-the-curriculum.* New York: Queensborough Community College. (ERIC Document Reproduction Service No. ED 362 216).

Perigo, D. J., & Upcraft, M. L. (1989). Orientation programs. In M. L. Upcraft & J. N. Gardner (Eds.), *The freshman year experience* (pp. 82–94). San Francisco: Jossey-Bass.

Rendon, L. I. (1994). Validating culturally diverse students: Toward a new model of learning and student development. *Innovative Higher Education, 19,* 33–51.

Rhoads, R., & Valadez, J. (1996). *Democracy, multiculturalism, and the community college: A critical perspective.* New York: Garland Publishing.

Robinson, D. A., Burns, C. F., & Gaw, K. F. (1996). Orientation programs: A foundation for student learning and success. In S. C. Ender, F. B. Newton, & R. B. Caple (Eds.), *Contributing to learning: The role of student affairs* (New Directions for Student Services, No. 75, pp. 55–68). San Francisco: Jossey-Bass.

Rodriquez, R. (1996). President's Hispanic education commission releases report. *Black Issues in Higher Education, 13,* 6–7.

Romo, H. (1998). Tracking programs derail minority and disadvantaged students' success. *Community College Journal, 69*(3), 12–17.

Roueche, J., & Roueche, S. (1993). *Between a rock and a hard place: The "at-risk" student in the open-door college.* Washington, DC: Community College Press.

Santa Rita, E. (1992). The freshmen experience and the role of student assistants. *Journal of College Admission, 136,* 19–22.

Santa Rita, E., & Bacote, J. B. (1997). The benefit of college discovery prefreshmen summer programs for minority and low-income students. *College Student Journal, 31,* 161–173.

Santiago, I. S. (1996). Increasing the Latino leadership pipeline: Institutional and organizational strategies. In R. C. Bowen & G. H. Muller (Eds.), *Achieving administrative diversity* (New Directions for Community Colleges, No. 94, pp. 25–38). San Francisco: Jossey-Bass.

Terenzini, P. T., Rendon. L. I., Upcraft, M. L., Millar, S. B., Allison, K. W., Gregg, P. L., & Jalomo, R. (1994). The transition to college: Diverse students, diverse stories. *Research in Higher Education, 35,* 57–73.

Ting, S. R. (1998). Predicting first-year grades and academic progress of college students of first-generation and low-income families. *Journal of College Admission, 158,* 14–23.

Tinto, V. (1993). *Leaving college: Rethinking the causes and cures of student departure* (2nd ed.). Chicago: University of Chicago Press.

Tinto, V. (1998). Colleges as communities: Taking research on student persistence seriously. *The Review of Higher Education, 21* (2); 167–177.

Tinto, V., Goodsell, A, & Russo, P. (1994). *Building learning communities for new college students*. State College: Pennsylvania State University, National Center on Postsecondary Teaching, Learning, and Assessment.

U.S. Department of Education. National Center for Education Statistics. (1998). *Digest of education statistics*. Washington, DC: Office of Educational Research and Improvement.

Upcraft, M. L. (1989). Understanding student development: Insights from theory. In M. L. Upcraft & J. N. Gardner (Eds.), *The freshman year experience* (pp. 40–52). San Francisco: Jossey-Bass.

Upcraft, M. L. & Gardner, J. N. (Eds.). (1989). *The freshman year experience*. San Francisco: Jossey-Bass.

Valadez, J. (1993). Cultural capital and its impact on the aspirations of nontraditional community college students. *Community College Review, 21* (3), 30–43.

Young, R. B., Backer, R., & Rogers, G. (1989). The impact of early advising and scheduling on freshmen success. *Journal of College Student Development, 30*, 309–312.

Zwerling, L. S. (1992). First generation adult students. In search of safe havens. In L. S. Zwerling & H. B. London (Eds.), *First-generation college students: Confronting the issues* (New Directions For Community Colleges, No. 80, pp. 45–54). San Francisco, CA: Jossey-Bass.

# Conclusion: The Future of Community College Policy in the 21st Century

*Susan B. Twombly and*
*Barbara K. Townsend*

In this volume we have attempted to provide an overview of the "state of the field" of selected federal, state and institutional policy issues affecting community colleges. While attempting to be comprehensive, we obviously have not been able to include in this single volume each and every possible policy affecting community colleges. Rather, we have attempted to focus on those policy issues and policy mechanisms that seem most salient for the community college at the turn of the century. We have two primary goals for this concluding chapter. First, we will look across the chapters in this book to assess the status of policies in the areas covered. Second, using ideas from poststructuralist and postmodern policy analysis, we will identify and discuss areas in need of attention for the future.

Social problems or needs, the mechanisms for determining policy, and the policy responses to those problems (i.e., solutions) occur within a particular historical and cultural context. The ways in which problems are defined and the range of solutions considered are, in some ways, limited by the "box" in which they occur. Scheurich (1997) refers to this as a "grid of regularities." For example, capitalism and democracy are fundamental shapers of those regularities in the United States. Capitalism has historically dominated educational policy, even from Harvard's earliest days, in that the institution sought to prepare professionals necessary for society. Thus, it is no surprise that at both the national and state levels, policy related to community colleges is, and has been, dominated by an overarching goal of workforce development (Grubb & Associates, 1999). Within this overarching goal, cultural values of equity, efficiency, quality, and choice dominate, as they do for educational policy in all sectors (Marshall, Frederick, & Wirt, 1989).

Most of the issues addressed by chapter authors are, directly or indirectly, related to this overarching concern for workforce development and the cultural values that underpin educational policy making. The policy issues discussed here also reveal how the goals of equity, quality, choice, and efficiency sometimes conflict. For example, remedial education addresses the goal of equity in access, and yet it conflicts with efficiency. Remedial education is seen by some as a way of maintaining quality in certain segments of the system and is seen by others as an indicator of poor quality. As we discuss the status of the policy issues included in this book, we will come back to these fundamental values.

However, before we assess the status of community college policy, it is important to focus briefly on globalization, a new force that seems to be changing fundamental cultural values that constitute the "the grid of regularities" within which problems are defined and policy solutions formed. In his book, *The Lexus and the Olive Tree, New York Times* reporter Thomas L. Friedman (1999) argues that globalization is an international system that is replacing the Cold War as the dominant paradigm for organizing the way in which we think and conduct business. He defines globalization as "a dynamic ongoing process: globalization involves the inexorable integration of markets, nation-states and technologies to a degree never witnessed before—in a way that is enabling individuals, corporations and nation-states to reach around the world farther, faster, deeper and cheaper than ever before" (pp. 8–9). Friedman goes on to say that, unlike the Cold War, globalization tends to encourage cultural homogenization.

Although community colleges are primarily local institutions, Levin in Chapter 5, reminds us that they are increasingly affected by forces of globalization. Even local industries and the local job markets are now part of a much larger global market and are therefore affected by global economic, informational, and cultural forces. Rural community colleges such as Garden City Community College, located in a Kansas community dominated by the meat-packing industry, are affected by the global market for that industry. For example, the meat-packing industry relies heavily on immigrant labor, whose presence results in a multicultural community requiring instruction in English as a second language.

In fact, the state of technology is such that no industry is further than a mouse-click from the nearest urban center whether in the same state or halfway around the world. Levin observes that community colleges are both buffeted by forces of globalization (e.g., changing nature and types of work, use of technology, effects of immigration, information technologies) and buffered (through policy) from direct impact. For example, the increasing shift of community colleges to an entrepreneurial focus and overt economic role is an outcome of direct government response to globalization forces. These forces, however, reorient the mission of education away from education of the whole person to workforce training and skill development. Federal, state and local policies are the key intermediaries that buffer (or fail to buffer) colleges from the direct impact of globalization. Thus, although individual colleges differ in the extent to which they are buffeted by or buffered from globalization, it is important for community college leaders to understand globalization and how the domains of globalization affect their colleges. This may be somewhat difficult because, unlike banks or for-profit businesses, community colleges are still only indirectly affected by forces of globalization. There is no doubt though that globalization is already having an impact on the world view or the "grid of regularities" that contribute to problems and their solutions. In many ways the federal and state policy trends discussed in this book directly reflect the forces of globalization described by Levin.

## STATUS OF COMMUNITY COLLEGE POLICY

### The Federal Government and Community Colleges

Although the impact of federal initiative is not as great for community colleges as it is for four-year colleges and universities, federal regulation has affected, and will continue to affect, how community colleges do business—particularly in the areas of access and of vocational and occupational education. At the federal level we clearly see the value of equity come into play in policy solutions. Well-known legislation and court actions reviewed by Cohen in Chapter 1 have promoted access by prohibiting discrimination in admissions and employment. Access has also been facilitated by federal financial aid policy. Although, as Lovell points out in Chapter 2, community colleges do not receive a majority of their revenues from federal financial aid, community college students have received 26 percent of Pell Grants awarded each year, and federal financial aid comprises the bulk of aid received by community college students. In her review of federal policy, Lovell notes that community college students have been affected by the gradual shift in reliance on loans as opposed to grants. This much-discussed trend has obvious negative potential outcomes for community college students. However, less well known are the problems community colleges face in dealing with federal financial aid: problems in the areas of satisfactory academic progress, remedial education and ability to benefit. For example, in order for their students to be eligible for federal financial aid, community colleges must assure that the students are enrolled in courses that count toward degrees. As primary providers of remedial education, community colleges must provide remedial courses within limits imposed by financial aid regulations. Finally, as open-access institutions, community colleges have to monitor, in a way that most selective institutions do not, the awarding of financial aid to students considered to be able to benefit from a program and have a reasonable chance to complete it. Recent federal initiatives are also intended to bring even more students into the post-secondary system. They include "Hope Scholarship tax credits, boosts to the Pell Grant and TRIO programs, savings incentives through education and Roth IRAs, and various kinds of partnerships" (Adelman, 1999, p. 21). It seems clear that the overall goal of federal policy is to provide the opportunity and means for the vast majority of U.S. residents to attain at least two years of post-secondary education.

Historically, community colleges have benefited tremendously from federally sponsored job training initiatives and acts that have supported occupational programs such as the Workforce Investment Act, the Job Training Partnership Act, and the Carl Perkins Vocational Act. These programs will continue to be essential to and have a great impact on community colleges. Many of these federal initiatives have a new twist and, as Laanan argues in Chapter 4, they are being used to achieve secondary goals such as accountability. However, it is the area of federal mandates, particularly unfunded mandates, that will increasingly influence community colleges. These unfunded mandates include such regulations and laws as the Integrated Post-secondary Education Data System (IPEDS), the Student Right to Know and Campus Crime Legislation, Americans with Disabilities Act, and Occupational and Safety Act. All these acts require institutions to devote resources to complying but provide no funds to assist colleges in doing so. One such initiative that may have particular influence on community colleges is the Workforce Investment Act, which, according to Lovell, is intended to provide "one-stop" assistance to workers. As she notes, community colleges will most likely be prime players in providing one-stop services. Questions remain as to how these centers will be funded. Lovell argues that, given their increase, it is essential for community college leaders to understand the scope and nature of these mandates.

In summary, it seems that federal initiatives are continuing to assist work force development and to support community college efforts to provide access to higher education to millions of economically disadvantaged students. Along with this support, two new trends are emerging: first, funding initiatives' requirements to provide accountability systems and, second, unfunded mandates. Although unfunded mandates address the values of quality and efficiency, their impact needs to be considered. Seeking to assure efficiency in other federal programs, unfunded mandates can often contribute to an increase in administrators to comply with the mandates.

### State Governance and Policy

Community colleges are primarily creatures of local and state governments. Accordingly, the vast majority of authors in this volume have addressed state policy issues. Until recently, articulation was one of the few state policy issues involving community colleges to receive policy makers' and scholars' attention. However, within the overarching policy goal of human capital development, the scope of state policy affecting community colleges has broadened. Three related issues seem to be of central importance in the state policy arena at the turn of the century: K-14 (or K-16) system building, workforce preparation, and re-

medial/developmental education. Secondary related issues include dual enrollment (high school students receiving both high school and college credit for
taking college-level courses sometimes offered in their high school), transfer
between and within higher education sectors, and technology. A concern for
state governance and accountability systems is also evident. These initiatives all
address equity, efficiency, quality, and choice.

Most of the issues cited here—a concern for workforce preparation, equity,
access, and shrinking resources—are converging to support partnerships between community colleges and K-12 and community colleges and universities.
Labor force forecasts suggest that occupations with the highest growth rates,
such as health care technicians and marketing and sales, will require what Grubb
(1999) calls subbaccalaureate degrees. To accommodate the projected demand
for such workers, K-14 (or K-16) system building will be necessary to assure
smooth transitions from high school to college and to enhance the rate of degree
completion. As Orr and Bragg indicate in Chapter 6, federal and state policy
initiatives, often in the form of seed grants, are essential to building collaborative
relationships between community colleges and school districts. Thus far, federal
policies in the form of Goals 2000, Tech Prep, and the School to Work Act of
1994 have promoted system building in some receptive states, whereas others
states have not used the potential of these policies to explicitly build relationships with K-12. On the other hand, Orr and Bragg conclude that current state
efforts are insufficient to provide the type and quality of collaboration that will
be demanded and necessary in the future. Evidence of the effectiveness of existing collaborative arrangements is mixed and the barriers to collaboration are
longstanding. Many community colleges fought for years to break away from
their association with local school districts and to establish themselves as part
of post-secondary education. Changes in attitude will not come easily. However,
arguments for efficiency, access and equity, and workforce development will
likely compel both systems, through federal and state policy initiatives, to engage collaborative problem solving. To date, many of the system-building efforts
have been targeted to vocational and occupational education. In the future, much
more will need to be done to create partnerships to facilitate basic skills development.

A concern for the development of basic skills is tied to one of the two most
visible policy issues currently facing community colleges: remedial/ developmental education (workforce training/vocational education is the other issues).
Remedial/developmental education is particularly controversial. The trend in
some states seems to be one of reassigning the majority of remedial education
to the community colleges. This trend has significant implications for four-year
colleges and universities, but it also opens opportunities (i.e., creates the necessity for) for K-16 system building, as Shaw indicates in Chapter 10. Although
some experts applaud the fact that community colleges are better positioned
than any other segment of the educational system to handle a significant portion
of all remedial work (Cohen, 1998), Shaw reminds us remediation is only partly

the responsibility of the postsecondary sector. She suggests that state policies should also hold the K-12 system responsible for graduating students that can not do college work. Moreover, careful attention needs to be paid to K-12 policies that affect what percentage of students enter colleges and university requiring remedial work. Remedial education is a case where the underlying values of equity, quality, and efficiency come into conflict. With increasing pressure for all persons to obtain at least some postsecondary education, no issue better illustrates the importance of a systematic, comprehensive approach to providing education for those students at risk of failure than does the issue of remedial education. No longer can the educational system afford to educate the same individuals multiple times for the same skills. Nor can the system pass them off to the next layer in without some accountability. We will return to this issue in the final section of this chapter.

Community colleges—and their junior college ancestors—have a long history of involvement in occupational training and workforce preparation. With the decline in blue-collar jobs and the rise of occupations requiring subbaccalaureate education, the community college role has grown (Grubb, 1999). State policy with respect to workforce preparation takes the form of independent state initiatives as well as decisions on how to enact federal policy. According to Dougherty in Chapter 7, states typically exert influence over preservice occupational and vocational preparation through financial incentives, technical assistance, regulation, and exhortation. Dougherty concludes that, despite such recent initiatives as the Workforce Investment Act of 1998 and the reauthorization of the Perkins Act, both of which attempt to create an integrated system for preparing the workforce of tomorrow, problems remain. Some of the problems identified include fragmentation of the system, inadequate accountability, and lack of knowledge on the part of students, community college personnel and state policy makers. In particular, workforce preparation suffers from what Grubb and associates (1999) call vertical and horizontal fragmentation. That is, students are currently unable to pass from one level of training to the next level in a consistently seamless fashion. In addition, effective workforce-training policies must address horizontal integration: providing access to the various kinds of learning necessary to training effective workers.

Two other issues considered in this book are closely related to K-16 system building: dual credit, or enrollment that links high schools and community colleges, and articulation policies that link community colleges with four-year colleges and universities. In Chapter 8 Girardi and Stein observe that states' approaches to dual credit are as varied as the states themselves. Some states are more active than others in setting policy to guide dual credit practice. Others set only the broadest of parameters. As the trend of offering dual credit programs grows, states often face the challenge of developing policy on top of existing practices. Although community colleges are well positioned to be the primary providers of dual credit programs, serious questions of admissions standards, quality and transferability remain to be resolved.

Just as states vary in their approach to dual credit, so too does their approach to transfer and articulation vary. Ignash and Townsend indicate this variance in Chapter 9 in their overview of current state-level articulation policies. A striking finding in their survey of these policies is that quite a few states do not even have state-level articulation agreements between two-year and four-year state institutions. Of the states that do, about half only cover transfer from the two-year sector to the four-year sector, thus ignoring the reality of current student enrollment patterns, which have been characterized as a "transfer swirl" (de los Santos & Wright, 1989). Additionally, most articulation policies fail to address emerging related issues such as transfer resulting from dual degree programs and to and from for-profit institutions.

Yet another area in which state policy is just emerging is that of technology. It seems clear from Cintrón, Dillon, and Boyd's review in Chapter 11 that state policy is not keeping up with the rapid pace with which technology is being incorporated into community colleges. Policy is needed with respect to access, teaching and learning, quality and technology infrastructure. As Cintrón, Dillon, and Boyd note, when state policies deal with access, they usually refer to providing educational opportunities to rural areas and to lowering the cost of education. Policies have little to say about how about how passing the costs of distance education to users affects equity and educational access to individuals from lower socioeconomic or minority groups. As the authors note, "The relationship between technology and educational equality remains unclear, if not problematic, as these [existing state] policies do not address an equation whereby full-cost recovery, access, and equality are offered to an increasingly diverse student population." Further, policies support investment in the technological infrastructure and have little to say about providing the educational infrastructure that can keep up with the technology. Policy responses to measuring quality in distance education is very much in its infancy but generally seem to rely on criteria established for other purposes (i.e., accreditation). Cintrón, Dillon, and Boyd characterize the debate as between fostering "intrastate competition" versus "intrastate cooperation." With respect to matters of infrastructure, the question seems to be one of control and centralization versus decentralization. Areas in need to attention include differentiation between open markets and duplication of programs, systematic approaches to faculty development, and priorities for the technology infrastructure itself.

State policy initiatives for community colleges exist within, and are products of, state governance structures and systems of accountability. As a result, governance and accountability systems themselves must be capable of facing new policy demands. Given the current environment of increasing demands on the educational system at all levels coupled with decreasing public support, the need for coordination is greater than ever. In Chapter 3, Richardson and Santos argue that states basing higher education governance on federal principles (i.e., having a central coordinating board or agency that works with a range of institutional governing boards) enjoy advantages over states with other governance structures.

Systems based on federal principles offer advantages such as flexibility, division of responsibility for representing the public interest from institutional advocacy, and ability to provide leadership on a variety of issues requiring collaboration of all segments of the post-secondary system. Most of the authors in this book have addressed issues that require closer coordination between all sectors of education. Federal systems have the greatest potential for providing the "better integrated, more synergistic, less bureaucratic state governance arrangements" necessary to respond to the challenges of the new century.

Accountability, not an entirely new issue to higher education, has recently taken center stage in community colleges. As Laanan notes in Chapter 4, federal initiatives such as the Perkins Act require continuous program improvement through the development of a state performance accountability system. Other states have developed accountability systems consistent with their state mission or regional accrediting bodies. In general, one notes a shift in focus from an input model of assessment to a system of measuring outputs. In some cases accountability processes allow state governance bodies to decentralize decision making while holding institutions responsible. In other words, accountability measures and systems can steer institutions toward desired goals without having explicitly stated policies. Creating and using effective accountability systems for community colleges poses particular challenges for state policy makers. These challenges include the existence of incredibly diverse student populations and lack of sophisticated institutional research offices that can keep up with the demands for data. Specifically, state policy makers must develop multiple measures of success for assessing community colleges, which must take into consideration community colleges' multiple missions and diverse student populations.

### Institutional Policies

Only two chapters in this book address institutional policies. In Chapter 12 Higginbottom and Romano show what happens when trustees either counteract or interpret state policy in a way that clashes with long-established institutional prerogatives. Fortunately, trustees seldom actually determine curricular content for colleges, as they are trying to do in New York. Governing boards typically use much more subtle means, such as outcomes assessment, performance indicators, and program review, to achieve their objectives. In addition to asking whether mandating a system-wide curriculum is the best way to achieve desired outcomes, we should be asking why states might engage in such summary actions, whether their behavior is likely to become the rule rather than the exception, and how these actions can be prevented in the future.

Student persistence or retention is an institutional issue, but of late it has taken on new public urgency for many of the same reasons as K-16 system building, the enhancement of remedial education, and workforce preparation. In his recent review of the economic benefits, Grubb (1999) shows that without doubt, degree completion leads to greater economic returns than either high school completion only or some college. He concludes, "With some exceptions, the results clarify that completing associate degree enhances wages, employment, and earnings by significant amounts" (p. 3). Conversely, the returns for those who fail to complete credentials or who have small amounts of higher education are small and uncertain. Thus, community colleges must find ways to increase retention to degree or transfer. In Chapter 13 Jalomo argues that student persistence poses challenges for community colleges that most of their four-year counterparts never dreamed of because community colleges are faced with an incredible diversity of students in almost every way one can measure diversity— ethnic background, preparation, goals, needs, and native language. A variety of programs have been effective in smoothing students' transition to community colleges and improving persistence: transitional bridge programs, orientation programs, freshman seminars, mentoring programs, and multifaceted approaches. Clearly, public and institutional policy must focus on transition *and* persistence to degrees. Here community colleges are at somewhat of a disadvantage in that the associate degree has been viewed as a desirable, but not necessary, goal for students. In explaining low graduation and transfer rates, community colleges frequently offer the rationale that students persist until they have completed individual goals, which may include skills but not degrees. Lack of degree completion or transfer has been considered acceptable from this perspective. If Grubb's (1999) data are correct, community colleges will now become more engaged in efforts to encourage persistence to graduation (either from external pressure or their own concern).

## PROSPECTS FOR THE FUTURE

Community colleges have been remarkably successful institutions within a policy environment that has, for the most part, failed to recognize their importance. For many of the reasons cited by the authors in this volume, that failure is being corrected and community colleges are emerging as an important player in the policy arena. Obviously, there is still much work to be done. It is clear from the chapters in this book that governance structures in some states may be ill prepared to deal with the rapid changes likely to occur in the future. Workforce preparation is not yet as seamless as it might be, not all states have created policy to manage high-quality dual credit programs, the location of remedial education is in transition, and some colleges are buffeted by globalization rather than buffered from its effects. Technology policy seems to be behind the rapid advance of hardware and software. Particularly important policy issues will have to be faced in this area, issues such as intellectual property rights, faculty development and training, and extending technology to disadvantaged students.

In this last section, rather than make specific policy recommendations for the future, we use ideas from postpositivist policy analysis and policy archaeology

(Scheurich, 1997) to suggest ways in which future policy choices and their implications can be better understood and, perhaps, better policy can be made. Throughout this section we will use two issues or problems to illustrate our points. First is the relationship of state and institutional policy decisions to teaching and learning in the community college. Second is remedial education. Before proceeding, it is important to reiterate that community colleges have carried out their multiple missions within a broad policy framework that encourages development of high-quality human capital (workforce preparation) for the broadest segment of society possible (access).

Policy analysis is the broad term for the methodology used to analyze social problems, link them to potential solutions, and assess the impact of policies. Scheurich (1997) points out that traditional policy analysis has proceeded in a very rational manner employing one of four areas: (1) descriptions of the problem, (2) discussion of competing policy solutions, (3) consideration of implementation problems, and (4) evaluations of policy implementations (p. 95). These four areas also represent the steps in the traditional, rational problem-solving cycle. In this traditional approach, problems are viewed as real, often as diseases to be cured. The traditional policy process reflects little understanding of potential for social problems to be either unnatural or socially constructed.

Viewed from the traditional policy perspective, system capacity, poor teaching, and remedial education are real, natural problems that need attention. In fact, perhaps with the exception of system capacity, these problems have been addressed through the traditional policy process. For example, poor teaching is assumed to be real and caused by the teacher's lack of motivation or preparation. Frequent responses to the problem are faculty development and awards for outstanding teaching. Seldom do we attempt to understand how the "problem of poor teaching" came to be defined as such. Moreover, we are even less likely to assume that policies could actually cause or contribute to poor teaching. Likewise, remedial education stems from the overriding commitment to equity and access. We recognize that not all students have the preparation to do college-level work, but our values hold that (1) everyone is capable of developing those skills, (2) everyone should have the right to attend college and (3) some college education is becoming essential to future economic success. Remedial education is a logical policy solution, a patch between high school and college for those who, for whatever reason, have not been successful in developing college-level skills. The dominant policy approach assumes that lack of college preparedness is a real, not a socially constructed, problem. Seldom do we consider that, rather that solving the problem of college preparedness, remedial education might be contributing to the problem.

Others seek to understand the complicated and symbolic nature of public policy formation. Kelly and Maynard-Moody (1993) argue that postpositivist approaches "conceive of policies as symbolic and interpretive rather than as efficient solutions designed to solve society's ills" (p. 135). The policy process becomes a struggle over symbols. From this approach those symbols (policies) are manifestations of "latent public concerns" (p. 135). Policies then are symbolic solutions to latent public concerns (Scheurich, 1997). From this perspective, policies surrounding remedial education can be seen as symbolic of forces either to overturn the existing social order or to maintain the power in the hands of a largely white elite depending on which side of the fence one sits.

Scheurich sees these two approaches—the traditional and the postpositivist—as variations on a theme. Both assume or accept the larger liberal worldview that conceives of modern, free-enterprise democracies as the best, if not yet perfect, societies. In this view progress is possible. Policy is, in fact, the mechanism by which democratically ordered societies gradually perfect themselves. He proposes yet another approach to policy analysis which he calls policy archaeology, after Michel Foucault. Although we question whether this approach is radically different from the postpostivist, Scheurich proposes a valuable way of thinking about social problems and policies that might help community colleges leaders plan and implement more effective policy for the future.

Scheurich divides his policy archaeology into four arenas: "(1) The education/social problem arena: the study of how education problems are socially constructed. (2) The social regularities arena: the identification of the network of social regularities across education and social problems. (3) The policy solution arena: the study of the social construction of the range of acceptable solutions. (4) The policies studies arena: the study of the social functions of policies themselves" (p. 97). The common element in these four arenas is the emphasis on social construction.

In the first arena, Scheurich argues that rather than accept a social problem as a given, policy makers should "examine closely and skeptically the emergence of the particular problem" (1997, p. 97). Rather than ask questions such as how big the problem is and where it exists, policy archaeology asks how a particular problem came to be defined as a problem and what makes it possible for this problem to become identified as a problem needing a policy solution (p. 97). By focusing on this "prepolicy" stage, one comes to understand better the "constitutive grid of conditions, assumptions, forces which make the emergence of a social problem . . . possible" (p. 98).

Thus, for remedial education and the problem(s) for which it is the solution, rather than focusing only on the size of the problem (how many students lack skills), the nature of the problem (what skills they lack), or location of the problem (e.g., rural or urban setting, a particular social class), policy archaeology suggests that we should be asking how and why the lack of skills became defined as a problem. Why has lack of skills become framed as it has? In the particular case of remedial education, some of this type of work has been done. For example, in his study of City College, James Traub (1994) illuminates the debates over the definition of social problems giving rise to remedial education. One way to label or define the root problem is in terms of deficits. That is, students lack certain skills necessary for success in college. This position tends to be taken by those labeled as conservatives who argue for standards. Another position is that individuals have different skills and that most attempts to assess those skills are really assessing race and class, not ability. For advocates of this "definition," standards are merely an obstruction to a democratic and equitable society. Traub illustrates how this debate played out at City College. Although it is impossible to recreate his book here, the dimensions of the debate offer an important perspective for those who are in a position to make policy regarding remedial education. In recent years a number of well-known arguments have emerged to contribute to the current definition of the problems in need of remedial education. One has only to look to history to understand this. Universities in this country have long had preparatory departments. In fact, not unlike most early public universities, the majority of students at the newly founded University of Kansas in the 1870s were registered in the preparatory department. The context, however, led to a very different understanding and construction of the "problem" of college preparedness. Another illustration of problem definition is to ask why is it that lack of preparedness for college became defined as the problem rather than the high level of expectations to succeed in college?

The second arena focuses on the "network of regularities" that constitute "what becomes socially visible as a social problem and what becomes socially visible as a range of credible policy solutions" (Scheurich, 1997, p. 99). As we understand Scheurich, this network of regularities might also be thought of the web of culture, or paradigm. As Scheurich points out, regularities are neither intentional nor consciously created. However, they do produce, or reproduce, practices. A second important point about regularities is that they do not create social problems or policy solutions as if they were an outside force. They are, to borrow a word from Lewis Menand, the "ambient fluid" that supports, sustains and gives rise to social problems and solutions. These regularities, according to Scheurich, do not literally create problems, but they do provide the environment in which problems are selected and made "real" (1997, p. 100). A third characteristic of regularities is that they are historically situated. The network of regularities changes and is particular to time periods and cultures. Friedman (1999), for example, argues that the Cold War provided one set of regularities (he uses the word *paradigm*) and that globalization is now creating a different set.

What are the regularities surrounding the emergence of college preparedness as a problem and remedial education as a solution? Certainly there are regularities associated with race/ethnicity, gender, and social class that contribute to the "ambient fluid" surrounding remedial education. But we argue that dominant ideas such as meritocracy and affirmative action also contribute to the mix. Additionally, ideas about higher education in the United States have been shaped by its history, namely, developing before elementary and secondary schooling, being rooted in the English liberal arts model, and coming to be seen as the vehicle of upward mobility for an aspiring middle class. Clearly, affirmative action and immigration patterns are two of the factors affecting how preparedness for college is defined today as opposed to how it was defined a century ago.

The third arena of policy archaeology brings together the first two arenas and studies how the grid of social regularities shapes the range of possible policy choices. Scheurich argues that this process is also not intentional or conscious, but rather "is like a preconceptual field that constitutes some policy choices as relevant and others as virtually invisible" (1997, p. 102).

This policy arena is particularly relevant to the issue of remedial education policy at two levels: at the institutional level and at the system level. For example, are community colleges to become the primary providers of remedial education, which Cohen (1998) argues, community colleges are in a unique position to do? Commentators at every level seem to agree. Why is this so? What regularities come together to make this a logical policy solution? The explanation must go beyond that of the traditional safety valve metaphor in which community colleges serve to preserve quality in the four-year sector by taking weaker students. What is the community college role in creating this policy alternative? At the institutional level, one must ask why certain approaches to preparedness come to be defined in one way versus another way. Traub (1994) illustrates this point well in his description of the debate over remedial education at City College. Although City College is a four-year university and the remedial debate he describes is supposed to be linked to admission to the regular college program, it is unlikely that the parameters of the debate are very different at most community colleges.

The fourth and final arena of policy archaeology seeks to examine the role of policy studies themselves. Policy studies, like policies and solutions, play a nonneutral role in the social order. For example, policy studies contribute to the way in which problems are understood. From this perspective it is important to analyze why policy studies focus on and use the methodologies they do. Here we modify Scheurich's model a bit to focus not only on the role of policy studies but also on the nature of policy studies.

For example, given the concerns Grubb and associates (1999) raise about the current state of teaching in community colleges, creating state policies that "dump" the primary responsibility for providing high-quality remedial education upon community colleges may be counterproductive. This policy approach becomes even more problematic if Adelman's assessment that the current system does not have the capacity to accommodate the new influx of students is correct. Community colleges can not easily achieve economies of scale by forcing remedial students into large lecture sections. If Grubb's portrait of teaching in community colleges is even partially accurate, one has to ask once again if the very students who need high quality remedial education, sometimes at very low levels, are once again receiving the short end of the stick. Can community colleges continue to provide high quality remedial and developmental education to even more students *and* serve the influx of good students in states such as Florida and California? If policy studies themselves do not reflect the complexity of the problem being considered, the solutions are likely to be shortsighted. We believe that Shaw is correct when she argues in Chapter 10 that remedial education must be viewed a problem that must be dealt with at all levels of the educational system. Policies that do otherwise are likely to put tremendous burdens on community colleges and result in greater gaps between the educationally advantaged and disadvantaged.

Community college leaders must also understand their institution's role in the "grid of regularities" that shape problem and solution definition. For example, community college leaders must decide what their reasonable role and mission in providing remedial education will be. Do they take all comers? Do they more clearly define their role in adult basic education as separate from remedial education? Or do they and policy makers put some pressures on high schools to be held accountable for the competencies of students who graduate? Remediating students who lack some college level skills seems to be a very different function than providing (for a second time) the equivalent of middle school or high school education to millions of comers. If community colleges and policy makers fail to delineate the community college role in this, taxpayers will continue to "pay twice" for basic education. Furthermore, state and institutional policies may unintentionally convey the message that high school performance is unimportant (Rosenbaum, 1999). Is it possible that a policy solution actually contributes to maintain the problem? If so, why is this so? Who benefits from this process? Sound educational policy requires answers to these questions. At the very least, these answers must be considered in the policy process.

In a recent Community College Research Center Brief, sociologist James Rosenbaum (1999) raises the question, "Are community colleges getting the right message to high school students?" The essence of his essay is that open-access policies, "college-for-all" rhetoric, and the "second-chance" reputation of community colleges may actually encourage students not to work hard in high school. What they fail to understand, says Rosenbaum, is that high school achievement predicts degree completion. This is not the message that students seem to understand and that state and institutional policies reinforce. Using data from the High School and Beyond Survey, Rosenbaum argues that grades, test scores, and homework time can soften the negative effects of race and class on attainment. That is, for disadvantaged students there is a positive payoff for studying hard in high school. Rosenbaum argues that community colleges should provide degree-completion rate information (maybe transfer rates, too) by high school grades, inform high school students that "second chances are second best" (p. 4), and build K-16 linkages. Both the dual credit programs and K-14 system building potentially address this concern. Here we come back to the need for a policy-making structure—state governance structure and accountability processes—that facilitates collaboration and high quality rather than competition and money grubbing. As Shaw says in Chapter 10, a systemic approach to the complicated issues of workforce preparation, in the broadest sense, is necessary for providing high-quality education for the 21st century.

Another example comes from the area of state policy aimed at efficiency. One of the more serious areas in which this can be seen is in the area of teaching.

In a recent book, *Honored but Invisible*, Grubb and his associates (1999) point out that federal and state policies have done very little to promote good teaching. However, some state and institutional policies actually have an indirect but negative impact on the quality of teaching in community colleges. Enrollment-based funding, for example, puts pressures on colleges to increase class sizes, while funding cuts encourages the hiring of part-time instructors. Under the enrollment-based model, non-credit-generating activities, such as faculty development, are frequently the first to go when funding is cut. At the institutional level, teaching load and the practice of hiring part-time instructors are of particular concern. Although when used appropriately and sparingly, part-time faculty can be quite effective in bringing "real world" experiences to the classroom, overuse can result in decline in quality of instruction. Part-time faculty typically have little time or commitment to improving teaching and learning new pedagogical techniques, and they have less time than their full-time colleagues for office hours. Grubb and his associates (1999) argue that institutional personnel policies also fail to provide support for high-quality teaching—for both full and part-time instructors. They provide a disturbing portrait of inattention to teaching in hiring, faculty evaluation, and merit pay policies that fail to promote high-quality teaching. This example illustrates how policy values can conflict with each other (Marshall, Mitchell, & Wirt, 1989).

It is clear from the chapters in this book that community colleges have come of age, so to speak, as a center of policy attention. They are now recognized as an essential part of the educational continuum, thanks in part to the role President Clinton has assigned to these colleges in workforce preparation. This new-found status will come at a price. The price is that community colleges will come under the same levels of public scrutiny and pressure as other segments of the educational system. Policy makers and community college leaders alike must not only address such important policy issues as the appropriate location for remedial education, the quality of dual credit, and workforce preparation; they must also understand the complex forces, such as globalization, that affect even locally based community colleges. Furthermore, they must anticipate and evaluate the intended as well as unintended consequences of policy options. One has only to read Grubb and associates' (1999) description of the "drill and kill" approach to teaching common in many remedial classrooms in community colleges (p. 181) or Traub's (1994) more balanced view of teaching in remedial programs and the low level of skills of students in these programs to realize the challenge that exists. It is clear that, no matter how wonderful they are, community colleges alone will not solve the problems behind remedial education or workforce preparation in this country. Not only will K-14 or K-16 system building be necessary, we believe that the policy process, and its attendant studies, will benefit from (and will need) the more complicated approach suggested by Scheurich's policy archaeology.

In this book we have begun the process of making explicit important policies affecting community colleges and the policy process necessary for achieving a

better understanding of how social problems and their policy solutions are socially constructed.

## REFERENCES

Adelman, C. (1999, January/February). Crosscurrents and riptides: Asking about the capacity of the higher education system. *Change*, pp. 21–26.

Cohen, A. (1998). *Projecting the future of the community college*. Available through
ERIC Clearinghouse for Community Colleges: www.gse.ucla/ERIC/digest/
dig9601.html

Friedman, T. L. (1999). *The lexus and the olive tree: Understanding globalization*. New
York: Farrar, Straus, Giroux.

Grubb, N. (1999, June). *The economic benefits of sub-baccalaureate education: Results
from national studies* (CCRC Brief No. 2). New York: Teachers College Community College Research Center.

Grubb, N., & Associates (1999). *Honored but invisible: An inside look at teaching in
community colleges*. New York: Routledge.

Kelly, M., & Maynard-Moody, S. (1993). Policy analysis in the post-positivist era: Engaging stakeholders in evaluating the economic development districts [*sic*] program. *Public Administration Review, 53*(2), 135–142.

Marshall, C., Mitchell, D., & Wirt, F. (1989). *Culture and education policy in the American states*. London: Falmer Press.

Rosenbaum, J. (1999, October). *Unrealistic plans and misdirected efforts: Are community
colleges getting the right message to high school students?* (CCRC Brief No. 4).
New York: Teachers College Community College Research Center.

de los Santos, A. G., & Wright, I. (1989). Maricopa's swirling students: Earning one-
third of Arizona State's bachelor's degrees. *Community, Technical, and Junior
College Journal, 60* (6), 32–34.

Scheurich, J. J. (1997). *Research method in the postmodern*. London: Falmer Press.

Traub, J. (1994). *City on a hill: Testing the American dream at City College*, Reading,
MA: Addison-Wesley.

# Index

# About the Editors and Contributors

TAMMY BOYD is a Ph.D. student in Historical, Social and Philosophical Foundations of Education at the University of Oklahoma. Her areas of interest are policy studies, international education, and anthropology of education.

DEBRA D. BRAGG, Associate Professor in the College of Education at the University of Illinois at Urbana-Champaign (UIUC), specializes in postsecondary education, policy analysis and evaluation, and leadership development. She directs the Office of Community College Research and Leadership as well as the Community College Leadership graduate program at UIUC. She is also the Site Director for the National Center for Research in Vocational Education, University of California at Berkeley.

ROSA CINTRÓN is Assistant Professor of adult and higher education at the University of Oklahoma. She specializes in the study of student personnel services and the American community college.

ARTHUR M. COHEN is Professor of Higher Education and Director of the Educational Resources Information Center (ERIC) Clearinghouse for Community Colleges at the University of California, Los Angeles (UCLA). His prior books include *The American Community College* (3rd ed.) and *The Shaping of American Higher Education.*

CONNIE DILLON is Professor of adult and higher education at the University of Oklahoma, where she specializes in the study of distance education and telecommunications.

KEVIN J. DOUGHERTY is Associate Professor of Higher Education at Teachers College, Columbia University. He has published widely on the community college and the educational excellence reform movement of the last 20 years. He recently completed a final report for the Sloan Foundation, *The New Economic Development Role of the Community College*," which addresses the forms, origins, and impacts of the community college's growing role in contract training, small business development, and local economic planning.

ANTHONY G. GIRARDI is a doctoral student in the Education Policy Studies Program at the University of Missouri–Columbia and a graduate intern with the Missouri Coordinating Board for Higher Education in Jefferson City, Missouri.

GEORGE H. HIGGINBOTTOM is Dean of the Liberal Arts and Human Services Division at Broome Community College, Binghamton, New York. He was a founding member of the Community College General Education Association and served on the State University of New York (SUNY). Joint Task Force on General Education.

JAN M. IGNASH is a former Assistant Director, Academic Affairs, for the Illinois Board of Higher Education. Her responsibilities included working with the Illinois Articulation Initiative. She is currently Associate Professor, Department of Educational Leadership, at the University of South Florida.

ROMERO JALOMO JR. is Assistant Professor of Higher Education Administration at New York University. His past research examined the transition to college and first-year experiences of first-generation college students. His current research examines how campus climate plays a role in student involvement on campus. Jalomo is the coauthor of book chapters, monographs, and articles relating to student transitions to college and culturally diverse students in community colleges.

FRANKIE SANTOS LAANAN is Assistant Professor of Human Resource Education at the University of Illinois at Urbana-Champaign. Before joining the University of Illinois faculty in 1999, he held positions at the Coast Community College District and the Center for the Study of Community Colleges. His publications have addressed transfer and articulation issues, community college accountability, and the economic benefits of a community college education.

JOHN S. LEVIN is employed at the Center for the Study of Higher Education at the University of Arizona in Tucson. He conducts research on organizational change, governance, culture, and leadership in higher education institutions. He is currently working on a book, *Reflection and Reproduction: The Community College and Globalization*, and has just completed a funded research project on globalization and the community college. Previously, Levin worked in community colleges as an instructor of English and an administrator.

CHERYL D. LOVELL is Assistant Professor of Education and Coordinator of the Master's Program in Higher Education and Adult Studies at the University of Denver. She teaches postsecondary public policy and college student development. In the public policy area, she focuses her research on state-federal relationships and the influence to postsecondary institutions. Previously she was Director of the State Higher Education Executive Officers/State Postsecondary Review Entity (SPRE) Technical Assistance Network, in Denver, Colorado, and Staff Associate with the National Center for Higher Education Management Systems (NCHEMS), in Boulder, Colorado.

MARGARET TERRY ORR is Associate Professor in the Department of Organization and Leadership, Teachers College, Columbia University. She is a Senior Research Associate with the Community College Research Center, where she has investigated the relationship between community colleges and secondary schools, focusing of workforce development issues and policies.

RICHARD C. RICHARDSON JR. is Professor of Higher Education at New York University and Professor Emeritus in the Department of Educational Leadership and Policy Studies at Arizona State University.

RICHARD M. ROMANO is Professor of Economics and Director of International Education at Broome Community College, Broome, NY. He is the founding director of the Institute for Community College Research.

GERARDO E. DE LOS SANTOS is Director of Programs at the League for Innovation in the Community College in Mission Viejo, California. In addition to his administrative and teaching contributions to community, colleges, de los Santos speaks and consults locally, regionally, and nationally on various educational topics ranging from community building and accelerated instructional delivery to adjunct faculty participation and information technology certification.

KATHLEEN M. SHAW is Assistant Professor and Coordinator of the Urban Education Program at Temple University in Philadelphia. Her research interests include issues of equity and access to postsecondary education for poor and minority students; the intersection between educational policy and broader social policy; and the subjective experience of social mobility among first-generation college students. She was the lead editor of *Community Colleges as Social Texts: Qualitative Explorations of Organizational and Student Culture* (1999). She is the codirector of a national study of urban community colleges and is currently completing, with Howard London, a book entitled *Where Dreams Cross: Urban Community Colleges and the Search for Educational Mobility.*

ROBERT B. STEIN is Associate Commissioner for Academic Affairs at the Missouri Coordinating Board for Higher Education. As the state's chief academic officer, he works to promote collaboration among public and independent colleges and universities in designing initiatives that support the board's goals for access, quality, and efficiency.

BARBARA K. TOWNSEND is Professor of Higher Education and Associate Dean for Research and Development at the College of Education at the University of Missouri–Columbia. A former community college faculty member and administrator, she has published extensively about the community college, including works on transfer, gender issues, and the distinctiveness of the community college as an institutional type. Her most recent books about the community college include the edited volumes, *Two-Year Colleges for Women and Minorities* and *Understanding the Impact of Reverse Transfers upon Community Colleges*.

SUSAN B. TWOMBLY is Professor of Higher Education and former chair of the Department of Educational Policy and Leadership at the University of Kansas. Her research interests include women in higher education, curriculum, community colleges, and higher education in Latin America. She served as a Fulbright Fellow in Ecuador in 1995. Her publications on community colleges have focused on administrator and faculty careers, leadership, and gender and have appeared in the *Community College Review, The Review of Higher Education*, and the *Journal of Higher Education*.